Sovereign Immunity from Execution and International Arbitration

International Arbitration Law Library

VOLUME 74

Editors

Professor Julian D.M. Lew QC has been involved with international arbitration for more than forty years as counsel, as arbitrator and as an academic. He is the founder and has been the Head of the School of International Arbitration, Centre for Commercial Law Studies, Queen Mary University of London since its creation in 1985. He is now an independent international arbitrator at 20 Essex Street, London.

Stavros Brekoulakis is the Michael & Laura Hwang Professor in International Arbitration at the National University of Singapore and a member of 3 Verulam Buildings (Gray's Inn). He is a leading academic in international arbitration and has led, or been involved in, several projects with ICCA, ICC Commission and ILA. He also acts as an independent arbitrator and has been appointed as a chairman, sole arbitrator, co-arbitrator and emergency arbitrator under all the major arbitration rules.

Introduction

Since its first volume published in 1993, this authoritative practitioner-oriented series has published in-depth and analytical works on niche aspects of international arbitration, authored by specialists in the field.

Objective

This authoritative and established series covering in-depth analyses of niche areas appeals to both practitioners and academics. The series includes specific monographs and PhD dissertations of high quality, which are practical and cover issues not fully explored in general texts.

Frequency

A volume is published whenever an interesting topic presents itself.

The titles published in this series are listed at the end of this volume.

Sovereign Immunity from Execution and International Arbitration

Theory and Practice

Ylli Dautaj

Wolters Kluwer

Published by:
Kluwer Law International B.V.
PO Box 316
2400 AH Alphen aan den Rijn
The Netherlands
E-mail: lrs-sales@wolterskluwer.com
Website: www.wolterskluwer.com/en/solutions/kluwerlawinternational

Sold and distributed by:
Wolters Kluwer Legal & Regulatory U.S.
920 Links Avenue
Landisville, PA 17538
United States of America
E-mail: customer.service@wolterskluwer.com

ISBN 978-94-035-0858-0

e-Book: ISBN 978-94-035-0868-9
web-PDF: ISBN 978-94-035-0878-8

About the Author

Dr. Ylli Dautaj currently teaches as an Associate Professor in Commercial Law and Commercial Arbitration at Durham Law School, U.K.

He previously taught at various institutions in the U.K., India, Sweden, and the U.S., including as an adjunct and visiting associate professor at Penn State Dickinson Law, U.S. He is a frequent guest lecturer at various legal institutions worldwide, including as part of the international adjunct faculty of Uppsala University's master's program in investment treaty arbitration.

Ylli graduated with a PhD from the University of Edinburgh (U.K.) as a stipendiary scholar of the Scottish Graduate School for Arts & Humanities.

Ylli practices with DER Disputes out of Stockholm, Sweden. He represents clients in primarily litigation and arbitration, domestic and international, commercial and investment. He represents individuals, private enterprises, State-owned enterprises, and States in various disputes, including matters incidental or ancillary to arbitration.

Table of Contents

Foreword

The book in your hand is designed to provide a deeper understanding of the complex intersection between arbitration law—particularly international investment arbitration—and sovereign immunity. It does so in a dense and comprehensible manner at the same time as it to a large extent uses a comparative approach to the topic.

The possibility of a non-state party to enforce arbitral awards against a state party which has promised to abide by an arbitration agreement is of great importance for a rule-based world order, as is sovereign immunity. I know it firsthand that it is a challenge to maintain a sensible balance between these two legitimate interests.

The problem of enforceability typically presents itself in state courts foreign to the defendant state. A judge in the court where enforcement is sought will look in vain for authoritative guidance in international conventions. He or she will have to figure out what customary public international law has to say about it (and what it has to say about other similar state defenses against recognition and enforceability). The judge will have to navigate by means of the reasons presented, mostly by other courts in foreign jurisdictions and check the soundness of the reasons against, among other things, subsequent developments in international law. He or she will also to a large extent use legal literature in the field, to which this highly concentrated piece of work is a significant contribution.

The concentrated style in which the book is written will, I think, make it a suitable starting point for advances students as well as a place to go to for practitioners when they strive to hammer out their arguments before showing up in court. Practitioners who will argue for enforcement may explore the virtues of a pragmatic and restrictive theory on sovereign immunity, whereas the practitioner who seeks arguments for an absolute theory can be well advised to use the book to meet the devil's advocate. In either position I am sure that the reader will find the exercise a worthwhile one.

Eric M. Runesson

Eric M. Runesson is since 2018 Justice of the Swedish Supreme Court, former Member of the Swedish Bar Association and assistant professor of commercial law.

Preface

This book navigates the intersection between international arbitration law and the law of sovereign immunity. More specifically, it deals with the back end of the arbitral procedure where an award-creditor is seeking to liquidate the arbitral award against a reluctant award-debtor State.

This book makes the subtle point that for investor-State dispute settlement (ISDS) and investment treaty arbitration (ITA) to remain a reliable and effective transnational dispute resolution regime, the norm of *voluntary compliance* must remain intact. Incidentally, when award-debtor States default, the enforcement of foreign arbitral awards must be sanctioned with coercive force. It is in that light that the doctrine of sovereign immunity presents a serious obstacle or a balance (depending on how you look at things). Not all assets of the award-debtor State can (nor should) be made available to the award-creditor.

Moreover, this book notes that the law on immunity from execution is still largely unchartered territory and one that continues to be in a state of flux. This includes immunity from enforcement and execution in the context of enforcing international arbitral awards. As a result, courts in various jurisdictions have battled with the doctrine for many years. Although some principles, rules and tests have been distilled and formulated, significant obstacles and issues remain largely unresolved in large parts of the world. The lack of harmonization and the constant state of flux further intensify the uncertainties embedded in law on sovereign immunity.

The research question and focus of this book are whether the doctrinal understanding of sovereign immunity from execution (*theory*) and its interpretation and application in the international arbitration context (*practice*) sit well with a twenty-first-century global marketplace.

To answer the question, this book investigates doctrinally (a) whether and how domestic legislators and courts have contributed to shaping the law on sovereign immunity from execution, in general, and in the arbitration context, in particular. Following the exploration of the substantive law, this book explores in a more practically driven study (b) whether and how domestic legislators and courts have facilitated award execution through its procedural rules and court practices. Consequently, this book provides the reader with both the theory and practice of the law on sovereign immunity from execution in the international arbitration context.

Finally, this book explores (c) whether and how non-legal solutions can assist an award-creditor when the award-debtor State refuses to comply voluntarily with a pecuniary award. Thus, this book also explores and underscores non-legal and pragmatically driven venues for redress.

To answer the questions posed forensically, this book employs the doctrinal and comparative law methodologies. Through a doctrinal methodological study, the author analyzes and maps the doctrinal/theoretical understanding of sovereign immunity and the interpretation and application of its sources. The study begins with a broad overview and then moves to a more specific exercise by comparing and contrasting the approaches of several jurisdictions in this respect. The subjects of study are China, France, India, Russia, Sweden, the U.K., and the U.S. Through a comparative legal methodology, the author compares and contrasts various domestic and international approaches in order to see whether and what theories, principles, rules, tests, and doctrines have emerged and whether these can (or should) be adopted in other jurisdictions (cross-fertilization leading to harmonization) and whether such approaches can or should be crystallized and consolidated into customary international law (e.g., by the International Court of Justice (ICJ)).

The study will provide a clear methodological framework by examining the selected jurisdictions' doctrinal understanding/approach of sovereign immunity from execution (substantive law/theory), on the one hand, and their respective application and interpretation (procedural rules/practice) of sovereign immunity from execution of foreign arbitral awards, on the other hand. The object of study will be divided into four colors: *Red*, *Orange*, *Yellow*, and *Green*:

- *Red list* countries are those that adhere to absolute immunity from execution. The said approach is "conservative."
- *Orange list* countries are those that adhere to restrictive immunity from execution in theory but not necessarily in practice. It can also include jurisdictions that cannot be mapped with relative certainty. The said approach is "quasi-liberal."
- *Yellow list* countries are those that adhere to restrictive immunity from execution in theory as well as in practice from a substantive law point of view. The said approach is "liberal."
- *Green list* countries are those that, like the yellow list, adhere to restrictive immunity from execution in theory as well as in practice. In addition to the yellow list, green countries not only adhere to restrictive immunity with respect to the substantive law but also provide award-creditors with procedural tools that make award execution possible. The said approach is "liberal" and "pragmatic."

It is hard—if not impossible—for the international lawyer tasked with a legal issue pertaining to sovereign immunity from execution to engage in a thorough analysis of various jurisdictions' approaches. It is undeniable that "the sheer size of the modern caseload makes it impossible for those engaged in the day to day business of adjudication to perceive and reflect upon the larger tensions underlying the law which they have to apply and the relative merits and demerits of the different directions in which it might be developed."[1] In that light, wearing the academic hat proudly, it is the author's belief that this book will benefit international lawyers who are currently or will in the future be tasked with navigating the maze of sovereign immunity law as it intersects with international arbitration law. It is believed that this book will answer many of the readers' inquiries in this regard or at least lead or steer them in the right direction.

1. Peter Birks et al., "Editor's Preface," in *What Are Law Schools For?* (1996) ix.

Acknowledgment

I remain immensely grateful to University College Cork (LLB), Uppsala University (LLM), Penn State Law (LLM), and Edinburgh Law School (PhD) for the journey that led to this book. Particularly, I remain thankful and indebted to Edinburgh Law School and the Scottish Graduate School for Arts & Humanities. I am indeed privileged and honored to have had the opportunity to study at Edinburgh Law School as an awardee of the Arts and Humanities Research Council scholarship. I have enjoyed and embraced every moment of my PhD tenure. Hopefully this book—once a dissertation—shows the fruits of my labor. Meanwhile, I remain grateful to the academic institutions where I have taught and undertaken research—Nirma University, Jindal Global University, Uppsala University, Brunel University London, Pennsylvania State University, and Durham University. Finally, I remain indebted to my clients who have put their trust in my hands in various arbitration and litigation matters.

This book would have been impossible to write but for the gracious mentoring and vital and instrumental feedback from my PhD supervisors. I remain forever indebted and grateful. Dr. Ana Maria Daza Vargas, Dr. Filippo Fontanelli, and Professor Christian J. Tams—thank you! I remain indebted to my PhD panel for their instrumental feedback and input at my viva in 2023—Professor Andrew Lang, Dr. Kabir Duggal, and Professor David Cabrelli. Finally, neither my project nor the PhD journey itself would have been possible without the gracious support and mentoring from my dear professor and mentor Kaj Hobér.

A sincere thanks to all my dear mentors, role models, or sources of inspiration—especially Professor William F. Fox, Assistant Dean Stephen G. Barnes, Professor Kaj Hobér, Dean Purvi Pokhariyal, Professor Jud Mathews, Professor Steffen Hindelang, former justice of the Swedish Supreme Court Göran Lambertz, Professor Lei Chen, Dr. Crina Baltag, and Professor Volker Röben.

Many thanks to my colleagues, too, including but not limited to Michaela Iosifidou, Sarah van der Stad, Johan Cederström, Katharina Wide, and others. Thanks also to my research assistants, Gurtej Grewal and Rushana Sadullaeva. Not only have they had class readings to take care of, but in between they have also edited hundreds of footnotes for me—for which I remain indebted.

A PhD and book journey is more than a purely academic exercise, it assumes an integral part of your life (willingly) and those around you (unwillingly). For that reason, I thank my girlfriend and family (Greta, Alban, Rreze, Aurora, Luan, Dielli, Guri), as well as my closest friends (Rawaz, Nima, Siddhart, Jan, Bruno, and many more). With so many canceled weekends, dinners spent with books and highlighters, gatherings with headphones and my computer, and canceled meetings, it is a wonder that I am not all alone in celebration. Perhaps they appreciate and embrace a good, collateral pursuit.

On a personal note, my parents were born in the former Republic of Yugoslavia and fled the war in Kosovo. Many were not as fortunate. I was born in safe harbors in Sweden. Thanks to Sweden's inclusiveness and community values I had the opportunity to achieve things that many of similar and much higher caliber could not. Doctrines that allow a break from past evil and enable fresh starts have recently been revisited in distaste (in Sweden and elsewhere), as is cyclically the case; however, we should not forget that better ideas always prevail. I have asked, sought, and knocked. Now it is time to serve. I hope to live by the pursuit of justice—where the rule of law is the core value of a civilized society and where access to justice is *never* undercut by policy objectives or political concerns. I take this oath to heart and hope not to cower down when confronted with peer pressure, financial incentives, fearmongering, or virtue signaling—i.e., when push comes to shove.

I dedicate this book to my mother, Aurora Pirraku, and to my dear mentor Professor William F. Fox.

I had a lot of time, so I wrote a short letter.

Dr. Ylli Dautaj
State College, U.S.
January 2025

CHAPTER 1

Introduction: Sovereign Immunity from Execution and International Arbitration

§1.1 INTRODUCTION

This book helps navigate the intersection between international arbitration law and the law of sovereign immunity. More specifically, it deals with the back end of the arbitral procedure where an award-creditor is seeking to liquidate the arbitral award against a reluctant award-debtor State. Going further, it answers practical issues such as: Under what circumstances can an award-creditor attach and execute an arbitral award against an award-debtor State that invokes sovereign immunity? Under what circumstances will the plea of immunity be granted/rejected by national courts? Under what circumstances will the enforcing forum court grant, qualify, or condition the general rule on immunity from execution?

To familiarize the reader with the context of the topic at hand, this book will start with a brief articulation of *(a) what* international arbitration is; *(b) what* international investment law (IIL) is; *(c) what* the doctrine of sovereign immunity is; and *(d) what* obstacles the doctrine of sovereign immunity may present in the arbitration context.

Through a doctrinal and comparative methodological exercise, the theoretical analysis and practical observations made in this book will culminate in a typology of the compared jurisdictions. Such typology will outline whether or not certain influential enforcement jurisdictions have a "conservative" or "liberal" doctrinal understanding of sovereign immunity and whether or not they have a "pragmatic" approach to facilitating award execution. In this book, the author looks at the approaches taken by courts in China, France, India, Russia, Sweden, the U.K., and the U.S. This study can grow to include many more jurisdictions.

(a) International Arbitration: International arbitration is an alternative dispute resolution method whereby the parties can settle a dispute outside of court, with appointed experts, pursuant to their own procedural directions, and yet with an outcome that is final and binding. The process has key characteristics that make it

unique. These characteristics are generally speaking why the system resonates well with its users; for example, party autonomy, expertise, neutrality, flexibility, finality, and enforceability.[1] International arbitration moves justice from the realm of court procedures (sometimes cumbersome, idiosyncratic, or even parochial) and places it in the hands of the parties' own procedure. Predominantly, however, the success comes from the effective multilateral enforcement conventions that make an international arbitral award final, binding, and directly enforceable (i.e., the International Centre for Settlement of Investment Disputes Convention, known as the "ICSID Convention," and the New York Convention on the Recognition and Enforcement of Foreign Arbitral Awards, known as the "New York Convention"). For the combined reasons, international arbitration is the preferred venue of dispute resolution for cross-border disputes.[2]

When a private party is arbitrating against a State vis-à-vis commerce, trade, and investment, there are two types of international arbitrations available: international commercial arbitration (ICA) and investor-State Dispute Settlement (ISDS). ISDS procedures where the substantive law is IIL are usually referred to as investment treaty arbitration (ITA). This is because the IIL is often found in international investment agreements (IIAs). Such treaties are often bilateral investment treaties (BITs) between two states, or multilateral investment treaties (MITs) between more than two states. IIL is also found in foreign direct investment laws (FDI Laws). What distinguishes ITA from ICA is that in the former (a) the respondent is almost always a State, and (b) the substantive dispute is one of IIL.

ISDS refers to an alternative dispute settlement mechanism between investors and States (e.g., arbitration, negotiation, mediation, early neutral evaluation, conciliation, etc.). Typically, ISDS clauses are found in either investor-State contracts, IIAs, or FDI Laws. Usually, the reference to ISDS is a reference to arbitration, and not to mediation, conciliation, or other means of settling investor-State disputes. This is also how this book will use the terminology. In fact, this book uses ISDS also interchangeably with ITA.

The most frequently used arbitration rules for ISDS are the International Centre for Settlement of Investment Disputes Rules (ICSID Rules). The ICSID Rules are the only arbitration rules specifically tailored for investor-State and investment disputes. ICSID arbitrations are governed by the ICSID Convention—making the regime a completely self-contained, detached system, free from domestic court interference (apart from in the enforcement and execution context). Other frequently chosen alternatives for ISDS include the International Chamber of Commerce Rules (ICC Rules), the Stockholm Chamber of Commerce Rules (SCC Rules), or ad hoc arbitrations pursuant to the United Nations Commission on International Trade Law Arbitration

---

1. *International Arbitration Survey: The Evolution of International Arbitration*, White & Case and Queen Mary School of International Arbitration (2018), https://www.qmul.ac.uk/arbitration/media/arbitration/docs/2018-International-Arbitration-Survey---The-Evolution-of-International-Arbitration-(2).PDF.
2. *Ibid.*

Rules (UNCITRAL Arbitration Rules). UNCITRAL ISDS procedures are often administered by the Permanent Court of Arbitration.[3]

Awards rendered pursuant to the ICSID arbitration regime are enforced under the ICSID Convention, while arbitral awards rendered pursuant to the other arbitration regimes are enforced pursuant to the New York Convention. In this book, the focus is on arbitral awards rendered against States primarily in the ISDS context. However, for the purposes of enforcement and execution, there is no major difference between ICA and ITA where the award-debtor is a State. Similarly, much of the book can also be applied, with important caveats, *mutatis mutandis* to the execution of judgments.

Despite the widespread use of ISDS, the regime is not free from obstacles, criticisms, and concerns. The legitimacy of the institution has been heavily criticized and a backlash movement has emerged.[4] Thus, on the one hand, while it can be argued that ISDS enforces a global rule of international economic law (IEL) and arguably de-politicizes investment disputes, provides adjudicatory neutrality, and facilitates economic development; it can be argued, on the other hand, that the regime is tilted in favor of investors and is proving hostile to States.[5] This book is not focused on discussing and analyzing the alleged shortcomings of international arbitration (neither commercial nor investment). However, this book does indeed focus on improving the regime by discussing the narrow shortcomings of ISDS in the execution phase, whereby an award-debtor State can invoke sovereign immunity to shield against an adverse arbitral award. For the purposes of this book, the author's starting point is that cross-border commerce, trade, and investment are crucial for prosperity, peace, and interdependence. A crucial premise is the author's position that such can only foster, entrench, and function with a reliable dispute settlement mechanism that enforces a global rule of law. The author is of the opinion that international arbitration represents

3. *See, e.g.*, Kaj Hobér & Joel Dahlquist, *Investment Treaty Arbitration: Problems and Exercises* 10 (2018).
4. For more on the "legitimacy crisis" of ITA/ISDS and the "backlash" against the regime, *See* Comprehensive Trade and Economic Agreement between Canada and the European Union, *Can.-E.U.* (signed October 30, 2016, not yet entered into force); European Federation for Investment Law and Arbitration (EFILA), *A Response to the Criticism Against ISDS*, 4-42 (2015); Ylli Dautaj, *Between Backlash and the Re-Emerging "Calvo Doctrine": Investor State Dispute Settlement in an Era of Socialism, Protectionism, and Nationalism*, 41 Nw. J. Int'l L. & Bus. 1 (2021); James H. Carter, "The Culture of Arbitration and the Defense of Arbitral Legitimacy," in *Practising Virtue: Inside International Arbitration* (David D. Caron et al. eds.) 97-105 (2016); Stephan W. Schill, "Conceptions of Legitimacy of International Arbitration," in *Practising Virtue: Inside International Arbitration* (David D. Caron et al. eds.), 106-124 2(016); Charles N. Brower & Sadie Blanchard, *From "Dealing in Virtue" to "Profiting from Injustice": The Case Against "ReStatification" of Investment Dispute Settlement*, 55 Harv. Int'l. L.J. 45 (2014); Chester Brown & Kate Miles, *Evolution in Investment Treaty Law and Arbitration* 3-4 (2011); Christoph Schreuer, "Investment Protection: Original Purpose and Features," in *The Future of Investment Treaty Arbitration in the EU: Intra-EU BITS, The Energy Charter Treaty, and the Multilateral Investment* (Crina Baltag & Ana Stanic eds.), 1, 5 (2020); and Charles H. Brower, *Politics, Reason, and the Trajectory of Investor-State Dispute Settlement*, 49 Loy. U. Chi. L.J. 271, 295 (2017).
5. *See, e.g.*, Crina Baltag & Ylli Dautaj, *Promoting, Regulating, and Enforcing Human Rights Through International Investment Law and ISDS*, 45 Fordham Int'l L.J. 1 (2021); Crina Baltag & Ylli Dautaj, *Investors, States, and Arbitrators in the Crosshairs of International Investment Law and Environmental Protection* (2020).

a successful cross-border adjudicatory framework—both for disputes stemming from trade and commerce (ICA) and for disputes stemming from investments (ISDS).

(b) International Investment Law: IIL applies in ITA disputes and sets out substantive standards protecting against illegitimate state measures/interference vis-à-vis the investor and/or the investment. IIL often includes protection ensuring, *inter alia,* no unlawful expropriation (direct and indirect), fair and equitable treatment (FET), full protection and security (FPS), the right to national and most-favored-nation treatment (NTS and MFN), the right to transfer funds and assets freely, etc. In order to avail of ISDS for hearing IIL grievances, the tribunal must have jurisdiction. For this purpose, a potential claimant must show that: (i) she is an investor as defined in the treaty (*ratione personae*); (ii) she has made an investment in the host State as defined in the treaty (*ratione materiae*); (iii) that the treaty applies from a temporal standpoint (*ratione temporis*); and (iv) that the State has given its consent to arbitration (*ratione voluntatis*).

(c) Sovereign Immunity Law: The law of sovereign immunity can be divided into two distinct regimes, namely, (i) immunity from *jurisdiction,* and (ii) immunity from *execution*. Moreover, sovereign immunity law can be said to be divided into two broad theoretical categories: (a) the theory of *absolute* immunity, and (b) the theory of *restrictive* immunity. The theory of absolute immunity means that a State cannot be sued (i.e., absolute immunity from jurisdiction) and that an award or judgment-creditor cannot execute against a State's assets (i.e., absolute immunity from execution). The theory of restrictive immunity, however, is based on a distinction of State actions as either: (1) an exercise of sovereign authority (governmental actions, better known as *acta iure imperii*), or (2) an act that a private person may perform (commercial actions, better known as *acta iure gestionis*). Under this theory, a State cannot be sued for its iure imperii actions but can be sued for its iure gestionis actions (i.e., restrictive immunity from jurisdiction). Similarly, an award or judgment-creditor cannot execute against a State's assets held for an iure imperii purpose but assets held for a iure gestionis purpose can be executed against (i.e., restrictive immunity from execution). When determining whether acts are commercial or governmental for purposes of jurisdictional immunity, the *nature test* must be used. When determining whether to execute against State assets, the *purpose test* must be used.

Outside the commercial context, other exceptions are prevalent too: e.g., when dealing with torts, employment matters, or terrorism. This book deals only with the commercial exceptions to immunity from execution in the international arbitration context.

(d) Sovereign Immunity & International Arbitration: A Bumpy Road Ahead: Even though the doctrine of sovereign immunity has mostly transitioned to the restrictive theory, "there exist[s] a significant diversity of State practice in matters of execution" and "even among those States which accept the restrictive doctrine," variations still persist.[6] As such, sovereign immunity from execution of arbitral awards can at times frustrate the legitimate expectations of an award-creditor as well as the underlying

6. Rosalyn Higgins, *Themes and Theories* 380 (2009).

object and purpose of ISDS.[7] The unresolved issue highlights serious questions about the future of ISDS and clearly demonstrates a major weakness in the system.[8]

Even though the rate of voluntary compliance with ISDS awards has been high—obviating much of the need for enforcement litigation—issues are prevalent and accelerating.[9] Thus, even though voluntary compliance is generally considered the norm, States continue to refuse enforcement, and this refusal appears to be occurring more frequently. Such lack of voluntary compliance leads to post-award proceedings and often to the invocation of a plea of immunity from execution. The consequence of successfully invoking sovereign immunity from execution is that a successful award-creditor may suffer a pyrrhic victory where assets used for a commercial purpose cannot be found.[10] Schill rightly explained that immunity in the back-end context "creates a loophole in the efficient protection of foreign investors" and that such "loophole[s] [are] amply illustrated by cases of investors struggling for years to enforce an award against assets not protected by enforcement immunity."[11] This is the crux of the matter that this book deals with.

This book makes the point that for investment arbitration to remain a reliable and effective transnational dispute resolution regime, the norm of voluntary compliance must remain intact. And if an award-debtor State defaults and fails to honor the outcome voluntarily, the enforcement of foreign arbitral awards must be sanctioned with coercive force when required.[12] It is in that light that the doctrine of sovereign immunity manifests a serious obstacle. This is only exacerbated by the fact that "[t]he law on immunity from execution remains an unchartered territory and one in a state of flux, [especially] in the context of enforcing foreign arbitral awards."[13] Courts in various jurisdictions have battled with sovereign immunity for many years now and many issues nevertheless remain outstanding.[14] It is for these reasons that sovereign immunity from execution has been said to represent "the last fortress, the last bastion of State immunity."[15]

7. *See* Julian D.M. Lew et al., *Comparative International Commercial Arbitration* 688 (2003).
8. *See* Alan S. Alexandroff & Ian A. Laird, "Compliance and Enforcement," in *The Oxford Handbook of International Investment Law* (Peter Muchlinkski, Federico Ortino & Christoph Schreuer, eds.), 1171 (2008).
9. Jorge A. Huerta-Goldman et al., *WTO Litigation, Investment Arbitration, and Commercial Arbitration* 372 (2013). *See also,* Hazel Fox & Philippa Webb, *The Law of State Immunity* 205 (2015).
10. *See, e.g.,* Matthew Saunders & Claudia Salomon, *Enforcement of Arbitral Awards Against States and State Entities* 469 (2007); *See also,* Huerta-Goldman, *supra* n. 9, at 372.
11. Stephan W. Schill, *Cross-Regime Harmonization through Proportionality Analysis: The Case of International Investment Law, the Law of State Immunity and Human Rights,* 27 ICSID Rev. 87, 101 (2012) https://doi.org/10.1093/icsidreview/sis002.
12. *See* Mark M. Cymrot, "Enforcing Sovereign Arbitral Awards: State Defences and Creditor Strategies in an Imperfect World," in *The Cambridge Handbook of Immunities and International Law* (Tom Ruys et al., eds.), 350, (2019).
13. Ylli Dautaj, "Sovereign Immunity from Execution of Foreign Arbitral Awards: Sweden's Liberal and Pragmatic Contribution," in *Stockholm Arbitration Yearbook* (Axel Callisendorf & Patrik Schöldström, eds.), 223 (2nd ed. 2020).
14. Kaj Hobér, *Selected Writings on Investment Treaty Arbitration* 497 (2013).
15. International Law Commission (ILC) Report, *Commentary to Art 18,* para. 1 (2001).

Notwithstanding this, as will be shown throughout this book, legislators, domestic courts, and the International Court of Justice (ICJ) have indeed clarified the law on sovereign immunity up to some point. It is this evolution that this book will identify and articulate for the benefit of award-creditors—in *theory* and in *practice*. Based on the study, future decisions or reforms can be reasonably approximated.

Conclusively, the object and purpose of this book is to produce scholarship that international lawyers can use when confronted with the plea of sovereign immunity from execution and when navigating its interpretation and application in the international arbitration context. In a sense, the author's mission is that of a research assistant working for the benefit of any and all international lawyers who are currently or will in the future be tasked with navigating the maze of sovereign immunity law as it intersects with international arbitration law.[16] It is believed that this book will answer many of the readers' inquiries in this regard or at least lead or steer them in the right direction.

§1.1.1 Illustrating the Crux of the Matter

The reader must understand the context we are dealing with. Hence, the "award-creditor situation" should be illustrated to better capture the crux of the matter. The reality is such that when an investor holds an investment award against a State, she has already successfully used several available legal means (judicial procedures and substantive standards) to get to that end (quantum):

(1) assumed a substantial risk in investing in the host-State;
(2) faced interferences with her investment, amounting to breaches of the State's international obligations (IIL), which may have rendered the business less profitable, not profitable, or even non-existent, and culminated in state responsibility (damages);
(3) invested efforts and resources into the ISDS procedure (and any other pre-condition or domestic litigation);
(4) faced the obstacle of non-compliance with the award and having to instead entertain miscellaneous and incidental post-award negotiations;
(5) possibly defended against set-aside/annulment efforts;
(6) reorganized her efforts and resources in order to bring post-award enforcement procedures (i.e., recognition and/or enforcement litigation), including having engaged in a time-consuming and costly asset hunt, perhaps culminating in having found some assets, somewhere, to attach against (perhaps even in several different jurisdictions in order to make up for the entire amount outstanding);
(7) sought enforcement in one or more relevant jurisdictions (sometimes unsuccessful and having to pay attorney costs); and finally

16. *See* Mathias M. Siems, "A World Without Law Professors," in *Methodologies of Legal Research: Which Kind of Method for What Kind of Discipline?* (Mark Van Houcke & Francois Ost, eds.), 81 (2011).

(8) reinvested efforts and resources in yet another post-award enforcement proceeding (i.e., execution litigation), having to respond to the plea of sovereign immunity and ultimately hoping to attach and execute against *commercial* assets.

Keeping in mind this scheme of mapping "means vs ends," the book already illustrates here the issue at hand by briefly outlining three ISDS stories. These "sagas" may help underscore the importance of embracing a commercially reasonable doctrine of sovereign immunity as domestic courts assume the role of facilitating and enabling award enforcement/execution where the award-debtor is a sovereign State. While the ISDS and IIL systems may perform well, it is ultimately for domestic courts to confirm that the last link of the ISDS procedure is not its weakest:

(1) *The Sedelmayer Saga*: In 1991, a German investor (Sedelmayer), through his business entity SGC International (SGC) signed a contract with the Police Department in Leningrad (GUVD) for the establishment of a joint stock company in Russia (KOC). The investment constituted, *inter alia,* police equipment, the building of training facilities, and the establishment of a private surveillance and protection agency. GUVD signed and transferred the strategically important property to KOC for the said purposes; SGC International was to lend capital and provide expertise. From 1992-1993 several procedures were initiated in the commercial courts of Russia against KOC, resulting in the ordered liquidation of the joint stock company. In 1994, then-President Boris Yeltsin ordered the transfer of the property from KOC to the Russian Administrative Department. Germany and the Soviet Union had signed a BIT for the protection of investors and investments. Apart from IIL protection, the BIT also contained an arbitration clause. The investor filed for ISDS in 1996 before the SCC pursuant to the SCC Rules. In 1998, the investor was awarded roughly USD 2.3 million.[17] The investor now had his arbitral award and had to collect. However, Russia did not pay voluntarily and instead defaulted on its debt. The investor was forced to commence post-award proceedings in national courts in Germany and Sweden. In these proceedings, the plea of sovereign immunity complicated matters immensely.

(2) *The Ascom Saga*: Between 1999-2003, two Moldavian and Romanian investors, via two companies (Ascom and Terra Raf), acquired shares in two Kazakh companies (TNG and KPM). TNG and KPM owned exploitation and prospecting rights to oil and gas fields in Kazakhstan. In 2010, Kazakhstan terminated the agreements regarding exploitation. Since Kazakhstan was a member of the Energy Charter Treaty (ECT)—an MIT—the investors and their investment enjoyed various IIL protections. Procedurally speaking, the ECT also contained an arbitration clause. The investors filed for ISDS in 2010 before the SCC pursuant to the SCC Rules. In 2013, the investors were

17. *Franz Sedelmayer v. The Russian Federation*, SCC Award at 118, (July 1998).

awarded roughly USD 500 million.[18] The investors had their award. Now they had to collect. However, Kazakhstan did not pay voluntarily and instead defaulted on its debt. The investors were forced to commence post-award proceedings in various national courts—e.g., in Sweden, Belgium, the Netherlands, the U.K., the U.S., etc. In these proceedings, the plea of sovereign immunity complicated matters immensely.[19]

(3) *The Crystallex Saga*: In 2002, a Canadian investor (Crystallex) invested in Venezuela for the exclusive right to develop and extract gold deposits at a mining facility. In 2011, Venezuela nationalized its gold mines and provided no compensation to the investor. Venezuela transferred the rights of developing and extracting gold deposits to a State-owned entity. Canada and Venezuela had signed a BIT for the protection of investors and investments. The BIT contained an arbitration clause. Crystallex filed for ISDS in 2011 before the ICSID and pursuant to the ICSID Rules. In 2016, Crystallex was awarded USD 1.202 billion.[20] "Crystallex had its award. Now it had to collect."[21] However, Venezuela did not pay voluntarily and instead defaulted on its debt. Crystallex was forced to commence post-award proceedings in national courts. In these proceedings, the plea of sovereign immunity complicated matters immensely.

The stories above help to illustrate why global merchants need IEL and international arbitration (ISDS) in a globalized world when operating in a cross-border context. Cynically, the stories also illustrate that once the award is finally rendered, the award-debtor State can nevertheless frustrate the effect of the law and utility in the procedure by defaulting on the debt. Thus, the stories also convey a darker picture of dealing with reluctant States. More specifically, it tells us that what works between commercial actors may not work as smoothly when a State is involved. One reason is the risk that sovereign immunity may be invoked by defaulting award-debtor States to obstruct the enforcement or execution of a favorable award. As Bjorklund noted, "the international community has created an elaborate international architecture with respect to investment protection but at the back end—the stage of actual payment—the edifice is built on shaky ground."[22]

To some extent then, the effectiveness of international arbitration as a mechanism sanctioning a global rule of international economic law largely rests with national courts. It is the national courts that are finally asked to turn arbitral awards into national judgments and then, if necessary, attach and execute against the assets of

18. *Anatolie Stati, Gabriel Stati, Ascom Group S.A., & Terra Raf Trans Traiding Ltd. v. Republic of Kazakhstan*, Case No. V (116/2010), (Stockholm Chamber of Commerce, 2013).
19. The matter has now been settled between the parties.
20. *Crystallex Int'l Corp. v. Bolivarian Republic of Venezuela*, Case No. ARB(AF)/11/2, (ICSID, 2016).
21. *See Crystallex Int'l Corp. v. Bolivarian Republic of Venezuela and Petroleos De Venezuela, S.A.*, Nos. 18-2797 & 18-3124, slip op. at 7 (U.S. 3d Cir., 2019).
22. Andrea K. Bjorklund, *Sovereign Immunity as a Barrier to the Enforcement of Investor-State Arbitral Awards: The Re-politicization of International Investment Disputes*, 21 Am. Rev. Int'l Arb. 211-212 (2011).

award-debtor State. The arbitral tribunals are by then *functus officio* and their product rests solely in the hands of domestic judges and the domestic legal order. That said, courts in various jurisdictions have at times proven to be both "liberal" and "pragmatic" in this context. For example, the end result of the award-creditor in at least two of the stories told above was ultimately a positive one, even though it came after years of asset hunting, litigation, and mounting legal fees.

Conclusively, with the right knowledge, persistence, and determination there is light at the end of the debt-tunnel, even when dealing with a reluctant award-debtor State. This book seeks to gather and share knowledge, along with stories of persistence and determination, so that the locomotive of ISDS/ITA can proceed relatively free from obstacles. At the same time, it highlights the other side of the coin by underscoring the importance of the doctrine of sovereign immunity and articulating why some States may adopt a more conservative approach to its doctrinal development.

§1.1.2 Research Question(s) and Problem Formulation

[1] Research Problem

The plea of sovereign immunity presents a serious obstacle when invoked by an award-debtor State in order to avoid compliance with an arbitral award.[23] In such a situation, sovereign immunity effectively turns into a "shield" used in order to prevent the award-creditor from having sovereign assets attached and executed against. The issues pertaining to sovereign immunity in international law, in general, and in the international arbitration context, in particular, are not new. Nonetheless, several aspects remain unresolved.

This book assesses the substantive law of sovereign immunity to provide an overview of the international doctrinal understanding of the doctrine. The study identifies and explores various—often divergent—interpretations and applications of the law before domestic courts. In turn, such mapping assists in analyzing divergences, scope for cross-fertilization, and room for harmonization. Consequently, the analysis provides data on whether and how potential reforms could be shaped and by whom (e.g., through legislation or case law, internationally or domestically, by treaty or consolidating the approaches as customary international law). But that is not the end of this book's forensic investigation. Several non-legal solutions to the issue of sovereign immunity from execution are outlined. It is suggested that such solutions can be, for example, market-based.

[2] Research Question

Does the *doctrinal understanding* of sovereign immunity from execution and its *interpretation and application* in the international arbitration context resonate with a twenty-first-century global marketplace?

23. *See, e.g.*, Schill, *supra* n. 11, at 102.

This book investigates (a) *whether* and *how* domestic legislators and courts have contributed to shaping the law on sovereign immunity from execution, in general, and in the arbitration context, in particular. Following the exploration of the substantive law, this book explores (b) *whether* and *how* domestic legislators and courts have facilitated award execution through its procedural rules and court practices. Finally, this book explores (c) *whether* and *how* non-legal solutions can assist an award-creditor when the award-debtor State refuses to comply voluntarily with a pecuniary award.

[3] Why Should the Reader Care?

Much of what this book focuses on is essentially the principle of effectiveness vis-à-vis international arbitration against States—i.e., strengthening the ends of the arbitration procedure by treating the arbitral award as final, binding, and directly enforceable even where the award-debtor is a State. The principle of effectiveness rests ultimately on *pacta sunt servanda*; that is, in the notion that agreements to arbitrate should be honored and consequently that the product of the procedure (adverse arbitral awards) should be carried out in good faith.

The crux of the matter is thus one of improving the trust in the regime of ISDS, and therefore increasing and strengthening its legitimacy. In that light, this book makes three important arguments (or assumptions) in favor of ISDS in order to justify the underlying study, to begin with—i.e., why the reader should even care about the research problem and want an answer to the research question. The author's axiom is that ISDS/ITA: (1) facilitates, promotes, protects and attracts much-needed foreign direct investments (FDIs); (2) provides for a neutral forum for disputes between investors and States; and (3) de-politicizes investment disputes by providing for a rules-based, private regime instead of diplomatic protection, state-to-state dispute settlement or domestic court solutions. Thus, the starting point of this book is that: (a) the legitimacy of ISDS/ITA is important, and (b) that much of the trust in and approval of the system rests on one of its key characteristics—effective enforcement. Conversely, the lack of compliance, on the one hand, and the lack of effective coercive force by domestic courts, on the other hand, breeds re-politicization of disputes. When host-States "fail to comply and where enforcement actions do not yield results, the investor has one recourse left: to turn to its own State."[24]

Due to shifting perspectives on globalization, growing political hostility toward multilateralism, and, more specifically, increasing hostility toward ISDS/ITA, it raises the question: Is ISDS still the most effective forum for resolving investment disputes in the twenty-first century? Primarily, one must ask whether IIL has evolved to solve the solution it purported to and whether it effectively considers (or at least does not present an obstacle to) challenges of imminent global concern, e.g., human rights, environmental law, public health, and labor standards. However, this issue is not the topic of this book. Instead, this book proceeds from the axiom presented above and responds

24. Emmanuel Gaillard & Ilija Mitrev Penusliski, *State Compliance with Investment Awards*, 36 ICSID Rev. 1, 52 (2021) https://doi.org/10.1093/icsidreview/siaa034.

to whether adverse awards against States can actually be enforced and, if so, how. This is the issue that this book addresses. It is an important caveat, especially for those who stop reading when they hear ISDS or start criticizing the current way, shape, or form of IIL/ISDS when encountered with the subject matter.

This book does not analyze the execution as a *mono*dimensional concept, i.e., considering only the award-debtor State or the award-creditor's interests. Instead, it approaches it as a *multi*dimensional concept through the prism of broader legitimacy and public interest concerns. Moreover, does not steer blindly at economic development and economic benefits. It also appreciates ideological differences.

§1.2 METHODOLOGY AND TYPOLOGY

It is important that the reader understands not only *what* will be investigated (research problem and question) but also *how* it will be investigated (research method).[25] The substantive law on sovereign immunity is a discipline that falls under the broader realm of public international law and is an area of law that has developed primarily through domestic case law. Thus, the doctrinal and comparative law methodologies are best suitable to answer the research question presented above.

Through a *doctrinal methodological* study, this book will analyze and map the doctrinal understanding of sovereign immunity and the interpretation and application of its sources, in general, and in the jurisdictions of China, France, India, Russia, Sweden, the U.K., and the U.S., in particular. Through a *comparative legal methodology*, this book compares and contrasts various approaches in order to see whether and what theories, principles, rules, and doctrines have emerged and whether these can (or should) be crystallized and perhaps even consolidated into international law. The primary research method has been the doctrinal methodology, with comparative methodology serving as the secondary one. The latter complements the former, but both reinforce each other.

The doctrinal method is utilized to distill the normative meaning and a conceptual understanding both in the substantive law of sovereign immunity as well as the procedural rules that facilitate its application. The comparative method is used to compare and contrast domestic approaches, while also underscoring areas of uniformity, potential for cross-fertilization, opportunities for harmonization, and where divergence persists. Combining the two methods allows the author to first assess the current law *de lege lata* (i.e., the doctrinal understanding and the contemporary interpretation and application) and in a second step propose areas for reform *de lege ferenda*.

It is important to highlight that the author takes an "internal point of view," i.e., analyzing the research problem from the position of a "jurist working from within the law."[26] Houcke rightly noted that "[w]hether a certain law 'exists' may be checked 'empirically', but what legal doctrine is mainly about is the *interpretation* of that law or

25. *See* Pauline C. Westerman, "Open or Autonomous? The Debate on Legal Methodology as a Reflection of the Debate on Law," in Houcke & Ost, *supra* n. 16, at 89.
26. *See* Geoffery Samuel, *An Introduction to Comparative Law Theory and Method* 35 (2014).

its balancing with other laws or legal principles."[27] In this light, the author first outlines the theory of sovereign immunity and the sources of substantive law and only then, in a second step, interprets these sources. Finally, in a third step, the author engages in arguing as to the differences and similarities pursued in the jurisdictions subject of the comparative exercise.

The research could thus be understood as both *hermeneutic* and *argumentative*. The argumentative discipline is applied to support or challenge interpretations of sovereign immunity from execution (i.e., the doctrinal understanding, interpretation, or application across various jurisdictions or internationally) and also maps these approaches using a typology of categorizing States as either conservative *or* quasi-liberal *or* liberal *or* liberal & pragmatic. Before drawing any conclusions, the author engages in: (a) an extensive interpretation of the sources collected (the empirical data, the normative sources, and authoritative sources);[28] (b) outlines hypotheses on the meaning, scope, and degree of the interpretation of the sources; (c) compares the case law, legislation, and other data against the questions/survey compiled (*see* below); (d) the hypothesis is then (re-)tested against case law and other sources in various jurisdictions; and (e) the author formulates an opinion on whether a particular jurisdiction's approach is either conservative *or* quasi-liberal *or* liberal *or* liberal & pragmatic.[29] This culminates in a typology.

The sources studied are divided by a strict hierarchy of which sources are to be given a higher epistemological value. For example, case law is given a higher value than scholarly work. Supreme Court judgments are given a higher value than decisions from the Court of Appeals. Scholarly work from an influential author is given more value than a less renowned scholar. Apart from "relevance," the author also analyzes the sources from a "validity" perspective, i.e., whether the source is still valid in the country of origin or internationally.

In this book, none of the subjects/jurisdictions in the comparative study adopts the absolute immunity theory. Such a position is relatively categorical and there would not be very much to analyze. China used to be absolutist but has changed course since 2024. Moreover, it is difficult to know which States are absolutist when there is no legislation to such effect and when there is no case law to confirm the position.[30]

27. Mark Van Hoecke, "Legal Doctrine: Which Method(s)?," in Houcke & Ost, *supra* n. 16, at 7.
28. *Ibid.*, at 11-12.
29. *Ibid.*, at 11.
30. For example, it is believe that Brazil and Saudi Arabia would accept absolute immunity from execution. However, it remains a speculation. It can also be speculated that other Latin American countries would adopt such position, e.g., Venezuela, Pery, and Ecuador. Such speculation can be strengthened by Colombia's absolutist stance. In *Rusoro v. Venezuela*, Colombia's Supreme Court accepted Venezuela's plea of sovereign immunity from execution. The court even went as far as to conclude that because Venezuela enjoys absolute immunity form execution, it would be impermissible to enforce the arbitral award *See* IAReporter, Analysis Colombia Supreme Court Refuses to Enforce ICSID Additional Facility Award against Venezuela, Citing State's Absolute Immunity from Execution, June 27, 2024: https://www.iareporter.com/articles/colombia-supreme-court-refuses-to-enforce-icsid-additional-facility-award-against-venezuela-citing-states-absolute-immunity-from-execution/.

§1.2.1 Doctrinal Methodology

The law on sovereign immunity has developed predominantly and primarily through treaty work,[31] domestic case law, national legislation, and scholarly work. Most influential for the development of the substantive law on sovereign immunity has been domestic case law. From such decisions, the substantive law of sovereign immunity has generated workable principles, doctrines, tests, and theories that have in turn been consolidated as part of customary international law by other courts or international institutions (most notably the ICJ). Thus, domestic case law builds—and at the same time tracks the emergence and evolution of—customary international law in this field. Put simply, domestic judges both crystalize principles and consolidate international law through their domestic decision-making. Domestic judges both interpret and make international law in this area. Through domestic case law we find evidence of judges' doctrinal understanding of sovereign immunity law as well as evidence of how they facilitate the law's effectiveness through interpretation and application juxtaposed to domestic procedural rules (e.g., discovery, lowering or reversing the burden of proof, allowing execution against mixed-use assets, etc.). More importantly for international law, domestic case law serves as evidence of how rules of customary international law concerning sovereign immunity "emerge, crystallize and consolidate."[32] As will become evident to the reader, judicial decisions now constitute a de facto primary source of the substantive law of sovereign immunity. Moreover, due to the scarcity of guidance on the evolution of the law, scholarly work is also "prolific" in this field of law.[33] For these reasons, the doctrinal research method is instrumental to the study of sovereign immunity law.

The author will trace, source, and map legislation, case law, and scholarly work in order to analyze and reveal the doctrinal understanding of immunity from execution, in particular as pertains to the international arbitration context. This will lead to a critical and systemically conceptual understanding of the substantive law as well as to the interpretation and application of the law by domestic courts. In doing so, the doctrinal methodology will assist in explaining the unresolved areas of divergence as well as assisting in predicting and suggesting possible future developments.[34] In turn, the doctrinal study (*de lege lata*) lays the ground for a comparative exercise. In turn, the two methodologies combined will generate enough data for reform suggestions (*de lege ferenda*). Thus, through distilling general theories, positions, interpretations, and applications, the doctrinal study will culminate in a coherent set of rules and exceptions to the rules at different levels of abstraction.[35]

The history, evolution, contemporary practices, and the direction of the substantive law of sovereign immunity from execution, as well as its implementation through

31. The term "treaty work" is used as opposed to "treaties" because the primary treaty on sovereign immunity has not yet entered into force.
32. Xiodong Yang, *State Immunity in International Law* 27 (2012).
33. Fox & Webb, *supra* n. 9, at 2.
34. *See* Terry Hutchinson, *The Doctrinal Method: Incorporating Interdisciplinary Methods in Reforming the Law*, 3 Erasmus L. Rev. 130 (2015) https://doi.org/10.5553/elr.000055.
35. *Ibid.*

interpretation and application of procedural rules and court practices, will be presented through a study of a series of cases, legislation, treaty work, and scholarly work. That being so, the author has not used a formula to be systemically applied for each case analyzed in this study. The author believes that the doctrinal method is (and needs to be) fluid to a certain degree. Moreover, given that several jurisdictions are the object of comparison (including various court instances), the author has made the conscious decision that it would be impossible to reduce the doctrinal analysis to an algorithm categorizing exactly what will be looked for in each case.[36] Thus, a more holistic doctrinal exercise has been undertaken.

The "current" law on sovereign immunity—i.e., the law as it is (*de lege lata*)—is analyzed not only to instruct the "international lawyer" (counsel) on the substantive law and procedural rules available in different jurisdictions when representing an award-creditor or award-debtor State but also in order to assist policy-makers, judges, and scholars to identify the possible law going forward—i.e., rethinking the law as it could or should be (*de lege ferenda*).[37] Thus, the aim is to go beyond identifying and analyzing current law, and therefore to also offer possible new tools, positions, amendments, and reforms.[38]

Notwithstanding the above-mentioned, truly understanding case law and legislation requires some theoretical understanding. Thus, before proceeding to a case law analysis, jurisdiction by jurisdiction, this book will analyze the conceptual framework of sovereign immunity by discussing the sources of the law and the theory that underlie the substantive rules (Chapter 3). The doctrinal method will then be better utilized when investigating, comparing, and contrasting various positions. The result of the doctrinal exercise in conjunction with a robust and thorough theoretical understanding will help answer the questions outlined in the comparative methodology and lead to a form of typology (i.e., the outcome of the analysis in Chapter 4).

§1.2.2 Comparative Methodology and Typology

The study of foreign laws and recourse to comparison in legal scholarship is as old as the science of law itself.[39] However, the utilization of a comparative method and the study of comparative law is a more recent phenomenon. Comparative studies of law are indeed vital and instrumental in the twenty-first-century scholarship and practice of law.

The studies of comparative law can be macro and micro, e.g., comparing entire legal systems (macro) or individual rules (micro).[40] The comparative methodology is a vital and integral tool and device in the practice of an international lawyer—especially such lawyers dealing with cross-border matters and international law. The study of comparative law and the usefulness of the comparative methodology is also intrinsic in

36. *Ibid.*
37. *See* Westerman, *supra* n. 25, at 97.
38. Hutchinson, *The Doctrinal Method* (2015).
39. René David & John Elmes Campbell Brierley, *Major Legal Systems in the World Today* 1 (1985).
40. *See, e.g.*, Samuel, *supra* n. 26, at 53.

understanding the performance of various national laws and international law. The use of comparative law and methodology is also essential and integral when proposing legal reforms and in seeking to achieve or propose harmonization or even unification of the law.[41]

In improving the law as "it is" legislators make use of comparative law in understanding what the law "could" or "should" be by looking at, for example, foreign case law, foreign legislation, and scholarly work. In this endeavor, comparative law and methodology assume the status of a science, indeed an autonomous branch of legal knowledge.[42]

For this book's purposes, it suffices to conclude that an international lawyer who engages with comparative legal studies or comparative legal practice is indeed a "comparatist." In being a comparatist, it is important to understand that the "principal task is to prepare the ground, so to speak, in order that others can, with profit, adopt the comparative method in their specific fields."[43]

As a comparatist, this author has studied foreign legislation and case law in the area of sovereign immunity from execution, and in particular in the context of execution of foreign arbitral awards. This is done for the readers' benefit. One of the main purposes of this book is to create conditions for a fruitful dialogue between internal and external stakeholders, i.e., both domestically rooted and international lawyers, as well as for lawyers from different areas of specialization.

The comparative methodology utilized in this book compliments the doctrinal study and is used to put together various approaches to the understanding, interpretation, and application of sovereign immunity law in order to examine the degrees of similarity and differences between jurisdictions so as to be able to draw conclusions that a study of each jurisdiction independently would not have enabled.[44] Put very simply, without having undertaken the doctrinal methodological exercise, there is nothing to compare, no commonalities or diverging viewpoints to observe, and no principles, theories, tests, or doctrines to distill and draw comparative inferences or conclusions from. One can consider the comparison to be a reflection, an argumentation, of the study that has been done through doctrinal research.

The author interprets and then compares various jurisdictions' doctrinal understanding, interpretation, and application by looking at various sources of law. Because the doctrine on sovereign immunity is formed by an amalgam of public international law and domestic law, the legal analysis and judicial pronouncements on the subject require "interpretative and comparative skills to detect the common international law rule" or the different rules that the various objects of comparison endorse.[45]

The "doctrinal understanding" will be distilled by asking and answering a series of questions to determine whether the approach in the said jurisdiction is "conservative," "quasi-liberal," "liberal," or "liberal & pragmatic" (*see* more below).

41. *See, e.g.*, John Bell, "Legal Research and Comparative Law," in Houcke & Ost, *supra* n. 16, at 157.
42. David & Brierley, *supra* n. 39, at 12.
43. *Ibid.*
44. *See, e.g.*, Samuel, *supra* n. 26, at 26.
45. Fox & Webb, *supra* n. 9, at 13.

[1] Selection Criteria

When engaging in the field of comparative law, the researcher must ask the crucial questions: "What is meant by comparison" and "What is meant by law"?[46] For this book's methodological purposes, the author had to determine what subject matter (or institution of law) was to be compared and what sources of law to use for such comparison (and why). The comparative methodological exercise is like the Socratic method of study, i.e., all about asking the right questions. By formulating the right questions, the examiner will have a clear set of data to effectively compare and contrast. Although, as previously stated, it was impracticable to reduce the study of case law into one single mechanical formula, it was possible to systematically break down the selection of comparative objects and formulate specific questions. This allowed for a methodologically consistent analysis, ultimately guiding the research toward answering the posed questions.

The objects of comparison (i.e., the chosen jurisdictions) were selected on three common denominators and several factors unique to the specific jurisdictions selected. This book engages in an in-depth analysis of the practice of the courts in: (1) the U.K., and (2) the U.S. Moreover, the book engages in a rigorous analysis of the practice of the courts in (3) France, (4) India, and (5) Sweden. Finally, this book engages—albeit in a less rigorous manner—with an analysis of the practice of the courts in (6) China and (7) Russia.

The common denominators of each object of study were: (i) market impact (size of economy primarily); (ii) ideological relevance (leaders of international governance and from various political theories; for example, all permanent five members of the Security Council represented); and (iii) geographical importance (geopolitically and arbitration-specific). Each jurisdiction was chosen for its strong economic positioning and relevance for international commerce, trade, and investment (outbound and inbound). Each jurisdiction was chosen also for purposes of ideological diversity, representing influential States with divergent political theory and market structuring. Finally, each country holds both geographic and geopolitical importance and is therefore influential in international affairs, generally, and in international arbitration, particularly. Sweden may be the exception in this regard but is included because it has historically played an instrumental role as a neutral State, and therefore as the seat of "East-West ISDS matters" since the aftermath of the Cold War. Therefore, it also has a rich body of jurisprudence on sovereign immunity in the international arbitration context.

The two main jurisdictions studied—i.e., the U.K. and the U.S.—have three common unique factors making such study practical: namely, (iv) language; (v) high frequency of cases; and (vi) influential case law for the consolidating of customary international law. Adding to that, the U.K. and the U.S. have (vii) enacted special legislation to deal with sovereign immunity. As a result, the U.K. and the U.S. courts have exercised global influence in this field. Given that both are financial centers of the

46. *See, e.g.*, Samuel, *supra* n. 26, at 13.

world, foreign States typically hold assets in these jurisdictions, making them both attractive enforcement venues for award-creditors. For example, the U.S. controls the world's reserve currency and is (still) the largest economy in the world. Furthermore, the World Bank, and therefore ICSID, is located in the U.S. Similarly, the U.K. is one of the world's largest economies and is a frequently chosen venue for settling disputes stemming from international commerce, trade, and investment—including ISDS matters.

Apart from the common denominators above, China was chosen because it is the world's second-largest economy and is the leading non-Western State that adheres to civil law (with traits of socialism and other Chinese characteristics). Moreover, China's legal system could play a significant role in regulating the doctrine on sovereign immunity outside the mainland, e.g., in Hong Kong and Macau. France was chosen because it is a Western State that adheres to civil law and has a rich experience dealing with enforcing arbitral awards, including the plea of sovereign immunity. France is also home to the largest international arbitration institution (the ICC). India was chosen because of the size of its economy and population and also because it is a non-Western country, a former colony, and a common law country with socialist roots. Russia was chosen because it is a non-Western country, a former Soviet/socialist state, and a defendant and award-debtor in many ISDS matters. The U.S., Russia, and China are all global superpowers—considering political, military, and economic powers. Moreover, China, France, Russia, the U.K., and the U.S. are permanent members of the UN. Sweden used to be a neutral jurisdiction, which was also the financial, political, and cultural center of Scandinavia, on the one hand, and recognized as a hub for ISDS, on the other. More than that, Sweden was chosen for comparative purposes because it adheres to the Scandinavian model of legal traditions—i.e., a form of mixture between the common law and civil law traditions. As a final note, France, Sweden, the U.K., and the U.S. are also some of the jurisdictions with the most important case law in the area, which have been cited in the ICJ, foreign courts, and by many influential scholars. To this list, one could have added Argentina, Saudi Arabia, Germany, the Netherlands, Nigeria, South Africa, Colombia, Japan, Switzerland, and many more. For the reasons mentioned in the selection criteria, and due to limitations in pages and time, it is not possible to cover every jurisdiction. It is hoped that the typology presented in this book will keep on growing with more and new jurisdictions in the future.

The reader may also wonder why the author chose India and Russia instead of, for example, Canada and Australia as objects of study. Admittedly, the latter two are potentially bigger enforcement markets for an award-creditor. The reason is that the book must also cover divergences in scope, degree, and nuance, especially stemming from different legal families and traditions. The author asserts that ideology and legal families play an important part in the evolution of sovereign immunity law. In the author's informed view, neither Canada nor Australia differs to a radical extent from other common law jurisdictions, such as the U.S. or the U.K. Sure, there may be some differences, but with a fair understanding of sovereign immunity law generally (the theory), and an understanding of the approaches taken by the courts in the U.S. and the U.K. (the practice), in particular, the reader will be capable of working toward a good understanding of the approaches in Canada and Australia too. Similarly, in order to understand the approaches taken in Sri Lanka and Nepal, one may have to understand the approach in India. On that note, in order to understand the approaches in Uzbekistan, Kazakhstan, and Belarus, one may have to understand the approach taken in Russia. Similarly, the jurisdictions from continental Europe are not too different from, for example, other jurisdictions on the continent (e.g., France). A fair understanding of France (and perhaps Sweden) would render the reader capable of understanding German, Belgium, and Switzerland, too.

[2] Comparative Elements and Elaborating a Typology

This book focuses strictly on immunity from execution. More specifically, this book deals with the plea of immunity from execution in the arbitral award enforcement context. Any reference to immunity from jurisdiction is illustrative, contextual, and for micro-comparative purposes only. For example, a reference of immunity from jurisdiction could be used for two reasons: (i) to explain the background/evolution before moving on to the topic at hand; and (ii) because if a State adheres to absolute immunity from jurisdiction, it typically does so with respect to immunity from execution too. The latter point is important because if a State, for example, accepts absolute immunity from enforcement of an arbitral award, then it can be inferred with relative certainty that it accepts absolute immunity from execution.

This book will divide the comparing objects' doctrinal understanding and application and interpretation of sovereign immunity from execution of international arbitral awards into four colors: Red, Orange, Yellow, and Green, in that order.

Red List: Red list countries are those that adhere to absolute immunity from execution. The said approach is "conservative" toward award-creditors. Even such States, however, can be more or less "conservative." A conservative State can still be "pro-arbitration." For example, States in this category differ on the answer to:

- whether the State has an arbitration law;
- whether the arbitration law is modeled after the UNCITRAL Model Law or shares important characteristics with it;
- whether courts have embraced a pro-arbitration attitude;
- whether the State is a Member State to the New York Convention;
- whether the State is a Member State to the ICSID Convention;
- whether the State has signed IIAs with ISDS clauses;
- whether the State respects the principle of voluntary payments of adverse awards;
- whether the State engages through diplomatic channels to assist award-creditors against award-debtor States;
- whether the State endorses a restrictive doctrine of immunity from jurisdiction; and
- whether the State endorses a restrictive doctrine of immunity from jurisdiction, including for recognition and enforcement of arbitration awards.

Thus, red list States can be pro-arbitration and still adhere to the theory of absolute immunity, and therefore be considered "conservative" for the purposes of this typology. Similarly, red list States can accept restrictive immunity for the purposes of confirming arbitral awards but not with respect to execution thereafter. These are two important caveats.

Orange List: Orange list countries are those that adhere to restrictive immunity from execution in theory. The said approach is "quasi-liberal" toward award creditors. This list includes States that adhere to restrictive immunity in theory but not necessarily in practice. Such lack of faithful observance of the restrictive immunity doctrine can be practiced domestically before its own courts when asked to apply the plea of sovereign immunity or else by the State's frequent invoking of immunity when assuming the role of an award-debtor. The quasi-liberal States also engage in politics to retaliate against other States for espousing a liberal (and perhaps pragmatic) attitude toward the award-debtor State. Some quasi-liberal States submit the question of whether or not to grant immunity to the executive branch, as opposed to having the matter determined by the judicial branch. Questions asked under this category are not only the same as those asked to fall under the yellow list (*see* below), but also:

- whether the State's courts have accepted the plea of sovereign immunity from execution and in what instances;
- whether the State has invoked sovereign immunity from execution in foreign courts;
- whether the State has retaliated or used "reciprocity" standards regarding sovereign immunity from execution;
- whether the State has moved decisions on immunity from execution from the judicial branch and to other branches of government.

Yellow List: Yellow list countries are those that adhere to restrictive immunity from execution in theory as well as in practice (from a substantive law point of view). The said approach is "liberal" toward award creditors. In this category, as well as in the orange list, we ask the following questions:

- whether the State adheres to restrictive immunity regarding execution;
- whether the State has signed and/or ratified the UN Convention on Jurisdictional Immunities of States and Their Property (UNCSI);
- whether the State has adopted legislation reflecting the restrictive theory of immunity from execution;
- whether the State has clarified the restrictive position on immunity from execution through case law;
- whether the State has clarified the restrictive position on immunity from execution through political undertakings; and
- whether the State has demonstrated its restrictive position on immunity from execution through its own actions.

In order to fall under the yellow list, a State must also have referred to the restrictive theory on sovereign immunity in practice, i.e., in favor of an award-creditor by making a reference to either:

- domestic legislation;
- the UNCSI;
- customary international law;
- general principles of law;
- foreign case law embracing the restrictive theory on sovereign immunity; and
- scholarly work in favor of the restrictive theory on sovereign immunity.

Green List: Green list countries are those that, like the yellow list, adhere to restrictive immunity from execution in theory as well as in practice. In addition to satisfying the yellow list criteria, green list countries not only adhere to restrictive immunity with respect to the substantive law but also provide award-creditors with procedural tools that make award execution possible. The said approach is both "liberal" and "pragmatic." In order to qualify as both liberal & pragmatic, the State in question must, in addition to what has already been stated under the yellow list embrace one or more of the following:

- a "nature test" with respect to immunity from execution;
- a "double-waiver doctrine";
- a low burden-of-proof or reversed it on the award-debtor State in a reasonable manner;
- a reasonable stance on "veil piercing";
- a reasonable stance on mixed-use assets;
- a means of identifying State assets (e.g., discovery); and
- a less rigid list of property immune *ipso facto.*

Finally, it must be mentioned that within each list, States can be more or less "conservative," more or less "liberal," and more or less "pragmatic."

It must be emphasized and clearly underscored that the methodology as presented above—culminating in a typology—is instrumental to answering the research question. The answer to the research question rests on the outcome of the comparative exercise as manifested in turn through the answers to the series of questions asked above under the various lists. If a State is "liberal," the *doctrinal understanding* of sovereign immunity from execution does indeed resonate with a twenty-first-century global marketplace—at least from a substantive law point of view. If a State is also "pragmatic," the *interpretation and application* of the doctrine when dealing with the execution of an international arbitral award is one that resonates undoubtedly with a twenty-first-century global marketplace—also from a procedural rules and court practice point of view. If the State is "conservative," the *doctrinal understanding* of sovereign immunity from execution and its *interpretation and application* in the international arbitration context does not resonate with a twenty-first-century global marketplace. If the State is "quasi-liberal," it is difficult—if not impossible—for the award-creditor to draw any conclusions on whether the State's attitude will be either conservative or liberal.

§1.2.3 Non-legal, Non-methodological Study

It has been said that "[a]lmost all nations observe almost all principles of international law and almost all of their obligations almost all of the time."[47] In that cynical light, an international lawyer dealing with reluctant States must at least consider approaching legal issues with non-legal solutions. Sometimes, it is surely worth the award-creditor's while. To some parties, justice delayed is justice denied. The very survival of award-creditors could be contingent on liquidity and the stream of income from the ISDS award may be the only amount that can save the entity as a going concern.

Apart from analyzing the law—and corresponding legal solutions to the presented issue—this book will investigate and explore non-legal approaches available to assist an award-creditor against an award-debtor State that invokes sovereign immunity to shield against attaching and executing against its assets.

Thus, this book explores the law of sovereign immunity through four lenses; that is: (1) substantive law (*law-based solutions*); (2) procedural law (i.e., legal/judicial structures and architecture available to an award-creditor; *structural-based solutions*); (3) behavioral norms (*norms-based solutions*); and (4) market-based venues for redress or assistance (*market-based solutions*).

47. Louis Henkin, *How Nations Behave: Law and Foreign Policy* 47 (2nd ed. 1979).

CHAPTER 2

Final, Binding, and Directly Enforceable Arbitral Awards & Sovereign Immunity

§2.1 INTRODUCTION

For a dispute resolution regime to be reliable and function effectively, the decision-making process must be legitimate and its product must be sanctioned with coercive force to overcome the eventuality of non-compliance.[1] ISDS, like any dispute resolution regime, must guarantee the quality if its processes while providing effective sanctioning of its outcomes. As Lew and others noted:

> Enforcement may function as a sword in that the successful party requests the assistance of the court to enforce the award by exercising its power and applying legal sanctions should the other party fail or refuse to comply voluntarily. The type of sanctions available will vary from country to country and may include seizure of the award debtor's property, freezing of bank accounts or even custodial sentences in extreme cases.

The enforceability of international arbitral awards represents one of the central pillars upon which the international arbitration system rests.[2] International arbitration

1. *See, e.g.*, Alan S. Alexandroff & Ian A. Laird, "Compliance and Enforcement" in *The Oxford Handbook of International Investment Law* (Peter Muchlinkski, Federico Ortino & Christoph Schreuer, eds.) 1, 171 (2008).
2. The New York Convention has been held to be "the pillar on which the edifice of international arbitration rests." J. Gillis Wetter, *The Present Status of the International Court of Arbitration in the ICC: An Appraisal*, 1 Am. Rev. Int'l. Arb. 91 (1990); *See also* Loukas A. Mistelis, *Award as an Investment: The Value of an Arbitral Award or the Cost of Non-enforcement*, 28:1 ICSID Rev. 64, 66 (2013) https://doi.org/10.1093/icsidreview/sis035; and *See* Emmanuel Gaillard & Ilija Mitrev Penusliski, *State Compliance with Investment Awards*, 36 ICSID Rev. 50-52 (2021) https://doi.org/10.1093/icsidreview/siaa034.

has largely been the preferred means of settling transnational disputes because arbitral awards are generally treated as final, binding, and directly enforceable.[3]

Apart from the legal framework, the legitimacy of international arbitration is further reinforced when participants view recourse to arbitration as an implied engagement to honor the outcome of the award in good faith.[4] Simply put, award-creditors expect that foreign arbitral awards are final, binding, and directly enforceable. In this light, renowned arbitration scholars rightly noted that:

> Unless parties can be sure that at the end of arbitration proceedings, they will be able to enforce the award, if not complied with voluntarily, an award in their favour will be only a pyrrhic victory. Further, the high degree of voluntary compliance is due to there being an effective system for the enforcement of awards in case of non-compliance.[5]

Thus, any obstacle with respect to post-award proceedings must be addressed with due seriousness. The system can remain reliable and effective only if its outcomes carry strong credibility.

§2.1.1 Background to the Enforcement Conventions and the Expectation of Voluntary Compliance

Two primary multilateral enforcement regimes exist for the enforcement of ISDS awards: the 1958 United Convention on the Recognition and Enforcement of Foreign Arbitral Awards (New York Convention) and the 1965 World Bank Convention on the Settlement of Investment Disputes between States and Nationals of Other States (ICSID Convention).[6]

Both conventions are widely adopted and implemented in letter as well as in spirit. However, despite the existence of a robust enforcement regime through multilateral enforcement conventions, award-creditors seldom need to pursue post-award proceedings. Generally speaking, award-debtors—including award-debtor States—mostly comply voluntarily with adverse awards.[7] This is likely due to the relative ease

3. Put differently, the enforcement of foreign arbitral awards positively distinguishes the procedure from other means of dispute settlement. Foreign arbitral awards can be enforced without engaging in a cumbersome legal procedure, such as that of enforcing foreign judgments. *See, e.g.*, *International Arbitration Survey: The Evolution of International Arbitration*, White & Case and Queen Mary School of International Arbitration (2018), https://www.qmul.ac.uk/arbitration/media/arbitration/docs/2018-International-Arbitration-Survey---The-Evolution-of-International-Arbitration-(2).PDF. *See also* Matthew Saunders & Claudia Salomon, *Enforcement of Arbitral Awards Against States and State Entities* 467 (2007).
4. *See* Aron Broches, *Awards Rendered Pursuant to the ICSID Convention: Binding Force, Finality, Recognition, Enforcement, Execution*, 2:2 ICSID Rev. 287, 289 (1987) https://doi.org/10.1093/icsidreview/2.2.287.
5. Julian D.M. Lew et al., *Comparative International Commercial Arbitration* 688 (2003).
6. New York Convention on the Recognition and Enforcement of Foreign Arbitral Awards, 330 U.N.T.S. 3; Convention on the Settlement of Investment Disputes Between States and Nationals of Other States, 575 U.N.T.S. 159.
7. Nigel Blackaby et al., *Redfern and Hunter on International Arbitration* 608 (fn 10) (2015); Saunders & Salomon, *supra* n. 3, at 467; Christoph H. Schreuer et al., *The ICSID Convention: A Commentary* 1107-1108 (2nd ed. 2009); and Mark M. Cymrot, "Enforcing Sovereign Arbitral

of enforcing arbitral awards, coupled with the reputational harm associated with defaulting on debt.[8]

The expectation of voluntary compliance has been so firmly entrenched that when the ICSID Convention was drafted, there was a general expectation that award enforcement "would not be a practical problem and that voluntary compliance would be a natural consequence of the treaty obligation."[9] Yang observed the legitimate expectations of award-creditors as follows:

> If, however, the foreign state, either through a waiver or voluntary submission (be it explicit or by implication) or through the operation of some pre-existing rules compelling non-immunity, enters into the judicial process, then it will be legitimately expected that the state should also obey the orders and decisions of the court. Such has been the expectation since ancient times. In the words of Blackstone, "the sentence of a court would be contemptible, unless that court had power to command the execution of it." (citations omitted) The law of state immunity, however, has come to hold otherwise.[10]

§2.1.2 Background to the Enforcement Conventions and the Obstacle of Sovereign Immunity

Although enforcement is a key characteristic and benefit of ISDS, and compliance remains the norm, in practice, enforcing an award against an award-debtor State poses greater challenges than enforcement against a private party. These challenges stem largely from the fact that the State can invoke the plea of sovereign immunity in the execution phase. If successfully invoked, such plea protects against the attaching and execution of State assets. Therefore, despite the common trajectory in IIL and the law of sovereign immunity to level the playing field between states and private parties, ISDS/ITA still falls short of offering efficient protection in enforcing arbitral awards.[11] As a result, "sovereign immunity remains a significant obstacle to obtaining forced satisfaction of awards against states."[12] This challenge is exacerbated by the fact that

Awards: State Defences and Creditor Strategies in an Imperfect World" in *The Cambridge Handbook of Immunities and International Law* (Tom Ruys et al., eds.) 351 (2019).

8. States engage in diligent cost-benefit analysis, often tilting in favor of compliance. *See* Lew et al., *supra* n. 5, at 803. At times, however, States default not due to bad faith but because they have been under severe economic hardship, i.e., akin to a form of "sovereign insolvency." It is not the author's place to claim the moral high ground in favor of either investors or States in such situations. It is mostly an unfortunate situation.
9. *See* Schreuer et al., *supra* n. 7, at 1107. This position was partly so because non-compliance would lead to, *inter alia*, adverse reactions by other states and, as Schreuer writes, "would affect the standing of the state concerned with the international business community."
10. Xiodong Yang, *State Immunity in International Law* 348 (2012).
11. Stephan W. Schill, *Cross-Regime Harmonization Through Proportionality Analysis: The Case of International Investment Law, the Law of State Immunity and Human Rights*, 27 ICSID Rev. 87, 101 (2012) https://doi.org/10.1093/icsidreview/sis002.
12. Philippe Fouchard et al., *Fouchard Gaillard Goldmn on International Commercial Arbitration* 377 (1999).

neither of the two major multilateral enforcement conventions addresses sovereign immunity in a substantive way.[13]

As a result of this interplay between enforcement and immunity, the enforcement regime of ISDS is shaped by an inherent public-private tension. Paradoxically, addressing this tension was a primary motivation behind the creation of ISDS. One of the underlying purposes was to foster de-politicization, shifting away from a "State-centric" perspective and instead "towards a rule of law based international law that takes individuals and their protection seriously."[14]

That said, sovereign immunity plays an important role in public international law. The adjudicator (arbitrators and judges) must carefully balance between public and private interests. Siding too much with one over the other can lead to unwelcome consequences. If the balance is not properly struck, States or private parties might no longer participate willfully in ISDS. The regime of ISDS is already facing serious legitimacy concerns and a backlash movement has ensued. If we reach a point where States increasingly refuse to voluntarily comply with adverse arbitral awards, the rules-based international legal order we rely on today would be seriously jeopardized.

§2.2 INVESTOR-STATE ARBITRATION: ENFORCING PRIVATE INTERESTS AND THE GLOBAL RULE OF LAW

The study of this book invokes two areas of international law; that is, (1) ITA/ISDS, and (2) sovereign immunity law. For that reason, some familiarity with international arbitration and IIL (substantive law in ITA procedures) is necessary before moving on to a detailed analysis of ISDS and sovereign immunity from execution.

International arbitration and IIL facilitate the enforcement of private economic interests (i.e., manifest as important vehicles of international economic law) while sovereign immunity retains the ability to protect public interests by fending off adjudication or the intrusion on State assets (i.e., manifests as an important public policy instrument). The balancing of the competing doctrines cannot be fully comprehended without understanding the importance of what the competing interests promote.

---

13. *See* Kaj Hobér & Joel Dahlquist, *Investment Treaty Arbitration: Problems and Exercises* 1 (2018); Phoebe D. Winch, "State Immunity and the Execution of Investment Arbitration Awards: A Review of the Plea of State Immunity and the Execution of Investment Arbitration Awards from the Viewpoint of the Forum State," in *Public Actors in International Investment Law* (Catharine Titi, ed.) 61 (2021); Mark C. Weidemaier, *Sovereign Immunity and Sovereign Debt*, 14:1 U. Ill. L. Rev. 67, 77 (2014). Another serious obstacle to award enforcement through execution is the separate legal personality of state entities and sovereign wealth funds, which often hold title over states' commercial assets. *See* Gaillard & Penusliski, *supra* n. 2, at 50-51. *See generally* Emmanuel Gaillard, "Effectiveness of Arbitral Awards, State Immunity from Execution and Autonomy of State Entities: Three Incompatible Principles" in *State Entities in International Arbitration* (Emmanuel Gaillard & Jennifer Younan, eds.) 1 (2008).
14. *See* Schill, *supra* n. 11, at 91.

§2.2.1 International Arbitration and Award Enforcement: ITA/ISDS

When a private party arbitrates against a State, two types of international arbitration are available: ICA and ITA/ISDS. ICA deals with pure commercial disputes. In an ICA procedure, the State may act like any other commercial party if it has signed a commercial agreement and has not in any way, shape, or form acted in its non-commercial governmental capacity. What distinguishes ICA from ITA is that, in the latter: (a) the respondent is almost always a State, and (b) international law is substantively applied in the proceedings (i.e., IIL). ITA is a type of ISDS. Investor-State mediation would also technically be ISDS. The most frequently used ITA/ISDS regime is ICSID. Other frequently chosen alternatives include the International Chamber of Commerce (ICC), the Stockholm Chamber of Commerce (SCC), or ad hoc arbitration pursuant to the UNCITRAL Arbitration Rules.[15] Awards rendered pursuant to the ICSID regime are enforced under the ICISD Convention, while arbitral awards rendered pursuant to the other regimes are enforced pursuant to the New York Convention.[16]

[1] ITA: History and Background

Historically, an investor could not sue a host-State for interfering with his investment, nor could he claim investor protection under customary international law against a State. Instead, the aggrieved investor had to turn to its home State for protection through the venue of diplomatic protection.[17] At times, the home State went as far as to engage in so-called gunboat diplomacy in order to protect its investors' rights and/or interests abroad. From the late 1800s until the end of World War II, there was a relatively regressive era regarding the enforcement of private economic rights against States. During this time period, sovereign immunity was considered absolute.

This regressive era saw its peak in 1889, when an Argentinian jurist and diplomat, Carlos Calvo, elaborated the infamous "Calvo doctrine." The ethos of the Calvo doctrine was to restrict the protections offered to foreign investors—both substantively and procedurally. The Calvo doctrine held that foreign investors should be strictly subjected to the exclusive jurisdiction of national courts and afforded the same treatment as domestic investors.[18] The Calvo era was marked by suspicion and a generally negative stance toward IIL and international arbitration.

The ethos of the Calvo doctrine became unsustainable as cross-border capital flow became essential, leading to a gradual shift from this doctrine that gained momentum at the Second International Peace Conference of the Hague in 1907.[19] However, it was not until the aftermath of World War II that the de-politicization of

15. *See, e.g.*, Hobér & Dahlquist, *supra* n. 13, at 10.
16. *Ibid.*, at 11.
17. *See* Blackaby et al., *supra* n. 7, at 441.
18. *Ibid.*
19. *See, e.g., Eiser Infrastructure Ltd v. Kingdom of Spain*, FCA 157, (2020), at para. 69 ("By providing [for ICSID arbitration], the Centre aims to improve the international investment climate and stimulate a larger flow of private international investment.") and *Kingdom of Spain v. Infrastructure Services Luxembourg S.á.r.l.*, FCAFC 112, (2021), at para. 2 (Stating that the

investment disputes started taking shape effectively. It is no coincidence that this shift followed the Bretton Woods Agreement and occurred during a new world order. In this new era, the ICSID Convention emerged, with its primary purpose—and perhaps its greatest achievement—being the attraction of FDI and the de-politicization of investment disputes through investor-State arbitration.[20] The liberalization that defined this world order, along with the establishment of regimes aimed at promoting, facilitating, and protecting transborder commerce, trade, and investment (e.g., ICC, ICSID, World Trade Organization, IMF, etc.) can find a clear expression in the Washington Consensus.

With these policies in mind, it was globalization that eventually led to the increased need for and use of international arbitration. It is rather evident that domestic laws and domestic legal procedures cannot cater to a global economy that transcends borders. Such domestic practices cannot facilitate the enforcement of a global rule of law. In this way, international arbitration enabled increased commerce, trade, and investment across borders. As a result, international arbitration has played an instrumental part in interconnecting the world and making our markets and economies largely interdependent. It has also helped create relative peace and stability by making "global business possible between Western parties and emerging States and countries that embrace different ideological and legal traditions."[21]

[2] The New York Convention

The New York Convention was crafted to facilitate the recognition and enforcement of international arbitral agreements and awards. It "significantly simplified the enforcement of foreign awards and harmonized the national rules for the enforcement of foreign awards."[22] It has surely achieved its intended purposes.

Article III of the New York Convention outlines the fact that arbitral awards are binding and should be final unless there are grounds for refusing enforcement pursuant to Article V. Thus, Article III makes it clear that states shall as a rule recognize arbitral awards as binding and enforce them accordingly.

However, several exceptions are available to the award-debtor. Arbitral awards can be refused recognition or enforcement on several grounds. Such few and mostly procedural grounds are enumerated exhaustively and exclusively in Article V. In short, international arbitral awards should be recognized and enforced unless they can be attacked on the narrow grounds outlined in the following Article V:

> 1. Recognition and enforcement of the award may be refused, at the request of the party against whom it is invoked, only if that party furnishes to the competent authority where the recognition and enforcement is sought, proof that:

ICSID Convention is an important international convention underpinning and supporting the flow of investment capital around the world.).

20. *See* Gaillard & Penusliski, *supra* n. 2, at 2.
21. Thomas E. Carbonneau, *The Law and Practice of Arbitration* 108 (2020).
22. Lew et al., *supra* n. 5, at 693.

(a) The parties to the agreement referred to in article II were, under the law applicable to them, under some incapacity, or the said agreement is not valid under the law to which the parties have subjected it or, failing any indication thereon, under the law of the country where the award was made; or
The party against whom the award is invoked was not given proper notice of the appointment of the arbitrator or of the arbitration proceedings or was otherwise unable to present his case; or
(b) The award deals with a difference not contemplated by or not falling within the terms of the submission to arbitration, or it contains decisions on matters beyond the scope of the submission to arbitration, provided that, if the decisions on matters submitted to arbitration can be separated from those not so submitted, that part of the award which contains decisions on matters submitted to arbitration may be recognized and enforced; or
(c) The composition of the arbitral authority or the arbitral procedure was not in accordance with the agreement of the parties, or, failing such agreement, was not in accordance with the law of the country where the arbitration took place; or
(d) The award has not yet become binding on the parties or has been set aside or suspended by a competent authority of the country in which, or under the law of which, that award was made.

2. Recognition and enforcement of an arbitral award may also be refused if the competent authority in the country where recognition and enforcement is sought finds that:
(a) The subject matter of the difference is not capable of settlement by arbitration under the law of that country; or
(b) The recognition or enforcement of the award would be contrary to the public policy of that country.

The Convention sets minimum formal requirements for the enforcement and maximum standards for which an award may be refused.[23] Moreover, a court embracing the pro-arbitration policy elaborated by the New York Convention will not engage in a merits review—neither will they add such grounds in domestic law nor will they exercise a "second review" through the public policy exception.[24] Bermann rightly questioned "whether leaving an ostensibly procedural matter entirely to domestic law risk undermining the efficacy of the Convention itself."[25] This is an important and broader concern which is reserved for proper debate in another forum. Here, the focus is more narrowly put on the obstacle of sovereign immunity and whether such doctrine undermines the efficacy of the convention.

Does the silence on sovereign immunity in the New York Convention, and therefore the delegation and deference to domestic approaches, serve as an antithesis to the pro-arbitration ethos unveiled by the convention and entrenched by court practices? Put differently, does sovereign immunity from execution undercut the

23. *Ibid.*, at 697.
24. *See, e.g.*, Andrew Stephenson et al., "Interference by a Local Court and a Failure to Enforce: Actionable under a Bilateral Investment Treaty?" in *Evolution in Investment Treaty Law and Arbitration* (Chester Brown & Katie Miles, eds.) 429 (2012).
25. George A. Bermann, *Recognition and Enforcement of Foreign Arbitral Awards, the Interpretation and Application of the New York Convention By National Courts* 74 (2017).

effectiveness of international arbitration? Despite the undeniable success of the New York Convention, it is undoubtedly the case that the option of an award-debtor State to invoke sovereign immunity may at times undermine the spirit, mission, and destiny of the Convention.

[3] The ICSID Convention

The ICSID Convention, like the New York Convention, is partly an enforcement instrument that renders an investment arbitration award under the ICSID Rules final, binding, and enforceable. In contrast to other kinds of arbitrations falling under the New York Convention umbrella, the ICSID regime is "detached" and "self-contained" from local courts. Simply put, an ICSID award is subject to a self-contained/detached enforcement mechanism free from other international and domestic rules and procedures dealing with the enforcement of foreign arbitral awards.[26] Thus, ICSID awards are not under the same post-award scrutiny by domestic courts as New York Convention awards, which can be challenged at the seat of arbitration under the law governing the arbitration and at the place of enforcement pursuant to the convention. Contrastly, in ICSID arbitrations, challenges are only possible in the form of "annulment procedures" which are decided by an ICSID annulment ad hoc committee. The only possibility for review—which is narrow and limited in and of itself—is at the annulment phase. The annulment phase is ICSID's equivalent to a "challenge" or "set-aside" procedure. The court cannot examine whether the tribunal had jurisdiction, whether it adhered to the proper procedure, whether the award is substantively correct, or whether it conforms to the state's public policy.[27] Important to note, however, is the fact that ICSID Additional Facility Awards (pursued under the separate ICSID Additional Facility Rules) do not form part of the self-contained system and are to be enforced like any other non-ICSID award.

When enforcing ICSID awards, domestic courts' authority is limited to recognition and enforcement, i.e., verifying the authenticity of the award and thereafter entering such award into judgment. ICSID's enforcement mechanism is contained in Articles 53, 54, and 55. The articles read as follows:

> **Article 53**
>
> (1) The award shall be binding on the parties and shall not be subject to any appeal or to any other remedy except those provided for in this Convention. Each party shall abide by and comply with the terms of the award except to the extent that enforcement shall have been stayed pursuant to the relevant provisions of this Convention.
>
> ...
>
> **Article 54**
>
> (1) Each Contracting State shall recognize an award rendered pursuant to this Convention as binding and enforce the pecuniary obligations imposed by that

26. *See* Schreuer et al., *supra* n. 7, at 1118.
27. *See, e.g.*, Rudolph Dolzer & Christoph Schreuer, *Principles of International Investment Law* 448 (2022).

award within its territories as if it were a final judgment of a court in that State. A Contracting State with a federal constitution may enforce such an award in or through its federal courts and may provide that such courts shall treat the award as if it were a final judgment of the courts of a constituent state.

(2) A party seeking recognition or enforcement in the territories of a Contracting State shall furnish to a competent court or other authority which such State shall have designated for this purpose a copy of the award certified by the Secretary-General. Each Contracting State shall notify the Secretary-General of the designation of the competent court or other authority for this purpose and of any subsequent change in such designation.

(3) Execution of the award shall be governed by the laws concerning the execution of judgments in force in the State in whose territories such execution is sought.

Article 55

Nothing in Article 54 shall be construed as derogating from the law in force in any Contracting State relating to immunity of that State or of any foreign State from execution.

As seen, Article 53 underscores the binding effect of the ICSID award and requires parties to abide by and comply with the award. Article 54 underscores the duty to recognize the pecuniary[28] award as final and binding as if it were a final judgment of a court in that State. Article 54(1) can be said to have established the award's enforceability, while 54(2) prescribes how enforceability must be invoked, and finally, 54(3) deals with the execution stage of enforcement.[29] Rightly so, Article 54 has been described as "one of the most important provisions of the Convention" because it "provides for recognition and enforcement of ICSID awards by all courts of all States parties to the Convention."[30] Meanwhile, Article 55 "states that the ICSID Convention does not seek to modify the laws of contracting states with respect to immunity from execution."[31]

Despite the ICSID Convention's unique a-national characteristics, its otherwise self-contained nature does not extend with the same detachment to the recognition and enforcement stage.[32] It is evident from the provisions that both Articles 54(3) and 55 preserve the matter of immunity from execution for domestic practices. Accordingly, despite the purpose of facilitating enforceability and elaborating a duty to honor ICSID awards through a detached and self-contained regime, Articles 54(3) and 55 present a potential obstacle, namely, that of sovereign immunity from execution. As a result, because a State can invoke sovereign immunity from execution, the legal obligation to enforce ICSID arbitral awards—similarly to the obligation under the New York

28. However, the entire award could be recognized and therefore constitute res judicata and technically be enforced even if not covered by Art. 54. Enforcing specific performance awards is completely different from enforcing pecuniary awards. The ICSID Convention expressly mentions that only pecuniary awards are directly enforceable. In *Hardy Exploration v. India*, D.C. District Court concluded that it would be contrary to public policy to enforce an arbitral award for specific performance (D.D.C. Memorandum Opinion, 16-140).
29. *See* Broches, *supra* n. 4, at 320-321.
30. *See* Schreuer et al., *supra* n. 7, at 1117.
31. *See* Winch, *supra* n. 13, at 61.
32. *See* Schreuer et al., *supra* n. 7, at 1120.

Convention—does not automatically ensure the realization of actual assets.[33] Saunders and Salomon illustrated the problem as follows:

> States continue to apply [sovereign immunity], with the consequence that a successful ICSID claimant may suffer a Pyrrhic victory unless assets owned by the state but not immune from enforcement/execution (commonly those in use for commercial purposes) can be identified. Having gone to the significant costs of obtaining an ICSID award and leave to enforce the award (pursuant to Article 54(2) of the ICSID Convention), the claimant may find itself unable to obtain satisfaction thereunder.[34]

§2.2.2 International Investment Law

Since the 1980s there has been a significant growth in promoting and attracting foreign investment by offering investors protection through IIAs.[35] The IIAs—both BITs and MITs, respectively—contain definitions of what a protected investor and investment is and the substantive protection (i.e., IIL). These treaties also contain the arbitration clause (offer to arbitrate) that the investor can unilaterally "trigger" (accept) by requesting arbitration subject to four pre-requisites.[36] The IIL part found in IIAs contains the subject matter law of an ITA procedure.[37] Redfern and Hunter summarized the typical substantive protections found in these IIAs:

- the protection against expropriation or measures equivalent to expropriation without compensation [i.e., indirect expropriation];
- the right to FET;
- the right to FPS;
- the protection against arbitrary or discriminatory treatment;
- the right to national and MFN treatment [NTS and MFN];
- the right to the free transfer of funds and assets; and

33. *See, e.g., LETCO v. Liberia,* 650 F. Supp. 73 (S.D.N.Y 1986) (aff'd by 2d Circuit with no published opinion), where it was held that the investor "have execution" but later found that Art. 55 subjects it to the FSIA, and therefore a second attempt to realize the assets failed on grounds of sovereign immunity; *See also* Jan H. Dalhuisen, *Dalhuisen on Transnational Comparative Commercial, Financial and Trade Law* 565 (2016).
34. *See* Saunders & Salomon, *supra* n. 3, at 469.
35. *See* Blackaby et al., *supra* n. 7, at 444-445.
36. (i) ratione voluntatis (there is a consent to arbitrate); (ii) ratione materiae (there is a protected investment); (iii) ratione personae (there is a protected investor); and (iv) ratione temporis (the treaty applies from a temporal standpoint). Notably, the ICSID Convention has an additional jurisdictional threshold in Art. 25 (commonly referred to as the "double-barreled test").
37. Whether the subject matter of IIL is to be adjudicated in "isolation" or whether other fields of public international law, such as international environmental law or international human rights law, become relevant in ITA/ISDS is much debated. *See, e.g.,* Crina Baltag & Ylli Dautaj, *Promoting, Regulating, and Enforcing Human Rights Through International Investment Law and ISDS*, 45 Fordham Int'l L.J. (2021); and Crina Baltag & Ylli Dautaj, *Investors, States, and Arbitrators in the Crosshairs of International Investment Law and Environmental Protection* (2020). Apart from this, better known as "regime interaction," also domestic laws on the environment, public health, human rights, and so on, may become relevant and applicable with respect to the merits of the ITA/ISDS dispute.

- the protection against a state's breaches of its investment obligations and undertakings [Umbrella Clause].[38]

IIL is one key component of what is known as international economic law. The other major part of international economic law is trade law, which is established by institutions like the World Trade Organization and various preferential trade agreements (e.g., USMCA).

When ISDS arbitrators deal with IIL—i.e., in ITA procedures—they are effectively enforcing international law. It can even be said that they are enforcing a global rule of law. However, there is a significant distinction between compliance with IIL found in treaties and compliance with enforcement and execution of the arbitral decisions.[39] Arbitrators become *functus officio* when the award has been delivered. Thus, while arbitrators can issue a binding award on liability stemming from violations of IIL and order damages accordingly, it ultimately falls to domestic courts to enforce these pecuniary awards. While arbitrators' adjudicatory role involves interpreting and applying substantive IEL (here, IIL), enforcement of their decisions relies on domestic laws, procedures, and international arbitration frameworks. At times, domestic courts are also asked to consider the public international law concept of sovereign immunity.

Thus, the doctrine of sovereign immunity emerges as a procedural hurdle—one which can complicate the execution phase.[40] As a result, an award-debtor State obstructing to honor her commercial obligations under international economic law can use the law to delay, and perhaps even evade, responsibility.[41] It is thus the unequivocal case that the plea of sovereign immunity from execution "offers a debtor [S]tate additional methods of denying [the award-]creditor execution in satisfaction of a valid award obtained in respect of a commercial transaction."[42] Incidentally, the enforcement of the global rule of law (here, IIL) is obstructed, while perhaps another principle of a global rule of law is upheld (sovereign immunity from execution). This presents a notable conundrum.

§2.2.3 Sovereign Immunity Law

The law on sovereign immunity is one of the classic branches of public international law.[43] Thus, sovereign immunity law is public international law. The sources of sovereign immunity law are the same sources as for other areas of public international law, which are to be found in Article 38(1) of the Statute of the International Court of Justice (ICJ Statute)—i.e., treaties, customary international law, general principles of

38. *See* Blackaby et al., *supra* n. 7, at 470; More generally on international investment law, *see* Dolzer & Schreuer, *supra* n. 27, at 186-295.
39. Alexandroff & Laird, *supra* n. 1, at 1172.
40. The immunity from execution generally includes immunity from provisional measures to attach or preserve assets.
41. Hazel Fox & Philippa Webb, *The Law of State Immunity* 536 (2015).
42. *Ibid.; See, e.g., Sedelmayer v. The Russian Federation*, Case No. Ö 170-10, (Swedish Supreme Court, 2011) (the creditor eventually was finally able to attach Russian assets after 17 years).
43. Jan Klabbers, *An Introduction to International Institutional Law* (2nd ed. 2009).

law, judicial decisions, and renowned scholarly work. Because a multilateral treaty framework is technically silent on the issue of sovereign immunity,[44] the law has primarily developed through either domestic case law, international decisions, or domestic and international legislation.[45] Much of this practice has generated agreed-upon principles and has been crystalized as customary international law (as will be discussed in Chapter 3). Therefore, while it is true that sovereign immunity exists as a rule (with multiple exceptions) of public international law, it is also equally true that its content and application depend substantially on domestic law developments and procedural rules of the enforcing domestic court.[46]

The law of sovereign immunity can be divided into two distinct regimes: (1) immunity from jurisdiction; and (2) immunity from execution. The difference is self-explanatory. Moreover, the theory of sovereign immunity law can largely be divided into two categories: (a) the theory of absolute immunity; and (b) the theory of restrictive immunity. The theory of absolute immunity means essentially that a State cannot sit in proceedings before foreign courts without its consent (i.e., absolute immunity from jurisdiction) and/or that an award or judgment-creditor cannot execute against a State's assets (i.e., absolute immunity from execution). The theory of restrictive immunity (in the commercial context), however, is based on a distinction of State actions as either an exercise of sovereign authority (*acta iure imperii*), or an act that a private person may perform (*acta iure gestionis*). This test is based on the *nature of the act*. In contrast, when the theory of restrictive immunity is applied in the execution context, it is based on a distinction between assets used for a commercial purpose (*iure gestionis*) or a non-commercial governmental purpose (*iure imperii*). In the execution context, the test is based on the *purpose of the assets* and not the nature of the underlying transactions.

This book focuses strictly on immunity from execution when enforcing an international arbitration award (although the law is in large part similar when enforcing a foreign judgment). However, this book will also briefly cover immunity from enforcement of international arbitral awards, which is actually a matter of

44. Albeit there has been an attempt to codify the law, *see* the 2004 United Nations Convention on Jurisdictional Immunities of States and Their Property, that convention will take effect and enter into binding force when ratified by thirty countries. That has not happened. Notwithstanding this, the convention has largely been treated as a codification of customary international law. *See, e.g., Jurisdictional Immunities of the State (Germany v. Italy: Greece Intervening)*, Judgment, I.C.J. 99 (February 3, 2012) (hereinafter *Jurisdictional Immunities*) and *Sedelmayer v. The Russian Federation*, Case No. Ö 170-10, (Swedish Supreme Court, 2011) at p. 475. Furthermore, it may be worth noting that two earlier treaties deal with sovereign immunity, namely, the Brussels Convention for the Unification of Certain rules Relating to the Immunity of State-Owned Vessels (adopted on April 10, 1926, additional protocol added on May 24, 1934) and the ECSI (adopted on May 1972). The former is narrow and specific, while the latter is entered into between few European States. The latter is still in force but to insignificant to count as a multilateral treaty on sovereign immunity for the purposes of this study. Customary international law has outgrown the ECSI.
45. *See, e.g.*, U.S. Foreign Sovereign Immunities Act 1976; U.K. State Immunity Act 1978; and *Jurisdictional Immunities*, *supra* n. 44.
46. *See, e.g.*, James Crawford, *Brownlie's Principles of Public International Law* 489 (8th ed. 2012). *See also* Hobér & Dahlquist, *supra* n. 13, at 11.

immunity from jurisdiction.[47] In a nutshell, an arbitration clause is treated as a waiver of immunity from jurisdiction, while the State still retains the right to invoke immunity from execution.

In practical terms, successfully invoking sovereign immunity from execution allows a State to protect public assets without being forced to disclose where they have commercial ones (unless, of course, rigorous discovery rules are in place, or a reversed burden of proof embraced by domestic courts).

§2.2.4 Sovereign Immunity and International Arbitration

The growth of ISDS/ITA as part of international economic law, along with the shift away from absolute immunity, reflects a broader movement from a State-centric international law order toward a rules-based legal framework.[48] However, the freedoms given to private actors remain limited, and protections for States have not been entirely diminished.

The ability to invoke sovereign immunity from execution underscores the fact that "international law does not accord unconditional primacy to the economic interests of foreign investors but ensure[s] the availability of procedural means to protect State interests against enforcement of investment treaty awards."[49] States have kept the plea of immunity from execution as a safety valve to protect legitimate public interests of the State and to serve the "legitimate purpose of shielding assets from attachment and seizure that States need in order to act in the public interest."[50] Thus, the liberal push of the new international world order is met with a sovereign pull.

§2.3 THE TRANSNATIONAL CURRENCY OF INTERNATIONAL ARBITRATION: FINAL, BINDING, AND DIRECTLY ENFORCEABLE AWARDS

Thanks to the two robust multilateral enforcement regimes—i.e., the New York Convention and the ICSID Convention—international arbitral awards are considered de jure near functional equivalents to court judgments.[51] In theory, an international arbitral award should therefore be both final and binding, as well as readily available for recognition and enforcement. In practice, this theory has largely been validated. However, aside from the challenges posed by annulment proceedings (ICSID arbitrations) and set-aside and enforcement issues (non-ICSID arbitrations), the primary post-award obstacle arises when the award-debtor is a State; namely, the issue of sovereign immunity. Such defensive plea can complicate the execution phase and actual asset realization. When this book refers to "post-award proceedings" in this broad sense it is encapsulating also execution, which is technically a "post-judgment proceeding" as enforcement/

47. This book does not look at other exceptions to sovereign immunity, such as vis-à-vis human rights, torts, employment, terrorism, etc.
48. *See* Schill, *supra* n. 11, at 91.
49. *Ibid.*
50. *Ibid.*
51. *See* Mistelis, *supra* n. 2, at 64.

confirmation of an international award leads to it being entered into as a judgment of the said jurisdiction. At times, when it is important to make a distinction between enforcement of an international award and execution, the narrower terminology of "post-judgment proceeding" will be used when referring to execution.

Notwithstanding this book's focus on immunity from execution, it is important to understand the role that post-award enforcement proceedings play in the chain of events leading up to the issue of immunity from execution. Broadly put, a "post-award proceeding" refers to the actions an award-debtor may take after an arbitral award is delivered to attack its legal effects.

In such situations, the award-creditor can first defend against the attacks against the award and later on (or simultaneously) turn to domestic courts to seek recognition, enforcement, and/or execution pursuant to the applicable enforcement convention or domestic laws/rules.[52]

In most trading-friendly nations, the enforcing court generally puts parochialism and idiosyncrasy aside in exercising a strong policy favoring arbitration. Such policy includes a pro-enforcement attitude, i.e., a form of "deference" to the arbitral decision-making procedure and its product. These domestic courts demonstrate a faithful application of the two multilateral enforcement convention and their deference to international arbitral awards (including ISDS-awards).

However, as previously mentioned, despite a generally pro-enforcement attitude, when the award-debtor is a State that refuses voluntary compliance, the doctrine of sovereign immunity can indeed frustrate the effectiveness of ISDS at the back end of the process.

§2.3.1 Final and Binding Arbitral Awards

The arbitral award is a product of the agreement to arbitrate. Both arbitration agreements and arbitral awards are binding and enforceable. The binding agreement or award creates rights and corresponding obligations to comply with the effects of the agreement/award. Despite being binding, an award must be final in order to be forcefully enforced (i.e., the award-debtor must have either forgone or pre-empted the limited ability to challenge the award). This book does not deal with the finality aspect of post-award proceedings and its many ramifications. The ICSID Convention provides for a number of remedies and review procedures, e.g., "supplementation and rectification" (Article 49), "interpretation" (Article 50), "revision" (Article 51), and "annulment" (Article 52). The annulment happens before an ad hoc annulment committee. In non-ICSID arbitrations, an award-debtor can seek to challenge (set-aside) an arbitral award at the seat of the arbitration pursuant to the provisions in the arbitration act (usually similar to those found in Article V of the New York Convention). Moreover, in non-ICSID arbitrations, the award-debtor can seek to challenge recognition and/or enforcement pursuant to Article V of the New York Convention. When the award is final and free from annulment/set-aside processes, the award-debtor must carry out its obligations.

52. Lew et al., *supra* n. 5, at 689.

Thus, international arbitration is grounded in two fundamental principles of law: namely, the obligation to carry out voluntary undertakings (*pacta sunt servanda*) and to do so in good faith (bona fide).

§2.3.2 Post-Award Proceedings: Recognition, Enforcement, and Execution

Despite the final and binding character of international arbitral awards pursuant to multilateral enforcement conventions, if an award-debtor does not comply voluntarily, the award-creditor must nevertheless bring the award to a national court for recognition and enforcement.[53] In that phase, we deal with recognition, enforcement, and execution of the arbitral award. Cymrot succinctly explained the concepts as follows:

> "Recognition" is the determination by a court that an arbitration award is entitled to preclusive effect, meaning the arbitral panel's determination resolved the dispute. "Enforcement" is the reduction of a foreign arbitral award to a domestic judgment, which makes judgment enforcement remedies available to the successful claimant. "Execution" is the process by which a court takes control of specific property.[54]

When an award-debtor State refuses to comply with an award, the award-creditor must first pursue recognition and enforcement. In a final "post-*judgment*" (as opposed to "post-*award*") step, the creditor must then "seek execution of the award by identifying non-immune assets of the debtor state which can be attached or seized in satisfaction of the debt arising under the award."[55] An international award that is confirmed or enforced is thereby converted into a judgment within that jurisdiction. However, unless specified otherwise, references to post-award proceedings in this book, include execution.

While this book primarily focuses on the broader issue of sovereign immunity from execution, sovereign immunity from enforcement has also proven problematic. Therefore, it is essential to address the latter, at least briefly.

[1] Sovereign Immunity in the Broader Enforcement Context: Enforcement and Execution

As seen above, this book makes a clear distinction between recognition, enforcement, and execution.[56] It is well-established that an agreement to arbitrate constitutes a waiver of immunity for actions seeking recognition and enforcement of an award,

53. *See* Committee on International Commercial Disputes of the New York City Bar Association, *Recommended Procedures for Recognition and Enforcement of International Arbitration Awards Rendered under the ICSID Convention*, 27(1) ICSID Rev. 207, 209 (2012); *See also* Cymrot, *supra* n. 7, at 354 https://doi.org/10.1093/icsidreview/sis021.
54. *See* Cymrot, *supra* n. 7, at 352; *See generally,* Gary Born, *International Commercial* Arbitration 3394-3731 (2nd ed. 2014). For a good early pronouncement on the meaning of recognition, *See Socobel Case*, PCIJ (ser A/B), Case No. 78 (1939) at 175.
55. *See* Winch, *supra* n. 13, at 63.
56. The distinction, and subsequently clarification of where and when a state may invoke the plea of immunity, matters for practical purposes of engaging in "asset hunting" and forced "forum shopping." *See, e.g.*, Weidemaier, *supra* n. 13, at 90.

however, it is now widely held that this same agreement does not constitute a waiver of immunity from execution.[57] Therefore, despite the pro-enforcement success of the multilateral enforcement conventions, execution is still subject to sovereign immunity laws of the enforcing jurisdiction.[58]

In the ICSID context, in particular, "[t]here has been much debate over the meaning of the term 'enforce' or 'enforcement' as used in Article 54, and whether it has a distinct meaning from either 'recognition' or 'execution,' both of which also are used in Article 54."[59]

The general consensus is that there is no scope for immunity from recognition. However, there is a level of disagreement still in the ICSID context on whether the immunity regime is limited to execution or also covers enforcement. This disagreement differs slightly on whether we are dealing with an award to be enforced pursuant to the New York Convention or the ICSID Convention. Under the New York Convention, an agreement to arbitrate translates to a waiver of immunity from jurisdiction, which includes enforcement jurisdiction. There is little debate about that. However, under the ICSID Convention, the matter is slightly more blurred due to the language of the Convention, in general, and due to the equally authentic Spanish and French versions. The remainder of this sub-section, therefore, deals exclusively with the ICSID Convention and ICSID arbitrations.

States have waived their right to invoke immunity from recognition and enforcement by having entered the ICSID Convention. Put differently, they have submitted to the jurisdiction of the enforcing court. Yet, many prominent practitioners and scholars disagree with this notion in scope, degree, and nuance.[60] Notably, the leading commentators on the ICSID Convention seem to be of the view that enforcement and execution are used interchangeably in Article 54, and that there should be no derogation from national sovereign immunity laws in this regard (Approach 1).[61] Notwithstanding this position, other leading commentators are of the opposing view; for example, Reed and Paulsson opined that enforcement is indistinguishable from recognition and that both are steps leading up to actual execution (Approach 2).[62] It has been noted that neither of these two approaches "attribute an autonomous, distinct meaning to the term 'enforcement.'"[63] Thus, a third position has grown from and

57. *See* Lew et al., *supra* n. 5, at 750; and Saunders & Salomon, *supra* n. 3, at 469.
58. *See* Broches, *supra* n. 4, at 304.
59. Committee on International Commercial Disputes of the New York City Bar Association, *supra* n. 53, at 212. *See also* Lucy Reed et al., *Guide to ICSID Arbitration* 180 (2004).
60. *See, e.g.*, Cymrot, *supra* n. 7, at 355. *See also* Ylli Dautaj, *Enforcing Arbitral Awards against States and the Defence of Sovereign Immunity from Execution*, 16 MJIEL 395 (2019); Lew et al., *supra* n. 5, at 750; and Saunders & Salomon, *supra* n. 3, at 750.
61. *See* Schreuer et al., *supra* n. 7, at 1136.
62. Reed et al., *supra* n. 59, at 180. This position was also endorsed by the ICJ (albeit not with respect to an ICSID Award). *See Jurisdictional Immunities, supra* n. 44 (the court held that there is a distinction between proceedings for the recognition and enforcement, on the one hand, and the execution of a foreign judgment, on the other). *See* cf. *Eiser Infrastructure Ltd v. Kingdom of Spain*, FCA 157 (2020) and *Kingdom of Spain v. Infrastructure Services Luxembourg S.á.r.l.*, FCAFC 112, (2021).
63. Committee on International Commercial Disputes of the New York City Bar Association, *supra* n. 53, at 213.

added to the Second Approach. This third approach was expressed by the Committee on International Commercial Disputes of the New York City Bar Association as follows:

> This Committee views recognition, enforcement and execution in the ICSID award context as points progressing along a single continuum as follows: (1) "recognition" refers to confirmation or certification of an ICSID award as a final and binding disposition of claims, with res judicata effect; (2) "enforcement" refers to converting the ICSID award into a judicial judgment that orders an award debtor to comply with the award, including paying any monetary sum due; and (3) "execution" refers to coercive measures that an award creditor may take when an award debtor refuses to pay the converted award voluntarily.[64] (Approach 3).

In this linguistic and interpretative conundrum, it would be wise to search for guidance from the "grand architect" of ICSID, former Secretary-General Aron Broches. Discussing the ICSID drafting history, Broches noted that:

> In replying I made a distinction between enforceability and forced execution. While the question of enforcement of awards had not been covered specifically in the original Working Paper there was not a clear provision which in effect equate a Convention award with a final judgment of domestic courts. Whether forced execution could be obtained against a government would depend on whether a final judgment in the country where enforcement was sought could be enforced by forcible execution.
>
> [...]
>
> The obligation of governments to abide by awards remains unaffected by the limitations of their forcible execution.[65]

It is this author's position that Articles 54 and 55 of the ICSID Convention were meant to limit the signatories' submission to a foreign State's jurisdiction only vis-à-vis enforcement and not execution. In other words, any waiver of immunity through an arbitration agreement does not cover execution but does, however, constitute a waiver of immunity for purposes of recognition and enforcement. The limitation on execution was expressly discussed.[66] This position is further entrenched by Broches in the following statement:

> A comment is in order on the use of the term "enforce" in Article 54(1) which, standing alone, might be considered as including execution. Paragraph (3) of Article 54 which deals separately with execution makes clear that that is not the intention, but a slight awkwardness remains. When that paragraph was added (in

64. *Ibid.; See also* Ylli Dautaj & Maxime Chevalier, "A Liberal Push and the Sovereign Pull: Recognition, Enforcement, and Execution in the ICSID Convention" in *American Review of International Arbitration* (2022); *See furthermore,* Cymrot, *supra* n. 7, at 356; and Winch, *supra* n. 13, at 62. For the French Court de Cassation clarifying this matter and making a distinction between enforcement and execution, *See SOABI v. Senegal,* Case No. 30 ILM, (1991), at 1167, 1169 ("A foreign state which has consented to arbitration has thereby agreed that the award may be rendered enforceable which, as such, does not constitute a measure of execution that might raise issues pertaining to the immunity from execution of the state concerned.").
65. *See* Broches, *supra* n. 4, at 301, 307 ("The Convention should not provide for forced execution against a state but would leave domestic law on the subject untouched.").
66. *Ibid.*, at 303, 332 (referring to legislative history at 342-344, highlighting that Mr. Lowenfield from the U.S. had noted that the ICSID Convention should not reserve immunity from execution, but that such position was rejected).

the first draft) the first paragraph should have been reworded and might, for example, have read as follows:

> An award rendered pursuant to this Convention shall be recognized as binding by each Contracting State, and the pecuniary obligations imposed by the award shall be enforceable within the territories of each such State, as if it were a final judgment of one of its courts.
>
> Such a formulation would have brought out more clearly the distinction between enforceability which is governed and decreed by the Convention and its implementation by execution which is governed by domestic law.[67]

Both Article 54(3) and Article 55 retain immunity from execution—not enforcement. Due to the linguistics of the provisions, and the actual content vis-à-vis execution, Articles 54 and 55 of the ICSID Convention have created uncertainties for award-creditors (dealing with enforcement), on the one hand, and uncertainties *and* a legal barrier (when dealing with execution), on the other hand. Put simply—when an award-creditor seeks to enforce an ICSID award against an award-debtor State, the preservation of immunity from execution manifests as the "Achilles' heel" of the ICSID regime.[68]

§2.4 SOVEREIGN IMMUNITY AS A BARRIER TO FINAL, BINDING, AND DIRECTLY ENFORCEABLE INTERNATIONAL ARBITRAL AWARDS

As explained above, when an arbitral award is rendered the next step is for the award-debtor to either comply, voluntarily or by coercion. The latter occurs when the award-creditor approaches a domestic court for enforcement purposes. The enforcement[69] (recognition)[70] by domestic courts seeks to confirm the product of the arbitration procedure and turn that product/award into a judgment of the court. In other words, "[a] private act is being empowered by a public act, a judgment of a state court."[71] When the enforcement process works as intended, the negatives of non-compliance are remedied by law and legal procedure.

Historically, the general perception and practice has been that the rate of voluntary compliance by award-debtor States has been high. This historical norm has obviated much of the need for post-award enforcement proceedings through national courts.[72]

67. *Ibid.*, at 318.
68. *See* Schreuer et al., *supra* n. 7, at 1154; *See also* Broches, *supra* n. 4, at 318.
69. Lew et al., *supra* n. 5, at 691.
70. Where an award is enforced, it is always recognized. The recognition procedure seeks to confirm the awards while enforcement seeks to mandate the outcome by coercive assistance. Recognition can be referred to as a defense, i.e., a party can object a lawsuit by invoking res judicate or lis pendens. It can be said that recognition is a shield and enforcement is a sword. *See* Blackaby et al., *supra* n. 7, at Ch. 11.
71. Lew et al., *supra* n. 5, at 689.
72. Jorge A. Huerta-Goldman et al., *WTO Litigation, Investment Arbitration, and Commercial Arbitration* 372 (2013).

While voluntary compliance is still largely the norm, one can identify a recent increasing trend of engaging in lengthy post-award proceedings.[73] In these proceedings, award-debtor States increasingly invoke immunity from execution in the post-judgment phase (i.e., after the award has been enforced). Resultingly, award-creditors may suffer a seemingly meaningless victory when assets used for a commercial purpose (*see* more in Chapter 3) cannot be found.[74] Schill rightly underscored the enforcement issue as follows:

> Enforcement immunity as "the last bastion of State immunity" [...] creates a loophole in the efficient protection of foreign investors. Although most States voluntarily comply with arbitral rulings against them, that loophole is amply illustrated by cases of investors struggling for years to enforce an award against assets not protected by enforcement immunity.[75]

In this light, it is interesting to track the evolution of non-voluntary compliance with ISDS-awards. Gaillard and Penusliski have gathered data on the outcome of investment arbitrations involving 32 States that have been sued more than 10 times (as of December 31, 2019) and their study concluded that "the instances of non-compliance have increased and, by all accounts, are likely to continue to do so ..."[76]

Given that ISDS/ITA is currently going through a backlash movement and there are so-called legitimacy concerns being ventilated, it is logical to reason that the negative trend of non-compliance and increased post-award proceedings may further accelerate if States endorse the "ideological and myopic attacks on the system."[77] The decision to refuse compliance could even be for non-legal, i.e., political, reasons. Such behavior could catch on. Put colloquially, award-debtor States may ask: "why should we comply when other States, including GDP capital exporting States are not?" States carefully observe each other's conduct, and as a result, further non-compliance may be the result.[78] One effective tool in the basket of non-compliance is the plea of sovereign immunity from execution. Invoking such plea can be used to frustrate the awards even for non-legal reasons and by legally valid means. This is a legal catch-22.

It therefore seems like a safe assumption that for ITA/ISDS to remain a reliable and effective transnational dispute resolution regime, the norm of voluntary compliance must remain intact. There are several ways in which the regime as such regains

73. *See* Broches, *supra* n. 4, at 303; Gaillard & Penusliski, *supra* n. 2, at 47; *See* Hazel Fox, *State Immunity and Enforcement of Arbitral Awards: Do We Need an UNCITRAL Model Law Mark II for Execution Against State Property?*, 23 Arb. Int'l 89, 90 (1996) https://doi.org/10.1093/arbitration/12.1.89.
74. *See, e.g.*, Saunders & Salomon, *supra* n. 3, at 469; and *See* Huerta-Goldman et al., *supra* n. 72, at 372.
75. *See* Schill, *supra* n. 11, at 101.
76. Gaillard & Penusliski, *supra* n. 2, at 8 and 54. (Moreover, the diplomatic pressure can yield legislative changes that makes it more difficult for an award-creditor to execute against state assets.) *See, e.g.*, the recent legislative amendments in France and Belgium—Loi no 2016-1691 du 9 décembre 2016 relative à la transparence, à la lutte contre la corruption et à la modernisation de la vie économique and Art. 1412 quinquies of the Belgian Code Judiciaire, respectively; *See also* Winch, *supra* n. 13, at 64-65.
77. *See* Gaillard & Penusliski, *supra* n. 2, at 55.
78. *Ibid.*

legitimacy, notably when the award-debtor States simply comply voluntarily. However, if the award-debtor State does indeed default on its debt, the enforcement of ISDS arbitral awards—like other international arbitral awards—must be sanctioned with coercive force.[79] This includes effectiveness in what is technically the "post-judgment" phase vis-à-vis execution.

Hence, due to the divergent, unclear, and at times, unpredictable regime of sovereign immunity from execution, the effectiveness of the international arbitration against States is at times frustrated. It is unfortunately the case that the law on sovereign immunity from execution "remains an unchartered territory and one in a state of flux in the context of enforcing foreign arbitral awards."[80]

Courts in various jurisdictions have battled with sovereign immunity from execution for decades, but the obstacles stemming from execution immunity remain largely unresolved.[81] However, there has been positive progress globally, especially in certain jurisdictions. As will be seen in Chapter 4, domestic courts have worked on clarifying the law up to some point. Such legal evolution is welcomed by award-creditors and will indeed serve as instrumental guidance when having to navigate around award-debtor States' non-compliance and more frequent and increased practice of invoking sovereign immunity from execution.

§2.4.1 The Expectation of Enforcement and the Last Fortress, the Last Bastion of Sovereign Immunity

As mentioned at the beginning of this chapter, the enforcement of international arbitral awards could lay claim as its greatest feature. The enforcement regimes created by the ICSID Convention and the New York Convention are unprecedented and unparalleled compared to other means of international dispute resolution.[82] In that light, an award-creditor can legitimately expect that the arbitral award can be coercively enforced if necessary.[83]

Notwithstanding this, as we have already seen in this chapter, time and again "thwarted judgment creditors have sought to attach assets of foreign States within the forum State territory, only to be refused orders for execution by national courts."[84] Despite the success of the multilateral enforcement conventions, sovereign immunity from execution of arbitral awards still remains a barrier to an award-creditor. Therefore, even though coercive measures may be expected, and even though the enforcement regime in international arbitration has been successful, the plea of sovereign immunity from execution can at times frustrate the legitimate expectations of an

79. *See* Cymrot, *supra* n. 7, at 350.
80. Ylli Dautaj, "Sovereign Immunity from Execution of Foreign Arbitral Awards: Sweden's Liberal and Pragmatic Contribution" in *Stockholm Arbitration Yearbook* (Axel Callisendorf & Patrik Schöldström eds.) 223 (2nd ed. 2020).
81. Kaj Hobér, *Selected Writings on Investment Treaty Arbitration* 497 (2013).
82. *See, e.g.*, Mistelis, *supra* n. 2, at 2.
83. *See* Yang, *supra* n. 10, at 348.
84. Fox & Webb, *supra* n. 41, at 484.

award-creditor.[85] This unresolved issue between award enforcement (in the broad sense) and the plea of immunity from execution underscores the major weakness in the system of ISDS/ITA.[86]

Coming back to the issue highlighted in Chapter 1, the ISDS processes "may drag out over years, through multiple court cases in multiple states and jurisdictions, and ultimately may not result in any payment by the [S]tate at all."[87] Thus, one is compelled to conclude that when the award-debtor State successfully invokes immunity from execution, it effectively circumvents the consequences of liability. As a result, from a practical standpoint, the award-credit is left with a judgment on paper but no real assets.[88] This is not always alleviated by the theoretical fact that immunity does not mean impunity. Certain award-creditors—compared to States—do not measure their existence or balance their budgets in decades or centuries. Therefore, one cannot escape the hard-told truth that when a State successfully invokes sovereign immunity from execution it has defeated much of the purpose of signing the IIA which accommodates the ISDS clause. The State has also undercut the enforcing of a global rule of law which levels the playing field between private and public. By forcing the award-creditor to re-invest energy and resources in order to either settle for less or re-locate assets and start the enforcement procedure from scratch in another jurisdiction, the award-debtor State is turning transborder best practices on its head. The award-creditor may be left with a substantial award but underwritten only by costs, risks of additional loss, uncertainties, and ineffective remedies.

Despite this pessimistic (or rather, cynical) depiction, it must be noted (as mentioned) that even if the award-debtor State successfully invokes the shield of sovereign immunity from execution, that does not itself equal impunity. Put differently, the successful plea of immunity does not alter the legal obligation stemming from the award. Consequently, the award can be recognized and enforced (i.e., turned into a domestic judgment) pursuant to the New York Convention or the ICSID Convention. The State will remain responsible for a breach of its international obligations and post-award/judgment will accrue over time. That "claim for money"—both awarded amount and interest—will be a commodity that can be traded on the market. Thus, there is some light at the end of the long award-debtor tunnel, even though the award-creditor is forced to navigate in the dark for some time and must stop and pay the toll fee several times.

Furthermore, as we will *see* in Chapters 4-6, there are several laws and procedural rules in place to assist aggrieved award-creditors in market-friendly and pro-arbitration jurisdictions. The ICJ has also played a role in consolidating the customary international law on sovereign immunity. Moreover, the aggrieved award-creditor may seek some remedy through market mechanisms (e.g., engaging third-party funders, assigning the award, or insuring the underlying investment).

---

85. Lew et al., *supra* n. 5 at 688.
86. *See* Alexandroff & Laird, *supra* n. 1, at 1,171.
87. Alexis Blane, *Sovereign Immunity as a Bar to the Execution of International Arbitral Awards* 41 N.Y.U.J. Int'l L. & Pol. 453, 474 (2009) https://doi.org/10.2139/ssrn.1522244.
88. *See* Mistelis, *supra* n. 2.

Dealing with the issue of sovereign immunity from execution, in this book, we will look at: (1) law-based solutions; (2) structural/procedural-based solutions; (3) norms-based solutions; and (4) market-based solutions.

Ultimately, it should be in the State's interest to voluntarily comply with an adverse arbitral award. After all, each State is contributing to the establishment of transborder trust and harmony, as well as the breaking down of legal, cultural, historical, political, and other sorts of barriers. If those goals are not lucrative in and of themselves, self-interest in successfully competing for international business should be enough to serve both as a carrot and a stick. The scenario in which a State benefits from transnational cooperation yet undermines the accompanying responsibilities can best be described by twenty-first-century readers as "sovereign fiction." Not participating in building a transborder legal civilization manifests as self-defeating behavior that leads to international isolation and economic impoverishment. That being said, invoking sovereign immunity from execution to shield public assets is not always a mere litigation tactic or strategy or expression of bad faith or ill will. Claiming sovereign immunity is, first and foremost, a legal right, which in some jurisdictions is absolute and in others is hardly set-aside (i.e., the rule of immunity is strong and the threshold for meeting an exception is high). Moreover, the plea for immunity can come due to severe financial distress, political turmoil, actual disagreements with the legitimacy of the procedure, and so on.

§2.4.2 Reasons Justifying Immunity from Execution

There are justifiable reasons as to why the doctrine of sovereign immunity, in general, and that from execution, in particular, is applicable in international law and legal practice. The reasons are primarily legal but even more deeply rooted in public policy and political concerns. Therefore, while shedding a (legal) light on the problems sovereign immunity presents, one must understand its normative underpinnings as well as its pragmatic appeal.

The drafting history of both the ICSID Convention and the UNCSI reveals that the relevant bodies avoided the question of immunity from execution as far as they could. Meanwhile, both working groups treated immunity from execution distinctively from immunity from jurisdiction and almost as an unquestionable rule—one with more limited and narrow exceptions than that of jurisdictional immunity.[89] In other words, even if the discussion on immunity from jurisdiction progressed on the basis of a more rapid commercial, market-based evolution, it was made clear in the work leading up to

89. *See, e.g.*, Schreuer et al., *supra* n. 7, at 1152-1154; *See also* Sompong Sucharitkul, *Preliminary Report on the Topic of Jurisdictional Immunities of States and Their Property*, Special Rapporteur, para. 83, U.N. Doc. A/CN.4/323 (1979) ("The general rule appears to be that the property of a foreign State—especially property in its possession or control—is exempt from provisional measures of seizure or attachment, as well as from execution."), https://legal.un.org/ilc/documentation/english/a_cn4_323.pdf.

the UNCSI that "[i]mmunities from execution form a different dimension of State immunities, requiring special attention and distinct treatment."[90]

Thus, in 1989 the working group of the UNCSI started to underscore two competing viewpoints—i.e., state-centered and commercially oriented ones. Highlighting the commercial view, the forty-first session noted that:

> [T]here are some writers who argue that allowing plaintiffs to proceed against foreign States and then withholding from them the fruits of successful litigation through immunity from execution may put them into the doubly frustrating position of being left with an unenforceable judgment and expensive legal costs.[91]

This view, which essentially justifies the commercial exceptions to the rule of immunity, is anchored primarily in market-based considerations and perhaps even in an ideological embrace of capitalism. Furthermore, the working group noted the growing State practice, as evidenced, *inter alia*, by the U.S. and the U.K. sovereign immunities acts (Foreign Sovereign Immunities Act (FSIA) and State Immunity Act (SIA), respectively). It was observed that certain States do indeed permit enforcement/execution of award-debtor States' commercial property.[92]

Even though immunity from execution was discussed in the work leading to the UNCSI, such discussions did not include a thorough debate on the normative basis of immunity from execution compared to immunity from jurisdiction and the possible exceptions. Although the eventual UNCSI, was motivated by the restrictive theory of immunity, which also prevailed in the execution context of influential States (e.g., the U.S. and the U.K.), a review of the final drafts and accompanying commentary in the UNCSI, reveals that the working group did not thoroughly address the justification of immunity from execution or the rationale behind its exceptions.[93] However, with respect to what became Article 21 (the list of property to be protected as immune; *see* Chapter 3) the working group concluded that it is important to be able to attach and execute against State assets—yet, there is no explanation as to why that is so.[94]

In fact, there are several reasons underlying the idea of no, or limited, execution against State property. One must thoroughly consider such normative basis for a more conservative approach to immunity when balancing the public interests against private ones in this public-private tension. The normative underpinning for sovereign immunity, in general, and immunity from execution, in particular, will be discussed more thoroughly in Chapter 3 (e.g., equality, independence, sovereign autonomy, public interest concerns, etc.).

---

90. *Yearbook of the International Law Commission*, vol. II, pt. 2, para. 23, (1978), https://legal.un.org/ilc/publications/yearbooks/english/ilc_1978_v2_p2.pdf.
91. Motoo Ogiso, *Second Report on Jurisdictional Immunities of States and Their Property*, Special Rapporteur, para. 42, U.N. Doc. A/CN.4/422 (1989), https://legal.un.org/ilc/documentation/english/a_cn4_422.pdf.
92. *Ibid.*
93. *Draft Articles on Jurisdictional Immunities of States and Their Property*, with Commentaries 56-57 (1991) (commentary to Art. 18, which later became Art. 19), https://legal.un.org/ilc/texts/instruments/english/commentaries/4_1_1991.pdf.
94. *Draft Articles on Jurisdictional Immunities of States and Their Property*, with Commentaries 58-59 (1991) (commentary to Art. 19, which later became Art. 21), https://legal.un.org/ilc/texts/instruments/english/commentaries/4_1_1991.pdf.

Despite compelling arguments in the private-interest-based direction, there are several public-interest-related reasons that justify retaining at least some immunity, for at least some State property. An illustrative but not exhaustive list includes:

(i) that there is no international law regulating State debts (e.g., no international law of insolvency for State debt);
(ii) due to external interests (e.g., citizens or the international community at large);
(iii) that execution against State property constitutes a greater interference with a State's freedom to manage its own affairs and to pursue its public purposes; and
(iv) that execution against State property has adverse consequences to the friendly relations of the States, and conversely is necessary for facilitating international relations.[95]

Another argument in favor of immunity is that "immunity" does not equal "impunity." As Schreuer explained by referring to the procedural history of the ICSID Convention:

> A successful invocation of State immunity does not alter the fact that non-compliance with an award is a violation of the Convention. State immunity is a procedural bar to measures of execution against a recalcitrant party. It does not affect in any manner the award debtor's obligation under Art. 53 to abide by and comply with the award (History, Vol. II, p. 763).[96]

Put differently, even if a State's assets are protected, the State is nevertheless liable, and often such liability is coupled with a rather generously accruing post-award interest. Thus, in the international arbitration context at least, the underlying assumption is that an award can indeed be recognized and enforced and that execution can only be limited vis-à-vis certain property; and, while the State can default, it remains liable with ticking interest. Seen in that light, the balancing exercise between public and private interests makes more sense even in the twenty-first century.

On the contrary, a good argument can be made that the plea of sovereign immunity can nevertheless place an award-creditor in a peculiar situation—and perhaps an unfair one. Yang rightly noted that:

> It almost seems as if the regime of State immunity is simply to declare a foreign State liable but leaves the enforcement of that liability to chance and the goodwill of the defendant State. Thus courts freely handing down judgments against foreign States without little prospect of enforcement will remain a constant feature of the law and practice on State immunity.[97]

The UNCSI (as discussed in depth in Chapter 3) is the result of a balancing exercise. The rule in the UNCSI (as in the U.S. FSIA and the U.K. SIA) is still immunity from execution. However, such immunity is subject to certain exceptions (e.g., express

95. Fox & Webb, *supra* n. 41, at 485.
96. *See* Schreuer et al., *supra* n. 7, at 1153.
97. *See* Yang, *supra* n. 10, at 422.

waiver, earmarking, or commercial purposes exception). In further balancing the interests of the public, the UNCSI expressly protects certain property as immune *ipso facto* (*see* Article 21). This is the case in domestic sovereign immunity laws too.

§2.5 CONCLUSION

One of the main advantages of international arbitration is the enforceability of awards.[98] Reliable and effective enforcement reinstates trust, legitimacy, and therefore sustainability into the algorithm of international arbitration.[99] The two multilateral enforcement regimes—the New York Convention and the ICSID Convention—make international arbitration the preferable venue for settling transborder disputes stemming from trade, commerce, and investment.

Consequently, any obstacle to final, binding, and direct enforcement is a serious threat to the regime of ISDS/ITA. This includes matters of execution of the award. If States refuse to comply voluntarily with adverse ISDS-awards, international arbitration against States will prove to be ineffective. If the non-complying State invokes immunity from execution, the award-creditor has a serious uphill battle to fight. The award-creditor is thus forced to engage in post-award proceedings in various jurisdictions in order to locate (if at all possible) attachable assets that can be executed against the State. Having done so, the award-creditor must hope that the relevant domestic court will apply the law on sovereign immunity liberally and perhaps even pragmatically.

When the State successfully circumvents or delays its legal liability by invoking sovereign immunity from execution, it has suspended the award-creditor's rights stemming from the award and correspondingly its obligations stemming from the same.

A scenario in which sovereign defaults are the norm and in which governments rarely repay their debts in full cannot be tolerated in the twenty-first century.[100] It is not surprising then that the issue of sovereign immunity in investment arbitration has been described as "the Achilles' heel of the [ICSID] Convention" and that "[t]he otherwise effective machinery of arbitration has its weak point when it comes to the actual execution against States of pecuniary obligations under awards."[101]

This book will show that the evolution of immunity from execution is uniform and harmonized to some extent, but serious divergences nevertheless exist—especially in scope, degree, and nuance. It will be shown that State practice and *opinio juris* differ in certain areas of immunity from execution, which frustrates attempts to crystalize nuances positions into customary international law.

98. *International Arbitration Survey: The Evolution of International Arbitration*, White & Case and Queen Mary School of International Arbitration (2018), https://www.qmul.ac.uk/arbitration/media/arbitration/docs/2018-International-Arbitration-Survey---The-Evolution-of-International-Arbitration-(2).PDF. *See also* Mistelis, *supra* n. 2, at 2.
99. Mistelis, *supra* n. 2, at 3 ("Ultimately, it is the enforceability and indeed the enforcement of the award that gives credence to the entire arbitration process and justifies the cost and time that the parties to a dispute have invested in the resolution process.").
100. Michael Waibel, *Sovereign Defaults Before International Courts and Tribunals* 13 (2011).
101. *See* Schreuer et al., *supra* n. 7, at 1154.

While this book sets out sovereign immunity from execution as an issue in international arbitration, the reader should keep in mind the underlying public-private tensions and the balancing of policies that must be considered at the intersection of sovereign immunity law and international arbitration (investment and commercial). Several scholars rightly noted that the immunity regime continues to be forged by competing forces, including, on the one hand, the deference to State sovereignty, the desire for stability in international relations or the need to protect the independent functioning of IOs, and, on the other hand, the advance of human rights and the fight against impunity, as well as the principle comprehensive nature of States' territorial jurisdiction.[102]

When the ICSID Convention was drafted, it was considered extremely unlikely that a State would not comply with an adverse award in the ISDS context.[103] Fast forward to today, and empirical data shows that the frequency of non-compliance is surging and that the plea of immunity from execution is used vividly by award-debtor States. Therefore, it is important not only to re-consider the arguments in favor and against a more limited immunity regime from a theoretical perspective but also to navigate the award-creditor in where and how to overcome the immunity obstacle in practice. This book does both of those things.

102. Tom Ruys, Nicolas Angelet & Luca Ferro, *Cambridge Handbook on Immunities and International Law* 5 (2019).
103. *See* Schreuer et al., *supra* n. 7, at 1152.

CHAPTER 3

Theory and Sources of the Substantive Law on Sovereign Immunity

§3.1 INTRODUCTION

The main objective of sovereign immunity is to ensure that the core functions of the State are not frustrated or put in gridlock. Differently put, the purpose of sovereign immunity is to relief the State from obstacles that would prevent it from performing its core governmental functions. Thus, the underlying premise of immunity is that the role of governance is so important for a State and its citizenry that the threat of litigation, or worse, interference with its assets should not be allowed to undercut the exercising of such critical functions. We can consider this the *horizontal object and purpose* of sovereign immunity. It protects the State within its territorial sovereignty. It protects the State in performing its sovereign responsibilities.

Another major objective of sovereign immunity is the respect for States' dignity, independence, and equality when acting among its equals. This objective leads to less conflict and therefore promotes stability, security, and peace. We can consider this the *vertical object and purpose* of sovereign immunity. It protects the State from interference from other States and preserves the equality of sovereigns. Fox and Webb articulated the objectives as follows:

> (i) as a method to ensure a "stand-off" between States where private parties seek to enlist the assistance of the courts of one State to determine their claims made against another State; (ii) as a method of distinguishing between matters relating to public administration of a State and private law claims; (iii) as a method of allocating jurisdiction between States in disputes brought in national courts relating to State activities in the absence of any international agreement by which to resolve conflicting claims to the exercise of such jurisdiction.[1]

1. Hazel Fox & Philippa Webb, *The Law of State Immunity* 1 (2015).

Notwithstanding this, whatever normative/theoretical justification we give the doctrine of sovereign immunity, it can hardly be denied that at its core it is a matter of policy objectives and political concerns. Such policy objectives and political concerns swing like a pendulum in big and in small—from discussions on absolute/restrictive immunity to the scope of the commercial exception. Given the global trajectory in political theory from World War II and onward, i.e., toward a (liberal) capitalist world order, the major dispute in the underlying theory of sovereign immunity has been relatively steady in moving in one direction—i.e., the rule of immunity has been carved-out with more and liberally construed exceptions. Hence, we are largely left with dealing with the—from a public international law standpoint—small steps (i.e., degree, scope, and nuance of any exceptions to sovereign immunity).

Thus, while sovereign immunity has been a useful and even necessary doctrine in insulating the power to administer and operate the public sphere, free from and without interference by another State in its internal affairs, we must critically examine where immunity ends and accountability commences.[2] It is undeniable that we now live in different times, where the State's sphere of functions has grown to encompass various trade, commerce, and investment matters. The State actively engages in global competition, including outbound and inbound FDI. Therefore, the doctrine of immunity had to adjust to new demands and new contextual realities.

In this doctrinal continuous evolution that sovereign immunity has embarked upon, competing interests have competed and some level of concessions between States inevitably decides the direction that the evolution takes. The direction of sovereign immunity can be observed through theoretical concessions (e.g., States adhering to the restrictive doctrine as opposed to absolute immunity). The direction can be traced in concessions on formulating the substantive law on sovereign immunity (e.g., States agreeing on absolutely protecting certain assets). Moreover, the direction can be studied considering domestic procedural rules enabling the theory and substantive law to be implemented in practice.

It must be emphasized, however, that the doctrinal evolution of sovereign immunity differs depending on the area of law that it intersects with. While capitalism in global commerce, trade, and investment dominates, it is not equally true that *liberal* capitalism dominates as resoundingly. This book deals with a rather narrow issue; that is, *does the doctrinal understanding of sovereign immunity from execution and its interpretation and application in the international arbitration context resonate with a twenty-first-century global marketplace?* As is evident, the focus is purely on international economic law and even more specifically on the international arbitration context.

§3.1.1 The Non-static Nature of Sovereign Immunity

Because global governance and mutual intercourse are not static and because fundamental political and economic disagreements exist, the theory of sovereign immunity

2. *Ibid.*, at 26.

has swung like a pendulum and likely will continue to be fluid. Therefore, the doctrine of sovereign immunity may constantly be in a *relative* state of "flux." Fox observed that the last 100 years have seen enormous changes in the doctrine and practice of sovereign immunity and that, in the last decade, the changes have accelerated in response to the changed priorities of society.[3]

The lack of global consensus on the theory and practice of sovereign immunity is exacerbated by the fact that the normative justification for the doctrine rests on different underpinnings—e.g., equality, dignity, independence, comity, or a combination of the mentioned. This author starts from the position that the theory, and more so the practical implementation, is the product of policy objectives and political concerns. As State objectives and politics shift and change, so does both the theory and practical implementation of sovereign immunity as a plea before domestic courts.

To reflect changed priorities—i.e., align with policy objectives and political concerns of the twenty-first century—in general, and in global commerce, trade, and investment, in particular, the theory underpinning the doctrine of sovereign immunity has moved from being absolute to being restrictive (i.e., including exceptions to immunity).

For the advocates of a more liberal theory and a more pragmatic application, the crux of the matter will remain whether, when, and how (in scope, nuance, and degree) to qualify the *general rule* on immunity. It must be clearly articulated that immunity is still the rule, albeit qualified by several and increasingly more exceptions. This group of advocates starts with a presumption that State and individual are equal (at least in certain areas) and that such is important for the preservation of democracy, the rule of law, and faithfully observing individual rights and liberties. There is merit to this private-centric worldview. There are indeed good policy considerations as to why exceptions to sovereign immunity must exist.

Meanwhile, for the advocates of lesser exceptions—or even absolute immunity—the crux of the matter will be to elevate the ensuring the key performances of the State and protection for its citizenry, on the one hand, and the aspect of comity and equality among States, on the other (i.e., the horizontal and vertical objects and purposes for immunity). This group of advocates starts from a presumption that State and individual are not equal. The State is responsible for the individual. The proponents of immunity believe that peace and harmony are best preserved if sovereignty prevails. There is merit to this more State-centric worldview. There are indeed good policy considerations as to why sovereign immunity exists.

§3.1.2 The Substantive Law of Sovereign Immunity

The substantive law of sovereign immunity falls under the broader realm of public international law. Thus, the sources of the law on sovereign immunity will be those of public international law enumerated in Article 38 of the ICJ Statute: (a) international

3. Hazel Fox, *Hazel Fox on State Immunity*, UN WEB TV (October 10, 2011), https://webtv.un.org/en/asset/k1u/k1uenbfivc.

conventions (i.e., treaties); (b) customary international law; (c) general principles of law; and (d) judicial decisions and scholarly work.[4]

Albeit the law of sovereign immunity is an area of substantive public international law, it has developed in its own right and primarily through domestic case law. And because the practical implementation/effect of the substantive law of sovereign immunity is largely dependent on procedural rules (e.g., decisions on burden of proof, discovery, pre-judgment attachment, etc.), such case law also forms part of sovereign immunity law considered more broadly. In other words, it is impossible to understand sovereign immunity law by simply looking at the substantive law from a pure public international law lens. Better put, it is not practical to undertake such an approach to the law of sovereign immunity.

As of today, the substantive law on sovereign immunity is far from uniform, let alone the procedural rules in various jurisdictions dealing with the plea. Domestic practice has developed differently and divergent positions exist. The differences are both substantive and procedural, but perhaps more evident in the procedural features enabling (or not) the execution of an arbitral award or judgment against a State invoking immunity.

The interpretation and application of sovereign immunity is indeed cumbersome. The issue that this book deals with is that of sovereign immunity from execution, in general, and with respect to execution of international arbitral awards, in particular. Because immunity from execution is less clear than that of immunity from jurisdiction, and because the test is narrower in scope (focusing on "purpose" rather than the "nature"), it remains a major obstacle to award-creditors and an area of uncertainty in public international law.[5]

This chapter discusses the theory and sources of the substantive law on sovereign immunity, with focus on the post-judgment/post-award context.

§3.2 THE THEORY OF SOVEREIGN IMMUNITY

The theory of absolute immunity focuses on the intrinsic characteristics of the State (*horizontal object and purpose*) as well as the relationship between States (*vertical object and purpose*). Explained simply, the theory of absolute immunity insulates the State from foreign courts from coercively adjudicating (immunity from jurisdiction) or enforcing/executing (immunity from execution) an award/judgment against a foreign State without its consent.

The approach espoused in the absolute theory came to be seen as impracticable in an increasingly interconnected and interdependent global world order. Especially in a world where transborder commerce, trade, and investment are mainstream practices. Increased market participation from all corners of the world required a shift from a

4. Thomas Buergenthal & Sean D. Murphy, *Public International Law in a Nutshell* 23 (2013) ("a rule cannot be deemed to be international law unless it is derived from one of [the] sources").
5. International Law Commission (ILC) Commentary, "United Nations Convention on Jurisdictional Immunities of States and Their Property" (UNCSI), Art. 18(1) adopted February 2, 2004; *see also* UNCSI, Art. 2, 19.

power-based to a rules-based world-order. Thus, globalization and the spread of capitalism have dictated the direction of the doctrine. It was therefore no surprise that the restrictive theory emerged in shaping the doctrine. In fact, even though the restrictive immunity got entrenched post-World War II, the idea that a State should not be absolutely immune in all respects can be traced back all the way to the beginning of the nineteenth century.[6]

The restrictive immunity theory espouses that the State is immune only with respect to transactions involving the exercise of governmental authority (*acta iure imperii*; immunity from jurisdiction) and that its assets are only immune where used for a governmental purpose (*iure imperii*; immunity from execution).[7] Conversely, the theory makes clear that the State is not immune when acting commercially or undertaking such other transactions that are not unique to the State (*acta iure gestionis*) and that its assets are not immune where used for a non-governmental commercial purpose.[8] Notwithstanding this, sovereign immunity manifests as a procedural plea and does not exonerate a State from legal liability.[9]

In practice, it is hard to tell what activities are taken *iure gestionis/iure imperii*, and what assets are used for a *iure gestionis/iure imperii* purpose. Such is the reality on the ground.

§3.2.1 The Legal Theory of Sovereign Immunity

To understand sovereign immunity, one must understand the concepts of *sovereignty* and *immunity*. Sovereignty represents the basic "constitutional doctrine" of the law of nations; that is, States enjoy legal personality and as sovereigns, they are *equal* in relation to each other.[10] The fact that sovereign States are equal, independent, and must be treated with such dignity was clearly articulated in the landmark *Lotus* case already in 1927, wherein the Permanent Court of International Justice (PCIJ) reasoned that:

> the first and foremost restriction imposed by international law upon a state is that—failing the exercise of a permissive rule to the contrary—it may not exercise its power in any form in the territory of another State. In this sense jurisdiction is

6. *The Schooner Exchange v. McFaddon*, 11 U.S. (7 Cranch) 116 (1812) (read the reasoning of the court and the arguments presented by both sides). *See* Fox & Webb, *supra* n. 1, at 146; and *see also* Ernest K. Bankas, *The State Immunity Controversy in International Law* 175 (2005) (The ILC's work with the UNCSI "was made possible after the Second World War in respect of the interests expressed by governments to promote a rapid growth and the progressive development of international law, with the ultimate aim of codifying the said law.").
7. James Crawford, *Brownlie's Principles of Public International Law* 1935 (8th ed. 2012, e-book). *See* Fox & Webb, *supra* n. 1, at 34 ("This distinction has in the main proved workable but the absence of objective criteria on which to base the distinction for the two types of acts has left it open to criticism and inconsistent application.").
8. *See, e.g.*, *Jurisdictional Immunities of the State (Germany v. Italy: Greece Intervening)*, Judgment, ICJ Rep. (February 3, 2012), at 99 (hereinafter "*Jurisdictional Immunities*").
9. *Ibid.*
10. Crawford, *supra* n. 7, at 2158.

> certainly territorial; it cannot be exercised by a State outside its territory except by virtue of a permissive rule derived from international custom or a convention.[11]

In modern usage, sovereignty generally refers to a collection of rights held by a State in exercising control over its territory and citizens (internally), and the State's capacity to represent the territory and its citizens on the international plane (externally).[12]

We move on to the concept of *immunity*. The law on immunity is one of the classic branches of public international law.[13] The law on immunity has evolved separately depending on what is to be protected and why. For example, diplomatic and consular missions and their representatives have separate rules of immunity (diplomatic immunity) compared to those governing international organizations (immunity for international organizations). Neither of these two immunity regimes is dealt with in this book.[14] This book deals with sovereign immunity. Sovereign immunity, as a separate branch of immunity law, operates on twin bases: (1) immunity *ratione materiae* (vis-à-vis the State); and (2) immunity *ratione personae* (vis-à-vis State certain officials highest).[15]

Despite the approval of sovereign immunity as a procedural barrier, it must be emphasized that it neither exonerates a State from liability nor does it mean that a sovereign State's court within its own territory lacks the competence to either adjudicate disputes or coercively enforce foreign awards/judgments against other States. The relevant question is not whether a State *can* exercise its inherent competence/ powers within its territorial sovereignty, but rather *when* and *why* its courts should refuse to do so.

As explained, sovereign immunity has the effect of limiting the competence and jurisdiction of a forum court. The court justifies the granting of such immunity on the basis of one or more normative bases. These *immunity justifications* are in turn underpinned by the object and purpose of sovereign immunity (i.e., the horizontal and vertical aspects mentioned throughout this chapter). It is in this light that sovereign immunity has mostly been justified as a result of States' independence, dignity, equality, independence, or due to comity.[16] Whether reliance on one or more of these

---

11. The Case of the S.S. "*Lotus" (France v. Turkey)*, PCIJ Series A No. 10, (1927) at 10.
12. Crawford, *supra* n. 7, at 2161.
13. Jan Klabbers, *An Introduction to International Institutional Law* 139 (2nd ed. 2009).
14. Albeit in the U.S., the International Organizations Immunities Act (IOIA) makes a reference to the law on sovereign immunity. *See* §288a(b) (the act grants international organizations "the same immunity from suit and every form of judicial process as is enjoyed by foreign governments." The ensuing issue has been whether "the same immunity"). For a discussion on this, *see* Ylli Dautaj, *Immunity from Suit for International Organizations: The Judiciary's New Que of Separating Lawsuit Sheep from Lawsuit Goats*, 27 Ind. J. Global Legal Stud. 207 (2020) https://doi.org/10.2979/indjglolegstu.27.2.0207.
15. Crawford, *supra* n. 7, at 1935-1936.
16. Fox & Webb, *supra* n. 1, at 26-27. *See also The Schooner Exchange, supra* n. 6, at 116, 136-137 ("The world being composed of distinct sovereignties, *possessing equal rights and equal independence*, whose mutual benefit is promoted by *intercourse with each other*, and by an interchange of those good offices which humanity dictates and its wants require, all sovereigns have consented to a relaxation in practice, in cases under certain peculiar circumstances, of that absolute and complete jurisdiction within their respective territories which sovereignty confers

immunity justifications leads to a logical, well-justified rule of law can be argued with different outcomes.[17] Does one justification suffice or is more than one needed? In real life, judges have cited one or more of these immunity justifications in order to justify their judicial pronouncements.[18] There is no universal agreement on the actual immunity justification. However, the ICJ has held that the customary international law on sovereign immunity is justified on the basis of equality.[19] This was probably not considered at great length or more of a decision taken out of convenience. For most practical purposes it does not matter what immunity justification you cloak immunity with. And in reality, neither of the normative bases can lay claim to represent "the true" legal basis of or justification for sovereign immunity.[20] Therefore, it has been said that "any doctrinal inquiry into the legal basis of immunity will lead to a dead end."[21]

It is this author's position that it is unnecessary to indulge in a doctrinal or historical analysis to find the "right" justification. That does not exist and all and any of the abovementioned bases work. There is simply no need to "probe into such metaphysical issues as the origin and basis" for immunity.[22] Some have suggested that

[...]. This *full and absolute territorial jurisdiction being alike the attribute of every sovereign*, and being incapable of conferring extraterritorial power, would not seem to contemplate foreign sovereigns nor their sovereign rights as its objects. One sovereign being in no respect amenable to another; and being bound by obligations of the highest character *not to degrade the dignity of his nation*, by placing himself or its sovereign rights within the jurisdiction of another, can be supposed to enter a foreign territory only under an express license, or in the confidence that the immunities belonging to his independent sovereign station, though not expressly stipulated, are reserved by implication, and will be extended to him. *This perfect equality and absolute independence of sovereigns*, and this *common interest impelling them to mutual intercourse*, and an *interchange of good offices with each other*, have given rise to a class of cases in which every sovereign is understood to waive the exercise of a part of that complete exclusive territorial jurisdiction, which has been stated to be the attribute of every nation.") and *I Congreso del Partido* [1983] 1 AC 244 at 262, [1981] 2 All ER 1062 at 1070, HL, 64 ILR 307 ("It is necessary to start from first principle. The basis on which one State is considered to be immune from the territorial jurisdiction of the courts of another State is that of 'par in parem non habet imperium', which effectively means that the sovereign or governmental acts of one State are not matters on which the courts of other States will adjudicate.").

17. Xiodong Yang, *State Immunity in International Law* 57 (2012) ("Thus such notions as sovereignty, equality, independence, dignity and reciprocity are but items on a random list, to be chosen á la carte, according to the predilections of whoever is making the choice but cannot be seriously identified as the theoretical underpinnings of State immunity. Ultimately, the discussion of the doctrinal basis or bases of immunity is neither profitable nor even necessary, and is at best of academic interest only, for courts regularly deal with the issue of State immunity without regard to any doctrinal consideration and this tendency is becoming more and more manifest.").
18. *See, e.g., Distomo Massacre Case*, Greece, 129 ILR, (2009) at 513, 516 ("In its contemporary version, the institution of sovereign immunity constitutes a consequence of the sovereignty, independence and equality of nations, whilst its aim is to avoid the disturbance of international relations."). Cf. *Rahimtoola v. Nizam*, AC 379, (England, 1958) at 418 per Lord Denning; 24 ILR, (1957) at 175, 196-197 ("It is more in keeping with the dignity of a foreign sovereign to submit himself to the rule of law than to claim to be above it, and his independence is better ensured by accepting the decisions of courts of acknowledged impartiality than by arbitrarily rejecting their jurisdiction.").
19. *See Jurisdictional Immunities, supra* n. 8, at 99.
20. *See* Yang, *supra* n. 17, at 57.
21. *Ibid.*, at 51.
22. *Ibid.*, at 56.

it breaks down to this: a State enjoys the privilege of immunity because it is a State.[23] This author tends to agree, but the reason for that is the horizontal and vertical object/purpose already outlined under §3.1. Hence, even if the practical utility of this "revelation" is limited, it seems as if the true immunity justification is the result of political concerns and policy objectives.[24] Therefore, as the world shifted to market economies competing for business in a global, free and open market, the theory on and the application of sovereign immunity has shifted in line with those policy objectives and anti-State-centric political concerns of the twenty-first century. This also means that the underlying theory of sovereign immunity, and therefore the law and its application can shift further in that direction or back in the reverse direction depending on broader global political winds.

For practical reasons, however, we can accept the ICJ's proposition and start with the presumption that sovereign immunity is based on *equality* between States (*par in parem non habet imperium*).[25] It not only serves the purpose as a logical justification for the doctrine but indeed also serves as a workable stepping-stone for legal method and analysis in this area of law. And because it works in practice, it makes sense in theory. The reversed—i.e., that it works in theory, but not in practice—can never be satisfactory to legal civilization.

[1] From Absolute to Restrictive Immunity

The main premise of absolute immunity is that the world is conceived of equally competing sovereign States, which enjoy bilateral relations with each other. The sovereign States enjoy exclusive internal competence (*horizontal object and purpose*) and external equality and independence (i.e., immunity from interference with its affairs-*vertical object and purpose*).[26] The absolute theory is said to be based on a "structuralist" or "status-oriented" idea of immunity, i.e., being concerned with the status of the party claiming immunity.[27] There are still States that adhere to the absolute doctrine.

---

23. *Ibid.*, at 45.
24. Fox & Webb, *supra* n. 1, at 35 (discussing the idea of restrictive immunity) ("the problem is once again that the distinction and the way it is applied rests 'on political assumptions as to the proper sphere of State activity and of priorities in State policies' which cannot easily be contained in formal rules.").
25. *See generally*, *Jurisdictional Immunities*, *supra* n. 8, at 99; *See also* Crawford, *supra* n. 7, at 1799, 1935; *see, e.g.*, *Al-Adsani v. UK*, Case No. 35763/97, (ECHR, November 21, 2001) (2002), 34 EHRR 11, at para. 54 ("[S]overeign immunity is a concept of international law, developed out of the principle par in parem non habet imperium, by virtue of which one State shall not be subject to the jurisdiction of another State."); and Declaration of Principles of International Law Concerning Friendly Relations and Co-operation Among States in Accordance with the Charter of the United Nations, GA Res 2625 (XXV) of 24 October 1970 ("All States enjoy sovereign equality and independence").
26. *See* Fox & Webb, *supra* n. 1, at 4; *See also* ILC, Commentary (3) on Part IV (Immunity from Measures of Constraint) to the UNCSI.
27. A.F.M. Maniruzzaman, "Sovereign Immunity and the Enforcement of Arbitral Awards Against State Entities: Recent Trends in Practice," in *ICDR Handbook on International Arbitration Practice* (Grant Hanessian et al., eds.), 382 (2017).

The restrictive theory makes a distinction between the exercise of governmental authority (*acta iure imperii*) and commercial actions (*acta iure gestionis*) vis-à-vis jurisdictional immunity.[28] This theory is said to be based on a "functionalist" idea, i.e., being concerned with the subject matter forming the basis for the claim of immunity.[29] However, when discussing property/assets rather than conduct, the distinction is made between property *used for commercial purposes* (*iure gestionis*) and property used for *governmental non-commercial purposes* (*iure imperii*).

Notwithstanding the evolution toward restrictive theory of immunity in many (if not most) jurisdictions, the problem of determining its precise boundaries remains unresolved.[30] This difficulty is only exacerbated in the execution phase when seeking to attach and execute against State property/assets.

The shift from absolute immunity to restrictive immunity is so important to the doctrine of sovereign immunity that it has been said that "[t]he history of the law of [sovereign] immunity is the history of the triumph of the doctrine of restrictive immunity over that of absolute immunity."[31] This transition has happened gradually but really took off from the 1970s and onward.[32] Some jurisdictions embrace the restrictive theory as a matter of customary international law, while others have codified a presumption of immunity and elaborated for context-specific exceptions (e.g., the commercial activity exception).[33]

The more practical explanation for the shift is that States can no longer enjoy absolute immunity when acting in the commercial or private law sphere. It is simply not compatible with modern trade, commerce, and investment.[34] Thus, the move toward a restrictive theory is primarily a result of States' active participation in the market and is in sync with ideas embedded in capitalism and the rules-based world-order. Hence, ideology has played a major role in the transition from absolute to restrictive immunity.[35]

---

28. Crawford, *supra* n. 7, at 1935; *See* Fox & Webb, *supra* n. 1, at 4. ("This distinction has in the main proved workable but the absence of objective criteria on which to base the distinction for the two types of acts has left it open to criticism and inconsistent application.").
29. Maniruzzaman, *supra* n. 27.
30. Crawford, *supra* n. 7, at 1939.
31. Yang, *supra* n. 17, at 6. *See, e.g., Englander v. Statni Banka Ceskoslovenska*, (France, 1969) 52 ILR 33; *see also Letter from Jack B. Tate, Acting Legal Adviser, Dept. of State, to Acting Attorney General Philip B. Perlman*, reprinted in 26 Dep't. St. Bull. 984 (1952).
32. Fox & Webb, *supra* n. 1, at 2. In fact, the theory was launched by Belgian and Italian courts much earlier.
33. Cf., e.g., Sweden with the U.S. (customary international law), the U.S. (FSIA) and the U.K. (SIA).
34. *See, e.g., Kuwait Airways Corp. v. Iraqi Airways Co.*, (U.K. House of Lords, January 16, 1995), 1 WLR 1147, at 117 (per Lord Mustill: "[t]he rationale of the common law doctrine of the restricted immunity, of which section 3 is the counterpart, is that where the sovereign chooses to doff his robes and descend into the market place he must take the rough with the smooth, and having condescended to engage in mundane commercial activities he must also condescend to submit himself to an adjudication in a foreign court on whether he has in the course of those activities undertaken obligations which he has failed to fulfil."). *See also The Schooner Exchange*, *supra* n. 6, at 116, 137 ("So if a sovereign descends from the throne and become a merchant, he submits to the laws of the country. If he contracts private debts, his private funds are liable. So, if he charter a vessel, the cargo is liable for the freight.").
35. There are disagreements on this point. *See, e.g.*, Yang, *supra* n. 17, at 23 ("It is doubtful whether ideological differences played any significant part in the evolution of State immunity rules.").

This arguably continuous transition now begs new questions and pushes for several additional exceptions and a more liberal/pragmatic approach with respect to already existent exceptions (e.g., when dealing with immunity from execution and specifically the arbitration exception or the commercial purpose exception). What this book will trace is whether such a *private push* has—or will—gain approval. Conversely, will such a push be met with a *public pull*? This book limits its research to a strict focus on immunity from execution in the international arbitration context (which is part of the broader umbrella "measures of constraint").[36]

[2] The Two Sovereign Immunities: Jurisdiction and Execution

As mentioned, in the now prevailing restrictive theory of immunity there is a distinction between *iure imperii* (i.e., "public acts" or "public use") and *iure gestionis* (i.e., "commercial acts" or "commercial use"). To enable the restrictive theory of jurisdictional immunity to truly anchor in workability, the implied consent (or waiver) doctrine gained approval. In other words, if the State concludes an agreement with a choice-of-forum clause, it has waived the right to claim immunity from jurisdiction. Whether and how a State waives immunity from execution is a separate and more complicated matter. Without the waiver doctrine, the transition to a restrictive theory of immunity would have been less likely and had less practical utility.

With the entrenched restrictive immunity theory a crucial debate emerged, namely, whether the commercial activity should be determined on the basis of the "nature of the act" (i.e., the *Nature Test*) or on the basis of the "purpose of the act" (i.e.,

---

The author titles a sub-section as "The irrelevance of ideologies." However, in the concluding remarks the same author writes that "[t]he true cause for the passing of absolute immunity is that international economic life, and with it the very conceptualization of the State itself, had undergone so phenomenal a change that the law inevitably and inexorably became out of step with the reality, and thus had to be discarded as a thing of the past. It is only for this reason—and not because of any philosophical breakthrough, that the doctrine of absolute immunity finally appeared so anachronistic and untenable: cessante ratione legis cessat ipsa lex." Yang, *supra* n. 17, at 31-32. This author agrees in point but not in reasoning. It is contended that the evolution of liberal democracies that embrace the free and open market is per definition a philosophical breakthrough. This philosophical breakthrough has paved the way from *command/centrally planned economies* to *market economies* in large parts of the world. As a corollary, international trade, investment, and commerce follow suit of such developments. And with increased economic activity across borders and a deepened sophistication in State practices as a market actor, a shift in the notion of the sovereign and sovereign prerogatives followed suit—the State became subject to foreign court's jurisdiction and their assets can no longer be out of reach for remedial purposes. Capitalism has prevailed over its competitors. The greatest philosophical battle of the twentieth-century saw one ideology defeated and another prevailing as superior for organizing a twenty-first-century citizenry.

36. Measures of constraint "encompass the full variety of pre- and post-judgment measures available in national legal systems"; among other things, injunctions, attachment, and execution. *See* Crawford, *supra* n. 7, at 1,962; *see also* Yang, *supra* n. 17, at 343 ("'Measures of constraint' is a generic term covering both interlocutory, interim or pre-trial measures prior to final judgments and the execution or enforcement of judgments. In the context of State immunity, these are coercive or enforcement measures taken by the court either to restrain the foreign State in the disposition of its property, normally in the form of interlocutory injunctions, or otherwise to attach, arrest or seize the property of the foreign State.").

the *Purpose Test*). In some jurisdictions, a *Context Approach Test* has emerged.[37] Notwithstanding this, in most jurisdictions, the test employed at the jurisdictional phase is the Nature Test.

The major outstanding issue vis-à-vis sovereign immunity from jurisdiction is how to determine what constitutes a commercial act or else elaborate additional exceptions to the general rule (e.g., due to human rights, torts, terrorism, etc.). The two most invoked exceptions are the *commercial activity* exception and the *implied waiver doctrine*. Apart from that, the use of domestic procedural rules to implement the substantive law rises to prominent importance.

Similar issues arise in the execution context; however, in that phase, the court looks at whether the property/assets targeted to satisfy the award-creditor are used for a *commercial purpose*. Moreover, the implied waiver doctrine is generally only acceptable as a waiver of jurisdiction and not to be treated as a "double waiver" also for execution. Such waiver of immunity from execution cannot be implied but must be express/explicit. It has been said that "[t]here is a general rule that, even if judgment against a State based on an act *jure gestionis* has been entered, measures of execution against that State's property may not be taken without the foreign State's consent if the asset in question serves governmental purposes."[38] Hence, in most jurisdictions, the test employed at the execution phase is the Purpose Test.

Because the Purpose Test is a significant barrier to award execution, it can be argued that while the restrictive theory has "laid open a wide area of procedural and substantive law to enable national courts to exercise jurisdiction over foreign states," sovereign immunity meanwhile "continues to bar to a very large extent the enforcement of judgments given by such courts against foreign states."[39]

Thus, oftentimes award-creditors find themselves in a situation where they can indeed have their awards recognized and enforced (i.e., turned into a judgment of the court), but nevertheless face insurmountable obstacles when seeking to attach and execute against the award-debtor State's assets. It was in this context that Fox and Webb noted that "again and again thwarted judgment creditors have sought to attach assets of foreign States within the forum State territory, only to be refused orders for execution by national courts."[40]

Conclusively then, even though most trading-friendly jurisdictions have transitioned to embrace the restrictive theory of immunity also in the execution phase, the exceptions to the general rule of immunity in the execution context are narrower compared to jurisdictional immunity. This is largely due to the more stringent Purpose Test, not accepting an implied double waiver, the growth of separate SOEs, and the

37. *See generally* Katherine Reece Thomas, *Enforcing Against State Assets: The Case for Restricting Private Creditor Enforcement and How Judges in England Have Used "Context" When Applying the "Commercial Purposes" Test*, 2 J. Int'l Compar. L. 1 https://doi.org/10.4337/9781803923468.00010. Some judges have found difficulty in favoring a distinction and have instead searched for an answer in the totality of the circumstances.
38. Roy Goode et al., *Transnational Commercial Law: Text, Cases, and Materials* 522 (2nd ed. 2015).
39. Fox & Webb, *supra* n. 1, at 484.
40. *Ibid.*

treatment of a certain property as immune *ipso jure*.[41] To this, one can add several domestic procedural barriers—e.g., lack of discovery, limited execution against asset with a mixed-use, and conservative burden of proof shifting.

Ultimately then, whether an award-creditor is successful against a reluctant award-debtor State will depend on the domestic court's readiness to apply public international law incisively and pragmatically, without excessive deference to State defenses. Already from the outset, however, it must be emphasized that domestic courts are less likely to grant coercive measures against States. Fox and Webb observed that:

> The application of coercive measures to a state and its property involves different and more directly intrusive mechanisms than the ruling of a national court as to liability. In consequence, the bar against coercive measures against a foreign state remains largely absolute, subject at the present time to the state's consent.[42]

It should not come as a surprise then that the area of sovereign immunity from execution remains largely unresolved and is loaded with major obstacles for creditors of award-debtor States.[43] Bjorklund expressed that States seem less interested in removing immunity from execution.[44] While it holds some truth and one does best in treating the area with some cynicism, one must also be careful in overplaying the pessimism. Many jurisdictions have indeed qualified the conservative rule of immunity from execution in a liberal and even in a pragmatic manner, resulting in the enabling of award satisfaction through execution. This book will give plenty of such examples.

The major outstanding issue vis-à-vis sovereign immunity from execution (like immunity from jurisdiction) is how to determine what constitutes commercial assets or else to elaborate additional exceptions to the general rule (e.g., a double waiver doctrine). The two most invoked exceptions are the *commercial activity* exception and the *implied double waiver doctrine*. The latter is nowadays almost never successful. Apart from that, the use of domestic procedural rules to implement the substantive law rises to prominent—even determinative—importance in this context.

§3.2.2 Sovereign Immunity from Execution

Sovereign immunity *ratione materiae* has been described as "a rule of international law that facilitates the performance of public functions by the State and its representatives by preventing them from being sued or prosecuted in foreign courts."[45] Put differently, "[i]ts rationale is to promote the functioning of all governments by protecting States

41. Julian D.M. Lew et al., *Comparative International Commercial Arbitration* 745 (2003).
42. Fox & Webb, *supra* n. 1, at 23.
43. "Draft Articles on Jurisdictional Immunities of States and Their Property" (ILC Draft Articles on State Immunity), Art. 18(1), 1991.
44. Andrea K. Bjorklund, *Sovereign Immunity as a Barrier to the Enforcement of Investor-State Arbitral Awards: The Re-Politicization of International Investment Disputes*, 21 Am. Rev. Int'l Arb. 211, 230 (2011).
45. Crawford, *supra* n. 7, at 1,993.

from the burden of defending litigation abroad."[46] Therefore, it has been described as a protection that enables States "to carry out their functions effectively."[47] This underlying ethos has received stronger support in the execution context than in the jurisdictional context. This is because an interference with State property/assets is considered a greater interference with—or infringement on—the State's sovereignty.

This book does not deal with jurisdictional immunity. In the international arbitration context, the plea of jurisdictional immunity is of considerably less practical importance. This is because it is a generally held position that when a State has signed an arbitration clause or is a signatory to a multilateral arbitration-enforcement treaty, it has waived its immunity from jurisdiction. Such a jurisdictional waiver is mostly considered to extend to ancillary enforcement matters, including recognition and the turning of the award into a judgment. Lew, Mistelis, and Kröll noted that:

> The fact that a state cannot claim immunity from jurisdiction does not necessarily mean that the state is not immune from the actual execution of the award. In most laws the exceptions to immunity from execution are narrower than the exceptions to immunity from jurisdiction.[48]

In some jurisdictions, though, like Switzerland, if the court exercises jurisdiction over an action to determine rights and obligations, "one must admit also that a foreign State may in Switzerland be subjected to measures intended to ensure the forced execution of a judgment against it."[49] Notwithstanding this, for such an extension of the waiver, the activity of the dispute and the property targeted for attachment must have a close connection to Switzerland and to the dispute at hand. Naturally, this limits the practical utility of such "double waiver" in the international arbitration context (unless, for example, an international arbitration is considered a close connection or at least an international arbitration seated in the jurisdiction is considered as such). Even with this more lenient approach, the waiver does not extend to certain specifically protected property used for public purposes. As of today, however, most jurisdictions do not accept an arbitration clause as an implied waiver of immunity from execution.[50] The so-called *double waiver doctrine* has not been met with widespread approval.

As mentioned already, the different treatment of immunity from execution rests on the understanding that "[e]nforcement against State property constitutes a greater interference with a State's freedom to manage its own affairs and to pursue its public purposes than does the pronouncement of a judgment or order by a national court of another State."[51] Thus, the evolution and approval of the restrictive immunity theory

46. Lew et al., *supra* n. 41 at 744.
47. Fox & Webb, *supra* n. 1, at 1.
48. Lew et al., *supra* n. 41, at 750.
49. Fox & Webb, *supra* n. 1, at 492; *see also Arab Republic of Egypt v. Cintelevision Trust*, (Switzerland, Federal Tribunal, July 20, 1979).
50. The most notable exception to this presumption was presented in France in *Creighton v. Qatar*, (France, Court of Cassation, July 6, 2000) where the court held that the arbitration agreement constituted a waiver for purposes of execution because the ICC rules provided for a duty to carry out the award and waive any appeal of it. In other words, the court accepted the theory on "double waiver of immunity."
51. Fox & Webb, *supra* n. 1, at 486.

have not been as prevalent with respect to execution. Albeit the doctrine on immunity from execution allows for certain qualifications to the general rule of immunity, the doctrinal development has grown in a slightly different direction compared to its twin immunity from jurisdiction. Yang observed that:

> An examination of relevant State practice shows that, even though, as a general rule, preventive measures and measures of forced execution against foreign States and their property are permitted, such measures are subject to a number of conditions and limitations. First, a clear distinction has been drawn between immunity from the adjudicative process [immunity from jurisdiction] and immunity from measures of constraint [immunity from execution] […]. […] Secondly, the "purpose" test, much discredited in the context of adjudicative jurisdiction, resurfaces as a determinative factor in the context of measures of constraint. Generally speaking, the property of a foreign State enjoys immunity from attachment, arrest and execution when it is used for sovereign or public purposes, but not when it is used for commercial purposes. Thirdly, the territorial nexus requirement is adhered to even more strictly in the process of enforcement and execution of judgments against foreign State property. Finally, certain categories of property still enjoy absolute immunity, even where the foreign State has expressly waived its immunity from execution.[52]

Thus, while the twin doctrine of immunity from jurisdiction relies on the Nature Test, the immunity from execution doctrine relies on the Purpose Test. This makes award execution significantly more difficult than bringing a sovereign to court or arbitration. The fact that an arbitration clause is a waiver of immunity from jurisdiction but not execution exacerbates this difference in treatment.

In this conundrum, we can observe a number of differences between the twin doctrines, including, but not limited to: (a) that there is a universally accepted distinction between immunity from jurisdiction and immunity from attachment and execution; (b) the Nature Test is used for jurisdictional immunity and the Purpose Test is used for execution immunity; (c) the nexus requirement can complicate award execution even further; and (d) certain categories of State property/assets are outright immune and *ipso jure* out of reach for an award-creditor.

Putting this in practical terms, in order for an award-creditor to successfully execute against the award-debtor State's assets when sovereign immunity is invoked, she might have to: (1) prove that an *explicit/express waiver* of immunity from execution exists; (2) show that certain property has been *earmarked*; (3) prove that assets are used for *commercial purposes*; (4) establish a territorial or entity connection; and (5) find assets that are not considered immune *ipso jure*.[53] Such *ipso jure* immune assets can include diplomatic property (e.g., premises and bank accounts), central bank property, military property (e.g., ships and aircraft), cultural heritage of States, State property forming part of an exhibition, etc.

52. Yang, *supra* n. 17, at 343.
53. *See* UNCSI, Art. 19, 21. For a good overview, *see* Fox & Webb, *supra* n. 1, at Ch. 17. (dealing with the three exceptions to immunity from enforcement and the five categories of state property listed as immune).

As has been stated, the two most frequently submitted exceptions to immunity from execution have been *(implied) waiver* and the *commercial exception*. The most frequently debated exception is the waiver; in particular, the implied waiver doctrine. There is a generally held view that a waiver from jurisdiction—for instance, through an arbitration clause—does not entail a waiver of immunity from execution.[54] In fact, it has even proved difficult for award-creditors to construe explicit waivers of immunity from enforcement to include execution.

In practice, the commercial purpose exception is the most successful exception and the one most commonly invoked because neither explicit waivers nor earmarking is standard State practice.[55] Even the commercial purpose exception, however, is conservatively applied in the immunity from execution context as courts "tend to respect the discretion of states in claiming that the property at issue is used for public purposes."[56] For the combined reasons, it can be argued that the law on immunity from execution is largely restrictive in theory but to some extent still semi-absolute in practice.

Fox and Webb eloquently highlighted yet another non-legal consideration that constitutes a fatal drawback with the supposed restrictive theory on sovereign immunity from execution as follows:

> Even where attachment of foreign State assets located in the forum State is legally possible, the political consequences to the friendly relations of the forum State with the foreign State may discourage the forum State's support for such enforcement.[57]
>
> There are also strong economic considerations in favour of a foreign State's immunity from enforcement; the secure placement of foreign reserves of China and other States with expanding economies lodged in the U.S. and western European States constitute a significant factor in the balance of payments and stabilization of currency rates.[58]

Therefore, it might be a stretch to treat the transition from absolute immunity to restrictive immunity as "a triumph" in the execution context. There are still several important and unresolved issues pertaining to sovereign immunity. Such issues are of a theoretical, doctrinal, and practical nature. This book deals with some of the unresolved issues in the international arbitration context.

I would not go as far as Lauterpacht, who argued that the doctrine of sovereign immunity "infuse[d] an element of artificiality into international law" and that it was now time to "free … international law of the shackles of an archaic and cumbersome doctrine of controversial validity and usefulness."[59] First a caveat, it is not completely clear whether Lauterpacht's argument dealt with immunity from execution as opposed

54. Crawford, *supra* n. 7, at 1961. (The most notable exception to this presumption was presented in France in *Creighton v. Qatar*, where the court held that the arbitration agreement constituted a waiver for purposes of execution, too.).
55. *See* Crawford, *supra* n. 7, at 1964.
56. *Ibid.*
57. Fox & Webb, *supra* n. 1, at 32.
58. *Ibid.*
59. Hersch Lauterpacht, *The Problem of Jurisdictional Immunities of Foreign States*, 28 BYIL 220, at 247 (1951).

to jurisdictional immunity. One should bear in mind why immunity from execution is approved (i.e., the *horizontal* and *vertical objects and purposes*) and why the doctrine of sovereign immunity is indeed treated as a dichotomy.

First, there is no international law dealing with the insolvency of States. States can find themselves in serious economic hardship, affecting their primary goal of securing the wellbeing of their citizens. Second, the world is dependent on global governance to tackle global threats (e.g., climate change, public health issues, human rights, economic crises, historical injustices, etc.), and therefore States need to respect international comity and a level of deference to the State's practices. Third, one should take into consideration external stakeholders in a dispute—i.e., the population. Finally, the primary goal, however, is political, i.e., avoiding conflict between States and solving the ultimate faith of compensation through diplomatic means.[60] The International Law Commission (ILC) working group on the UNCSI noted that "[t]he seizure of a gunboat or military aircraft of another State may spark an endless process of hostilities of international conflict."[61] Moreover, aspects such as cultural identity, historical features, and the aspect of mutual global intercourse all justified a doctrine of immunity from execution that offers protection to States as regards their assets abroad.

Seen in this light, the doctrine of immunity from execution can be both justified as fending-off intrusive attachment and execution against State assets. At the end of the day, compared to exercising jurisdiction over a State, "[e]nforcement against State property constitutes a greater interference with a State's freedom to manage its own affairs [i.e., the *horizontal object and purpose*] and to pursue its public purposes [i.e., the *vertical object and purpose*]."[62]

§3.3 THE SOURCES OF SOVEREIGN IMMUNITY FROM EXECUTION

Sovereign immunity is a rule of public (customary) international law which has developed both domestically and internationally. There is no multilateral convention in force dealing with the law on sovereign immunity. One regional treaty exists—the European Convention on State Immunity (ECSI). Furthermore, there has been a serious attempt to enact a multilateral convention—culminating in the UNCSI. Even though the UNCSI never entered into force, it nevertheless represents a codification of customary international law in some parts.

Moreover, even though sovereign immunity is a field of public international law, the law has largely developed through the interpretation and application of the doctrine by domestic courts.[63] Thus, sovereign immunity law lies at the intersection between international law and national law and this makes it "imperative to examine how the international legal framework is further refined and implemented at the level of

60. *See* Fox & Webb, *supra* n. 1, at 88.
61. *Ibid.*, at 532.
62. *Ibid.*, at 486.
63. Crawford, *supra* n. 7, at 1,934.

national legislation and case law."[64] And apart from applying the substantive law of sovereign immunity, domestic courts apply procedural rules when dealing with the plea of immunity and the award-creditor's request to apply an exception.

Therefore, it can be said that "[i]mmunity exists as a rule of international law, but its application depends substantially on the law and procedural rules of the forum."[65] That being so, every now and then "these issues are being elevated to an international level, including through international litigation."[66]

Some jurisdictions have legislation dealing with sovereign immunity (e.g., the U.S., the U.K., Australia, and Pakistan). For jurisdictions with dedicated domestic codes, the courts engage mostly with statutory interpretation. Notwithstanding this, all judges dealing with sovereign immunity must know the boundaries set by public international law.[67] For the jurisdictions where legislative acts regulating immunity are lacking (as is the case in the vast majority of States), courts are more directly obligated to apply international law by "work[ing] out the parameters of immunity by referring to a variety of international sources, such as cases decided by foreign courts, treaties and other international instruments, government statements, and scholarly writings."[68]

The sources of public international law are: (a) treaties; (b) customary international law; (c) general principles of law; and (d) judicial decisions and scholarly work.

§3.3.1 Treaty Law

The idea of creating a multilateral framework dealing with sovereign immunity has been long-lived. There has been no shortcoming in attempts to elaborate a multilateral framework.[69] The attempts can be traced all the way back to the 1926 International Convention for the Unification of Certain Rules relating to the Immunity of State-owned Vessel. This was a subject-specific treaty that had limited scope and reach but nevertheless proved to be an important stepping-stone for further developments.[70] Such treaty was followed by another, more successful treaty, namely, the ECSI. These

64. Tom Ruys et al., "Introduction: International Immunities in a State of Flux?" in *Cambridge Handbook on Immunities and International Law* (Tom Ruys, Nicolas Angelet, & Luca Ferro, eds.), 3 (2019).
65. Crawford, *supra* n. 7, at 1934.
66. *Ibid.*
67. Yang, *supra* n. 17, at 37.
68. *Ibid.*, at 36.
69. Alexander Orakhelashvili, "Treaties on State Immunity: The 1972 and 2004 Conventions," in *Research Handbook on Jurisdiction and Immunities in International Law* (Roger O'Keefe & Christian J. Tams, eds.), 274 (2015) ("[T]he low participation of states in these treaties is a matter that cannot be overlooked. The 1972 European Convention on State Immunity is in force as between eight states only; while the 2004 UN Convention on Jurisdictional Immunities of States and Their Property is not in force yet, and it is uncertain when it will be …").
70. It has been said that "[a]s far as State immunity is concerned, the first real breakthrough came in 1926" with the 1926 International Convention for the Unification of Certain Rules relating to the Immunity of State-owned Vessels. *See* Yang, *supra* n. 17, at 445. (*See* in particular Art. 3 denying immunity from adjudication and execution for states vis-á-vis non-warship, non-governmental ships used for commercial activity.).

two earlier efforts laid the ground for the UN-led multilateralization work, which culminated in the UNCSI. The UNCSI has so far resulted in 22 ratifications and 14 signatures.[71] The UNCSI will enter into force upon 30 ratifications. Even though the UNCSI has not yet entered into force, the convention has proved to be a success; this is because the convention has been treated as constituting in certain parts a codification of customary international law by the ICJ and domestic courts. Therefore, it is probably the most significant instrument of sovereign immunity law and most certainly a starting point for any analysis in this field of law (bar in jurisdictions that have enacted legislation).

[1] European Convention on State Immunity

The ECSI was concluded in 1972 and remains the only treaty on sovereign immunity currently in force.[72] As such, ECSI has exerted considerable influence over the evolution of sovereign immunity law.[73] For example, the convention applied the restrictive theory of immunity as opposed to absolute immunity.

Notwithstanding ECSI's relative success, the convention faced two major challenges: (1) it was homogenous/regional in that it applied only in certain Western European States with cultural similarities; and (2) "it could not solve the problem of execution into the property of foreign states."[74] Hafner and Köhler observed that "even the Western European states could not yet get acquainted with the possible encroachment into their property by foreign courts, measures of constraint being viewed as the most intensive intrusion into state sovereignty."[75] As a result, the ECSI excludes "any measure of constraint against a foreign State in the absence of express consent."[76] Article 23 of the convention reads as follows:

> No measures of execution or preventive measures against the property of a Contracting State may be taken in the territory of another Contracting State except where and to the extent that the State has expressly consented thereto in writing in any particular case.[77]

71. UNCSI, Art. 30 ("1. The present Convention shall enter into force on the thirtieth day following the date of deposit of the thirtieth instrument of ratification, acceptance, approval or accession with the Secretary-General of the UN. 2. For each State ratifying, accepting, approving or acceding to the present Convention after the deposit of the thirtieth instrument of ratification, acceptance, approval or accession, the Convention shall enter into force on the thirtieth day after the deposit by such State of its instrument of such ratification, acceptance, approval or accession.").
72. Yang, *supra* n. 17, at 445. (It has entered into force in eight countries (Austria, Belgium, Cyprus, Germany, Luxembourg, Netherlands, Switzerland, and the United Kingdom), and has been signed but not ratified by one (Portugal).) *See* https://www.coe.int/en/web/conventions/full-list/-/conventions/treaty/074/signatures?p_auth = lSciW1vs.
73. *Ibid.*
74. Gerhard Hafner & Ulrike Köhler, *The United Nations Convention on Jurisdictional Immunities of States and Their Property*, 35 NYIL 5 (2004) https://doi.org/10.1017/s0167676804000030.
75. *Ibid.*
76. *Ibid.*, at 37.
77. "European Convention on State Immunity" (ECSI), Art. 23, 1972, 74 ETS 8.

In 2006, most signatories to the ECSI declared their intention of signing and ratifying the UNCSI, with the intention that the latter would supersede the former.[78] Even though the UNCSI has not yet entered into force, in practice it takes precedence over the ECSI. This is because ECSI is not all-encompassing and is largely outdated. Conversely, the UNCSI in certain crucial parts represents a codification of customary international law. This includes Article 19 UNCSI entrenching restrictive immunity from execution.

[2] The UN Convention on Jurisdictional Immunities of States and Their Property

The UNCSI builds on the ECSI.[79] The UNCSI sought to consolidate State practice and accommodate divergent views. Like the ECSI does with respect to jurisdictional immunity, and as legislation in certain trade-friendly jurisdictions (e.g., the U.S. and the U.K.), the convention adopts the restrictive theory of immunity. The UNCSI embraces the restrictive theory of immunity by first elaborating a general rule of immunity and then enumerating exceptions. Compared to the ECSI, the UNCSI qualifies the rule of immunity with exceptions both with respect to immunity from jurisdiction and immunity from execution ("measures of constraint" more broadly).[80]

The work leading up to the UNCSI initially took place in the ILC. The work by the ILC was completed already in 1991 when the ILC submitted 22 draft articles to the UN General Assembly (UNGA). The UNGA, in turn, established a Sixth Committee working group (UNGA Working Group). The UNGA Working Group was asked to consider the following issues:

> (1) the definition of the terms "State" and "commercial transaction," including the question of the criterion for determining whether a contract or transaction is a "commercial transaction"; (2) the question of the legal distinction between a State and certain of its entities in respect of State immunity; (3) contracts of employment; (4) the question of immunity from measures of constraint.[81]

78. Fox & Webb, *supra* n. 1, at 294.
79. David P. Stewart, *Introductory Note on the UN Convention on Jurisdictional Immunities of States and Their Property*, 44 ILM 801 (2005).
80. *See* Crawford, *supra* n. 7, at 489.
81. Yang, *supra* n. 17, at 448. Another interesting discussion that is slightly outside the scope of this dissertation is whether the work of the ILC should culminate in a convention or as a "model law." *See also* Hafner & Köhler, *supra* n. 74, at 8. Fox and Webb outlined the outstanding issues as divided in five and with two further items added by Professor Hafner in 1999, namely, "(i) the concept of a State for the purposes of immunity in the definition article; (ii) criteria for determining the commercial character of a contract or transaction; (iii) the concept of a State enterprise or other entity in relation to commercial transactions; (iv) contracts of employment; and (v) measures of constraint against State property." The two additional items were: "(vi) the possible form which the outcome of the work should take. Differing views as to a convention, a model law, or guidelines were expressed; (vii) the existence or non-existence of immunity in the case of violation of jus cogens norms." Fox & Webb, *supra* n. 1, at 290.

This book focuses strictly on the last question, namely, immunity from measures of constrained and more specifically on immunity from execution.[82] At that time, there was "no great enthusiasm to tackle the core problem of execution of judgments given by national courts against states."[83] Put in general terms, the clash was "between supporters of no execution and those favoring restricted immunity."[84] There was no strong support of—let alone effective advocacy for—absolute immunity.

Even though there was a general consensus that immunity from execution should be qualified by exceptions, many issues remained in defining the scope; for example, what kinds of State assets could be executed against, could an award-creditor execute against the assets of a State-owned entity, and should the commercial exception be qualified to adopt the Purpose or Nature Test?[85]

In 2000, the UNGA set up an Ad Hoc Committee (UNCSI Committee) to be chaired by Professor Hafner. Remarkably, the controversial aspects that had previously been met by unwavering divergence were settled—the participants made concessions.[86] This propelled the UNCSI Committee to finally deliver its proposal and the Draft UNCSI. Shortly thereafter, the UNGA adopted the UNCSI on December 2, 2004, and it was opened for signature on January 17, 2005.[87]

In a nutshell, the UNCSI adopts a general rule of immunity from jurisdiction and a separate rule of immunity from execution. Articles 19-21 of the UNCSI deal with sovereign immunity from post-judgment measures of constraint (including execution). Article 19 establishes a general prohibition against measures of constraint and qualifies it with three exceptions. Article 20 deals with the effect of consent in the post-judgment context. Article 21 establishes five categories of property considered *ipso jure* immune from execution. The said articles read as follows:

Article 19

State immunity from post-judgment measures of constraint

No post-judgment measures of constraint, such as attachment, arrest or execution, against property of a State may be taken in connection with a proceeding before a court of another State unless and except to the extent that:

(a) the State has expressly consented to the taking of such measures as indicated:
  (i) by international agreement;
  (ii) by an arbitration agreement or in a written contract; or
  (iii) by a declaration before the court or by a written communication after a dispute between the parties has arisen; or
(b) the State has allocated or earmarked property for the satisfaction of the claim which is the object of that proceeding; or

82. *See* Bankas, *supra* n. 6, at 200 ("Delegates were simply divided as to whether the denial of immunity means that enforcement measures should be taken against state property.").
83. Fox & Webb, *supra* n. 1, at 496.
84. *Ibid.*
85. *See* Yang, *supra* n. 17, at 449.
86. *Ibid.*, at 453; *see also Summary Record of the Sixth Committee, Fifty-Seventh Session*, 21 October 2003, A/C.6/58/SR.12, para. 12 (Hafner).
87. Yang, *supra* n. 17, p. 453 (On the 25 October 2004 the UN Sixth Committee met and considered the ad hoc work, culminating the UNGA adopting the final text as a convention.).

(c) it has been established that the property is specifically in use or intended for use by the State for other than government non-commercial purposes and is in the territory of the State of the forum, provided that post-judgment measures of constraint may only be taken against property that has a connection with the entity against which the proceeding was directed.

Article 20

Effect of consent to jurisdiction to measures of constraint

Where consent to the measures of constraint is required under Articles 18 and 19, consent to the exercise of jurisdiction under Article 7 shall not imply consent to the taking of measures of constraint.

Article 21

Specific categories of property

1. The following categories, in particular, of property of a State shall not be considered as property specifically in use or intended for use by the State for other than government non-commercial purposes under article 19, subparagraph (c):
   (a) property, including any bank account, which is used or intended for use in the performance of the functions of the diplomatic mission of the State or its consular posts, special missions, missions to international organizations or delegations to organs of international organizations or to international conferences;
   (b) property of a military character or used or intended for use in the performance of military functions;
   (c) property of the central bank or other monetary authority of the State;
   (d) property forming part of the cultural heritage of the State or part of its archives and not placed or intended to be placed on sale;
   (e) property forming part of an exhibition of objects of scientific, cultural or historical interest and not placed or intended to be placed on sale.
2. Paragraph 1 is without prejudice to article 18 and article 19, subparagraphs (a) and (b).

Thus, the UNCSI adopts the restrictive theory on immunity from execution, although it makes it considerably more difficult to execute against State property than to bring a suit against a State.[88] Thus, despite some degree of liberalization vis-à-vis issues of execution against State assets, not many can deny that on the whole, the UNCSI is relatively State-centric and not as liberal as in many trading-friendly jurisdictions.[89] It is important to understand that Article 19 does not prejudge the

88. *See* Hafner & Köhler, *supra* n. 74, at 36 ("In state practice, immunity from execution and immunity from jurisdiction are treated separately.").
89. Bankas, *supra* n. 6, at 309; *see* Fox & Webb, *supra* n. 1, at. 298 ("Despite the wide recognition, following the German decision in The Philippine Embassy case and the US and UK legislation, that State property used for commercial purposes was liable to attachment, the Convention's provisions on execution are cautious: no attachment pre-judgment without consent or specific allocation of State property, and attachment post-judgment only in respect of property used for commercial purposes 'that has a connection with the entity against which the proceeding was directed' (rt. 19(c)). The first Special Rapporteur appears to have been strongly influenced in 'his treatment of immunity from execution by the fears of developing countries that execution by

question of "piercing the corporate veil" as a step precedent to attaching and executing against the assets of, for example, State-owned entities for the debt of the State (and vice versa).[90]

In that light, some could argue that the UNCSI could have: (a) included a provision stating that an arbitration clause constitutes a waiver of sovereign immunity from execution of arbitral awards; (b) further clarified the law and adopted the Nature Test vis-à-vis post-judgment measures of constraint; (c) made Article 21 less categorical by including fewer types of assets as inherently immune, and most importantly (d) treated all property in Article 21 based on functionality and not categorically. It is my submission that international economic law would have benefited from a more liberal attitude that goes beyond the relative consensus struck by the UNCSI.

Despite what some could perceive as shortcomings, the UNCSI is indeed the best universal attempt to this day and overall, it does indeed push the evolution of the substantive law of sovereign immunity from execution in the right direction. It is no surprise then that national courts and the ICJ have referred to the UNCSI when applying the doctrine of sovereign immunity.[91] By way of illustration, in 2006, Lord Bingham stated that the UNCSI "[d]espite its embryonic status [...] [was] the most authoritative statement available on the current international understanding of the limits of state immunity in civil cases."[92] The UNCSI is nowadays considered in part a reflection/codification of customary international law.[93] Notwithstanding this, as will be seen below throughout this book, there are still areas of the UNCSI that are not considered to have been codified—e.g., whether there should be a nexus requirement (Article 19(c)) and which assets are immune *ipso jure* (Article 21). We will now look specifically at Articles 19 and 21 of the UNCSI.

[i] Article 19

Article 19 contains a general rule of immunity and three exceptions to it—i.e., no execution *unless*. Sub-section (a) makes it clear that immunity can always be waived,

unscrupulous creditors of commercial ventures would unfairly take the form of attachment of diplomatic and central bank assets.'").

90. Fox & Webb, *supra* n. 1, at 518.

91. *See, e.g., Jurisdictional Immunities, supra* n. 8; and *Sedelmayer v. The Russian Federation*, Case No. Ö 170-10, (Swedish Supreme Court, 2011), at 475.

92. *Jones v. Ministry of the Interior of the Kingdom of Saudi Arabia*, (U.K. House of Lords, June 14, 2006), 129 ILR 629, at 17, para. 26.

93. However, not everyone agrees with the standing of the UNCSI as a source of public international law. *See, e.g.*, Orakhelashvili, *supra* n. 69, at 292 ("It is, however, unclear how a Convention which is not ratified nor in force, including non-ratification by the forum state, can be the 'most authoritative' statement of the legal position or any of its understandings. It could well be a statement of the intention of the body that adopted the Convention as to the future state of the law after the Convention enters into force. But before then, it cannot be taken as a source of law, even if it conceptually reinforces the judges' own perception as to the required legal position."). Excellent as he is and considering that he writes from a good place and with the everlasting issues of transnational human rights litigation in mind, I must respectfully disagree with the analysis by Dr. Orakhelashvili. This disagreement comes even though I do not believe that the UNCSI goes far enough and also that I do not believe that the convention is a codification of customary international law in its entirety.

but that a separate (express and/or explicit) waiver is required for execution. This is made clear by Article 20. Sub-section (b) is more difficult to discern any inherent meaning from and its practical utility has been limited. Is earmarking to be explicit or can it be inferred from some other act?[94] It is this author's understanding that earmarking is expected to be explicit and that such is uncommon. Practically speaking, it serves as a form of express/explicit waiver and security/collateral combined.

The most important provision is found in Article 19(c). The major difficulty in the commercial exception is to determine what is used for a commercial purpose (*iure gestionis*) and what is used for a non-commercial governmental purpose (*iure imperii*). Courts have been tasked with working this out on an ad hoc, case-by-case basis.

Much of Chapter 4 deals with a comparative analysis of courts trying to discern meaning from the restrictive theory and elaborating a workable test for determining when property is considered to be used *jure gestionis*. Moreover, both Chapters 4 and 5 illustrate how courts have developed procedural tools to either facilitate or make it more difficult for award-creditors to execute against the assets of award-debtor States.

[ii] Article 21

Article 21 can be said to be the result of a concession between competing positions on sovereign immunity—i.e., no immunity, absolute immunity, and some immunity. All gained something they desired through Articles 19 and 21. While Article 19 established the commercial purpose exception, Article 21 establishes *ipso jure* (near absolute) immunity for a certain category of property.[95] Thus, the very purpose, objective and effect of Article 21 is to defeat some of the purpose, objective, and practical effect of the commercial purpose exception in Article 19(c).[96] The ILC Commentary to the UNCSI articulates this fairly well:

> This protection is deemed necessary and timely in view of the trend in certain jurisdictions to attach and freeze assets of foreign States, especially bank accounts, assets of the central bank or other instrumenta legati and specific categories of property which equally deserve protection.[97]

The property enjoying virtually absolute immunity is: (a) diplomatic property; (b) military property; (c) central bank property (or other monetary authority of the State); (d) property forming part of the cultural heritage of the State; or (e) property forming part of an exhibition. The list is non-exhaustive, which can be understood from the use of "in particular."

Given that Article 21 was a concession between competing positions of different States, it underscores the diverging State practice. Given that the UNCSI never entered into force, we are left wondering whether—and what parts of—Article 21 constitute a

94. *See* Fox & Webb, *supra* n. 1, at 518.
95. ILC Commentary, UNCSI, Art. 21 ("Each of these specific categories of property, by its very nature, must be taken to be in use or intended for use for governmental purposes removed from any commercial consideration").
96. The article sets out what assets are protected *ipso facto* despite the commercial exception.
97. *See* ILC Commentary, UNCSI, Art. 21.

codification of customary international law. This author's position is that Article 21 does not represent a codification of customary international law due to the divergence in positions and its language being essentially a result of concessions to get the UNCSI sort of speaking "through the door."

That does not exclude that there may be compelling arguments as to why certain property should remain virtually immune—primarily views expressed by the developing world, once colonialized and subject to brutal imperialism. Even though this book does not deal with such historical regret, it is important to note that international law, in general, and IIL, in particular, has been developed largely by Western capital-rich and capital-exporting countries. When the UNCSI was drafted, it was noted that:

> The process of decolonialisation is irreversible. The opposite is not permissible worth or without the consent of the State. A State may consent to give up its immunity from attachment and execution up to a certain limit beyond which no national jurisdiction or power is recognised. In this connection there exists a standard from which there can be no derogation.[98]

The positions espoused as righteous in the West may simultaneously be understood as an extension of imperialism in the Global South or by TWAIL scholars. This is not a book on historical injustices in law or what it means for a society to treat certain ideas as the norm and any opposing view as the exception/deviation. What can be said is that we should be open to studying law also as a historical feature and through the lens of structural inequities and social injustices. For example, such considerations must be part of a determination of whether and to what extent cultural heritage property should be immune.

(a) Diplomatic Property

The provision is written in such a manner as to limit execution against diplomatic property which is used or intended to be used for the purposes (i.e., in the performance) of diplomatic functions. This sub-section is less absolute than sub-section (c) on central bank assets in that it is not categorical and therefore does not cloak diplomatic assets *used or intended to be used* for commercial purposes in immunity (e.g., embassy accounts used to settle commercial debts). Difficulties often arise, however, where the accounts may have dual purposes; that is, where the assets have a so-called mixed use or intended use.[99] Some jurisdictions have made it more difficult to dissect the purposes of diplomatic property, while others have been more liberal in their approach.

(b) Military Property

This provision is meant to protect military equipment and objects from attachment and execution (e.g., ships, aircraft, etc.). The provision was probably added to protect countries that may have military bases and military presence in foreign nations (e.g.,

98. Fox & Webb, *supra* n. 1, at 532.
99. *See* James Crawford, *Execution of Judgments and Foreign Sovereign Immunity*, 75 Am. J. Int'l L. 820, 863 (1981) https://doi.org/10.2307/2201355.

the U.S. and the U.K.). It has been noted that this wide category was included in order to "avoid the possibility that a foreign State might permit execution on military property of the United States abroad under a reciprocal application of the act."[100]

(c) Central Bank Property or Other Monetary Authority

Article 21(1)(c) dealing with central bank assets is drafted *categorically*. As we can *see* in Article 21, the other types of protected property are drafted *functionally*. There is a major difference between the application of a functional as opposed to a categorically protected type of asset.

Central banks and other monetary authorities keep accounts with foreign banks for various activities and purposes. Whether a judgment or award creditor may attach and execute against central bank assets, or the assets of other monetary authorities, is treated as a very sensitive topic because such type of attachment may cause the award/judgment debtor-State serious financial problems and may therefore lead to significant harm to friendly relations between States.[101]

For these reasons, Article 21(1)(c) of the UNSCI makes the property of central banks and other monetary authorities absolutely immune. The express language is striking and actually unambiguous, namely, "property of a State *shall not* be considered as property specifically in use or intended for use by the State for other than government non-commercial purposes under Article 19, subparagraph (c)" when it is the "property of the central bank or other monetary authority of the State." In other words, central bank (and other monetary authorities) property is to be considered in use or intended for use by the State for governmental non-commercial purposes *ipso facto*, and therefore immune *ipso jure*.

Notably, this is the position in the UNCSI and does not necessarily reflect a codification of customary international law. Today, when it comes to the treatment of central bank assets, States are divided among those States that: (1) provide for "near-absolute immunity" from execution; (2) adopt a "middle-approach"; and (3) offer "no special protection." This lack of uniformity renders the proper level of protection under customary international law uncertain.[102] It is safe to say that there is "seemingly no general acceptance in State practice for the higher degree of immunity for its property conferred by UNCSI, Article 21 than that which applies to the property of other State entities."[103]

100. Fox & Webb, *supra* n. 1, at 526.
101. *See* Yang, *supra* n. 17, at 410 ("Therefore it is little wonder that, in the practice of some states, special considerations apply to the immunity of foreign central banks. In these states the property of foreign central banks is accorded absolute or near absolute immunity from execution.").
102. This debate was a vivid one already in 1981, *see, e.g.*, Crawford, *supra* n. 7, at 865 ("In practice, foreign central bank funds are usually mixed funds (*i.e.*, bulk accounts not earmarked for any specific purpose), and it is likely to be difficult to distinguish central bank funds as set aside for commercial purposes. On the other hand, no magic attaches to the label 'central bank'; the question must always be whether a particular function or use of property is immune in accordance with the criteria suggested here. There is no reason why a special or earmarked fund held for nonimmune purposes by a central bank should not be liable to execution. This is, however, an unlikely possibility.").
103. Fox & Webb, *supra* n. 1, at 529.

However, when interpreting Article 21(1)(c) as is, one cannot include language that is not there; for example, that central bank property be specifically protected only when using the property for "central bank functions" or when used for "governmental non-commercial purposes" is wrong. Such a functional approach would read-in the clause something that is not there. The UNCSI explicitly provides for a categorical position and the purpose of Article 21 is to provide an additional set of protection on top of the general rule of immunity as partly qualified by Article 19.[104] The bottom line is that Article 21 was an explicit and conscious decision taken against the backdrop of concessions among those States in favor of absolute immunity and those States advocating for limited immunity.

Fortunately for award-creditors, the buck does not stop with the UNCSI. First and foremost, one must ask whether Article 21—as part of Article 19—actually reflects a codification of customary international law. It is this author's opinion that it does not. Thus, domestic courts and international courts/tribunals are not bound by the categorical approach in Article 21 until and unless the UNCSI is ratified and enters into force. Thus, judges are free to apply the more functional approach that better reflects customary international law. There is one major caveat, i.e., that the categorical position may have been codified in a given jurisdiction (e.g., the U.K.).

Even where the functional approach is endorsed, a major issue is whether the assets have a mixed-use purpose. Earlier decisions allowed for attachment of mixed accounts in certain circumstances, but current practice seems to consider such accounts to be immune unless the use clearly tilts toward the commercial side of things.[105] All in all, one can easily conclude that the presumption is that central bank property enjoys immunity and that the burden of proving otherwise is a difficult one and sometimes an impossible one.[106]

(d) Cultural Heritage Property or Property Forming Part of an Exhibition

It is the author's position that this provision is very important since it deals with national identity and is only exacerbated by the fact that many underdeveloped or developing States have been subjected to and suffered from imperialism and/or colonialism. When drafting the UNCSI, developing States feared interference with property constituting the cultural heritage of the nation.[107]

104. *See The Republic of Kazakhstan and the National Bank of Kazakhstan v. Stati, Ascom, et al.*, Case No. ÖÄ 7709-1, (Swedish Supreme Court, June 17, 2020), at 21 (referring to the expert report by Professor Wrange).

105. *See* Philipp Janig & Sara Mansour Fallah, *Certain Iranian Assets: The Limits of Anti-terrorism Measures in Light of State Immunity and Standards of Treatment*, 59 GYIL 1 (2016) https://doi.org/10.17265/1548-6605/2021.04.002. (citing District Court of Rotterdam, *State of the Netherlands v. Azeta BV*, (District Court of Rotterdam, May 14, 1998), 128 ILR 688, at 688-689; *Alcom v. Republic of Colombia*, (U.K. House of Lords, April 12, 1984), 1 AC 580, at 604; *Iraq v. Vinci Constructions*, (Court of Appeal of Brussels, October 4, 2002), 127 ILR 101, at 105-106.).

106. *See, e.g., Ascom, Terra et al. v. The Republic of Kazakhstan*, Case No. Ö 3828-20, (Swedish Supreme Court, December 10, 2021), NJA 2021, s. 850; cf. *AIG Capital Partners Inc v. Kazakhstan*, ICSID Case No. ARB/01/6, (ICSID, November 20, 2005) EWHC 2239 (Comm).

107. *See* Fox & Webb, *supra* n. 1, at 532.

Specifically designed rules on cultural heritage and property may also complicate the analysis of sovereign immunity from execution in the context of certain property that at times is specifically protected. This book does not deal with the 1970 UNESCO Convention or other similar kinds of conventions or legislation.

§3.3.2 Customary International Law

It is well established that sovereign immunity is "a general rule of customary international law rooted in the current practice of States."[108] The law on sovereign immunity will continue to derive its legal authority from customary international law until the UNCSI comes into force.[109]

Having concluded that the substantive law on sovereign immunity is a general rule of customary international law, it nevertheless must be applied and the law and principles established. The ICJ has undertaken its important task of consolidating part of the law and in doing so crystallized some principles as constituting customary international law. For example, the court has held that: (1) sovereign immunity is "a general rule of customary international law rooted in the current practice of States";[110] (2) the "rules of State immunity are procedural in character and are confined to determining whether or not the courts of one State may exercise jurisdiction in respect of another State";[111] and (3) that the UNSCI represents, in part, customary international law, which includes rules on sovereign immunity from measures of constraint.[112]

Put simply, a judge dealing with the plea of sovereign immunity is obliged to consider customary international law unless she is (or in addition to being) tasked to interpret legislation on sovereign immunity (e.g., FSIA in the U.S. or SIA in the U.K.).[113]

---

108. *Jurisdictional Immunities, supra* n. 8, at para. 56.
109. Fox & Webb, *supra* n. 1, at 1.
110. *Jurisdictional Immunities, supra* n. 8, at para. 56.
111. *Ibid.*, at paras. 93, 82 ("Immunity from jurisdiction is an immunity not merely from being subjected to an adverse judgment but from being subjected to the trial process. It is, therefore, necessarily preliminary in nature. Consequently, a national court is required to determine whether or not a foreign State is entitled to immunity as a matter of international law before it can hear the merits of the case brought before it and before the facts have been established. If immunity were to be dependent upon the State actually having committed a serious violation of international human rights law or the law of armed conflict, then it would become necessary for the national court to hold an enquiry into the merits in order to determine whether it had jurisdiction. If, on the other hand, the mere allegation that the State had committed such wrongful acts were to be sufficient to deprive the State of its entitlement to immunity, immunity could, in effect be negated simply by skillful construction of the claim.").
112. *Ibid.*, at paras. 117-118.
113. This presents an interesting academic question of whether customary international law should nonetheless fill the gaps of sovereign immunity legislation and whether such domestic codification can in fact deviate from customary international law (and if so, how much). This is a discussion for another day but generally speaking it has been said that "customary law may be called on to mold and even modify texts which cannot realistically be amended, however desirable amendment might be." *See, e.g.*, Crawford, *supra* n. 7, at 428. It is this author's position that Jurisdictions with a codified law on sovereign immunity should not outright refuse to interpret their acts in light of customary international law.

[1] The International Court of Justice

This section will deal with the two ICJ cases that directly address sovereign immunity; that is, *Germany v. Italy (Greece intervening)* and *Iran v. U.S.*[114] Recently, the 2012 *Germany v. Italy* dispute has been revived.[115] That new proceeding will be discussed too.

There is no doubt that the ICJ has had an enormous impact on the development of the law of sovereign immunity. The ICJ has the role and standing of analyzing various domestic court decisions and thereafter consolidating the law and crystallizing certain principles. One learned scholar rightly noted that:

> The results of the Court's forays into the law of interstate immunities have been, variously, to crystallize, to catalyze the further formation of, to consolidate, and to set the seal on the customary rules at issue. Not all, however, of the Court's statements on jurisdictional immunities have touched on controversy. Many have represented no more than textbook expositions of doctrinal principle as to the nature and implementation of such immunities. Dicta of this sort have served usefully to affirm or clarify certain fundamentals of the law of jurisdictional immunities and have been restated since in a range of fora.[116]

Surely domestic court practice is important for the development of customary international law, and therefore the law on sovereign immunity. However, given ICJ's standing as the leading court of interpreting public international law, its judgments hold the highest currency.

Accordingly, apart from domestic courts and legislative branches being forced to deal with sovereign immunity laws, it is ultimately the role of the ICJ to shape the law of sovereign immunity. Sovereign immunity issues are often of "primordial importance in present-day international society but still are largely obscure from a legal point of view."[117]

[i] Germany v. Italy

In 2012, the ICJ delivered the "*Jurisdictional Immunities decision.*" In the decision, the court partly consolidated customary international law—at least with respect to immunity from jurisdiction.[118] As is the case with customary international law, much of the law that was consolidated was already an expression of practices in domestic courts and legislative action. The consolidation also considered renowned scholarly

---

114. *Jurisdictional Immunities, supra* n. 8, at para. 56*; see also Islamic Republic of Iran v. United States, Certain Iranian Assets,* Preliminary Objections, Judgment, ICJ Rep. (February 13, 2019), at 1 (hereinafter "*Certain Iranian Assets*").
115. *Germany v. Italy, Certain Questions of Jurisdictional Immunity and Enforcement of Judgments,* Application Instituting Proceedings and Request for Provisional Measures, ICJ Rep. (April 29, 2022), at 1.
116. Roger O'Keefe, "Jurisdictional Immunities," in *The Development of International Law by the International Court of Justice* (Christian J. Tams & James Sloan, eds.), 107 (2013).
117. Pieter Kooijmans, *The ICJ in the 21st Century: Judicial Restraint, Judicial Activism, or Proactive Judicial Policy,* 56 Int'l & Compar. L. Q. 750-751 (2007) https://doi.org/10.1093/iclq/lei223.
118. O'Keefe, *supra* n. 116, at 111-115.

work. But most notably perhaps, the decision by the ICJ treated the UNSCI as partly codifying customary international law and as a stepping-stone for further analysis of the substantive law of sovereign immunity.

In several important observations, the court reasoned, *inter alia,* that:

(1) immunity from jurisdiction had been "adopted as a general rule of customary international law solidly rooted in the current practice of States"[119] and that there are elaborate exceptions to such rule;
(2) there is a distinction between proceedings for the recognition and enforcement, on the one hand, and the execution of a foreign judgment on the other;[120] and
(3) parts of Article 19 of the UNSCI (on post-judgment measures of constraint) represent customary international law.[121]

Germany claimed that Italy had violated public international law by denying sovereign immunity to Germany in proceedings relating to: (1) liability for war damage caused by German armed forces during World War II (such disputes were to be heard by Italian courts and the plea of immunity from jurisdiction was invoked); (2) the attachment and execution of German property in Italy; and by (3) the Italian courts' failure to consider jurisdictional immunity when recognizing and enforcing foreign judgments. Thus, Germany's application included a request to: (a) grant immunity from jurisdiction; (b) grant immunity from execution; and (c) declare that Italian courts were obliged to consider immunity from jurisdiction when recognizing or enforcing foreign judgments.[122]

In the execution context, which is the focus of this book, the UNCSI "provides a comprehensive regime of rules covering immunity from … [execution] of a state."[123] And even though not yet having entered into force, the court referred to UNSCI Article 19, in general, and Article 19(c) in particular. Although the court was careful not to endorse the article as mandatory customary international law, "the ICJ shaped, by reference to that article's exception (c), the standards to be applied by a third state's court in proceedings for recognition of a judgment given against a foreign state in the national court of another state."[124] Thus, in a kind of indirect endorsement of the

119. *Jurisdictional Immunities, supra* n. 8, at para. 26, where the Court observed this by citing International Law Commission Yearbook of 1980.
120. *Ibid.*, at paras. 128, 130.
121. The Court did not find it necessary to determine whether the entirety of Art. 19 reflects current customary international law. *Ibid.*, at paras. 117-118. But the ICJ seems to have made a serious mistake in closing off additional discussion on implied waiver from execution. The court seems to have created a caveat by stating that this reflected only "current" customary international law, and therefore the discussion may remain open.
122. *Jurisdictional Immunities, supra* n. 8, at paras. 15, 17.
123. Hazel Fox, "When Can Property of a State Be Attached to Enforce a Foreign Judgment Given Against It in Another Country? Some Guidance in the ICJ Judgment in the Jurisdictional Immunities Case," in *Contemporary Developments in International Law* (Rüdiger Wolfrum & Frauke Lachenmann, eds.), 46-47 (2016).
124. *Ibid.*

treaty, the court crystalized and consolidated the law as written in the convention, holding that:

> When the United Nations Convention was being drafted, these provisions gave rise to long and difficult discussions. The Court considers that it is unnecessary for purposes of the present case for it to decide whether all aspects of Article 19 reflect current customary international law.
>
> [...]
>
> Indeed, it suffices for the Court to find that there is at least one condition that has to be satisfied before any measure of constraint may be taken against property belonging to a foreign State: that the property in question must be in use for an activity not pursuing government non-commercial purposes, or that the State which owns the property has expressly consented to the taking of a measure of constraint, or that that State has allocated the property in question for the satisfaction of a judicial claim (citations omitted).[125]

However, it is important to note that the court did not decide whether all parts of Article 19 constitute customary international law. That being so, the court did indeed approve the main exception to immunity from execution reflected in Article 19(c) in the UNCSI, namely, that property not used for governmental non-commercial purposes may be executed against despite the plea of sovereign immunity.

The standard and test having been set, the court then held that the property in dispute was clearly in use for sovereign functions (i.e., used for governmental non-commercial purposes). The property in dispute was used for cultural exchanges between Germany and Italy.[126]

With respect to immunity from execution, Germany alleged that Italy was in breach of international law because the Italian courts had granted execution with respect to a judgment delivered by a Greek court. The Greek court withheld Germany's immunity prior to delivering its judgment on the merits.[127] The execution was ordered against German-owned property that was used for cultural purposes.[128] There are two types of separate pleas: (1) execution is unlawful because the underlying judgment is reached unlawfully (i.e., violating immunity from jurisdiction); and (2) execution on a particular asset is unlawful because that asset is covered by immunity from execution. This book deals only with the latter.

On the topic of execution, the court held that "the rules of customary international law governing immunity from enforcement are distinct from and go further than those governing jurisdictional immunity and must be separately applied."[129] The court reasoned that:

> Before considering whether the claims of the Applicant on this point are well-founded, the Court observes that the immunity from enforcement enjoyed by

125. *Jurisdictional Immunities, supra* n. 8, at paras. 117-118.
126. *Ibid.*, at para. 119. (Going even further, the ICJ may have indirectly recognized Article 21 (1)(d) of the UNSCI in that the property forms "part of the cultural heritage of the State" and is "not placed or intended to be placed on sale.").
127. The case concerned a massacre of the villagers of "Distomo" by German military.
128. *See* Section dealing with cultural property below.
129. *Jurisdictional Immunities, supra* n. 8, at para. 131.

> States in regard to their property situated on foreign territory goes further than the jurisdictional immunity enjoyed by those same States before foreign courts. Even if a judgment has been lawfully rendered against a foreign State, in circumstances such that the latter could not claim immunity from jurisdiction, it does not follow *ipso facto* that the State against which judgment has been given can be the subject of measures of constraint on the territory of the forum State or on that of a third State, with a view to enforcing the judgment in question. Similarly, any waiver by a State of its jurisdictional immunity before a foreign court does not in itself mean that that State has waived its immunity from enforcement as regards property belonging to it situated in foreign territory. The rules of customary international law governing immunity from enforcement and those governing jurisdictional immunity (understood *stricto sensu* as the right of a State not to be the subject of judicial proceedings in the courts of another State) are distinct and must be applied separately.[130]

The court applied this to "determine whether a measure of constraint—such as the legal charge [on the property]—violated Germany's immunity from enforcement."[131] Guided by Article 19 of the UNSCI, the court had no trouble determining that the property was used for a governmental non-commercial purpose and thus that the execution of the property was in violation of the immunity that Germany should enjoy.[132] Put differently, the property enjoyed immunity because it was used for governmental non-commercial *purposes* "regardless of the validity of the judgment on which it was based."[133] Italy was found to have violated its obligations to respect immunity from execution under customary international law by having taken measures of constraint against German State-owned property (the "Villa Vigoni").[134]

The judgment was limited in its coverage and many outstanding issues remain when seeking to articulate the scope of application with respect to post-judgment measures of constraint and immunity from execution.

[ii] Iran v. U.S.

In 2019, the ICJ was again presented with a case where the plea of sovereign immunity was invoked at the execution stage. At the outset, it must be mentioned that the case did not necessarily deal with customary international law of immunity from execution. Any possible statement/reflection by the court on immunity from execution is at best dicta.

Writing before the ICJ's decision in the *Certain Iranian Assets Decision*, two young scholars rightly noted that "a range of questions might arise in this case which unfortunately did not arise in the 2012 *Jurisdictional Immunities* case, and therefore

130. *Ibid.*, at para. 113.
131. *Ibid.*, at para. 124.
132. *Ibid.*, at para. 120 ("In these circumstances, the Court finds that the registration of a legal charge on Villa Vigoni constitutes a violation by Italy of its obligation to respect the immunity owed to Germany.").
133. *See* Fox, *supra* n. 123, at 51.
134. *Jurisdictional Immunities, supra* n. 8, at para. 139.

had been left unanswered."[135] They argued that the court would be in a position to, *inter alia,* "shed light on matters such as the exact regime relating to the property of central banks," in particular between the stricter provisions of the UNSCI and those of more "liberal" State practice.[136] Unfortunately, the court seems to have turned down that opportunity.

The United States has taken several direct and indirect measures against Iran for, on the one hand, its alleged support of groups labeled by the United States as "terrorist organizations"[137] and, on the other hand, for other human rights-related violations.[138] To give practical effect to their policy undertaking, the United States has created an additional exception to the jurisdictional immunity for States that allegedly are "sponsors of terrorism."[139] This is better known as the "terrorism-exception." In elaborating on such exception, the United States has blocked certain Iranian assets and property, while making these assets available for attachment and execution outside the "ordinary" regime where governmental non-commercial property would have been protected pursuant to the Foreign Sovereign Immunities Act of 1976. Thus, by way of both legislative and executive action, the United States has provided victims of terrorism with a judicial forum to remedy their grievances in full. In most cases, these actions have led to claims that are essentially in the form of either restoration or reparation. As expected, these measures have been challenged by Iran first through political means and later before U.S. courts, before finally asserting its case before the ICJ.

When it comes to the terrorism-exception matters, the United States Congress first amended the Foreign Sovereign Immunities Act of 1978 to include an exception for terrorist activities. In a second action, the President as head of the executive branch issued an executive order to freeze property of Iran and its financial institutions.[140] In a third step, and in order to make the blocked assets of a State sponsor of terrorism available for execution, the U.S. enacted the "Iran Threat Reduction and Syria Human Rights Act of 2012."[141] Subsequent to this, assets of the Central Bank of Iran ("Bank Markazi") were blocked and made available for execution to judgment-creditors. In *Bank Markazi v. Peterson*, the Supreme Court of the United States declared the Iran Threat Reduction Act to be valid and constitutional.[142] Having faced defeat in the United States' Supreme Court, Iran took the dispute to the ICJ, arguing that the United

135. *See generally* Janig & Fallah, *supra* n. 105.
136. *Ibid.*
137. Moreover, the U.S. State Department must classify the state as a "state sponsor of terrorism."
138. *See, e.g.*, Executive Order 13599, "Blocking Property of the Government of Iran and Iranian Financial Institution" (February 5, 2012) 77 Fed. Reg., at 6659. (hereinafter "Executive Order 13599").
139. *See* 28 U.S.C. § 1605A (Terrorism Exception to the Jurisdictional Immunity of a Foreign State), "Jurisdictional Immunities of Foreign States," 1976, ("FSIA 1976").
140. Executive Order 13599.
141. 22 U.S.C. §§ 8701 et seq.
142. 136 S. Ct. 1310, 578 U.S. 212 (2016).

States' actions against the Iranian assets violate the 1955 Treaty of Amity, Economic Relations, and Consular Rights between the U.S. and Iran ("Treaty of Amity").[143]

The court could, albeit in dicta, clarify the standing of the five categories listed as immune *ipso facto* in Article 21(1) of the UNCSI. The list includes sub-section (c) on "property of the central bank or other monetary authority of the State." Whether this exception is properly to be a part of customary international law is debatable.[144]

Thus, a proper discussion of public international law would have to turn to the crosshairs of domestic-international law issue of to what extent a State can create its own exceptions to sovereign immunity without simultaneously violating public international law. The ICJ has remained silent on this point in the *Jurisdictional Immunities* case and in *Certain Iranian Assets* alike. This issue is still unresolved.

The heart of the dispute before the ICJ involved an alleged violation by the United States of the Treaty of Amity. The ICJ's decision on jurisdiction was handed down on February 13, 2019. The case has now moved to the merits phase. The United States had presented several jurisdictional objections, i.e., to: (a) dismiss Iran's claims in their entirety as *inadmissible*; (b) dismiss as outside the Court's jurisdiction all claims that the United States measures that block or freeze assets of Iran or its financial institutions violate any provision of the treaty; (c) dismiss as outside the court's jurisdiction all claims that are predicated on a purported failure by the United States to accord sovereign immunity from jurisdiction or enforcement to Iran, Bank Markazi, or Iranian State-owned entities; and (d) dismiss as outside the court's jurisdiction all claims of purported violations of Articles III, IV, or V.[145]

Iran claimed that the measures imposed by the United States fall within the scope of the Treaty. In turn, the United States "consider[ed] that the question of immunities is outside the court's jurisdiction *ratione materiae*, since the rule on the central bank immunities is a rule of customary international law and is not covered by the 1955 Treaty."[146] Iran claimed that the U.S. had failed to respect the immunity from jurisdiction and execution for its entities that were controlled by the State. As a response, the United States argued that there is no protection for such immunity in the Treaty.

The court aligned with the United States[147] and accordingly essentially shut the door for elaborating on the content of sovereign immunity under customary international law in any of the contested parts.

143. At least two authors raise an interesting point on these issues. *See* Janig & Fallah, *supra* n. 105 ("Overall, Iran's line of argumentation appears somewhat oxymoronic, as it seeks to incorporate a right exclusively enjoyed by States–i.e. State immunity–into provisions intended to protect individuals' rights.").
144. *Ibid.* ("Yet, again, judicial as well as legislative State practice so far have been reluctant to award special protection to property of a central bank. Only a limited number of States enacted legislation as to that effect. Thus, the customary nature of this provision is 'contentious', and courts usually apply the general rules to property of the central bank as well.").
145. *Certain Iranian Assets*, *supra* n. 114, at para. 15.
146. *Ibid.*, at 3 (separate opinion of Judge Gevorgian).
147. *Ibid.*, at 11 (separate Opinion of Judge Momtaz) ("In my opinion, the violation of the sovereign immunities of Bank Markazi in relation to its activities *jure imperii* is capable of impeding freedom of commerce between Iran and the United States and thus depriving the Treaty of its object and purpose.").

[iii] Germany v. Italy II

As we saw above, the 2012 *Jurisdictional Immunities* case was prompted by Italy refusing to grant jurisdictional immunity to Germany and having taken execution measures against German property ("Villa Vigoni") located in Italy. Italy was found in violation of customary international law by not respecting Germany's immunity from jurisdiction and from execution.[148]

Fast-forward some 10 years, to April 29, 2022, Germany instituted new proceedings against Italy before the ICJ regarding the alleged failure to respect its sovereign immunity.[149] Germany alleges that Italy has, despite the *Jurisdictional Immunities* case, entertained a significant number of new claims against Germany and that such actions constitute a violation of the customary international law on sovereign immunity as pronounced by the ICJ.[150]

The issue stems from an Italian Constitutional court ruling that declared the ICJ's findings in the *Jurisdictional Immunities* case to be incompatible with Italian constitutional principles in certain cases (i.e., where judicial protection for victims of international crimes and where no other remedies are available).[151] This resulted in Italian courts refusing to grant Germany jurisdictional immunity despite the 2012 judgment by the ICJ.

Subsequently, when judgments were rendered, Italian courts approved the attachment against German property (real estate).[152] The attachment led to the threat of public auctions of the State property, which in turn prompted Germany to take the case back to the ICJ.[153]

Germany asked the court to—on an interim basis—prevent Italy from subjecting State-owned property to public auctions pending a final judgment by the ICJ.[154] The measures of constraint were undertaken to satisfy the judgments in *Giorgio v. Germany*[155] and *Cavallina v. Germany.*[156] In the former, "four German State-owned properties located in Rome were seized and attached."[157] The latter judgment-creditor

148. *Jurisdictional Immunities, supra* n. 8, at para. 139.
149. *See* ICJ Press Release, "Germany Institutes Proceedings Against Italy for Allegedly Failing to Respect Its Jurisdictional Immunity as a Sovereign State" (No. 2022/16, 29 April 2022), https://www.icj-cij.org/public/files/case-related/183/183-20220429-PRE-01-00-EN.pdf; *see also Germany v. Italy, supra* n. 115.
150. Reportedly, at least 25 new cases have been brought against Germany and two judgments have been subject to measures of constraint in order to satisfy the debt. *See Ibid.*, at paras. 8, 22, and 24.
151. Lorenzo Gradoni, *Is the Dispute Between Germany and Italy over State Immunities Coming to an End (Despite Being Back at the ICJ)?*, EJIL:Talk! (May 10, 2022), https://www.ejiltalk.org/is-the-dispute-between-germany-and-italy-over-state-immunities-coming-to-an-end-despite-bein g-back-at-the-icj/.
152. *Ibid.*
153. *Ibid.*
154. For a good and brief discussion, *see* Pietro Franzina, *Jurisdictional Immunities: Germany v. Italy*, EAPIL (May 4, 2022), https://eapil.org/2022/05/04/jurisdictional-immunities-germany-v-italy-again/; *see also Germany v. Italy, supra* n. 115.
155. Court of Bologna, Judgment No. 2892 of 2011.
156. Appellate Court of Rome, Judgment No. 5446 of 2020.
157. *Germany v. Italy, supra* n. 115, at para. 25.

joined the former in the enforcement process. The property included: (a) a German Archeological Institute in Rome; (b) a German Cultural Institute in Rome; (c) a German Historical Institute in Rome; and (d) a German School in Rome.[158] On July 12, 2021, the Court of Rome appointed a judicial custodian for the properties and on May 25, 2022, the custodian was to decide on whether to authorize the German properties for forced sale by public auction.[159]

Germany challenged the Italian action as a violation of customary international law of sovereign immunity. Germany was eventually, according to itself, "compelled to seek provisional measures from the [ICJ] in order to safeguard its rights against irreparable harm."[160] However, the interest of the provisional measure is now lacking since Italy, as a result of Germany's request before the ICJ, adopted the "Italian Decree-Law of 30 April 2022."[161] The decree "aims to shield Germany from the institution or the continuation of new and pending proceedings (including enforcement proceedings) in connection with acts perpetrated by [Germany during World War II]."[162] The decree "addressed the [request for provisional relief] made by Germany and 'essentially eliminate[d] the matter of the dispute'."[163] It does so by setting "up a Fund for the reparation of injuries suffered by victims of war crimes and crimes against humanity" committed during world war II and in so doing "protects Germany from non-recognition of immunity from jurisdiction."[164] For that reason, Germany withdrew its request for provisional measures.[165]

[2] Reflective Remarks on Customary International Law

It must be emphasized that [1] above constitutes an assessment of what is generally considered to be customary international law, and primarily as pronounced by the ICJ. Thus, it represents an approximation of a *de lege lata* analysis of the current law as far as possible to discern in public international law. Chapter 4 continues this doctrinal exercise; such schematic exercise can simultaneously be used to question or qualify the current understanding in a *de lege ferenda* manner. Comparing, contrasting, and mapping various jurisdictions will show that there are indeed divergences in approach, in both the substantive law on sovereign immunity as well as in the procedural rules incidental or ancillary to the plea being invoked before a domestic court.

158. *Ibid.*, at para. 26.
159. *Ibid.*, at para. 27.
160. *Ibid.*
161. Italian Decree-Law No. 36, Art. 43 (April 30, 2022) converted into Law No. 79 (June 29, 2022) Italy.
162. Franzina, *supra* n. 154.
163. Order May 10, 2022, *Questions of Jurisdictional Immunity and Enforcement of Judgments* (*Germany v. Italy*), https://www.icj-cij.org/public/files/case-related/183/183-20220510-ORD-01-00-EN.pdf (hereinafter "*Questions of Jurisdictional Immunity*").
164. Gradoni, *supra* n. 151.
165. *Questions of Jurisdictional Immunity, supra* n. 163 ("whereas Germany agreed with Italy that *Decreto-Legge 30 aprile, n. 36* addressed the central concern informing the Request for provisional measures made by Germany, and whereas, as a result, Germany had decided to '[withdraw] its Request for the indication pf provisional measures ...'.").

The bottom line is that what constitutes customary international law is not easy to discern, even though ICJ has delivered its take on the matter to some extent. We must still deal with questions such as: What constitutes State practice? What is *opinio juris* and how is it expressed? When is the State practice and *opinio juris* uniform enough to crystalize as a statement of either a general rule or current law?

After a careful examination of case law (primarily domestic), treaty and statutory provisions (UNCSI, ECSI, FSIA, SIA, etc.), state practice (executive, legislative, and judicial), and literature, the ICJ has effectively suggested that there is: (a) a general rule of immunity from execution; and (b) that such is qualified (i.e., the restrictive theory).[166] The ICJ has made a reference to Article 19 of the UNCSI as a manifestation, indeed a crystallization, of customary international law.[167] The court justified its position by referring to State practice and *opinio juris*, as they must.

This consolidation of State practice and *opinio juris* crystalizing the restrictive theory of immunity as a rule of customary international law can, however, be questioned. This is partly because a relatively low number of parties have ratified the UNCSI, and partly because there exist States that do not adhere to restrictive immunity in the execution context.[168] Moreover, we do not know what the exceptions are nor the material scope of the commercial exception in the various jurisdictions worldwide. Thus, the exact contours of the substantive law on sovereign immunity from execution (let alone the procedural rules enabling execution) are undefined, uncertain, and in a state of flux.[169]

It is in light of the divergences in State practice and *opinio juris* that questions on "whether the restrictive rule has attained customary status" have been raised.[170] It is indeed a legitimate question, even with the ICJ judgment in mind. By illustration, studying China, Russia, Brazil, and some Middle Eastern States, Shan and Wang argues that "[d]espite the general trend towards a restrictive doctrine, it has yet to be established as a rule of customary international law as both the objective (State practice) and subjective (*opinion juris*) requirements are yet to be met."[171] When it comes to *opinio juris*, the authors argue that a subjective approach can be justified for ideological reasons or for more pragmatic reasons.[172] By illustration of State practice, the authors explain that some countries still adhere to the absolute doctrine with respect to immunity from execution (e.g., China, Brazil, United Arab Emirates, etc.) and also that the scope and standard for exceptions to sovereign immunity are unclear

166. *Jurisdictional Immunities*, *supra* n. 8, at paras. 117-118.
167. *Ibid.*, at paras. 117-120. This is also the position taken in domestic courts of certain jurisdictions (*see* Chapter 4).
168. *See* Philippa Webb, *The United Nations Convention on Jurisdictional Immunities of States and Their Property* 3 (2019).
169. *See, e.g.*, Jean-Marc Thouvenin & Victor Grandaubert "Material Scope of Immunity from Execution," in *Cambridge Handbook on Immunities and International Law* (Tom Ruys, Nicolas Angelet & Luca Ferro, eds.), 246 (2019).
170. Ruys et al., *supra* n. 64, at 5.
171. Wenhua Shan & Peng Wang, "Divergent Views on State Immunity in the International Community," in *Cambridge Handbook of Immunities and International Law* (Tom Ruys, Nicolas Angelet & Luca Ferro eds.), 63-88 (2019).
172. *Ibid.*, at 67.

under the restrictive theory.[173] It should be mentioned that China has now changed course (*see* more in Chapter 4).

If the requirement is for *all* states to adhere to restrictive immunity for a trend to be crystalized into a rule, then the assessment by Shan and Wang is indeed accurate. If, however, that is not so, then the assessment must be qualified. Even if it is enough that the majority State practice and *opinio juris* illustrates customary international law, it must be questioned if such position can be maintained where large parts of the globe adhere to absolute immunity from execution. Put differently, can it be the case that the ICJ was wrong in treating Article 19 of the UNCSI as a manifestation of customary international law? That could potentially be so. It is not an argument without merit. However, this book does not deal with that question per se.

For the sake of transparency, this author's position is that the commercial exception in Article 19 of the UNCSI represents more than a mere "trend." It is indeed a reflection of customary international law. Hence, the substantive law on sovereign immunity does in fact rest on the distinction between *jure imperii* and *jure gestionis*, even though some divergences in approach may exist and even though the divergence is evident in some economically important jurisdictions.

Finally, and importantly, the substantive law on sovereign immunity from execution is not limited to whether or not a restrictive theory is embraced. There are divergences among States on the scope of exceptions to sovereign immunity and its material content.[174] For example, the commercial exception is just one among other exceptions such as employment, tort, human rights, anti-terrorism, etc. Even within the commercial exception, divergent approaches exist, *inter alia,* with respect to the test for determining commerciality and what property may be treated immune *ipso facto*. For example: should a judge determine whether property is commercial on the nature of the use or based on its purpose? What property is considered immune *ipso facto*? How and when to qualify the immunity for specific property (e.g., central bank property, diplomatic property, cultural property, etc.). Moreover, different jurisdictions embrace different procedural rules that may enable award-creditors to execute against award-debtor States (e.g., discovery, interim injunctions, lowering the burden of proof, accepting a double-waiver theory, accepting a mixed-use application, etc.).

§3.3.3 Domestic Case Law as Part of Customary International Law

Because sovereign immunity cases rarely reach the ICJ, it is—and will likely remain—domestic courts that are asked to apply the substantive law of sovereign immunity. Thus, it is domestic courts and domestic legislators that are in a position to embrace a particular theory on sovereign immunity and decide what direction the substantive law should take. Moreover, domestic courts and legislators are in a position to exercise domestic procedural rules in order to facilitate judgment and award-creditors in attaching and executing against the assets of a judgment or

173. *Ibid.*, at 65-67.
174. Shan & Wang, *supra* n. 171, at 67.

award-debtor State. Thus, State procedural rules and the courts' application of such can have a prevalent effect on the implementation of the substantive law of sovereign immunity.

Domestic courts have been asked to either embrace or reject the restrictive theory on immunity and when having made that decision of *whether* immunity should be qualified, *when* and *how*.[175] Judges direct the contours of the doctrine and determine its scope, degree, and extent.

Thus, as will be seen in Chapter 4, despite being a branch under public international law, the law on sovereign immunity has developed primarily and predominantly in domestic case law. Moreover, when interpreting and applying the substantive rule of sovereign immunity, the domestic courts rely on the sources of public international law, including foreign case law, but also on its own procedural rules. It is this author's position that it is difficult to navigate the substantive law of sovereign immunity without being skilled in comparative legal methodology and in public international law. That said, the more domestic courts are confronted with sovereign immunity law, the less they need to refer to the sources of public international law and can instead refer to previous case law from within.

§3.4 CONCLUSION

Having gone over the sources of sovereign immunity, it must be noted that the law on sovereign immunity (substantively speaking) cannot be understood without analyzing domestic courts' approaches and domestic legislation on sovereign immunity. Moreover, when the plea of sovereign immunity is invoked against award execution, judges are inevitably invited to engage in a discourse on the application of both substantive law of sovereign immunity and simultaneously to deal with domestic procedural rules (procedurally speaking). Having found a rather broad universal consensus on the substantive law evolution, much of its actual positive effect for award-creditors will depend on the scope of its application domestically as well as on the facilitation by domestic procedural rules. Thus, the practical effect of the substantive law of sovereign immunity largely depends on domestic application and on domestic procedural intricacies. Thus, domestic judges are now asked to exercise a comparative legal methodology when dealing with the plea of sovereign immunity and consequently when deciding *whether* and *how* the rule of immunity should be qualified. In doing so, several important principles have indeed been developed in international comparative law through a relative consensus on its substantive application. Yang eloquently presented the main principles firmly entrenched with respect to the substantive law on sovereign immunity as follows:

(1) States enjoy immunity before foreign national courts as a principle of customary international law.

175. *See* Yang, *supra* n. 17, at 3.

(2) International law prescribes a presumption of immunity; that is, first, immunity is the norm rather than the exception, and it can be denied only when one or more exceptions allowed by international law are present; and, second, immunity must be given due effect even if the defendant State does not appear before the court.
(3) States enjoy immunity for sovereign, or public, or governmental acts (acta jure imperii) but not for commercial, or private, or non-governmental acts (acta jure gestionis).
(4) The characterization of and distinction between these two types of acts are performed primarily by reference to domestic law, i.e., the law of the forum State.
(5) The exceptions to immunity are almost exclusively based on territorial jurisdiction; and the restrictions on territorial jurisdiction become more stringent and extensive where attachment or other enforcement measures against foreign State property are involved.
(6) The immunity enjoyed by a foreign State encompasses two distinct immunities in connection with the two distinct stages of the judicial process: immunity from adjudication and immunity from execution; loss of immunity from adjudication does not automatically lead to a loss of immunity from execution.
(7) Immunity can be waived by the defendant State either expressly or impliedly. Two separate waivers are needed for the adjudicatory and the executory stages unless the defendant State has made a clear and unmistakable indication of a combined waiver.[176]

However, the practices of interpreting and applying the doctrine and the various principles differ from one jurisdiction to the other, on the one hand, and the plea of immunity from jurisdiction is treated vastly differently from immunity from execution, on the other hand.[177] Notwithstanding this, many of the principles above have been codified in the UNCSI. Thus, a rather compelling case can be put forth that the UNCSI as interpreted by progressive domestic courts more or less reflects an international consensus on the customary international law of sovereign immunity.[178]

---

176. *Ibid.*, at 34.
177. *See Jurisdictional Immunities, supra* n. 8.
178. *See, e.g.*, Crawford, *supra* n. 7, at 1938-1939. *See Germany v. Italy* (Greece Intervening), 2012 (the Court held that part of the 2004 Convention represent customary international law). *See also Sedelmayer v. The Russian Federation, supra* n. 91, at 475 (where the court relied on the 2004 Convention as constituting in part customary international law).

CHAPTER 4

The Practice of Sovereign Immunity: A Comparative Study

§4.1 INTRODUCTION

As explained in Chapter 3, the application of the doctrine on sovereign immunity from execution is largely an exercise before domestic courts, and to some extent for domestic legislators to deal with. In some jurisdictions, the determination of whether to grant or reject the plea of immunity is left to the executive branch to determine.

The task of a domestic court dealing with the plea of sovereign immunity is essentially to determine whether the award-debtor State's assets: (1) fall under one of the possible exceptions to immunity; and if necessary (2) whether a State-owned entity (or equivalent) can be held liable for the State's debt. In so doing, the court must navigate the substantive law of sovereign immunity, on the one hand, and also determine what procedural features to deploy and how they apply when interpreting and applying the law, on the other hand.

These domestic court decisions largely make up the theory and practice on the law of sovereign immunity. Thus, the decisions from foreign domestic courts are "of considerable importance for legal practitioners in a wide range of national jurisdictions."[1] Put differently, for the public international law on sovereign immunity, domestic case law assumes the status of a primary source.

Unfortunately, but perhaps inevitable due to the widespread application of the doctrine across different legal cultures, the application of the law has resulted in a relative lack of uniformity. Considering that the law of sovereign immunity is one branch of public international law, such a lack of harmonization is somewhat problematic. This is evident when analyzing the case law from various domestic

1. Tom Ruys et al., "Introduction: International Immunities in a State of Flux?" in *Cambridge Handbook on Immunities and International Law* (Tom Ruys, Nicolas Angelet & Luca Ferro, eds.), 1 (2019).

courts. This is what this chapter deals with. Chapter 4 will underscore the diversity in application within and between States, yet distill principles that are indeed shared and could serve as yardsticks to consolidate a moderately or somewhat uniform application of the law.

Thus, this chapter maps the current *doctrinal understanding* of sovereign immunity from execution and its *interpretation and application* in various important enforcement forums. At the end of the day, when an award-debtor State invokes immunity from execution, the success of an award-creditor "will depend on the immunity law of the state in which he is seeking execution."[2]

§4.1.1 Research Question and Methodology

It is necessary to repeat in a succinct manner the research question and methodology (as outlined more comprehensively in Chapter 1).

The research question is:

- Does the *doctrinal understanding* of sovereign immunity from execution and its *interpretation and application* in the international arbitration context resonate with a 21st century global marketplace?

This book investigates (a) *whether* and *how* domestic legislators and courts have contributed to shaping the law on sovereign immunity from execution, in general, and in the arbitration context, in particular. Following the exploration of the substantive law, this book explores (b) *whether* and *how* domestic legislators and courts have facilitated award execution through its procedural rules and court practices. Finally, this book explores (c) *whether* and *how* non-legal solutions can assist an award-creditor when the award-debtor State refuses to comply voluntarily with a pecuniary award. This chapter deals with (a) and (b).

Through a *doctrinal methodological* study, this book will analyze and map the doctrinal understanding of sovereign immunity and the interpretation and application of its sources, in general, and in the jurisdictions of China, France, India, Russia, Sweden, the U.K., and the U.S., in particular. Through a *comparative legal methodology*, this book compares and contrasts various approaches in order to see whether and what theories, principles, rules, and doctrines have emerged and whether these can (or should) be crystallized and perhaps even consolidated into international law.

The objects of comparison (i.e., the chosen jurisdictions) were selected on three common denominators and several factors unique to the specific jurisdictions selected; that is, market impact, ideological relevance, geographical importance, language, frequency of cases, and influential case law.

This book focuses strictly on immunity from execution. More specifically, this book deals with the plea of immunity from execution in the arbitral award enforcement

2. Andrea K. Bjorklund, *Sovereign Immunity as a Barrier to the Enforcement of Investor-State Arbitral Awards: The Re-Politicization of International Investment Disputes*, 21 Am. Rev. Int'l Arb. 211, 213 (2011).

context. This book will divide the comparing objects' doctrinal understanding and application and interpretation of sovereign immunity from execution of international arbitral awards into four colors: Red, Orange, Yellow, and Green, in that order. Red list countries are those that adhere to absolute immunity from execution. The said approach is "conservative" toward award-creditors. Orange list countries are those that adhere to restrictive immunity from execution in theory. The said approach is "quasi-liberal" toward award creditors. Yellow list countries are those that adhere to restrictive immunity from execution in theory as well as in practice (from a substantive law point of view). The said approach is "liberal" toward award creditors. Green list countries are those that, like the yellow list, adhere to restrictive immunity from execution in theory as well as in practice. In addition to satisfying the yellow list criteria, green list countries not only adhere to restrictive immunity with respect to the substantive law but also provide award-creditors with procedural tools that make award execution possible. The said approach is both "liberal" and "pragmatic."

The reader is advised to revisit Chapter 1 and the questions in §1.2.2[2] before reading Chapter 4.

Finally, the reader must bear in mind that this is a book focusing on sovereign immunity from execution and not on sovereign immunity from jurisdiction, which includes immunity from enforcement (*see* Chapter 2). A State's immunity from execution is different than immunity from enforcement. The former is only relevant at a stage after the enforcement proceedings when the award-creditor seeks to enforce the award against particular State assets. Even though sovereign immunity from execution is much more of an obstacle in the execution phase, the award-creditor should be aware that sovereign immunity from execution is not unlimited and has its own and separate exceptions and tests. Whether and to what extent the award-debtor State can rely on immunity from execution depends entirely on the sovereign immunity law of the State and on the nature of the assets. This is not a matter that can—or should—be prejudged at the enforcement stage. This chapter deals with several jurisdictions' approaches to sovereign immunity from execution.

§4.2 THE UNITED STATES

U.S. has an old arbitration act (the 1925 Federal Arbitration Act), which is not based on the UNCITRAL Model Law. However, a pro-arbitration attitude has been developed through case law.[3] Moreover, many states in the U.S. have adopted the Model Law, e.g., California, Florida, Ohio, and Texas.[4] The U.S. is, furthermore, a Member State to both the New York Convention and the ICSID Convention. U.S. has also signed ISDS clauses; for example, as found in various of its IIAs with other States. There is no

3. *See* William F. Fox & Ylli Dautaj, *The Life of Arbitration Law Has Been Experience, Not Logic: Gorsuch, Kavanaugh, and the Federal Arbitration Act*, 21 Cardozo J. Conflict Resol. 1 (2019). *See also* Ylli Dautaj, *The Act Is Not the Entire Story: How to Make Sense of the U.S. Arbitration Act*, Kluwer Arbitration Blog (April 4, 2018), http://arbitrationblog.kluwerarbitration.com/2018/04/04/act-not-entire-story-make-sense-u-s-arbitration-act/.
4. Tibor Várady et al., *International Commercial Arbitration: A Transnational Perspective* 85-88 (7th ed. 2019).

reason to believe that the U.S. would not voluntarily comply with an adverse arbitral award. For the combined reasons, it can be said that the U.S. is indeed a "pro-arbitration jurisdiction."

This book deals with the issue of sovereign immunity and whether the U.S. is "liberal" and/or "pragmatic," i.e., is it a red, orange, yellow, or green list State. In the U.S., the move away from the absolute theory of immunity to the restrictive one came with the so-called Tate Letters. These were essentially a series of communications by which the State Department explained that it was from that moment and onward aligning with the restrictive theory of immunity.[5] The move was finally entrenched with the enactment of the Foreign Sovereign Immunities Act in 1976.[6] The act was said to codify the international law on sovereign immunity. It should be noted that the Tate Letters referred to immunity from jurisdiction and that it was first through the FSIA that the restrictive theory of immunity was embraced also for purposes of execution. The U.S. is not a signatory to the UNCSI.

As will be seen below, it can most definitely be said that the U.S. lives up to the doctrine of restrictive immunity from execution in both theory and practice. Through case law, the substantive law on sovereign immunity has been supplemented by a pragmatic judicial attitude, which has culminated in several liberal and progressive decisions. U.S. courts have indeed facilitated award-creditors against award-debtor States when seeking to attach and execute against State assets.

§4.2.1 Sovereign Immunity from Execution of Arbitral Awards in the U.S.

The doctrine of sovereign immunity initially grew out of common law and was a matter of grace and comity.[7] Chief Justice Marshall struggled with the justification of sovereign immunity already in 1812.[8] At that time, courts typically looked to the State Department for a recommendation on whether a foreign government should enjoy immunity. The courts normally deferred to State Departments' determination and incorporated the latter's decisions in their own.

5. *See generally Letter from Jack B. Tate, Acting Legal Adviser*, Dept. of State, to Acting Attorney General Philip B. Perlman, reprinted in 26 Dep't. St. Bull. 984, 984-985 (1952). (explaining that the state department was from then on aligning with the restrictive theory on immunity). *See also* David P. Stewart, "International Immunities in U.S. Law," in *The Oxford Handbook of Comparative Foreign Relations Law* (Curtis A. Bradley, ed.), 625, (2019) ("Over time, the U.S. approach evolved significantly, not least by adopting the so-called 'restrictive' theory in 1952."); and Dautaj, *supra* n. 3, at 207.
6. *See also Jam v. Int'l Fin. Corp*, 139 S. Ct. 759, 766 (2019). Stewart, *supra* n. 5, at 625-626 ("The rules for sovereign (or state) immunity were codified … in the 1976 [FSIA] and are now applied directly by the courts rather than the executive.").
7. *See, e.g., Samantar v. Yousuf*, 560 U.S. 305, 311-312 (2010).
8. *The Schooner Exchange v. McFaddon*, 11 U.S. (7 Cranch) 116, 136-137 (1812) (emphasis added). For a more recent pronouncement, *see* generally, *Playa Larga*, (U.K. House of Lords, 1983), 1 AC, at 262. (displaying a more recent pronouncement of the above case and displaying that the sovereign or governmental acts of one state are not matters upon which the courts of other states will adjudicate).

Fast-forward to today, the U.S. has not signed the UNCSI but has nevertheless codified the law of sovereign immunity through the 1976 FSIA.[9] Albeit the FSIA was adopted some time back it has been amended several times. Furthermore, U.S. courts have been active in applying the law to add flesh to the bones of the provisions therein. This is largely due to the high frequency of cases litigated before U.S. courts, and in particular due to the fact that foreign States typically have assets in the U.S. Due to the market standing of the U.S. and its robust rule of law, it remains a lucrative enforcement venue for award-creditors.

[1] Foreign Sovereign Immunities Act 1976

The FSIA was enacted in part to rectify some of the shortcomings of the common law era. The purpose and objective of enacting the FSIA were said to: (1) codify the restrictive theory of sovereign immunity; (2) ensure the application of the doctrine by courts and not by the State Department; (3) provide a statutory service procedure to establish jurisdiction; and (4) remedy the inability to obtain execution of a judgment obtained against a foreign State.[10] The FSIA also transferred "the primary responsibility for immunity determinations from the Executive to the Judicial Branch."[11] Prior to the enactment of the FSIA, a foreign State enjoyed virtually absolute immunity from execution of its property in the U.S. The restrictive theory of immunity as laid out in the Tete Letters applied only with respect to jurisdictional immunity. Nowadays, the FSIA is "the sole basis for obtaining jurisdiction over a foreign state in [US] courts."[12] Thus, the FSIA places any decision on immunity in the hands of the judiciary and away from the executive branch.[13] Notwithstanding this, the FSIA "was expressly understood to reflect and codify principles of international law."[14]

Due to the move toward the restrictive theory of immunity as entrenched in the FSIA, a foreign State is nowadays neither absolutely immune from suit/adjudication nor from execution of its assets.[15] As stated, prior to the FSIA—and even post the Tate Letters—a State was considered absolutely immune from execution even if restrictive immunity applied vis-à-vis jurisdiction.[16] Thus, such shortcoming in the execution phase was rectified with the FSIA. Brower II rightly noted that in order to "ensure a

9. *See* Stewart, *supra* n. 5, at 627 ("while the [U.S.] is not party to the [UNCSI], the FSIA is largely consistent with its approach and (together with the many judicial interpretations of the statute) is generally reflective of, and helps to contribute to, the relevant rules of customary international law.").
10. *See* Hazel Fox & Philippa Webb, *The Law of State Immunity* 241-242 (2015).
11. *Republic of Austria v. Altmann*, 541 U.S. 677, 691 (2004).
12. *Argentine Republic v. Amerada Hess Shipping Corp.*, 488 U.S. 428, 434 (1989).
13. *See* Stewart, *supra* n. 5, at 626. However, note that today courts sometimes consider (e.g., as amicus briefs) the executive branch's views in certain cases. *See Schermerhorn v. Israel*, 235 F. Supp. 3d 249 (D.D.C. 2017), *aff'd*, 876 F.3d 351 (D.C. Cir. 2017).
14. Stewart, *supra* n. 5, at 626.
15. *See Walters v. Industrial and Commercial Bank of China*, 651 F.3d 208 (U.S. 2d Cir. 2011) (The Circuit Court clearly articulated that there is a distinction between immunity from jurisdiction and immunity from execution.).
16. Charles H. Brower II, *Mitsubishi, Investor-State Arbitration, and the Law of State Immunity*, 20 Am. U. Int'l Rev. 907, 923 (2005) ("For example, before the enactment of the FSIA, the United

greater coincidence of moral and practical victories for the vast run of cases, the FSIA's drafters established a closer alignment between the rules on immunity from jurisdiction and the rules of immunity from execution of judgments."[17]

The FSIA has separate regimes for immunity from jurisdiction and immunity from execution. Both regimes articulate a general rule on immunity and qualify the rule with exceptions. Moreover, the FSIA deals differently with pre-judgment attachment and post-judgment execution as well as different principles relating to execution against State property or against property of State agencies or instrumentalities.[18] Immunity from jurisdiction is regulated in §§ 1604, 1605, 1605A, and 1605B (e.g., the commercial activity exception, waiver, arbitration exception, terrorism exception, etc.). Immunity from execution is dealt with separately under §§1609-1611, as outlined below:[19]

> **§ 1609**
>
> Subject to existing international agreements to which the United States is a party at the time of enactment of this Act the property in the United States of a foreign state shall be immune from attachment arrest and execution except as provided in sections 1610 and 1611 of this chapter.
>
> **§ 1610**
>
> (a) The property in the United States of a foreign state, as defined in section 1603(a) of this chapter, used for a commercial activity in the United States, shall not be immune from attachment in aid of execution, or from execution, upon a judgment entered by a court of the United States or of a State after the effective date of this Act, if—
> (1) the foreign state has waived its immunity from attachment in aid of execution or from execution either explicitly or by implication, notwithstanding any withdrawal of the waiver the foreign state may purport to effect except in accordance with the terms of the waiver, or
> (2) the property is or was used for the commercial activity upon which the claim is based, or
> (3) the execution relates to a judgment establishing rights in property which has been taken in violation of international law or which has been exchanged for property taken in violation of international law, or
> (4) the execution relates to a judgment establishing rights in property—
> (A) which is acquired by succession or gift, or
> (B) which is immovable and situated in the United States: Provided, That such property is not used for purposes of maintaining a diplomatic or consular mission or the residence of the Chief of such mission, or
> (5) the property consists of any contractual obligation or any proceeds from such a contractual obligation to indemnify or hold harmless the foreign

States applied the doctrine of restrictive immunity to *claims* against foreign states, but the doctrine of absolute immunity to the execution of resulting *judgments* ...").

17. *Ibid.*, at 924. However, due to the fact that property used for governmental purposes are protected, the theoretical proximity has less practical effect. *See, e.g.*, Restatement (Third) Of the Foreign Relations Law of the United States § 460, cmt. B (Am. Law Inst. 1987).
18. *See* Sun Jin, *Immunity from Execution of Judgments under the FSIA: Moderate Balance to the New UN Convention*, 4 U.S.-China Law Rev. 13, 14-15 (2013).
19. *See, e.g., Walters*, 651 F.3d at 288 ("First, the FSIA's provisions governing jurisdictional immunity, on the one hand, and execution immunity, on the other, operate independently.").

state or its employees under a policy of automobile or other liability or casualty insurance covering the claim which merged into the judgment, or

(6) the judgment is based on an order confirming an arbitral award rendered against the foreign state, provided that attachment in aid of execution, or execution, would not be inconsistent with any provision in the arbitral agreement, or

(7) the judgment relates to a claim for which the foreign state is not immune under section 1605A or section 1605(a)(7) (as such section was in effect on January 27, 2008), regardless of whether the property is or was involved with the act upon which the claim is based.

(b) In addition to subsection (a), any property in the United States of an agency or instrumentality of a foreign state engaged in commercial activity in the United States shall not be immune from attachment in aid of execution, or from execution, upon a judgment entered by a court of the United States or of a State after the effective date of this Act, if—

(1) the agency or instrumentality has waived its immunity from attachment in aid of execution or from execution either explicitly or implicitly, notwithstanding any withdrawal of the waiver the agency or instrumentality may purport to effect except in accordance with the terms of the waiver, or

(2) the judgment relates to a claim for which the agency or instrumentality is not immune by virtue of section 1605(a)(2), (3), or (5) or 1605(b) of this chapter, regardless of whether the property is or was involved in the act upon which the claim is based, or

(3) the judgment relates to a claim for which the agency or instrumentality is not immune by virtue of section 1605A of this chapter or section 1605(a)(7) of this chapter (as such section was in effect on January 27, 2008), regardless of whether the property is or was involved in the act upon which the claim is based.

(c) No attachment or execution referred to in subsections (a) and (b) of this section shall be permitted until the court has ordered such attachment and execution after having determined that a reasonable period of time has elapsed following the entry of judgment and the giving of any notice required under section 1608(e) of this chapter.

(d) The property of a foreign state, as defined in section 1603(a) of this chapter, used for a commercial activity in the United States, shall not be immune from attachment prior to the entry of judgment in any action brought in a court of the United States or of a State, or prior to the elapse of the period of time provided in subsection (c) of this section, if—

(1) the foreign state has explicitly waived its immunity from attachment prior to judgment, notwithstanding any withdrawal of the waiver the foreign state may purport to effect except in accordance with the terms of the waiver, and

(2) the purpose of the attachment is to secure satisfaction of a judgment that has been or may ultimately be entered against the foreign state, and not to obtain jurisdiction.

(e) The vessels of a foreign state shall not be immune from arrest in rem, interlocutory sale, and execution in actions brought to foreclose a preferred mortgage as provided in section 1605(d).

(f) (1) (A) Notwithstanding any other provision of law, including but not limited to section 208(f) of the Foreign Missions Act (22 U.S.C. 4308(f)), and except as provided in subparagraph (B), any property with respect to which financial transactions are prohibited or regulated pursuant to section 5(b) of the Trading with the Enemy Act (50 U.S.C. App.

5(b)),[1] section 620(a) of the Foreign Assistance Act of 1961 (22 U.S.C. 2370(a)), sections 202 and 203 of the International Emergency Economic Powers Act (50 U.S.C. 1701-1702), or any other proclamation, order, regulation, or license issued pursuant thereto, shall be subject to execution or attachment in aid of execution of any judgment relating to a claim for which a foreign state (including any agency or instrumentality or such state) claiming such property is not immune under section 1605(a)(7) (as in effect before the enactment of section 1605A) or section 1605A.

(B) Subparagraph (A) shall not apply if, at the time the property is expropriated or seized by the foreign state, the property has been held in title by a natural person or, if held in trust, has been held for the benefit of a natural person or persons.

(2) (A) At the request of any party in whose favor a judgment has been issued with respect to a claim for which the foreign state is not immune under section 1605(a)(7) (as in effect before the enactment of section 1605A) or section 1605A, the Secretary of the Treasury and the Secretary of State should make every effort to fully, promptly, and effectively assist any judgment creditor or any court that has issued any such judgment in identifying, locating, and executing against the property of that foreign state or any agency or instrumentality of such state.

(B) In providing such assistance, the Secretaries—

(i) may provide such information to the court under seal; and

(ii) should make every effort to provide the information in a manner sufficient to allow the court to direct the United States Marshall's office to promptly and effectively execute against that property.

(3) Waiver.—

The President may waive any provision of paragraph (1) in the interest of national security.

(g) Property in Certain Actions.—

(1) In general.—Subject to paragraph (3), the property of a foreign state against which a judgment is entered under section 1605A, and the property of an agency or instrumentality of such a state, including property that is a separate juridical entity or is an interest held directly or indirectly in a separate juridical entity, is subject to attachment in aid of execution, and execution, upon that judgment as provided in this section, regardless of—

(A) the level of economic control over the property by the government of the foreign state;

(B) whether the profits of the property go to that government;

(C) the degree to which officials of that government manage the property or otherwise control its daily affairs;

(D) whether that government is the sole beneficiary in interest of the property; or

(E) whether establishing the property as a separate entity would entitle the foreign state to benefits in United States courts while avoiding its obligations.

(2) United states sovereign immunity inapplicable.—

Any property of a foreign state, or agency or instrumentality of a foreign state, to which paragraph (1) applies shall not be immune from attachment in aid of execution, or execution, upon a judgment entered under section 1605A because the property is regulated by the United States

Government by reason of action taken against that foreign state under the Trading With the Enemy Act or the International Emergency Economic Powers Act.

(3) Third-party joint property holders.—
Nothing in this subsection shall be construed to supersede the authority of a court to prevent appropriately the impairment of an interest held by a person who is not liable in the action giving rise to a judgment in property subject to attachment in aid of execution, or execution, upon such judgment.

§1611

(a) Notwithstanding the provisions of section 1610 of this chapter, the property of those organizations designated by the President as being entitled to enjoy the privileges, exemptions, and immunities provided by the International Organizations Immunities Act shall not be subject to attachment or any other judicial process impeding the disbursement of funds to, or on the order of, a foreign state as the result of an action brought in the courts of the United States or of the States.

(b) Notwithstanding the provisions of section 1610 of this chapter, the property of a foreign state shall be immune from attachment and from execution, if—
  (1) the property is that of a foreign central bank or monetary authority held for its own account, unless such bank or authority, or its parent foreign government, has explicitly waived its immunity from attachment in aid of execution, or from execution, notwithstanding any withdrawal of the waiver which the bank, authority or government may purport to effect except in accordance with the terms of the waiver; or
  (2) the property is, or is intended to be, used in connection with a military activity and
    (A) is of a military character, or
    (B) is under the control of a military authority or defense agency.

(c) Notwithstanding the provisions of section 1610 of this chapter, the property of a foreign state shall be immune from attachment and from execution in an action brought under section 302 of the Cuban Liberty and Democratic Solidarity (LIBERTAD) Act of 1996 to the extent that the property is a facility or installation used by an accredited diplomatic mission for official purposes.

Thus, as a general rule, the property of a foreign State is immune against execution in the U.S. (§1609), unless an exception is applicable (§1610), and unless the property is not immune *ipso jure* (§1611).[20] Section 1610(a) deals with immunity from execution of property belonging to a foreign State, while section 1610(b) deals with immunity from execution of property belonging to an agency or instrumentality of a foreign State. Section 1610(a) deals with property that is both in the U.S. and is used for a commercial activity/purpose in the U.S. section 1610(b) deals with property that is in the U.S. but does not require it to be used for a particular purpose. There is no need to identify the purported use of the assets to be attached pursuant to section 1610(b). It

20. *See, e.g.*, Brower, *supra* n. 16, at 920 ("Consistent with the procedural, substantive, and practical justifications for incremental deference to foreign states, the FSIA's drafters intentionally adopted a presumption of immunity as a means of protecting foreign states from liability in doubtful cases.").

was established in *Conn. Bank of Commerce v. Republic of Congo*[21] that there is a distinction between the commercial activity requirements in section 1610(a) and 1610(b) in the FSIA.[22]

As will be further demonstrated below, the "execution immunity afforded sovereign property is broader than the jurisdictional immunity afforded the sovereign itself."[23] It has been noted that the statutory construct "reflect a pivotal purpose of the FSIA," namely, "to limit execution against property directly belonging to a foreign state."[24] It should also be mentioned that the situation for an award-creditor and a judgment-creditor is significantly different. For judgment-creditors, the only assets available are such "used for the commercial activity upon which the claim was based." This obstacle is not placed on an award-creditor, which in turn makes the international arbitration regime more effective compared to transnational litigation for enforcement/execution purposes. Notwithstanding this, award-creditors do face various obstacles and difficulties at the execution phase. An award-creditor must demonstrate that the pre-requisites of the property being: (1) in the U.S., and (2) being used for a commercial activity in the U.S. are both met. These prerequisites render the property that is subject to attachment and execution a significantly smaller category.

The award-creditor must either seek to attach and execute against State assets on the basis of confirming an arbitral award or else (if applicable) on the basis of a waiver. According to section 1610(a)(1) the waiver can be both "explicit" or "implicit." It has been noted that an explicit waiver "must be clear, complete, unambiguous, and unmistakable manifestation of a sovereign's intent to waive its immunity."[25] The explicit waiver can be found in contracts or treaties (the latter is less common), while implicit waivers are typically to be deduced from conduct that implies an intention to waive the right to invoke immunity.[26]

The "arbitration exception" is dealt with both in the jurisdiction and execution context. However, generally speaking, section 1605(a)(6) represents an exception to jurisdictional immunity, which cannot be considered a "waiver" from execution immunity. The arbitration exception deals with some arbitration-related matters but not execution issues. As was stated in *Crystallex International Corporation v. Bolivarian Republic of Venezuela*, when a party has established an exception to immunity from jurisdiction, the same party does not have to demonstrate yet another exception for "ancillary jurisdiction" of enforcing the award by registering it as a judgment.[27] As stated in *First City, Texas Houston, N.A. v. Rafidain Bank*, the court's jurisdiction

21. *Connecticut Bank of Commerce (CBC) v. Republic of Congo*, 309 F.3d 240, 252 (5th Cir. 2002).
22. *See also Walters*, 651 F.3d at 29 ("Third, the property of an agency or instrumentality of a foreign state is afforded narrower protection from execution than the property of the foreign state itself.").
23. *Ibid.*, at 289.
24. *Af-Cap Inc. v. Republic of Congo*, 475 F.3d 1080 (9th Cir. 2007) (citing *CBC, supra* n. 21).
25. Fox & Webb, *supra* n. 10, at 258.
26. *Ibid.*
27. *Crystallex Int'l Corp. v. Bolivarian Republic of Venezuela*, Case No. 18-2889, 14-15 (July 29, 2019) (Citing *Peterson v. Islamic Republic of Iran*, 627 F.3d 1117, 1123 (9th Cir. 2010); IFC *Interconsult, AG v. Safeguard Int'l Partners, LLC*, 438 F.3d 298, 311 (3d Cir. 2006); and *Peacock v. Thomas*, 516 U.S. 349, 356, 359 & n.7 (1996)).

sustains through proceedings to aid collection of a money judgment.[28] Thus, when a party seeks to recognize and enforce an arbitral award pursuant to the arbitration exception to jurisdictional immunity, the ensuing action is considered a "continuation of the action" in the district court to confirm the award.[29] This is not to be confused with execution of the award as such. It is important to note that this book deals with immunity from execution and therefore does not analyze more recent case law in the U.S. dealing with immunity from enforcement (whether dealing with "intra-EU awards," alleged lack of "minimum contacts," "forum non conveniens," or otherwise).[30] Similarly, this book does not deal with the objection that the arbitration exception in the FSIA does not apply when the State has acted in its sovereign capacity.[31]

When it comes to the actual execution of an arbitral award, section 1610(1)(6) becomes relevant. In order to prevail as an award creditor, you need to: (i) demonstrate an order confirming an arbitral award; and (ii) identify and locate assets to attach that are used for a commercial activity in the U.S. It is important to note that when the award-debtor is a sovereign agency or instrumentality as opposed to the State itself, it suffices to demonstrate that the award-debtor engaged in commercial activity, irrespective of whether the property is used for such purpose.

Moreover, as seen in section 1611, some property is considered immune *ipso jure*, e.g., property of a central bank or monetary authority held for its own account and property that is used or intended to be used in connection with a military activity. Furthermore, section 1610(1)(4)(B) cloaks in immunity property used for purposes of maintaining a diplomatic or consular mission or the residence of the Chief of such mission.

[2] Federal Rules on Civil Procedure

This book does not deal with the process of attaching and executing against assets under domestic rules. Rather, this book deals with whether property can be executed against, or conversely, whether and when sovereign immunity presents itself as an obstacle. It is, however, true that such focus invites not only a substantive law analysis but also to some degree a focus on procedural aspects enabling execution. As has

28. *First City, Texas-Houston v. Rafidain Bank*, 281 F.3d 48, 53-54 (2d Cir. 2002).
29. *See Crystallex, supra* n. 27, at 16.
30. For the readers information: The U.S. Court of Appeals for the District of Columbia have ruled that the intra-EU issue cannot thwart the arbitration exception in the FSIA vis-à-vis ICSID and non-ICSID awards and also refused to apply the forum non conveniens doctrine (as non-applicable in the context of confirming foreign arbitral awards)—*NextERA Energy v. Spain*, Cir. D.C., No. 23-7031 (August 16, 2024). Put simply, the State has waived its sovereign immunity when ratifying the enforcement conventions. Several U.S. district court cases have concluded the same, i.e., that the three conditions for the arbitration exception under the FSIA are: (i) the existence of an arbitration agreement; (ii) the existence of an arbitration award; and (iii) the existence of a treaty potentially governing the award's enforcement.
31. For the readers interest: U.S. courts have rejected such argument and applied the arbitration exception in the FSIA. *See Zhongshan Fucheng v. Nigeria*, No. 23-7016 (D.C. Cir. 2024).

rightly been noted, once an award-creditor satisfies an exception, she must nevertheless satisfy the relevant domestic rules requirements in order to attach and execute against the assets at issue.[32] For that reason, State procedural laws can indeed represent a final obstacle to execution.[33] Conversely, it can assist in such process. In the U.S., the States can have different rules on attachment and execution, e.g., with respect to royalties, debt, taxes, securities, trusts, and so on.

§4.2.2 Case Law

Even though the FSIA is the stepping-stone for any analysis of sovereign immunity law in the U.S., the act cannot be understood without engaging in a doctrinal study of case law. While the law on sovereign immunity has been codified, the area remains dynamic and continues to evolve.[34] In that light, the FSIA has been the subject of both statutory amendments as well as judicial interpretations.[35] Thus, to distill meaning from the statute, we must understand the case law. This exercise is the explicit design of the FSIA.[36] In the legislative work leading up to the FSIA it was stated that the legislative branch had "decided to put [their] faith in the U.S. courts to work out progressively, on a case-by-case basis ... the distinction between commercial and governmental" activities.[37] In so doing, it was said that the judge must bear in mind that the rules on sovereign immunity as found in the FSIA expressly reflect and codify principles of international law.[38] Moreover, it should be understood that the FSIA not only was based on principles of international law but also that it "continues to reflect basic principles of international law."[39] One could say that it is designed to be a "living" or "breathing" statute.

In this book, the author focuses on case law dealing with the statutory exceptions to execution immunity, which have been the subject of extensive judicial interpretation.[40] The cases below deal with the interpretation and application of the substantive law of sovereign immunity, i.e., with:

32. *See* Brian King et al., "Enforcing Awards Involving Foreign Sovereigns," in *International Commercial Arbitration in New York* (James H. Carter & John Fellas, eds.), 433, (2010).
33. *See Ibid.*
34. David P. Stewart, *Recent Developments in U.S. Law on Foreign Sovereign Immunity*, 18 YPIL 171, 172 (2016/2017) https://doi.org/10.9785/9783504385637-009.
35. *Ibid.*
36. *See* Legislative history of FSIA. *Jurisdiction of U.S. Courts in Suits Against Foreign States: Hearings on H.R. 11315 Before Subcomm. On Admin Law and Governmental Relations of the House Comm. On the Judiciary, 94th Cong. 24 (1976); H.R. REP. NO. 94-1487 (1976); and S. REP. NO. 94-1310 (1976).*
37. Monroe Leigh in *Jurisdiction of U.S. Courts in Suits Against Foreign States: Hearings on H.R. 11315 Before Subcomm. On Admin Law and Governmental Relations of the House Comm. On the Judiciary, 94th Cong. 24 (1976)* at 53.
38. *Bolivarian Republic of Venezuela, et al., Petitioners v. Helmerich & Payne International Drilling Co., et al.*, 137 S. Ct. 1317 (2017) ("The Act for the most part embodies basic principles of international law long followed both in the United States and elsewhere."). *See* Stewart, *supra* n. 5, at 626.
39. *Bolivarian Republic, supra* n. 38.
40. Stewart, *supra* n. 5.

(1) the waiver and implied waiver doctrines;
(2) the commercial activity exception; and
(3) certain property protected specifically.

The case law analyzed will also deal with procedural features enabling and facilitating the remedy that the exception establishes, e.g., through:

(4) the piercing of the corporate veil;
(5) discovery; and
(6) the lowering or reversing of the burden of proof.

At the outset it must be noted that the obstacle of immunity from execution is not one "despite of" the FSIA, it is there precisely "because of" the FSIA. Leaving certain award or judgment creditors without remedy is foreseen and intentionally designed by the legislators in order to protect States. This is a reflection of the situation under public international law. By way of illustration, in *De Letelier v. Republic of Chile*, the 2nd Circuit heard a matter where a judgment-creditor sought to attach and execute against the Chilean national airline, Linea Aerea Nacional-Chile (LAN), for Chile's debt.[41] The district court had reasoned that if jurisdictional immunity is lifted, the presumption is that immunity from execution should be lifted too. The rationale being that a statute should not be interpreted to create a right without a remedy.[42] The Circuit court held otherwise and explained that "when drafting the FSIA Congress took into account the international community's view of sovereign immunity," and therefore that the "Congress did in fact create a right without a remedy" in some circumstances.[43] It is an explicit design that "the execution immunity afforded sovereign property is broader than the jurisdictional immunity afforded the sovereign itself."[44] That is to say that in some instances, there may be a right to hold the State accountable but no asset to execute against because it may be protected *ipso jure*.

[1] Waivers

The FSIA requires separate and distinct waivers for submitting a case to the U.S. courts and to pursue execution of a judgment.[45] An explicit waiver of immunity from jurisdiction is not considered an implied waiver of immunity from execution and

41. *Letelier v. Republic of Chile*, 748 F.2d 790 (2d Cir. 1984).
42. *See Ibid.*, at 792.
43. *Ibid.*, at 798-799. The court also engaged in a comparative analysis, comparing, *inter alia*, the SIA 1978 and the ECSI's execution regime.
44. *Walters*, 651 F.3d at 289. *See also CBC*, 309 F.3d at 255-246 ("at the time the FSIA was passed, the international community viewed execution against a foreign state's property as a greater affront to its sovereignty than merely permitting jurisdiction over the merits of an action.") and *Republic of Philippines v. Pimentel*, 553 U.S. 851, 866, 128 S. Ct. 2180, 171 L.Ed.2d 131 (2008) ("pre-FSIA common-law doctrine dictated that courts defer to executive determination of immunity because 'the judicial seizure' of the property of a friendly state mat be regarded as 'an affront to its dignity and may [therefore] affect our relations with it.").
45. Jin, *supra* n. 18, at 14.

vice-versa.[46] In *Walters v. Industrial and Commercial Bank of China*, the court reasoned that nothing in the FSIA signals that the Congress intended a low standard for a waiver of sovereign immunity and, to the contrary, that the legislative history of section 1610(a)(1) indicates that the "Congress contemplated that waiver of execution immunity would be accomplished by some affirmative act of the foreign state."[47]

In *Liberian Eastern Timber Corporation v. Liberia*, the State had waived its sovereign immunity with respect to enforcement.[48] Such waiver meant that the award-creditor could recognize and enforce the award, but it did not translate to being treated as a waiver from execution immunity. Thus, assets like the tonnage fees, registration fees, and other taxes, were out of reach for the award-creditor because they were considered not to be used commercially, but rather to be used for the "support and maintenance of governmental functions" and as such were "an exercise of powers particular to a sovereign."[49]

In *Af-Cap Inc. v. Republic of Congo*, the 5th Circuit agreed with the district court that had reasoned that "even when a foreign state purports to waive completely its immunity, the FSIA only permits execution on property that is 'commercial'."[50] To some extent then, with this logic, waivers are rendered rather irrelevant. Even without a waiver, commercial assets in the U.S. are attachable, and even with a waiver, non-commercial assets are non-attachable. Whether such draconian reading of waivers will stand needs to be determined by future courts.

The 9th Circuit, in *Af-Cap Inc. v. Republic of Congo*, agreed with the 5th Circuit and held that an explicit waiver of immunity from "suit, execution, attachment, or other legal process" was an exception pursuant to section 1610(a)(a) to the general rule of immunity found in section 1609 and that a "waiver merely triggers the exception to the immunity from execution that would otherwise be in effect."[51] Thus, the waiver means that the court's inquiry continues to: (1) whether the property is in the U.S.; and (2) whether it is used for a commercial activity in the U.S. In other words, a waiver does not necessarily constitute a waiver with respect to all of the State's property in the U.S.[52] The explicit waiver of immunity from execution was not treated as going beyond and above section 1610(a). Such reasoning could be questioned and we have to see whether other circuits, and eventually the Supreme Court, agree.

In *Corporacion Mexicana De Servicios Maritimos, S.A. De C.V. v. M/T RESPECT*, it was held that the waiver provisions in the FSIA must be construed narrowly.[53] In

46. *See, e.g.*, *Walters*, 651 F.3d at 288 (referring to Restatement (Third) of Foreign Relations Law of the United States "a waiver of immunity from suit does not imply a waiver of immunity from attachment of property, and a waiver of immunity from attachment of property does not imply a waiver of immunity from suit."). *See also* Jin, *supra* n. 18, at 14.
47. *Walters, supra* n. 46, at 295-296.
48. *LETCO v. Republic of Liberia*, 650 F. Supp. 73 (1986).
49. *Ibid.*
50. *Af-Cap Inc. v. Republic of Congo*, 383 F.3d 361, 365 (5th Cir. 2004).
51. *Af-Cap Inc.*, 475 F.3d at 1087.
52. *See* Inna Uchkunova & Oleg Temnikov, *Enforcement of Awards under the ICSID Convention: What Solutions to the Problem of State Immunity?*, 29 ICSID Rev. 187, 203 (2014) https://doi.org/10.1093/icsidreview/sit038.
53. *Corporacion Mexicana de Servicios Maritimos, S.A. de C.V. v. The M/T Respect*, 89 F.3d 650, 655 (9th Cir. 1996).

Export-Import Bank of China v. Grenada, Granada had signed a waiver of immunity from execution in the following terms:

> [Grenada] represents and warrants that this Agreement and the Loan being made hereunder is a commercial ... act and that the Borrower is not entitled to claim immunity from legal process with respect to itself or any property owned by it ... on the ground of sovereignty ... [and] [t]o the extent that [Grenada] or any property owned by it ... has or hereafter may acquire any right of immunity from ... attachments or execution of judgment ... [Grenada] hereby irrevocably waives such right to immunity for itself and such property ... .[54]

As the law on waivers is currently construed, the crucial question is whether a waiver adds anything at all for an award-creditor since there is already an arbitration-exception in the execution context. Put simply, a waiver from execution does not seem to displace the execution immunity in the FSIA. Put differently, a waiver is one of the exceptions pursuant to section 1610(a) and nothing above and beyond that.[55] This was put clearly by the court in *Connecticut Bank of Commerce v. Republic of Congo*, where it reasoned that "[e]ven when a foreign state completely waives its immunity from execution, courts in the U.S. may execute only against property that meets these two statutory criteria."[56]

Thus, a waiver of immunity from execution applies only against property that is used for a commercial activity in the U.S. and is to be found in the U.S.[57] In this light, one may have reason to argue that the waiver doctrine is merely another form of the commercial activity exception. But because a judgment-creditor has it more difficult in the U.S. than in many other jurisdictions due to section 1610(a)(2) (i.e., that the property was "used for the commercial activity upon which the claim is based"), the waiver plays an important role for judgment-creditors. In the arbitration context, as mentioned, section 1610(a)(6) renders the issue moot. Thus, the waiver exception under the FSIA seems more relevant to judgment-creditors and does little to assist award-creditors.

[2] Commercial Purposes Exception

Pursuant to section 1610(a) of the FSIA, a court can only withhold or restrict immunity from execution with respect to the State's property if the property: (1) is in the U.S.; and (2) is used for a commercial activity in the U.S. "Used for" means something more than "in connection with," "related to," "integral to," or equivalent.[58] The property must be "put into action, put into service, availed or employed for a commercial activity" and must be so by the State and not a private, third party.[59] These prerequisites must be met

54. *Export-Import Bank of China v. Grenada*, 768 F.3d 75 (2d Cir. 2014).
55. *See also* (the decision in the District Court) 876 F.Supp.2d 263, 264-265 (S.D.N.Y. 2012).
56. *CBC*, 309 F.3d at 247.
57. *See Af-Cap Inc.*, 383 F.3d at 365.
58. *See Af-Cap Inc.*, 475 F.3d at 1089.
59. *Ibid.*, at 1090-1091. *See also EM Ltd v. Republic of Argentina*, 473 F.3d 463 (2007) (2d Cir. 2007) ("Because a nation state's borrowing relationship with the IMF takes place outside of the commercial marketplace, it cannot be considered 'commercial' in nature.").

even where there is, for example, an explicit waiver (the waiver exception) or where the judgment is based on an order confirming an arbitral award (the arbitration exception). Thus, where one of the mentioned exceptions applies, the property must be used for a commercial activity in the U.S., and the property must also be located in the U.S. (a nexus requirement). This can be especially problematic where the property is intangible in nature.[60]

In the U.S., as in other jurisdictions, the Purpose Test is prevalent in the execution context as opposed to the Nature Test which is used for jurisdictional immunity. As stated in *Export-Import Bank of China v. Grenada*, the focus is not on how a State generates the assets, but on how the State uses them.[61]

In *Af-Cap Inc. v. Republic of Congo*, the Congo had asserted immunity from execution for attachment of property held by ChevronTexaco in the form of intangible obligations (bonuses, taxes, and royalties from extraction of natural resources).[62] The 9th Circuit concluded that the property was not used for a commercial activity in the U.S., and therefore that it was "not subject to execution or collection under § 1610(a) of the FSIA."[63]

In real life, whether property is used for a commercial or governmental purpose is not always easy to discern. In fact, *Af-Cap Inc* had already litigated a similar matter in the 5th Circuit, where the court had reasoned differently, i.e., that property held by the oil company (CMS), in the form of debt (also tax and royalty obligations), was used to pay a commercial loan and was therefore used for commercial purposes in the U.S.[64] In the 5th Circuit, the judgment-creditor sought to execute through garnishment actions for intangible property held by third parties that was due/owed to Congo for payment of taxes and royalties. The third party (CMS) was the successor and is now the operator of a joint venture to extract oil in Congo in exchange for payments of royalties and taxes.[65] The property attached were these payments. In that case, whether property was considered used for a commercial purpose was determined through a "holistic approach" that examined the "totality of circumstances." The court reasoned as follows:

> Like the district court, we have similar reservations about defining property use as commercial in nature solely by reference to past single and/or exceptional commercial uses. Instead, we agree that determining the commercial (or non-commercial) status of a property's use requires a more holistic approach. Specifically, we think that an analysis applied to such a question should examine the

60. *See, e.g.*, *Af-Cap Inc.*, 383 F.3d at 361. The complications are even more cumbersome where the state can choose to be paid in royalties or "in-kind." Such latter payment could be, for example, barrels of oil instead of royalties. However, the task has been lessened since the holding in *U.S. Industries, Inc v. Gregg*, 540 F.2d 142, 151 n.5 (3rd Cir. 1976), where the court held that the attaching of a situs to intangible property is context-specific and requires embodying a common-sense appraisal of the requirements of justice and convenience in the particular circumstances and conditions.
61. *Export-Import Bank of China*, 768 F.3d at 89. The Court cited to, *inter alia*, *Af-Cap Inc.*, 475 F.3d at 1080.
62. *Af-Cap Inc.*, 475 F.3d at 1080.
63. *Ibid.*
64. *Af-Cap Inc.*, 383 F.3d at 361.
65. *Ibid.*, at 364.

> totality of circumstances surrounding the property. This analysis should include an examination of the uses of the property in the past [citations omitted] as well as all facts related to its present use, with an eye toward determining whether the commercial use of the property, if any, is so exceptional that it is "an out of character" use for that particular property.[66]

The court entertained evidence of past use in order to inquire into the predominant use or the future use of the property. Moreover, the court went as far as stating that it would be appropriate to consider whether the property has been manipulated by a sovereign in order to avoid being subject to garnishment.[67] Resultingly, in this case, the property of Congo was amenable to execution pursuant to the commercial activity exception in the 5th Circuit. The 5th Circuit also concluded that the situs for the tax and royalty payments was in the U.S. (nexus requirement) and refused arguments such as the one that Congo often elected payments in-kind instead.[68]

However, as already stated, in *Af-Cap Inc. v. Republic of Congo*, the 9th Circuit was faced with a similar plea of immunity from execution as a defense to the attempted execution of property held by a third party (Chevron-Texaco).[69] The 9th Circuit did not agree with the 5th Circuit. In the 9th Circuit, the property likewise included intangible obligations owed to the Congo for various taxes, bonuses, and royalties related to extraction of natural resources. The 9th Circuit, however, refused to adopt the same holistic inquiry/totality of circumstances test that included a backward-looking test to include "past single and/or exceptional commercial uses."[70] The court focused strictly on the "use" of the property. The 9th Circuit concluded that the nexus or connection to a commercial activity in the U.S. is insufficient for the purposes of execution.[71] It was held that "in order to satisfy [section] 1610(a), the property must have been 'used' [for a commercial activity in the U.S.]; the mere fact that the property has a 'nexus or connection to a commercial activity in the [U.S.]' is insufficient."[72]

In both circuits mentioned above, the courts focused on the difference between the narrower terminology "used for a commercial activity" in section 1610(1) dealing with execution immunity as opposed to the broader language of "in connection with" that can be found in section 1605(a)(2) with respect to jurisdictional immunity. Moreover, both courts shared a conceptual understanding and culminated in the same test as to how to determine whether property was used for a commercial activity in the U.S. The 9th Circuit reasoned as follows:

> The Fifth Circuit emphasized that "what matters under the statute is how the foreign state uses the property, not how private parties may have used the property in the past ..." [citation omitted], reasoning that, "[i]f we were to allow a private party's commercial use of the property to count for § 1610(a), we would erase the commercial/noncommercial use distinction for almost all of a foreign state's

66. *Ibid.*, at 369.
67. *Ibid.*, at 369 (fns 7-8).
68. *Ibid.*, at 372-373.
69. *Af-Cap Inc.*, 475 F.3d at 1080.
70. *Ibid.*, at 1091.
71. *Ibid.*, at 1080.
72. *Ibid.*

> tangible property." [citation omitted] We agree that to allow a private party's commercial use of the property to waive a foreign sovereign's immunity would not only frustrate "one of the principal goals of the FSIA"—to restrain, to the extent practicable, "judicial interference with the jus imperii, or sovereign acts, of a foreign state," [citation omitted]—but would also effectively eviscerate the protections of the FSIA by essentially placing the power to waive the foreign sovereign's immunity in the hands of private parties.
>
> ...
>
> Like the Fifth Circuit, we conclude that property is "used for a commercial activity in the United States" when the property in question is put into action, put into service, availed or employed for a commercial activity, not in connection with a commercial activity or in relation to a commercial activity.
>
> ...

The 2nd Circuit has joined the reasoning shared by the two circuits, stating that "[w]e agree with the Fifth and Ninth Circuits' interpretation. [We] understand the word 'used,' read literally, to require not merely that the property at issue relate to commercial activity in the [U.S.], but that the sovereign actively *utilize* that property in service of that commercial activity."[73] The 9th Circuit, however, disagreed slightly with the 5th Circuit as follows:

> We expressly decline, however, to incorporate the Fifth Circuit's articulated "reservations about defining property use as commercial in nature solely by reference to past single and/or exceptional commercial uses." Af-Cap, 383 F.3d at 369. In our view, attempting to quantify the number of commercial uses associated with the property, or to embark upon characterizing property use as exceptional or unexceptional, would unnecessarily complicate the determination to be made under § 1610(a).

Later on, in *Export-Import Bank of China v. Grenada*, the judgment-creditor sought to restrain taxes, fees, and other charges from certain private entities to be made to State entities for use of facilities located in Grenada.[74] Grenada claimed that: (A) the State entities are separate legal entities that cannot be held responsible; and (B) the funds are immune from attachment anyway. The issue of piercing the corporate veil is discussed below. This section deals with the issue of immunity vis-à-vis commercial property. The District Court had held that the funds were immune because the funds were not property in the U.S. of a foreign State and were not used for a commercial activity in the U.S.[75] The circuit court agreed and also found that the property was not "used for commercial activity in the [U.S.]."[76] It was reiterated that the analysis of the commercial activity exception must focus on how the State uses its money and not on how it was made.[77] The court reasoned that:

> For the most part, the application of this framework to the facts presented here is relatively straightforward. We do not consider the nature of the services provided in Grenada by the Statutory Corporations in exchange for the Restrained Funds,

73. *Export-Import Bank of China*, 768 F.3d at 90.
74. *Ibid.*, at 75.
75. 876 F.Supp.2d at 264-265.
76. *Export-Import Bank of China*, 768 F.3d at 78.
77. *Ibid.*, at 75.

> because the source of the property is irrelevant to the section 1610(a) analysis. Instead, we focus on the use to which Grenada puts—or clearly intends to put, by virtue of some formal designation or other specific means—the funds at issue. Even if, as Ex-Im Bank argues, the services provided by the Statutory Corporations are "precisely the kinds of services purchased from private vendors around the world," [Citations omitted] funds that the Restrained Entities pay to the Statutory Corporations for those services in Grenada are immune from attachment because they are not used by the Statutory Corporations for commercial activity that takes place in the United States. As the District Court found and the record supports, the Restrained Funds (with the possible exception of the IATA Funds, as discussed below), are devoted to "carrying out public functions in Grenada," and "used for the maintenance of facilities and services in Grenada." [Citations omitted] They fail both the "commercial use" and the "in the United States" prongs. They therefore do not meet the "commercial activity" exception to attachment provided by section 1610(a).

In this case, the funds that the creditor sought to execute the judgment against were considered to be used for public purposes and used for the maintenance of facilities in the home State. For a part of the funds, the court held that they were not used for a commercial activity in the U.S. Therefore, the property to be attached and executed against was either not commercial, not used commercially in the U.S., or not in the U.S. at all.

[3] *Certain Property Immune* **Ipso Jure**

Certain categories of property are considered immune *ipso jure* pursuant to section 1611. Such property includes funds held in the name of a foreign central bank or monetary authority for its own account and property used for certain military activities.

As an important caveat, however, certain property is considered amenable to execution due to the nature of the preceding underlying action—i.e., if a judgment is entered under section 1605A (terrorism exception), the property of the State is subject to execution regardless of, *inter alia*, the level of economic control over the property by the foreign State, whether the profits of the property go to that government, whether that government is the sole beneficiary, etc.

[4] *Mixed Use Property*

In *Birch Shipping Corp. v. The Embassy of the United Republic of Tanzania*, the District Court of D.C. held that:

> The only significant question, then, is whether it is proper to attach an account which is not used solely for commercial activity. Certainly the statute places no such restriction upon property which may be attached, nor is there anything in the legislative history indicating that Congress contemplated such a limitation. Central bank accounts are exempt, but that exception is not applicable to accounts used for mixed purposes. [Citations omitted] Indeed, a reading of the Act which exempted mixed accounts would create a loophole, for any property could be made immune by using it, at one time or another, for some minor public purpose. Defendant

> asserts, however, that failure to find this property immune will make it impossible for foreign countries to maintain embassies. Even if it could be shown this was actually a problem, the solution would not be the broad immunity defendant asks, but segregation of public purpose funds from commercial activity funds. Holding otherwise would defeat the express intention of Congress to (provide, in cases of commercial litigation such as this, that a "judgment creditor [would have] some remedy if, after a reasonable period, a foreign state or its enterprise failed to satisfy a final judgment." [Citations omitted]. Accordingly, the property at issue here is not immune from attachment, and the motion to quash the writ is denied.[78]

Here, the court clearly stated that such mixed use that is predominantly used commercially can be executed against, or at least that the commercially used part can be severed out.

In *Af-Cap Inc. v. Republic of Congo*, the 5th Circuit was not directly dealing with so-called mixed-use assets, but the reasoning may nevertheless prove helpful in such context.[79] In reasoning on whether property was used for commercial or sovereign purposes, the court outlined a holistic approach focusing on the "totality of circumstances."[80] Such test included looking both at past use, but also at whether the State has manipulated the use of the assets to avoid garnishment.[81] The court referred to the *Eastern Timer Corp. v. Republic of Liberia*, where the District Court of D.C. had reasoned that the property was a bank account primarily in use to fund diplomatic and consular activities, but where some portions had been used for commercial activities.[82] However, it is important to note that in the same case, the court held that a State does not lose its immunity because a portion of the property is used for a commercial activity.[83] In *Af-Cap Inc. v. Republic of Congo*, however, the 5th Circuit reasoned that Congo had "used at least fifty percent of [the property in question, i.e., royalties and taxes] to repay a commercial debt" and had at least once contemplated doing so again.[84]

Trying to distill meaning from these cases and going into the future, it seems that a relevant test is whether the property is predominantly used for a commercial or sovereign purpose and that assets with mixed-use can at times be executed against. Notwithstanding this, there seems to be no clear-cut doctrine on severing out what is commercial for purposes of attachment and execution. It is this author's belief that U.S. courts would endorse a predominant-use test and sever-out commercially used assets only where they constitute the major part of the assets.

[5] Piercing the Corporate Veil

A judge may be asked to address under what circumstances—if any—the agencies, instrumentalities, or even State-owned entities' assets may—or should—be executed

78. *Birch Shipping Corp. v. United Republic of Tanzania*, 507 F.Supp. 311 (D.D.C. 1981).
79. *See Af-Cap, Inc.*, 383 F.3d at 361.
80. *Ibid.*
81. *Ibid.*
82. *Ibid.*, at 370 (citing *LETCO*, 659 F.Supp. at 606).
83. *LETCO*, 659 F.Supp. at 610.
84. *Af-Cap, Inc.*, 383 F.3d at 370.

against for the award-debtor States' liabilities. Put differently, when should the separate juridical existence be ignored, thereby treating its property as that of the debtor State?

It is important to understand that where an arbitral award has been rendered and confirmed as a judgment in the U.S. against a State, the award is entered against that State only and not against any of its agencies or instrumentalities. In *First Nat'l City Bank v. Banco Para El Comercio Exterior de Cuba*, the Supreme Court held that "government instrumentalities established as juridical entities distinct and independent from their sovereign should normally be treated as such."[85] This presumption of affording separate legal status to agencies, instrumentalities, and State-owned enterprises is known as the "Bancec rule."[86] This is a rigorous presumption that must be overcome and can only be so under exceptional circumstances.[87]

However strong the presumption may be, in the *Bancec* case the Court outlined two exceptions to the rule: (1) the "corporate entity is so extensively controlled by its owner that a relationship of principal and agent is created"; or (2) that the recognition of the legal distinction "would work fraud or injustice."[88] Thus, the *Bancec* case elaborated on two exceptions to the presumption of separateness: (a) the "alter ego test/prong"; and (b) the "equity test/prong." For the former, the court elaborated certain factors to consider. Such factors are not to be treated mechanically.

In short, the *Bancec* case elaborated for: (1) the presumption of separateness (the Bancec Rule); (2) exceptions to the Bancec Rule under two separate prongs (the Bancec Exceptions); and (3) a fact-intensive inquiry of factors as pre-requisites to meet the exception (the Bancec Test).[89]

In *De Letelier v. Republic of Chile*, the 2nd Circuit heard a matter where a judgment-creditor sought to attach and execute against the Chilean national airline, LAN, for Chile's debt.[90] Relying on the Bancec Rule, LAN moved to dismiss, claiming

85. *First Nat'l City Bank v. Banco Para el Comercio*, 462 U.S. 611, 103 S. Ct. 2591, 2600 (1983).
86. *Ibid.*
87. *Crystallex, supra* n. 27, at 44 ("Under the [FSIA], there is a strong presumption that a foreign sovereign and its instrumentalities are separate legal entities. But the Supreme Court made clear in *Bancec* and *Rubin* that in extraordinary circumstances—including where a foreign sovereign exerts dominion over the instrumentality so extensive as to be beyond normal supervisory control—equity requires that we ignore the formal separateness of the two entities."). *See, e.g., Walters*, 651 F.3d at 298 ("The record in this case is bereft of any reason to conclude that the separate legal status of any agency or instrumentality of China should be disregarded for purposes of allowing petitioners to execute the judgment against assets of such entities.") *See also Export-Import Bank of China v. Grenada*, 768 F.3d 75 (2nd Cir. 2014) where the judgment-creditor sought to restrain taxes, fees, and other charges from certain private entities to be made to state entities for use of facilities located in Grenada. Grenada claimed that the funds are not subject to attachment since the state entities are distinct legal entities and separate from the state. Such entities cannot be held responsible for the debt of Grenada.
88. *First Nat'l City Bank*, 462 U.S. at 629 (1983).
89. *Ibid.* (Prong 1: "where a corporate entity is so extensively controlled by its owner that a relationship of principal and agent is created, we have held that one mat be held liable for the actions of the other.") (Prong 2: "the broader equitable principle that the doctrine of corporate entity, recognized generally and for most purposes, will not be regarded when to do so would work fraud or injustice."). These two prongs were approved in *Rubin v. Islamic Republic of Iran*, 138 S.Ct. 816, 823 (2018).
90. *Letelier*, 748 F.2d at 790.

that it should not be held responsible for the debt of Chile.[91] The district court had found an abuse of corporate form and therefore disregarded the presumption of separateness. In this case, the Circuit Court reversed the lower court's decision by reiterating that the burden of piercing the corporate veil is a difficult one and, moreover, a burden that the plaintiff (i.e., creditor) bears.[92] The court concluded that the burden of proving abuse "sufficient to overcome the presumption of separate existence" had not been met.[93] The court noted that both "Bancec and the FSIA legislative history caution against too easily overcoming the presumption of separateness."[94] Hence, LAN's assets could not be attached and executed against Chile's debt.[95]

In *Crystallex International Corporation v. Bolivarian Republic of Venezuela*, the 3rd Circuit stated that the Bancec doctrine was a "federal common-law outgrowth" of the FSIA and that it can, "in certain circumstances, [be used] to disregard the corporate separateness of foreign sovereigns to avoid the unfair results from a rote application of the immunity provisions provided by the [FSIA]."[96] Before that, in *Rubin v. Islamic Republic of Iran*, the Supreme Court had essentially confirmed the Bancec Rule, the Bancec Exception, and the Bancec Test when interpreting and applying the FSIA.[97]

In *Crystallex International Corporation v. Bolivarian Republic of Venezuela*, then, the 3rd Circuit heard a case on whether assets of Venezuela's State-owned entity, PDVS, should be attachable to satisfy the debt of Venezuela pursuant to an ICSID arbitration award.[98] The ICSID award of USD 1.4 billion had been confirmed in the U.S. As a matter of stepping-stone, the court outlined the Bancec Test, namely, that "a judgment creditor of a foreign sovereign may look to the sovereign's instrumentality for satisfaction when it is 'so extensively controlled by its owner that a relationship of principal and agent is created'."[99] The District Court concluded that the control was sufficient to attach PDVSA's shares in PDVH in satisfaction of the arbitral award and the Circuit Court affirmed.[100] It did so on the "alter ego" prong established as one of the Bancec Exceptions.

The way the court took to come there is of significant interest. The circuit court first found that it had jurisdiction over Venezuela pursuant to the arbitration exception (section 1605(a)(6)) and that such jurisdictions extend to "ancillary jurisdiction" to enforce their judgments through, for example, attachment and garnishment.[101] The

91. *Ibid.*, at 792.
92. *Ibid.*, at 795 ("A creditor seeking execution against an apparently separate entity must prove 'the property to be attached is subject to execution' [citations omitted].").
93. *Ibid.*
94. *Ibid.*
95. *Ibid.*, at 799.
96. *Crystallex, supra* n. 27, at 18-19.
97. *Rubin v. Islamic Republic of Iran*, 138 S. Ct. 816, 823 (2018).
98. *Crystallex, supra* n. 27.
99. *Ibid.*, at 6 (citing *First Nat'l City Bank*, 462 U.S. at 629).
100. *See Crystallex Int'l Corp. v. Bolivarian Republic of Venezuela ("Del. Crystallex")*, 333 F. Supp. 3d 380, 414 (D. Del. 2018). The district court held that it had jurisdiction to order attachment against PDVSA and that it could attach its shares of PDVH to satisfy the judgment against Venezuela.
101. *Crystallex, supra* n. 27, at 14 (Citing *IFC Interconsult, AG v. Safeguard Int'l Partners, LLC*, 438 F.3d 298, 311 (3d Cir. 2006) and *Peacock v. Thomas*, 516 U.S. 349, 356, 359 & n. 7 (1996)).

circuit then extended this jurisdiction to assets held by the State-owned entity, PDVSA. Referring to *Rubin v. Islamic Republic of Iran*, the circuit moved on to state that the judgment holder "may reach the assets of the foreign judgment debtor by satisfying the *Bancec* factors [i.e., the Bancec Test]."[102] Thus, if the State-owned entity is an "alter ego" of the State (i.e., qualifies under one of the Bancec Exceptions), the court has jurisdiction to proceed through its ancillary jurisdiction with execution, unless the assets are immune.

Moreover, *Rubin* and *Crystallex* clearly illustrate that U.S. courts have refused to develop a "mechanical formula" for when a State agency, instrumentality, or State-owned entity may be held liable for the debt of the State.[103] Instead, circuit courts have developed a case-by-case analysis on the basis of factors referred to as "the Bancec factors"—i.e., the Bancec Test—in aiding this analysis.[104] The factors to aid—not to be treated as decisive—courts in their analysis are:

(1) the level of economic control by the government;
(2) whether the entity's profits go to the government;
(3) the degree to which government officials manage the entity or otherwise have a hand in its daily affairs;
(4) whether the government is the real beneficiary of the entity's conduct; and
(5) whether adherence to separate identities would entitle the foreign state to benefits in United States courts while avoiding its obligations.[105]

In *Crystallex*, the 3rd Circuit went through the Bancec Test vis-à-vis the extensive control prong and analyzed the factors in light of the facts and circumstances at hand. In that case, the factors were satisfied.[106]

However, even where the presumption of separateness has been overcome by an exception, the last obstacle is still that of sovereign immunity; that is, whether the assets held by the State-owned entity—now considered assets of the State—are immune from attachment and execution. Put differently, the Bancec Exceptions deal with treating the State-owned entity and/or its assets as part of the State or State's assets, but the defense of sovereign immunity does not disappear if that turns out to be so. In *Crystallex*, the award-creditor argued that the property should not be immune pursuant to the commercial purpose exception, i.e., that the property is in the U.S., is used for a commercial activity in the U.S., and is sought to be attached in aid of execution pursuant to confirming an arbitral award under section 1610(a)(6). The test for determining whether State assets enjoy immunity or not has been discussed above.

102. *Rubin* 138 S.Ct. at 823.
103. *See Crystallex, supra* n. 27, at 21 and *Rubin*, 138 S.Ct. at 823.
104. *See Rubin*, 138 S.Ct. at 822-823.
105. *See Ibid.*, at 823. *See Crystallex, supra* n. 27, at 23-24 ("We use these factors identified in *Rubin* to structure our analysis here. At the same time, we recognize that they, like the other extensive control tests our sister circuits have adopted, are meant to aid case-by-case analysis rather than establish a 'mechanical formula' for identifying extensive control.").
106. *Crystallex, supra* n. 27, at 44 ("Indeed, if the relationship between Venezuela and PDSVSA cannot satisfy the Supreme Court's extensive-control requirement, we know nothing that can.").

Applying the law, in *Archirodon v. General Company for Ports of Iraq*, the U.S. District Court of D.C. accepted the arbitration exception to reject the immunity plea and granted the award-creditor's application for attachment and execution.[107] It was concluded that the award-debtor was an agent of the Ministry of Transport, which in turn is an organ of the State and hence is the State. The court relied on the "Bancec factors" in making its determination. Similarly, in *Amaplat v. Zimbabwe Mining Development Corporation*, the U.S. District Court of D.C. ruled that the waiver of sovereign immunity in the FSIA applied to the SOE because it was considered an alter ego of the State.[108]

Conclusively then, even where the corporate veil is pierced, the assets must nevertheless qualify under one of the exceptions in section 1610(a) since the assets are now treated as the State's property for purposes of execution. Seeing it in that light, the second step of the analysis is to determine whether the property at hand is used for the commercial activity upon which the claim is based (if it is a judgment that is to be enforced), whether a waiver exists, or whether the judgment is entered on the confirmation of an arbitral award. When the immunity can be qualified, the property must also be used for a commercial activity in the U.S. and be located in the U.S. section 1610(b) with its lower threshold of merely engaging in commercial activity in the U.S. is not applicable since the property is treated as that of the State following the veil piercing. This is a significant caveat.

[6] Burden of Proof and Post-Judgment Discovery

Post-judgment discovery in aid of execution belongs to a court's jurisdictional ambit. Meanwhile, one must also bear in mind that there is a major difference between general discovery and extraterritorial discovery.

Historically, U.S. courts were hesitant to approve extraterritorial (i.e., world-wide) asset discovery. In *Société Nationale Industrielle Aérospatiale v. United States*, the Supreme Court reasoned that "extraterritorial asset discovery in cases involving foreign states raises comity concerns, and courts ordering discovery should demonstrate due respect for any sovereign interest expressed by a foreign state."[109] This position was reiterated in 2011, in *Rubin v. Republic of Iran*, when the 7th Circuit Court held that a general asset discovery against a State's property violates the FSIA.[110]

This position came to change in 2014 when the Supreme Court rendered a landmark decision in the *Republic of Argentina v. NML Capital, Ltd.*[111] The Supreme Court reasoned that "the FSIA does not restrict the discovery of a foreign state's extraterritorial assets in aid of post-judgment attachment." It was clarified that "[t]here is no … provision forbidding or limiting discovery in aid of a foreign-sovereign

107. (D.D.C. August 16, 2024).
108. (D.D.C. February 9, 2024).
109. *Societe Nationale v. District Court*, 482 U.S. 522, 546-547 (1987).
110. *Rubin v. Islamic Republic*, 637 F.3d 783 (7th Cir. 2011), *cert. denied*, 133 S. Ct. 23 (2012).
111. *Republic of Argentina v. NML Capital, Ltd.*, 134 S.Ct 2250 (2014).

judgment debtor's assets …"[112] Accordingly, post-judgment discovery should be no different when the award-debtor is a sovereign State compared to a private award-debtor. Thus, without an explicit statement to the contrary, the ordinary rules on discovery apply. Any concerns not rooted in statutory interpretation, the Court reasoned, "are better directed to that branch of government with authority to amend the Act—which, as it happens, is the same branch that forced our retirement from the immunity-by-factor-balancing business nearly 40 years ago."[113] The Court held that "any sort of immunity defense made by a foreign sovereign in an American court must stand on the [FSIA's] text. Or it must fall."[114] In the U.S., "[t]here is no third provision forbidding or limiting discovery in aid of execution of a foreign sovereign judgment debtor's assets," the court reasoned.[115]

Not all justices agreed, however. Justice Ginsburg dissented. She was not in favor of the textual interpretation that, according to her, undercuts the purpose of the FSIA and does not consider fairly the consequences of such construction. She wrote that the U.S. courts should not "indulge the assumption that … the sky may be the limit for attaching a foreign sovereign's property."[116]

It is important to bear in mind that the discovery as such does not mean that the assets identified and located are automatically executable. Whether the assets in question are then immune is another, separate matter. This may be confusing to many. In *Aurelius Capital Master, Ltd. v. Rep. of Argentina,*[117] the 2nd Circuit Court refused a discovery objection on the grounds that the assets would be immune from execution. The court was simply wrong because seeking to rely on immunity comes at a later stage, i.e., where the award-creditor seeks to attach and execute against the assets. The Supreme Court highlighted this in the *NML* case, where it reasoned that:

> [The creditors] ask for information about Argentina's worldwide assets generally, so that NML can identify where Argentina may be holding property that *is* subject to execution. To be sure, that request is bound to turn up information about property that Argentina regards as immune. But NML may think the same property *not* immune. In which case, Argentina's self-serving legal assertion will not automatically prevail … .[118]

By granting post-judgment—and even extra-territorial—discovery, it can be said that the U.S. courts are truly facilitating creditors procedurally.[119] Put simply, the Supreme Court has made it easier to locate attachable assets and therefore made execution against a defaulting award-debtor State easier than before such widening of

112. *Ibid.*, at 2256.
113. *Ibid.*, at 2258.
114. *Ibid.*, at 2256.
115. *Ibid.*
116. *Ibid.*, at 2259.
117. *Aurelius Capital Master, Ltd. v. Republic of Argentina,* 589 F. App'x. 16 (2d Cir. 2014) ("To our knowledge, every court to consider whether awards issued pursuant to the ICSID Convention fall within the arbitral award exception to the FSIA has concluded that they do …").
118. *Republic of Argentina,* 134 S.Ct at 2258.
119. *See* Adriana T. Ingenito & Christina G. Hioureas, *Carving Out New Exceptions to Sovereign Immunity: Why the NML Capital Cases May Harm U.S. Interests Abroad,* 30 Md. J. Int'l 118 (2015).

the discovery tools. The decision in the *NML* case allows award-creditors to access previously unavailable legal/procedural mechanisms to seek satisfaction of outstanding debt from an award-debtor State.[120] Some authors have written negatively about the decision, including by highlighting that the U.S. Justice Department and the U.S. State Department had taken contrary positions during the proceedings.[121] To this, one could respond by stating that the FSIA was meant to achieve exactly this, i.e., turn any matter of sovereign immunity away from the executive branch and political considerations and instead to the judicial branch for proper legal interpretation and application.

Circuit courts and district courts have taken note of the precedent, as they must. In *Export-Import Bank of China v. Grenada*, the 2nd Circuit remanded a matter on discovery back to the district court in light of the decision in the *Republic of Argentina v. NML Capital, Ltd.*[122] The court held that "any lingering concern that the FSIA alone might presumptively bar further discovery has been eliminated by the Supreme Court in *NML Capital.*"[123] Thus, the court vacated the denial of post-judgment discovery to specific funds and remanded the district court to reassess whether to permit further discovery in light of the new precedent.

Another interesting development took place in *Walters v. Industrial and Commercial Bank of China*, where the 2nd Circuit held that where the petitioners had not yet "exhausted their powers of discovery pertaining to the judgment debtor's assets" pursuant to federal laws on civil procedure, it was not unreasonable for the burden of identifying specific, recoverable assets to remain with the petitioner.[124] One cannot but wonder what happens when the discovery powers are exhausted. Will the burden of identifying specific, recoverable assets shift to the State or third party holding State debt or assets? If so, such a position would be a massive game-changer in favor of award-creditors. It appears unlikely that such precedent will be unveiled by U.S. courts anytime soon.

[7] Injunctive Relief

In the *NML Capital, Ltd. v. Republic of Argentina* (*Equal Treatment Case I*), the 2nd Circuit Court affirmed an injunctive relief requesting Argentina to refrain from making payments with respect to its restructured bonds and not also make payments on the defaulted bonds.[125] The 2nd Circuit thus affirmed the decision in which the Southern District of New York had held that "whenever Argentina pays a percentage of what is due on the Exchange Bonds, it must pay plaintiffs the same percentage of what is then due on the FAA Bonds."[126] Specific performance was ordered because no adequate

120. *Ibid.*
121. *Ibid.*
122. *Export-Import Bank of China*, 768 F.3d at 92.
123. *Ibid.*, at 93.
124. *Walters*, 651 F.3d at 297.
125. *NML Capital, Ltd. v. Republic of Argentina (Equal Treatment Case I)*, 699 F.3d 250 (2d Cir. 2012).
126. *NML Capital, Ltd. v. Republic of Argentina*, No. 08 Civ. 6978 (TPG), 2012 WL 5895784 (S.D.N.Y. 21 November 2012).

monetary remedy was available.[127] Thus, because monetary damages were ineffective, and because Argentina simply refused to pay despite judgments, the court effectively assisted the judgment-creditor without undercutting the substantive law on sovereign immunity. The Supreme Court denied a writ for *certiori* on the injunction matter.

It is important to note that the injunction should not lead to an attachment, arrest, or execution as such. For example, in *Thai Lao Lignite (Thailand) Co. v. Gov't of Lao People's Democratic Republic (Laos)*, the Southern District of New York held that the remedies sought (i.e., restraining notices of flying fees) violated the FSIA.[128] The court held that the restraints would be "functionally the equivalent to the attachment of [Lao's] property because they involve court-ordered seizure and control."[129]

§4.2.3 Concluding Remarks

Today, because immunity from jurisdiction is treated differently from immunity from execution, a foreign State may be immune from the execution of a foreign judgment or foreign arbitral award even in a jurisdiction that embraces the restrictive theory on immunity (such as the U.S.).[130] Adding to that, the immunity from execution regime is broader and more difficult to penetrate than that with respect to immunity from jurisdiction.[131] Creditors can at times be left without a remedy. In fact, this is not "despite of" the FSIA. I am afraid to say that this is "because of" the FSIA. The 2nd Circuit hit the nail on its head in *De Letelier v. Republic of Chile* where it reasoned as follows:

> Congress passed the FSIA on the background of the views of sovereignty expressed in the 1945 charter of the United Nations and the 1972 enactment of the European Convention, which left the availability of execution totally up to the debtor state, and its own understanding as the legislative history demonstrates, that prior to 1976 property of foreign states was absolutely immune from execution. [Citations omitted] It is plain then that Congress planned to and did lift execution immunity "in part." Yet, since it was not Congress' purpose to lift execution immunity wholly and completely, a right without a remedy does exist in the circumstances here. Our task must be to read the Act as it is expressed, and apply it according to its expressions.[132] [Citations omitted].

127. *Equal Treatment Case I*, 699 F.3d at 261.
128. *Thai-Lao Lignite Co. v. Gov't of the Lao People's Democratic Republic*, No. 10 CIV. 5256 KMW DCF, 2013 WL 1703873 (S.D.N.Y. April 19, 2013) at 4.
129. *Ibid.*
130. *See* William S. Dodge, *Jurisdiction, State Immunity, and Judgments in the Restatement (Fourth) of US Foreign Relation Law*, 19 Chin. J. Int'l L. 101, 129 (2020) https://doi.org/10.1093/chinesejil/jmaa004.
131. *See, e.g.*, *Walters*, 651 F.3d at 289 and *CBC*, 309 F.3d at 255-256 ("at the time the FSIA was passed, the international community viewed execution as a greater affront to its sovereignty than merely permitting jurisdiction over the merits of an action.").
132. *Letelier*, 748 F.2d at 790. *See also Walters*, 651 F.3d at 289 ("Indeed, our court has observed that the asymmetry between jurisdiction and execution immunity in the FSIA reflects a deliberate congressional choice to create a 'right without a remedy' in circumstances where there is jurisdiction over a foreign state for purposes of obtaining a judgment, but its property is immune from attempts to execute the judgment ...").

Notwithstanding this, the U.S. is considered to be a creditor-friendly forum in which to enforce an international arbitral award and execute against the losing party's assets.[133] This is also the case where an award-debtor is a sovereign State. The FSIA has been a cornerstone in allowing the U.S. to serve as a worldwide financial hub, including as a hub for award enforcement purposes. Two authors rightly noted that:

> By making immunity determinations more predictable, the FSIA allows the United States to serve as a financial market to the world, where investors can make contracts knowing that they will be honored under law. The ability to sign agreements that will be enforced benefits sovereigns, especially those whose volatile histories make creditors wary of lending money secured only by the sovereign's promise.[134]

While true that the FSIA does not altogether alleviate the problem of States shielding their assets by invoking sovereign immunity, the FSIA as interpreted and applied by U.S. courts has truly made judgment/award execution significantly easier compared to other jurisdictions. Broadly put, before the FSIA was enacted, litigation against States had close to zero value and after its enactment, it had at least a non-zero value.[135] This is evident by the rise in cases post the Tate Letters and the FSIA enactment. This enabled the courts—and the courts took that opportunity—to elaborate on the liberal framework with pragmatic procedural tools and devices to assist the substantive law in achieving its objectives and purposes. Conclusively, as is evident from the U.S. courts' experiences with the FSIA, U.S. judges have given much-needed liberal and pragmatic flesh to the skeleton-like FSIA.

Conclusively, the U.S. could be considered both "liberal" and "pragmatic" for award execution purposes. Thus, the U.S. falls in Level 3 and is a "Green List" jurisdiction (*see* §1.2.2[2]).

§4.3 THE UNITED KINGDOM

The U.K. has a modern arbitration act (the 1996 English Arbitration Act). The 1996 English Arbitration Act is influenced by the UNCITRAL Model Law but differs from it in some ways and is generally considered arbitration-friendly.[136] England being a pro-arbitration jurisdiction is evident by London being a hub for international arbitration matters. Moreover, the U.K. is a Member State to both the New York and the ICSID Conventions. The U.K. has also signed ISDS clauses; for example, as found in various

133. Edward G. Kehoe, "The Enforcement of Arbitral Awards Against Foreign Sovereigns: the United States," in *Enforcement of Arbitral Awards Against Sovereigns* (Raymond Doak Bishop, ed.), 241-242, note 63, (2009).
134. Matthew D. McGill & Alexander N. Harris, *NML Capital v. Argentina: Enforcing Contracts in the Shadow of the Foreign Sovereign Immunities Act*, 30(1) Md J. Int'l L. 1, 4 (2015). *See, e.g.*, *Walters*, 651 F.3d at 288.
135. Mark C. Weidemaier, *Sovereign Immunity and Sovereign Debt*, 14 U. Ill. L. Rev. 67, 91 (2014) https://doi.org/10.2139/ssrn.2180228.
136. *See* Malis Acuner et al., "International Arbitration Laws and Regulations: England & Wales," in *International Comaraptive Legal Guide* (2021-2022).

IIAs. There is no reason to believe that the U.K. would not voluntarily comply with an adverse arbitral award. It can be said that the U.K. is a "pro-arbitration jurisdiction."

That being said, this chapter analyzes whether the U.K. is "liberal" and/or "pragmatic" with respect to sovereign immunity in the execution context. The U.K. has codified the law on sovereign immunity through the 1978 SIA. The SIA codified the restrictive theory—including in the execution context.[137] The act was established to bring the substantive law of sovereign immunity in the U.K. in line with the current international practice and to enable the ratification of the ECSI and the 1926 Brussels Convention and 1934 Protocol on State-owned ships.[138] The SIA extends to the whole of the U.K. and its dependent territories.[139] Furthermore, the U.K. is a signatory to the UNCSI.

Due to the SIA, the law on sovereign immunity in the U.K. is subject to statutory interpretation. Much of the law has developed in and can be found through case law. Moreover, U.K. courts have endorsed UNCSI as constituting largely, but not exclusively, a codification of customary international law.

In the U.K., as is the case internationally, the courts have been more hesitant—and at times even reluctant—to allow for attachment and execution against State property. As will be seen below, at times it can be questioned whether U.K. courts actually live up to the restrictive doctrine of sovereign immunity from execution as much in practice as in theory. Compared to the U.S. courts (*see* above in §4.2), the substantive law has not been applied as liberally, and neither has it been supplemented by a pragmatic judicial attitude vis-à-vis procedural rules. As will be seen, at times this has even resulted in non-liberal case law.

Put simply, the plea of sovereign immunity from execution is strong and presents a serious obstacle to award satisfaction in the U.K. For example, U.K. courts have placed the burden of proof onerously high for award-creditors, endorsed a State-friendly stance on so-called mixed-use assets, and have approved a rather conservative approach vis-à-vis certain property considered immune *ipso jure*.

§4.3.1 Sovereign Immunity from Execution of Arbitral Awards in the U.K.

In terms of terminology, the SIA uses "enforcement" as opposed to "execution." Therefore, it is important to set things straight at the outset on enforcement of judgments or arbitral awards, i.e., that "[p]roceedings to recognize a foreign judgment given against a foreign State, to register a foreign judgment [...] or to enforce a foreign judgment or arbitral award, relate to the exercise of the court's adjudicative jurisdiction."[140] This is different from execution. Execution is a post-judgment phase. This book's focus is on immunity from execution. Neither this book as such, nor this chapter

137. However, attention should be had to the fact that the act has not replaced the common law in every respect, and therefore the substantive law of sovereign immunity can in some respects grow outside the scope of the act. This has limited—if any—relevance to immunity from execution. *See also Holland v. Lampen-Wolfe* [1998] 1 WLR 188, CA; [2000] 3 All ER.
138. Fox & Webb *supra* n. 10, at 167.
139. *See* State Immunities (Overseas Territories) Order 1979.
140. Fox & Webb, *supra* n. 10, at 176.

within it, deals with immunity from recognition/enforcement; rather, it deals strictly with immunity from execution. Notwithstanding this, English courts and the SIA use the terminology "enforcement" synonymously with "execution." The reader must consider this while reading the SIA and English/U.K. case law.

[1] State Immunity Act 1978

Before the SIA, the doctrine of sovereign immunity applied only as a matter of common law in English courts.[141] Like the UNCSI and FSIA, the SIA treats immunity from jurisdiction differently than immunity from execution (albeit using the terminology "enforcement"). The SIA codified the law and the transition away from absolute immunity toward the theory of restrictive immunity—both with respect to immunity from jurisdiction and from execution. The SIA lays down the rule on immunity in both branches and articulates the exceptions thereto. Moreover, similarly to global practice, while the major commercial activity exception to jurisdictional immunity is determined on the Nature Test, the commercial exception to execution immunity is determined on the Purpose Test.[142]

The general rule of immunity is preserved in section 1 but is subject to several exceptions. Sections 2-11 deal with exceptions from jurisdictional immunity, while sections 13-14 deal with exceptions from execution immunity. Sections 13-14 read as follows:

> **13 Other procedural privileges.**
>
> (1) No penalty by way of committal or fine shall be imposed in respect of any failure or refusal by or on behalf of a State to disclose or produce any document or other information for the purposes of proceedings to which it is a party.
>
> (2) Subject to subsections (3) and (4) below—
>
> (a) relief shall not be given against a State by way of injunction or order for specific performance or for the recovery of land or other property; and
>
> (b) the property of a State shall not be subject to any process for the enforcement of a judgment or arbitration award or, in an action in rem, for its arrest, detention or sale.
>
> (3) Subsection (2) above does not prevent the giving of any relief or the issue of any process with the written consent of the State concerned; and any such consent (which may be contained in a prior agreement) may be expressed so as to apply to a limited extent or generally; but a provision merely submitting to the jurisdiction of the courts is not to be regarded as a consent for the purposes of this subsection.
>
> (4) Subsection (2)(b) above does not prevent the issue of any process in respect of property which is for the time being in use or intended for use for commercial purposes; but, in a case not falling within section 10 above, this subsection applies to property of a State party to the European Convention on State Immunity only if—

141. Katherine Reece Thomas, *State Immunity. Insight* (2016).
142. Fox & Webb, *supra* n. 10, at 216.

(a) the process is for enforcing a judgment which is final within the meaning of section 18(1)(b) below and the State has made a declaration under Article 24 of the Convention; or
(b) the process is for enforcing an arbitration award.

(5) The head of a State's diplomatic mission in the United Kingdom, or the person for the time being performing his functions, shall be deemed to have authority to give on behalf of the State any such consent as is mentioned in subsection (3) above and, for the purposes of subsection (4) above, his certificate to the effect that any property is not in use or intended for use by or on behalf of the State for commercial purposes shall be accepted as sufficient evidence of that fact unless the contrary is proved.

(6) In the application of this section to Scotland—
(a) the reference to "injunction" shall be construed as a reference to "interdict";
(b) for paragraph (b) of subsection (2) above there shall be substituted the following paragraph—

"(b) the property of a State shall not be subject to any diligence for enforcing a judgment or order of a court or a decree arbitral or, in an action in rem, to arrestment or sale."; and
(c) any reference to "process" shall be construed as a reference to "diligence," any reference to "the issue of any process" as a reference to "the doing of diligence" and the reference in subsection (4)(b) above to "an arbitration award" as a reference to "a decree arbitral."

14 States entitled to immunities and privileges.

(1) The immunities and privileges conferred by this Part of this Act apply to any foreign or commonwealth State other than the United Kingdom; and references to a State include references to—
(a) the sovereign or other head of that State in his public capacity;
(b) the government of that State; and
(c) any department of that government, but not to any entity (hereafter referred to as a "separate entity") which is distinct from the executive organs of the government of the State and capable of suing or being sued.

(2) A separate entity is immune from the jurisdiction of the courts of the United Kingdom if, and only if—
(a) the proceedings relate to anything done by it in the exercise of sovereign authority; and
(b) the circumstances are such that a State (or, in the case of proceedings to which section 10 above applies, a State which is not a party to the Brussels Convention) would have been so immune.

(3) If a separate entity (not being a State's central bank or other monetary authority) submits to the jurisdiction in respect of proceedings in the case of which it is entitled to immunity by virtue of subsection (2) above, subsections (1) to (4) of section 13 above shall apply to it in respect of those proceedings as if references to a State were references to that entity.

(4) Property of a State's central bank or other monetary authority shall not be regarded for the purposes of subsection (4) of section 13 above as in use or intended for use for commercial purposes; and where any such bank or authority is a separate entity subsections (1) to (3) of that section shall apply to it as if references to a State were references to the bank or authority.

(5) Section 12 above applies to proceedings against the constituent territories of a federal State; and Her Majesty may by Order in Council provide for the other

provisions of this Part of this Act to apply to any such constituent territory specified in the Order as they apply to a State.

(6) Where the provisions of this Part of this Act do not apply to a constituent territory by virtue of any such Order subsections (2) and (3) above shall apply to it as if it were a separate entity.

The SIA also includes an arbitration exception (section 9). Submitting to arbitration constitutes a waiver of immunity from jurisdiction. As explained in Chapter 2, the arbitration exception extends to proceedings that "relate to arbitration" (e.g., recognition/enforcement), but not to the execution of an already recognized and enforced award.[143] Importantly, "[a] distinction has to be made between seeking to have a foreign arbitral award recognized by the English courts where immunity is precluded by [section 9] and seeking to enforce against assets of the State to give effect to the award which would be covered by [Section 13] ..."[144] Award enforcement is not to be confused with execution of the award as such—despite terminological similarities. It is important to note that this book deals with immunity from execution, and therefore does not analyze more recent case law in the U.K. dealing with immunity from enforcement (whether dealing with "intra-EU awards" or otherwise).[145]

The general rule is still one of immunity. Section 13 then lists measures of constraint available as well as exceptions that can be invoked; for example, either consent or that the property is being used or intended to be used for a commercial purpose (*see*, e.g., section 13(4)). Section 13(1) is a total prohibition on committals and fines.[146]

Moreover, section 13(2) prohibits other types of enforcement or execution measures (e.g., injunctions and specific performance) unless there is an express consent pursuant to section 13(3). The "express" consent must target both pre-judgment and post-judgment measures as well as immunity from jurisdiction and immunity from execution.[147] Mann expressed his concern with such prohibition, stating that it is both a serious and a worrying aspect.[148] To illustrate, he argued that to

143. *See* discussion in *NML Capital v. Argentina* [2011] UKSC 31 and *Svenska Petroleum Exploration AB v. Lithuania and Another* [2006] EWCA Civ 1529.

144. Reece Thomas, *supra* n. 141, at para. 13. *See also Gold Reserve Inc v. Venezuela* [2016] EWHC 153; *Pearl Petroleum Co Ltd v. Kurdistan Regional Government of Iraq* [2015] EWHC 3361; and *Ecuador v. Occidental Exploration and Production Company* [2006] 2 WLR 70.

145. For the reader's interest: In *Yukos v. Russia* ([2023] EWHC 2704 (Comm)), the English High Court determined that Russia cannot rely on sovereign immunity with respect to award enforcement. This case was a bit peculiar in the sense that the court determined that immunity from enforcement was precluded (issue estoppel).

146. For example, a state cannot be fined for refusing to comply with a discovery order. *See* Derek William Bowett, *The State Immunity Act 1978*, 37 Cambridge L. J. 193, 195 (1978) ("As to other procedural privileges. Section 13 protects the state against committal or fine for non-disclosure of documents or information, against injunctions or orders for specific performance, and against execution of any judgment on the property of the state, provided the property is not in use or intended for use for commercial purposes.").

147. *See A Company v. Republic of X* [1990] 2 Lloyd's Rep. 520 (where a general waiver of immunity from jurisdiction and for the state's property was considered a waiver for immunity from pre-judgment measures.).

148. Frederick Alexander Mann, *The State Immunity Act 1978*, 50 BYIL 43, 59 (1979) https://doi.org/10.1093/bybil/50.1.43.

deny a party the right to a *Mareva Injunction* (i.e., a freezing order) "will frequently render proceedings nugatory and deprive a successful plaintiff of the fruits of his victory."[149] He went on to state that "in most cases proceedings in England against a foreign State may prove pointless even if the defendant is not entitled to immunity and the action succeeds."[150] A fuller discussion on measures of constraint on an interim basis or in the pre-judgment phase is—albeit much more interesting—a bit outside the scope of this book. However, it will be touched upon briefly in Chapter 5.

Section 13(4) is the "commercial purpose" exception, i.e., the manifestation of the restrictive theory of immunity in the execution phase. Pre-judgment attachment can be rendered with express consent only and not against property used for a commercial purpose.[151] Section 13(4) focuses on the actual, current use or intended use—and not on past use.[152] As will be seen in the case law below, this is an important distinction and clarification to understand.

Moreover, section 17(1) makes a reference to "commercial purposes" as being "purposes of such transactions or activities as are mentioned in section 3(3)." Section 3(3) in turn reads as follows:

> (3) In this section "commercial transaction" means—
>
> (a) any contract for the supply of goods or services;
> (b) any loan or other transaction for the provision of finance and any guarantee or indemnity in respect of any such transaction or of any other financial obligation; and
> (c) any other transaction or activity (whether of a commercial, industrial, financial, professional or other similar character) into which a State enters or in which it engages otherwise than in the exercise of sovereign authority;
>
> but neither paragraph of subsection (1) above applies to a contract of employment between a State and an individual.

In practice, the exceptions to jurisdictional immunity are generally based on a Nature Test while the exceptions to execution immunity are based on the Purpose Test.[153] The distinction between "nature" and "purpose" makes it more difficult to attach and execute against State property compared to litigating or arbitrating against a State. It also makes attaching and execution more difficult than award recognition and enforcement procedures.

149. *Ibid.*, at 60.
150. *Ibid.*
151. *See* Fox & Webb, *supra* n. 10, at 218.
152. *See SerVaas Inc. v. Rafidan Bank* [2012] UKSC 40.
153. Even though in the Court of Appeals in *Alcom Ltd v. Republic of Colombia*, determined the use of assets in a bank account based on the nature test as opposed to the purpose test. Finally, the case reached the House of Lords and was reversed. *Alcom v. Republic of Colombia*, [1984] AC 580, [1984] 2 WLR 750, [1984] 2 Lloyds Rep 24, [1984] 2 All ER 6. If the position by Donaldson MR. would gain approval, embassy accounts would never be immune in a jurisdiction that embraces restrictive immunity because money in a bank account can never per se be used for other purposes than commercial transactions. It is the purpose of the transaction that renders them immune, e.g., to "run and operate" the embassy.

In fact, in the English practice, the judges have not strictly adopted the Purpose Test but have been said to have developed a form of "purpose in context test."[154] It has been said that this test has, in practice, led to "favouring of States when a technical application of the statutory language might have favoured the creditor."[155]

The SIA makes immunity from execution even more cumbersome through the enactment of section 13(5), where the burden of proof is made highly onerous for an award-creditor. The section elaborates a high burden of proof on the award or judgment creditor; that is, for the purposes of determining whether property "is" or "is intended" for use for commercial purposes, the award or judgment-debtor State's head of mission's certificate of the property's use or intended use constitutes evidence unless the contrary is proven. Fox and Webb rightly noted that this "burden of proof is a difficult one to discharge when cross-examination of the ambassador is barred by his diplomatic immunity."[156] One should add to this that discovery cannot be followed up by contempt or a fine, but only by mere "adverse inferences."

Finally, section 14(4) introduces special provisions for certain categories of property being protected *ipso jure*. This means that even if a central bank or monetary authority is considered a separate entity, the special protections in section 13(1)-(3) shall nevertheless apply. More than that, "whether or not the central bank [or monetary authority] is a separate entity, the last-mentioned consequence is fortified by the express provision that even the bank's property used or intended to be used for commercial purposes is unavailable for execution."[157] Thus, central bank or monetary authority assets are protected categorically and *ipso jure*. Mann expressed his concerns also with section 14(4), stating that it has "rendered proceedings against a central bank almost wholly illusory ..." and that "[t]he mercenary attitude towards central banks ... remains a matter for great regret."[158] Albeit Mann's writing is relatively old, as we will *see* below, more recent case law and scholarship have confirmed the analysis and his speculative fears being true.

§4.3.2 Case Law

Given that the law on sovereign immunity is codified in the U.K., the courts engage in statutory interpretation as opposed to "common law." Late Mann rightly noted that the

---

154. *See, e.g.*, Reece Thomas, *supra* n. 141.
155. Reece Thomas, *Enforcing Against State Assets: The Case for Restricting Private Creditor Enforcement and How Judges in England Have Used "Context" When Applying the "Commercial Purposes" Test*, 2 J. Int'l & Compar. L. 1, 16 (2015) https://doi.org/10.4337/9781803923468.00010. *See also I Congreso del Partido*, [1983] 1 AC 244, 267 ("The conclusion which emerges is that in considering, under the 'restrictive' theory whether state immunity should be granted or not, the court must consider the whole context in which the claim against the state is made, with a view to deciding whether the relevant act(s) upon which the claim is based, should, in that context, be considered as fairly within an area of activity, trading or commercial, or otherwise of a private law character, in which the state has chosen to engage, or whether the relevant act(s) should be considered as having been done outside that area, and within the sphere of governmental or sovereign activity.").
156. Fox & Webb, *supra* n. 10, at 216.
157. Mann, *supra* n. 148, at 61.
158. *Ibid.*, at 61-62.

enactment of SIA "initiates a new era in the field of sovereign immunity in English law, an era which will throw up problems of a new and different kind that have to be solved by way of statutory interpretation."[159] Nowadays, "underpinned by four decades of interpretation and practice" it can be said that the U.K. approach represents an international "middle ground in the evolving landscape of immunity."[160] With "middle ground," this author refers to somewhere between non-liberal/conservative and liberal and pragmatic (*see* §1.2.2[2]).

Prior to the SIA, Lord Lloyd-Jones explained that the courts had to "define the rules as best they could, seeking guidance from the decisions of courts of other countries, from jurists, from conventions and by defining the rule in terms which are consonant with justice rather than adverse to it."[161] Such comparative exercise should not be seen as a "thing of the past" only. Even with the SIA fully enacted and applied, the comparative methodology informs the statutory interpretation and the English courts have, by way of illustration, cited the UNCSI in support of their decisions.[162] For example, in *Jones v. Saudi Arabia*, where the judge observed that the UNCSI, despite its embryonic status, is "the most authoritative statement available on the current international understanding of the limits of state immunity in civil cases."[163] Thus, the evolution of the law of sovereign immunity is not limited to domestic considerations given that it is indeed an area of public international law.

[1] Waivers

The consent to arbitrate serves as a waiver of immunity from jurisdiction, but not as a waiver of immunity from execution. Additionally, an arbitration agreement removes any "jurisdictional connection" requirement as it applies to domestic as well as foreign arbitral awards.[164] The rationale applies with the same force with respect to ICA as well as ISDS. However, in order to waive immunity from execution, a separate, express waiver is required.[165]

For illustrative purposes, in *A Company v. Republic of X*, the High Court (Queen's Bench Division), the State had signed a waiver clause waiving "sovereign immunity for itself or its property."[166] Such waiver was construed to be one of immunity from adjudication as well as from execution. Had it been a general waiver of immunity without expressly waiving immunity for its property, it would likely not have stood the test.

159. *Ibid.*, at 43.
160. Philippa Webb, "International Immunities in English Law," in *The Oxford Handbook of Comparative Foreign Relations Law* (Curtis A. Bradley, ed.), 1 (2019).
161. David Loyd Jones, *Forty Years On: State Immunity and the State Immunity Act 1978*, 3 (18 October 2018).
162. Fox & Webb, *supra* n. 10, at 173.
163. *Jones* [2007] 1 AC 270, para. 26.
164. *AIC Ltd v. Nigeria & Anor* [2003] EWHC 1357 and *Svenska Petroleum Exploration AB v. Lithuania and Another* [2006] EWCA Civ 1529.
165. *See A Company*, 2 Lloyd's Rep. at 520; *Sabah Shipyard (Pakistan)* [2002] EWCA Civ 1643; and *Svenska Petroleum*, EWCA Civ 1529.
166. *Ibid.*

More recently, in *General Dynamics v. Libya*, the English High Court concluded that where parties include language of the effect "wholly enforceable," such language indeed constitutes an effective waiver of sovereign immunity from execution.[167] Resultingly, the award-creditor could attach a property held by the State in London.

[2] Commercial Purposes Exception

Due to political ramifications and ingrained notions of dignity and sovereign equality, the immunity offered at the execution stage is more rigorous than that offered with respect to jurisdiction.[168] Professor Reece Thomas rightly notes that the widely accepted restriction on immunity from execution are such assets used or intended to be used for "commercial purposes," but that "[t]he scope and application of the commercial purpose test is … uncertain … ."[169] Below is the analysis of the English courts' application of the commercial purpose test. Commercial property has been defined broadly in the U.K., including "any right or interest, whether legal, equitable, or contractual, in assets, including those which other parties also have rights."[170]

Determining the purpose of State property is cumbersome. And so is the award-creditor's task of showing that property is in use or intended for use for commercial purposes.[171] This is especially true given that many States deposit assets "in accounts held in the name of their diplomatic missions or of their central banks."[172]

In *AIC Ltd v. The Federal Government of Nigeria and the Attorney General of the Federation of Nigeria*, the bank accounts of Nigeria were "dormant" as they had not been in use for over 18 months.[173] However, the previous use of purchase of books for Nigerian schools was not considered a commercial use and neither was the awarding of scholarships.[174] Thus, the accounts were immune. Thus, the court looked at past use—not only current or intended future use.

In *AIG Capital Partners Inc v. Kazakhstan*, the High Court of Justice heard a case that concerned a claim of sovereign immunity for the State and its central bank (the National Bank of Kazakhstan/NBK).[175] The award-creditor had been awarded a favorable ICSID arbitral award of approximately USD 10,000,000. The award was enforced as a judgment of the English court and the award-creditor, now turned judgment holder, sought to obtain both a third-party debt order and a discharging order against cash and securities held in London for the NBK.[176] The NBK managed a

167. [2024] EWHC 472 (Comm).
168. *See, e.g.*, Reece Thomas, *supra* n. 155, at 17.
169. *Ibid.*, at 2.
170. *See AIG Capital Partners Inc. v. Kazakhstan* [2005] EWHC 2239 (Comm), para. 45.
171. Webb, *supra* n. 160, at. 8.
172. *Ibid.*
173. *AIC Ltd.*, EWHC 1357.
174. *Ibid.*
175. *AIG Capital Partners Inc*, EWHC 2239.
176. I will not go into the Charging Orders Act 1979 and Part 72—Third-Party Debt Orders (Civil Procedure Rules). Its application is irrelevant for our purposes. However, it merits to say that the court found that it could not issue a third-party debt order against the financial service provider because it was not Kazakhstan that it had a debt to, but rather the national bank.

sovereign wealth fund (National Fund) that sought to stabilize fiscal policy and save portions of extraction of natural resources. The funds were then held in custody by financial service providers. The court had to determine: (1) whether the property belonged to the NBK; and (2) whether the property enjoyed immunity from execution pursuant to sections 13(2)(b), 13(4), and 14(4) of the SIA.[177] The construction of section 14(4) will be analyzed under the sub-section "*Property Immune Ipso Jure*" below since it deals with the categorical immunity of central bank assets. In the case at hand, the court also heard whether section 14(4) of the SIA has an adverse impact on the meaning of Article 6(1) of the ECHR so that the former should be reconstructed in a "purposive manner."[178] The author will not deal with that particular issue here. Under this sub-section, the author focuses on the reasoning with respect to commercial purposes.

The court looked at the natural resources funds and stated that such funds can be used as "stabilization funds" (i.e., for governmental purposes, *iure imperi*), "savings funds" (i.e., for commercial purposes, *jure gestionis*), or a "combination" of both (i.e., for mixed purposes).[179] In making its determination of whether the funds were used or intended to be used for commercial or governmental purposes, the court also looked at the ambassador of the State's certificate pursuant to section 13(5), stating that the "National Fund is designed to ensure economic stability of Kazakhstan and to accumulate funds for future generations by way of investment in securities" and that the "assets held in custody in [the national bank's] accounts with [the financial services provider] have never been used for commercial purposes ..." and that they were "not intended to be used for such purposes."[180]

The court outlined a test for determining whether enforcement against the State's assets should follow; that is, "(a) proof that the State concerned does have an interest in the particular asset; (b) proof that the State's property comes within the exception expressed in section 13(4); and (c) the nature of the property to be the subject of enforcement and the scope of the particular enforcement process under English law."[181]

Thus, if section 14(4) of the SIA did not exist or if the provision was interpreted functionally (as opposed to categorically), the courts would be asked to determine on a case-by-case basis whether the particular assets were used for commercial purposes pursuant to section 13(4). Since SIA reads the way it does, however, the court takes a more categorical position.

Thus, the court did not consider it necessary to determine whether the property at hand was used for a commercial purpose due to section 14(4). Notwithstanding this, Aikens J explained that he nevertheless did not believe that the assets were in use or intended for use for a commercial purpose. It was considered that the assets formed part of the national fund and that such fund was "created to assist in the management

177. *See AIG Capital Partners Inc*, EWHC 2239, at para. 1.
178. *See Ibid.*, at paras. 62-88.
179. *Ibid.*, at para. 11.
180. *Ibid.*, at para. 25.
181. *Ibid.*, at para. 51.

of the economy and government revenues of [the State], both in the short and long term."[182] Hence, the dealings with the assets were "all part of the overall exercise of sovereign authority by [the State]."[183]

In *Orascom Telecom Holding SAE v. Republic of Chad*, the bank account in question was considered in use for commercial purposes because the payments were made into separate accounts and one of the accounts held the revenues (oil royalties) paid into the bank and later to be used for paying loans owned to the World Bank.[184] In this case, however, the court focused largely on the nature of the way in which the assets were generated as opposed to how they were used or going to be used.[185] Burton J focused on the fact that the bank account had been established and operated for the purposes of a commercial transaction.[186] In fact, the set-up had a sovereign purpose. The decision is an anomaly and subsequent case law will better reflect the current position in the U.K. Whether immunity is warranted is determined by the current or intended use and not by the nature of the transaction.

In *SerVaas Incorporated v. Rafidain Bank and Others*, the U.K. Supreme Court was asked to construct section 13(4), i.e., the expression "property which is for the time being in use or intended for use for commercial purposes."[187] The property at hand was debt from a commercial bank to commercial creditors that had been purchased by Iraq. Thus, the claim of the funds and dividends arose from commercial transactions, and therefore a commercial activity. The court had to address the central question of "whether the nature of the origin of the debts [was] relevant to the question whether the property in question was in use for commercial purposes."[188] The court held that it does not matter how the State obtained the property, but rather what matters is what the State uses them for or how it intends to use them.[189] The court did not consider a retrospective analysis of the circumstances giving rise to the property to be necessary.[190] The court reasoned that SIA does not refer to "in connection with" or "related to" a commercial transaction in section 13(4).[191] The section deliberately focuses on "in use or intended for use." Thus, the court explained, "[t]he essential distinction is between the origin of the funds on the one hand and the use of them on the other."[192]

Put simply, what the court looks at is not the "nature" or origin, but the "purpose." The ultimate question before the court was thus whether Iraq "bought the debts in order to make a profit and as part of a commercial venture, or whether ... they

182. *Ibid.*, at para. 92.
183. *Ibid.*
184. *Orascom Telecom Holding v. Chad and Sotel Tchad*, [2008] EWHC 1841 (Comm) 2 Lloyds Rep 396, [2009] 1 All ER (Comm) 315.
185. *See* Reece Thomas, *supra* n. 155, at. 25.
186. *Orascom*, EWHC 1841, at para. 23.
187. *SerVaas Inc.*, UKSC 40, para. 1.
188. *Ibid.*, at para. 15.
189. *Ibid.*
190. *Ibid.*, at para. 16.
191. *Ibid.*, at para. 17.
192. *Ibid.*, at para. 19.

were bought in the exercise of sovereign authority as part of a huge restructuring of debts incurred in the Saddam Hussein era."[193] Focus was to be had on how the property is "currently" used or intended to be used.[194] It was not excluded that inferences can indeed be drawn from past or recent use, "but the older the use in evidence, the weaker the inference that may be drawn as to the use or intended use of the account."[195] The court explained that "[t]he focus is throughout on actual use."[196]

Having set this standard, the court concluded that the purchased debt "are simply the means to the end of the dividends" and that these "are nothing more than a legal mechanism."[197] The Supreme Court articulated its position clearly, namely, that the nature of the underlying transaction is irrelevant and that what matters pursuant to section 13(4) is the current use or intended use for commercial purposes is what matters. Neither the origin nor some distant future purpose matters. Moreover, pursuant to section 13(5), the Iraqi Ambassador had stated that the intended use was governmental.[198] In such a situation, the burden of proof shifts to the creditor (*see* more on this below).

More recently, in *Zhongshan Fucheng v. Nigeria*, the English High Court refused the plea of sovereign immunity from execution and enforced the award against real estate property used or intended to be used for commercial purposes.[199]

[3] *Certain Property Immune* Ipso Jure

Certain categories of property are considered immune *ipso jure*. What this means is that such property is virtually absolutely immune from attachment and execution. In the U.K., the SIA provides for *ipso jure* immunity from execution against the balances in the accounts of central banks or monetary authorities.[200] This means that assets of a central bank or monetary authority could never (*ipso facto*) be considered to be in use for commercial purposes.[201] This was not the position in common law prior to SIA.[202]

193. *Ibid.*, at para. 12.
194. *Ibid.*, at para. 23. (The court also looked at U.S. case law and explained that the same distinction between the source of the property and its use has been drawn there.).
195. *Ibid.*, at para. 21.
196. *Ibid.*
197. *Ibid.*, at para. 32.
198. *Ibid.*, at para. 7 ("1. The Admitted Scheme Claims of Iraq under the Scheme [of arrangement in respect of Rafidain] have never been used, are not in use, and are not intended for use, by or on behalf of the State of Iraq for any commercial purpose. 2. Any assets or distributions received in respect of any Admitted Scheme Claim of Iraq under the Scheme are not intended for use by or on behalf of the State of Iraq for any commercial purpose. 3. The State of Iraq has directed the Scheme Administrators, and intends to continue to so direct the Scheme Administrators, to transfer any assets or distributions in respect of any Admitted Scheme Claim of Iraq under the Scheme to the Development Fund for Iraq.").
199. [2024] EWHC 1503 (Comm).
200. Reece Thomas, *supra* n. 141, at para. 19.
201. *Ibid.; See also AIG Capital Partners Inc.*, EWHC 2239 and *Thai-Lao Lignite (Thailand) Co Ltd v. Laos* [2013] EWHC 2466.
202. *See Trendtex v. Central Bank of Nigeria* [1977] QB 529.

In *AIG Capital Partners Inc v. Kazakhstan*, it was held that the assets were not in use for commercial purposes *ipso facto* since the assets were considered property of the central bank and therefore *ipso jure* immune pursuant to section 14(4) of the SIA.[203] The fact that the funds were traded did not make them used for a "commercial purpose." According to Aikens J, "[t]he dealings of the securities accounts must, in my view, be set against the background of the purpose of the global custody agreement … In my view the dealings are all part of the overall exercise of sovereign authority by Kazakhstan."[204] Thus, the word "property of a central bank" meant all its property and not such parts that were used for governmental purposes only, which was contrary to what the award-creditor claimed. Aikens J clearly held that:

> 57. In my view the wording of *section 14(4)* is clear and imperative; hence the wording *"The property of a State's central bank … shall not be regarded … ."* The words are, in their natural meaning, not capable of qualification. When they are set in their context, as I have tried to do, it is clear that they should not be qualified. This has the following consequences:
> (1) All *"property"* of a State's central bank or other monetary authority is covered by *section 14(4)*. The only question is whether the central bank (etc) has one of the types of interests in the property concerned, as I have described the interests above, so that the assets concerned can be described as the *"property"* of the central bank concerned.
> (2) It does not matter whether the central bank is a department of the State or a separate entity. In all cases the central bank's property *"shall not be"* regarded as in use or intended for use for commercial purposes *"for the purposes of [section 13(4)]."*
> (3) Given the wording of *section 14(4)*, then the property of a State's central bank (or other monetary authority) must enjoy complete immunity from the enforcement process in the UK courts.
> (4) If the central bank (etc) has an interest in the property concerned, but the State of the central bank has another interest in the same property, then in my view the effect of *section 14(4)* is that the relevant property is immune from enforcement in respect of a judgment against that State, whether the property concerned is in use or intended for use for commercial purposes or not.
>
> …
>
> 61. Therefore I conclude that the words "Property of a State's central bank or other monetary authority" in section 14(4), when construed using common law principles of construction, mean any asset in which the central bank has some kind of "property" interest as I have described, which asset is allocated to or held in the name of a central bank, irrespective of the capacity in which the central bank holds it, or the purpose for which the property is held.[205]

Thus, the court did not consider it necessary to determine whether the property at hand was actually used for a commercial purpose due to the categorical position enacted in section 14(4).

203. *AIG Capital Partners Inc.*, EWHC 2239.
204. *Ibid.*, at para. 92.
205. *Ibid.*, at paras. 57, 61.

[4] *Mixed Use Property*

In *Alcom Ltd v. Republic of Colombia*, the judgment-creditor had identified a bank account in London which was held by or for the State's diplomatic mission.[206] In the first instance, the garnishee order was discharged because the ambassador had provided a certificate of non-commercial use. Generally speaking, property in the bank account of an embassy is presumed to be used for non-commercial governmental purposes. Even if property is partly used for commercial purposes, it can meanwhile be used for non-commercial governmental purposes too. The Court of Appeal had reasoned that the property in question was used for purposes outlined in section 3(3), i.e., in use or intended for use for a commercial purpose. The Court of Appeals reached this decision focusing on the nature of the use rather than the purpose. The House of Lords reversed the decision in the Court of Appeals. The House of Lords emphasized the distinction between immunity from jurisdiction and immunity from execution. The court did not break down the various purposes for which the accounts were used. It approached the matter more categorically by making a reference also to the German Federal Constitutional Court in the *Philippine Embassy* case. Somehow confusingly, though, the court made references to diplomatic immunity in the SIA (section 16) and the VCDR (Article 3). The bottom line is that the House of Lords refused to allow attaching the account of the bank embassy even though it was evident that the account was used partly to settle commercial debts. "While some of the funds in the accounts were used to pay commercial debts, the use was mixed and the [House of Lords] concluded that the [SIA] excluded attachment unless the account was 'solely' in use for commercial purposes."[207] Important to note is that the SIA does not contain the words "solely" or "solely used" and neither does the general position under international law impose such stringent requirement. The position in *Alcom Ltd v. Colombia* is at odds with other jurisdictions' position on assets used for mixed purposes.[208]

Adding to the difficulty of attaching and executing against property of mixed-use, the House of Lords found the ambassador's certificate to be conclusive, and therefore ultimately held that the property was in use for non-commercial purposes.

Notwithstanding such semi-conservative decision, in *Orascom Telecom Holding SAE v. Republic of Chad*, the bank account in question was considered to be in use for commercial purposes because the payments were made into separate accounts and one of the accounts held the revenues (oil royalties) paid into the bank and later to be used for paying loans owned to the World Bank.[209]

[5] *Piercing the Corporate Veil*

The House of Lords clearly articulated a distinction between State-owned entities and the State already in 1983, where Lord Wilberforce in *I Congreso del Partido* held that:

206. *Alcom*, [1984] AC 580, [1984] 2 WLR 750, [1984] 2 Lloyds Rep 24, [1984] 2 All ER 6.
207. Reece Thomas, *supra* n. 141, at para. 17.
208. Cf. Swedish jurisdiction below.
209. *Orascom*, EWHC 1841.

> State-controlled enterprises, with legal personality, ability to trade and to enter into contracts of private law, though wholly subject to the control of their state, are a well-known feature of the modern commercial scene. The distinction between them, and their governing state, may appear artificial: but it is an accepted distinction in the law of England and other states: *see C. Czarnikow Ltd. v. Centrala Handlu Zagranicznego Rolimpex* [1979] A.C. 351. Quite different considerations apply to a state-controlled enterprise acting on government directions on the one hand, and a state, exercising sovereign functions, on the other.[210]

The question is whether, why, when, and how the distinctness/separateness can be overcome.[211] The leading case is not one from the English courts as such but rather from the Privy Council, namely, *La Générale des Carrières et des Mines v. F.G. Hemisphere Associates LLC* (the *Gécamines* case).[212] *F.G. Hemisphere* had purchased two arbitral awards against the Democratic Republic of Congo and sought to attach and execute against the assets of *La Générale*, Congo's State-owned company. Before reaching the Privy Council, both the Royal Court and the Court of Appeal found in favor of the assignee award-creditor. In other words, the courts had "pierced the corporate veil." In so doing, the State-owned company was found liable for the debt of the award-debtor State, despite its separate and distinct legal existence.

In the *Gécamines* case, the Board asked itself what the correct approach is by distinguishing between an organ of the State and a separate legal entity and whether such distinction is relevant not only to questions of immunity but also to questions of substantive liability and enforcement.[213] The Board then reflected on the strong presumptive rule of distinctness or separateness and on such exceptional situations where the rule may indeed be overcome. In paragraphs 29-30, the Board offers the following analysis:

> 29. Separate juridical status is not however conclusive. An entity's constitution, control and functions remain relevant: paragraph 25 above. But constitutional and factual control and the exercise of sovereign functions do not without more convert a separate entity into an organ of the state. Especially where a separate juridical entity is formed by the state for what are on the face of it commercial or industrial purposes, with its own management and budget, the strong presumption is that its separate corporate status should be respected, and that it and the state forming it should not have to bear each other's liabilities. It will in the Board's view take quite extreme circumstances to displace this presumption. The presumption will be displaced if in fact the entity has, despite its juridical personality, no effective separate existence. But for the two to be assimilated generally, an examination of the relevant constitutional arrangements, as applied in practice, as well as of the state's control exercised over the entity and of the entity's activities and functions would have to justify the conclusion that the affairs of the entity and the state were so closely intertwined and confused that the entity could not properly be regarded for any significant purpose as distinct from the state and vice

210. *I Congreso del Partido*, 1 AC 244, at 258.
211. The domestic approach is found primarily in *Ben Hashem v. Ali Shayif* [2008] EWHC 2380 (Fam). The question is whether that approach should also be applicable in the international context. The courts rarely accept veil piercing. The threshold is a high one.
212. *La Générale des Carrières et des Mines v. F.G. Hemisphere Associates LLC*, [2012] UKPC 27.
213. *Ibid.*, at para. 28.

> versa. The assets which are (subject to waiver and to the commercial use exception in s.13(4) of the 1978 Act) protected by state immunity should be the same as those which against the states' liabilities can be enforced. This was, rightly, recognised by Pleming JA in the Court of Appeal (para 255).
>
> 30. There may also be particular circumstances in which the state has so interfered with or behaved towards a state-owned entity that it would be appropriate to look through or past the entity to the state, lifting the veil of incorporation. But any remedy should in that event be tailored to meet the particular circumstances and need. That is the position under domestic law (as to which *see* Munby J's final point in his para 164 quoted in paragraph 23 above). It must equally be so in the Board's view under international law. Merely because a state's conduct makes it appropriate to lift the corporate veil to enable a third party or creditor of a state-owned corporation to look to the state does not automatically entitle a creditor of the state to look to the state-owned corporation. Lifting the veil may mean that a corporation is treated as part of the state for some purposes, but not others.

Looking at both *Trendtex Trading Corporation v. Central Bank of Nigeria*[214] from the English jurisdiction and *First Nat'l City Bank v. Banco Para El Comercio Exterior de Cuba*[215] from the U.S. jurisdiction, the Board reasoned that "the existence of state control will not be a sufficient criterion, that the possession of a range of functions coupled with independence in their exercise will militate against a conclusion that an entity is an organ, and, generally, that caution is required before treating a separate legal personality as an organ."[216] The Board then concluded that the lower instance courts had treated the "Trendtex test" too generally and based on that treatment established an exception on "the existence of governmental control and the exercise of governmental functions."[217] Instead, the Board referred to the *I Congreso del Partido* and the fact that "governmental control is an ever present aspect of state-controlled enterprises which are not part of the state."[218] Even though control exists and some exercise of governmental functions visible, that does not in and of itself suffice to treat the state-owned entity as the State.[219] The Board reasoned that:

> There is no doubt that Gécamines had responsibility for operations in a sector of vital importance to the national economy of the DRC, but that may be said of many state-owned corporations in centrally planned or dirigist economies. It was true in I Congreso del Partido of Mambisa and Cubazucar, yet Lord Wilberforce recognised without hesitation the distinction between them and their governing state (to the control of which they were "wholly subject"): paragraph 9 above. There is no

214. *Trendtex Trading Corp. v. Credit Suisse*, [1980] Q.B. 629 (C.A.).
215. *First Nat'l City Bank* 462 U.S. at 611.
216. *La Générale des Carrières et des Mines*, UKPC 27 at para. 34.
217. *Ibid.*, at para. 43.
218. *Ibid.*
219. *Ibid.*, at para. 45. The Royal Court was of an opposite opinion, however. *See Ibid.*, at 53 ("The conclusion drawn by the Royal Court was that (para. 69): 'Overall, however, we find it impossible to avoid the conclusion that, as a matter of constitutional provision prior to recent attempts at reform, the exceptional degree of power accorded to the state over the affairs of Gécamines, at all levels, was such that the company was no more, in truth, than an arm of the state with responsibility for operations in a sector of vital importance to the national economy'.").

doubt that Gécamines' assets originated in the State, but there is nothing surprising or significant about that. Once it acquired them, they became its assets, albeit that dispositions and acquisitions were liable to veto by State authorities. Those in day-to-day charge of Gécamines' affairs were vulnerable to having any important decisions which they took reviewed and vetoed by other State authorities. But that does not mean that Gécamines had no real existence as a separate entity, or that it should be viewed for all purposes as assimilated to the DRC.[220]

Thus, the ultimate question for the Board was whether the circumstances show that the State-owned entity's juridical personality "and its apparently separate commercial assets and business were so far lacking in substance and reality as to justify assimilating Gécamines and the State for all purposes."[221] The Board refused to do so and concluded that "[i]n international law as in domestic law, lifting the corporate veil must be a tailored remedy, fitted to the circumstances giving rise to it."[222] Thus and overall, the Gécamines Case offers a strong presumption that a State and its State-owned entities are to be considered separate and that the latter does not bear the liabilities of the former and vice-verse. This separateness and distinction is made clear by the SIA.

In a recent case from the High Court of Justice in the British Virgin Islands, *Tethyan Copper Company PTY Limited v. Islamic Republic of Pakistan et al*, the court articulated the strong presumption established in the Gécamines Case.[223] In *Tethyan Copper*, the award-creditor had an arbitral award against the Islamic Republic of Pakistan and sought to attach and execute against one of its State-owned enterprises including its subsidiaries. The award-creditor claimed that the State-owned enterprise was "in effect, a governmental department of [Pakistan], and in consequence, [the State-owned entity's] assets are amenable to enforcement by [the award-creditor] towards satisfaction of the debt owed by Pakistan ..."[224] The court considered several factors as indicators of the State-owned entity being part of the State (e.g., the treatment of its assets as "national assets," 92% ownership by the State, its leadership and management structure, the financial support, political interference, etc.).[225] However, the court pointed out "other factors which point in the opposite direction ..."[226] Most notably, the court highlighted that the State-owned entity was a publicly listed company with some 56,000 other shareholders.[227] Having undertaken a thorough analysis of the *Gécamines* case, the court refused to apply veil piercing any less stringent in international law than in the domestic context.[228] Resultingly, the court did not equate the State-owned entity with the State as assimilated for all purposes.

Significantly, in both the *Gécamines* case and the *Tethyan Copper* case, the purported "control of the state-owned entity"—be it constitutional or factual—was not

220. *Ibid.*, at para. 54.
221. *Ibid.*, at para. 74.
222. *Ibid.*, at para. 77.
223. *Tethyan Copper Co. Ltd. v. Islamic Republic of Pakistan*, [2021] BVIHC (Comm) 2020/0196.
224. *Ibid.*, at para. 8.
225. *Ibid.*, at para. 69.
226. *Ibid.*, at para. 70.
227. *Ibid.*
228. *Ibid.*, at paras. 86-88.

considered to constitute proof of an "alter ego" or equivalent in and of itself. Such control, it was stated, is a common feature of State-owned entities.

More recently, in *Crescent v. National Iranian Oil Company*, a slightly different case dealing with the SOE transferring property away, the English High Court ordered the transfer of a property in London to the award-creditor.[229] The Iranian SOE had transferred the property to a pension fund under the State's supervision and control. The transfer was considered fraudulent and done for the purpose of avoiding enforcement. Therefore, it was ordered that the property be handed over for the debt of the SOE. A large portion of the case dealt with who was the rightful owner—the fund or the SOE.

[6] *Burden of Proof*

Pursuant to section 13(5) it is made clear that a certificate from the Head of Mission is sufficient evidence of the use of the assets. Such certificate creates a presumption *ipso facto* of non-commercial governmental use. Resultingly, where an award-creditor seeks to attach and execute against assets declared by the head of mission to be in use for a governmental purpose or intended for such, the award-creditor bears the burden of disproving such presumption. This is an onerous procedural obstacle placed on the award or judgment creditor. This obstacle proved instrumental in *Alcom Ltd v. Republic of Colombia,*[230] *AIC Ltd v. The Federal Government of Nigeria and the Attorney General of the Federation of Nigeria,*[231] *AIG Capital Partners Inc v. Kazakhstan,*[232] and *SerVaas Incorporated v. Rafidain Bank and Others.*[233] Professor Reece Thomas rightly noted that "[i]t will be hard, if not impossible to obtain evidence to rebut the Head of Mission's assertion, and so the claimant is greatly disadvantaged in trying to argue in favour of enforcement and against immunity."[234]

In *SerVaas Incorporated v. Rafidain Bank and Others*, the Supreme Court articulated exactly how meticulous the application of section 13(5) is where they stated that "the particular issue to be resolved in the appeal is whether there is any real prospect of SerVaas rebutting the presumption created by the Certificate that Iraq's right to receive payment of dividends from the Scheme in respect of the Admitted Claims as at October 13, 2010 was property which was not for the time being in use for commercial purposes within the meaning of section 13(4) of the Act."[235] Having set the burden of proof, after applying the facts to the law, the court reasoned that:

> On the facts of the instant case SerVaas cannot show that the Admitted Claims were property in use for a commercial purpose. It does not say that Iraq intended or intends to draw them down for commercial purposes. On the contrary, it accepts that they were intended to be used for sovereign purposes. By section 13(5) of the

229. [2024] EWHC 835 (Comm).
230. *Alcom*, [1984] AC 580, [1984] 2 WLR 750, [1984] 2 Lloyds Rep 24, [1984] 2 All ER 6.
231. *AIC Ltd*, EWHC 1357.
232. *AIG Capital Partners Inc.*, EWHC 2239.
233. *SerVaas Inc.*, UKSC 40.
234. Reece Thomas, *supra* n. 155, at 20.
235. *SerVaas Inc.*, UKSC 40, para. 10.

> Act, the burden is on SerVaas to prove that the Certificate that the property is not in use for commercial purposes is not correct. It cannot do so unless it can show that it is entitled to rely upon the source of the Admitted Claims and can show that the source is commercial and not sovereign.[236]

This shows that overcoming the presumption is difficult. That being so, it is far from impossible. In *Orascom Telecom Holding SAE v. Republic of Chad*, the court reached a decision against the State despite the contrary position being taken by the ambassador of Chad in his certificate.[237]

§4.3.3 Concluding Remarks

Speaking about the SIA, Lord Lloyd-Jones expressed that "[a]s the [SIA] enters early middle age, I think it is worth recording that, in general, it has stood the test of time reasonably well."[238] Whether such statement is accurate depends on one's position on the doctrine of sovereign immunity (theory and practice), what expectations one had on the SIA, and what aspect of the doctrine's scope is discussed (e.g., jurisdiction or execution). In the execution context, in general, and in execution as a result of an international arbitral award, in particular, the relative optimism for award-creditors is indeed shunned by the regressive treatment of the "commercial purposes" test, the onerous burden of proof with respect to the asset's destination, and the categories of assets treated immune *ipso jure*. As Reece Thomas notes and the doctrinal analysis of English case law above shows, the "[c]ourts are taking into account of the wider concerns by interpreting the 'commercial purposes' test in English law by reference to the broader international issues at stake which include a traditional deference towards foreign sovereigns."[239] This seemingly non-liberal/conservative attitude—or at least the lack of pragmatism—toward immunity from execution likely rests on the rationale that the "attachment of assets is a more serious erosion of immunity and can only be justified in very limited circumstances."[240] Therefore, the immunity from execution regime in the U.K. at times creates a situation which may leave a judgment- or award-creditor without a remedy.[241] One must not forget that this is also by design and is justified by important policy considerations.

Conclusively, the U.K. could, despite the aforementioned, still be considered a "liberal" jurisdiction for award enforcement purposes. The U.K., thus, falls in Level 2 and is a "Yellow List" jurisdiction. Quite frankly, this is barely so. The U.K. was close to falling in the orange, quasi-liberal category. Notably, this book's focus is limited to the study of enforcing arbitral awards against reluctant award-debtor States invoking sovereign immunity. This is indeed a conceptual caveat that is important to understand

236. *Ibid.*, at para. 30.
237. *Orascom*, EWHC 1841.
238. Loyd Jones, *supra* n. 161, at 24.
239. Reece Thomas, *supra* n. 155, at 4.
240. Reece Thomas, *supra* n. 141, at para. 16.
241. *Ibid.*, at para. 17.

in order to not read-in unnecessary or too wide conclusions to the "listing" of States (*see* §1.2.2[2]).

§4.4 SELECTED JURISDICTIONS

§4.4.1 China[242]

China has a modern arbitration act (the 1994 Arbitration Law of the People's republic of China), which was inspired by the UNCITRAL Model Law but is different from it in important aspects.[243] China is a Member State to the New York and the ICSID Conventions. China has also signed ISDS clauses; for example, in various IIAs.[244] China has thus far not been in the position to voluntarily comply with an adverse arbitral award, but there is no reason to believe that it would not.[245] Quite the opposite, China has a reputation for being pro-settlement and early dispute mitigation and prevention. China is most certainly a "pro-arbitration jurisdiction."

This section will analyze the issue of sovereign immunity and more specifically whether China is "conservative," "liberal" and/or "pragmatic."

As of January 1, 2024, the Foreign State Immunity Law (FSIL) of the People's Republic of China entered into force.[246] Before that, there was no Chinese law nor court case dealing specifically with sovereign immunity,[247] apart from the specific Law on Judicial Immunity from Measures of Constraint for the Property of Foreign Central Banks 2005 (the Central Bank Property Law) and case law from Hong Kong Special Administrative Region (HKSAR).[248] Moreover, China became a signatory to the UNCSI on September 14, 2005.

Notwithstanding signs of moving toward a restrictive theory of immunity already by signing the UNCSI in 2005, in 2011 the Standing Committee of the Chinese Congress

242. On the topic of China and sovereign immunity, this author has previously written a pretty negatively-oriented paper. This previously rooted conservative approach and absolute attitude has changed in the country, and therefore the author's perception as well. Hence, a new and modified paper is in progress that more accurately reflects China's current position. This section is a shorter version of that lengthier paper. For this chapter, I owe an extensive gratitude to Professor Lei Chen.
243. *See* Xu Guojian, "International Arbitration Laws and Regulations: China," in *International Comparative Legal Guide*, § 2.3 (2021-2022), https://iclg.com/practice-areas/international-arbitration-laws-and-regulations/china.
244. *Ibid.*, at § 14.2 ("China is a party to more than 130 BITs.").
245. Ning Fei, Wueyu Yang & Mariana Zhoing, "Investor-State Arbitration Laws and Regulations: China," in *International Comparative Legal Guide*, § 4.2 (2021-2022).
246. The People's Republic of China Foreign States Immunity Law (Passed by the 14th National People's Congress Standing Committee on September 1, 2023 and come into force on January 1, 2024), https://www.fmprc.gov.cn/wjb_673085/zfxxgk_674865/zcfg/fl/202309/t20230901_11137076.shtml.
247. Kaj Hobér, *Selected Writings On Investment Treaty Arbitration* 507 (2013).
248. The law was adopted for the protection of property of central banks in HKSAR but is applicable in the People's Republic of China and Macao SAR as well. However, *see ibid.*, at 509 ("The [Central Bank Property Law] does not deal with sovereign immunity in general, and therefore, does not shed more light on China's overall position on sovereign immunity, nor could it serve as a legal basis for the People's Courts to deal with a lawsuit in China [...].").

declared that "China's position on state immunity is normally referred to as 'absolute immunity', which has been reflected in the formal declarations and practices of the Chinese Government, as a legal fact widely acknowledged by the international community."[249]

To help underscore and understand China's traditional and evolved position on sovereign immunity, it may be helpful to understand the five principles underlying China's foreign policy: (i) peaceful co-existence; (ii) mutual respect of state sovereignty and territorial integrity; (iii) mutual non-aggression; (iv) mutual non-interference in each other's internal affairs; and (v) equality and mutual benefit.

[1] Legislation

In China, provisions related to state immunity can be found in four categories of legal sources: (1) general procedure law, such as Article 272 of the PRC Civil Procedure Law;[250] (2) Regulations issued by the State Council, for example, the *Regulations of the People's Republic of China on Diplomatic Privileges and Immunities* issued in 1986; (3) laws specifically enacted for specific matters, such as the *Law on Immunity of the Property of Foreign Central Banks in China* issued in 2005; and (4) relevant international conventions that China has signed.

Although Article 272 of the Civil Procedure Law, being a referral clause, does not provide substantive provisions on state immunity, it at least provides a legal basis for judicial authorities in China to follow when dealing with cases where foreign governments are defendants. The Foreign Central Banks Property Law was enacted to fill the legislative gap regarding whether the property of foreign central banks enjoys judicial immunity after the return of Hong Kong. When Hong Kong was handed over back to China, the U.K. SIA no longer applied, leaving a legislative gap in protecting the property of foreign central banks in the HKSAR. Notwithstanding this, if a foreign country does not grant immunity to the property of the People's Bank of China or the financial regulatory authorities of the HKSAR, or the granted immunity is lower than stipulated in this law, China will handle it based on the principle of reciprocity.

Later on, China's signing of the UNCSI in 2005 demonstrated its acceptance of the restrictive immunity theory. Nonetheless, before the FSIL, in 2011 the Standing Committee of the Chinese Congress declared that "China's position on state immunity is normally referred to as 'absolute immunity', which has been reflected in the formal declarations and practices of the Chinese Government, as a legal fact widely acknowledged by the international community."[251]

249. *See generally* Wenhua Shan & Peng Wang, "Divergent Views on State Immunity in the International Community," in *The Cambridge Handbook Of Immunities And International Law* (Tom Ruys et al., eds.), 67 (2019).
250. Article 272: Civil lawsuits filed against foreign individuals, foreign organizations, or international organizations enjoying diplomatic privileges and immunities shall be handled in accordance with the relevant laws of the People's Republic of China and the provisions of international treaties concluded or acceded to by the People's Republic of China.
251. *See generally* Shan & Wang, *supra* n. 249.

In summary, the legislative attitude of China toward national immunity has previously adhered to the principle of absolute immunity, but a shift toward restrictive immunity is evident. Since September 1, 2023, China enacted the FSIL which entered into force on January 1, 2024.

Generally, the FSIL states that a foreign State is entitled to immunity from legal proceedings (Article 3) and its assets are protected from enforcement/execution actions (Article 13) within the PRC. The FSIL then elaborates on specific exceptions. In addition to the primary exemptions, the FSIL introduces the principle of reciprocity, stipulating that the immunity granted to a foreign state may be diminished if that state provides a lower level of immunity to the PRC and its assets and vice-versa (Article 21). Furthermore, the law emphasizes that in cases of discrepancy, the provisions of an international treaty entered into or joined by the PRC shall take precedence over the FSIL (Article 22).

The term foreign State encompasses the foreign sovereign state itself and its entities or components, such as government departments or ministries, and extends to any organization or individual authorized by the State to exercise/engage in sovereign authority (Article 2). State-owned entities do not inherently enjoy state immunity. Interpreting the FSIL literally suggests that their immunity status hinges on their authorization to wield sovereign powers on behalf of the foreign state. It is important to note that under the FSIL, the Ministry of Foreign Affairs (MFA) can determine conclusively who is a "foreign State" by issuing certificates (Article 19). This gives the MFA a significant role in the foreign state immunity framework.

Four major exceptions to immunity from suits are provided in Article 12 of FSIL: (1) the validity of an investment arbitration agreement contained in an investor-state contract or a BIT; (2) the recognition and enforcement of the arbitral award rendered based on such arbitration agreement; (3) setting aside the arbitral award; and (4) other arbitration-related matters prescribed by law that are subject to the PRC courts' review. This is in line with international practice since arbitration proceedings are not directly affected by state immunity as they do not involve the exercise of jurisdiction by the court of one state over another state. The ambit of arbitration exception under Article 12 of the FSIL is not confined to arbitrations seated in the PRC or Hong Kong. Article 12 expressly provides that if a foreign state has agreed in an international investment treaty or otherwise in writing to submit an investment dispute between the foreign State and an organization or an individual of another State, including the People's Republic of China, to arbitration, that foreign state would no longer enjoy immunity from suit in these arbitration-related proceedings before the PRC courts including Hong Kong courts. In tandem with Article 305 of the PRC Civil Procedure Law, Article 12 of the FILS empowers the PRC courts to review investor-state arbitrations in civil proceedings.[252] This provides a legal basis from a domestic law perspective for

252. Mariana Zhong & Zeyu Huang, *PRC Foreign State Immunity Law: A Gateway to Judicial Review of Investor-State Arbitration by the PRC Courts?*, Kluwer Arbitration Blog (December 1, 2023), https://arbitrationblog.kluwerarbitration.com/2023/12/01/prc-foreign-state-immunity-law-a-gateway-to-judicial-review-of-investor-state-arbitration-by-the-prc-courts/.

investors to seek recognition and enforcement of investor-state arbitration awards (including ICSID awards) against foreign states in the PRC.

Moreover, as articulated in Article 7, a State may not be immune from legal proceedings related to a "commercial activity" if the said commercial activity involves the State and an entity or individual from another State (including the PRC) and either occurs within or directly impacts the territory of the PRC. Immunity for States in either of these circumstances is waived automatically, unless there are exceptions within each of these categories as well, e.g., if the property used belongs to the State's diplomatic and special missions, their central banks, or is of a military character (Article 15). Other exceptions include situations where a foreign state and its natural/legal persons expressly waive immunity in a case, submit a defense or counterclaim in a case being tried before Chinese courts, or engage in any issue pertaining to intellectual property rights where Chinese courts may have the right to exercise jurisdiction (Article 5).

The provisions in the FSIL dealing with sovereign immunity and execution are Articles 3, 13-15, and 21, as outlined below (google translate):

Article 3

Unless otherwise provided by this Law, a foreign State and its property enjoy immunity from the jurisdiction of the courts of the People's Republic of China.

Article 13

The property of a foreign State enjoys immunity from compulsory judicial measures in the courts of the People's Republic of China.

Submission by a foreign State to the jurisdiction of the courts of the People's Republic of China shall not be considered as its waiver of immunity from compulsory judicial measures.

Article 14

The property of a foreign State shall not enjoy immunity from compulsory judicial measures in the courts of the People's Republic of China if:

1. the foreign State has expressly waived immunity from compulsory judicial measures by an international treaty, a written agreement, a written document filed with a court of the People's Republic of China, or other means;
2. the foreign State has allocated or earmarked the property for the enforcement of compulsory judicial measures; or
3. the compulsory judicial measures are taken to enforce a valid judgment or ruling rendered by a court of the People's Republic of China, and the property of the foreign State is located in the territory of the People's Republic of China, used for a commercial activity, and connected to the proceedings.

Article 15

The following property of a foreign State shall not be considered as property used for a commercial activity provided for in sub-paragraph 3 of Article 14 of this Law:

1. property, including bank account, of diplomatic missions, consular posts, special missions, missions to international organizations, and delegations to international conferences, which is used for the performance of official functions or intended for such use;

2. property of a military character, or property which is used for military purpose or intended for such use;
3. property of the central bank or a financial regulatory administration exercising central bank functions of a foreign State or of a regional economic integration organization, including cash, notes, bank deposits, securities, foreign exchange reserves, gold reserves, and the immovable property and other property of the central bank or a financial regulatory administration exercising central bank functions;
4. property which forms part of the cultural heritage or archives of a foreign State, and which is not placed or intended to be placed for sale;
5. object of scientific, cultural or historical value used for exhibition, which is not placed or intended to be placed for sale as property; and
6. other property which a court of the People's Republic of China considers as not being used for a commercial activity.

Article 21

If the immunity accorded by a State to the People's Republic of China and its property is less favorable than those provided by this Law, the People's Republic of China applies the principle of reciprocity.

[2] Case Law

The case law in China may be misleading given the changes with the FSIL. Thus, the case law below illustrates the legal scenery before the changes in 2024.

Before the FSIL, China had made a declaration that it adheres to absolute immunity. This was the case despite having signed the UNCSI and was primarily evidenced by the reasoning and decision in the *FG Hemisphere v. DR Congo* (the "*FG Hemisphere* case"), where the Chinese MFA had sent several intervention letters to the HKSAR courts.[253]

The *FG Hemisphere* brought action before the HKSAR High Court in November 2008 against an award-debtor state as an arbitration enforcement matter. Initially, the DR. Congo challenged the jurisdiction of the court. The plea of sovereign immunity was brought up. Hence, the HKSAR High Court was confronted with which theory of immunity was to be embraced in HKSAR—i.e., the absolute or restrictive.[254]

253. *FG Hemisphere Associates LLC v. DRC* [2011] 14 H.K.C.F.A.R. 395. The office of the Commissioner of the Chinese MFA sent three letters. One on November 20, 2008 (quoted in the *FG Hemisphere* case at para. 197 (majority opinion)); one on May 21, 2009; and the last on August 25, 2010. All letters clearly articulating China's absolutist position *vis-á-vis* state immunity, stating that China adheres to absolute immunity and that it "has never applied the principle of restrictive immunity." *See generally* Hobér, *supra* n. 247, at 514-518. In one of the letters, the Chinese MFA in HKSAR had sought to articulate China's position vis-á-vis the UNCSI. It held, *inter alia*, that "3. [...] until now China has not yet ratified the Convention, and the Convention itself has not yet entered into force. Therefore, the Convention has no binding force on China, and moreover it cannot be the basis of assessing China's principled position on relevant issues. 4. After signature of the Convention, the position of China in maintaining absolute immunity has not been changed, and has never applied or recognized the so-called principle or theory of 'restrictive immunity' [...]." Hobér, *supra* n. 247.

254. *See* Volterra Fietta, *Absolute Immunity in Hong Kong* (2011), https://www.volterrafietta.com/absolute-immunity-in-hong-kong/ ("In 2004, FG Hemisphere Associates LLC ('FGH'), a so-called vulture fund dealing in distressed assets, obtained the rights in two arbitration awards

The High Court did not settle the issue on the theory of immunity to be embraced, but it did hold that the Congo had not waived immunity simply by agreeing to arbitrate and that the payment at hand was not "commercial" in nature.[255] The decision was appealed and heard before the HKSAR Court of Appeal, whereby a majority reversed the decision by concluding that the law in HKSAR is one of restrictive immunity. Moreover, it also held that the DR. Congo had waived its immunity, including immunity from execution. This was the law in place before 1997 and would remain applicable subsequently, unless, of course, it was inconsistent with "Chinese Basic Law." The Court went on to state that "no later inconsistent legislation had been enacted [and nor] had the Central People's Government applied any national law on state immunity to Hong Kong via Annex III of the Basic Law."[256]

The matter proceeded for final appeal before the HKSAR Court of Final Appeal with the outstanding questions on: (a) whether HKSAR could adopt a restrictive theory of immunity, (b) whether such position was consistent with the Basic Law, and therefore indirectly and ultimately (c) whether China adhered to absolute or restrictive immunity. The last question was especially interesting considering China's ratification of the UNCSI. The main take away from the eventual decision of the Court of Final Appeal can be summarized in the following two points:

> (a) The HKSAR cannot, as a matter of legal and constitutional principle, adhere to a doctrine of state immunity which differs from that adopted by the PRC. The doctrine of state immunity practiced in the HKSAR, as in the rest of China, is accordingly a doctrine of absolute immunity.
>
> (b) There is no basis in law for holding that [the DR. Congo] has waived its immunity before the courts of the HKSAR. Prior to rendering a final judgment in this matter, the court is under a duty pursuant to [the Basic Law] to refer and does hereby refer, the questions set out [in this judgment] to the Standing Committee of [China], being questions relating to the interpretation of Articles 13 and 19 of the Basic Law [...].[257]

In this light, a Chinese scholar described the continuing reluctance to accept the restrictive doctrine of immunity as a result of primarily three reasons:

given against the Democratic Republic of the Congo ('DRC'). FGH sought to enforce the arbitration awards against various assets belonging to the DRC in Hong Kong. The DRC acknowledged service for the purposes of disputing jurisdiction. The dispute raised two issues to be determined by the courts of Hong Kong. The first concerned the nature of sovereign immunity: which doctrine of immunity, 'absolute' or 'restrictive', is followed in Hong Kong? The second issue concerned waiver: had the DRC waived its immunity before the Hong Kong courts?"). For a more elaborate case note, *see* Shen Wei, *FG Hemisphere Associates v. Democratic Republic of the Congo [2011] 14 H.K.C.F.A.R. 395*, 108 Am. J. Int'l L. 776-782 (2014) https://doi.org/10.5305/amerjintelaw.108.4.0776.

255. For a good discussion, *see* Emmanuel Gaillard, "Effectiveness of Arbitral Awards, State Immunity from Execution and Autonomy of State Entities: Three Incompatible Principles," in *State Entities In International Arbitration* (Emmanuel Gaillard & Jennifer Younan, eds.), 179-193, (2008); *see also* Hobér, *supra* n. 247, at 511.

256. Hobér, *supra* n. 247, at 512.

257. *Ibid.*, at 512-513.

> The first, and most technical, arises from the arbitrary and inconsistent approach to distinguishing between sovereign and non-sovereign practices. The second, historical reason is that for many years China endured the imposition of extraterritorial rules by the West, resulting in an array of "unequal treaties" concluded under duress. The third, and a more cogent, reason is the vast number of Chinese state-owned enterprises (some of which are among the Global Fortune 500), which aggressively invest overseas and actively conduct a large number of cross-border commercial transactions.[258]

This reluctance was not new. China had agreed to the UNCSI as a matter of concession and it never entered into force. In UNCSI, China made "specific comments" to certain provisions in the convention in order to accept it, *inter alia*, Article 2(2); Article 10; and Article 18 (different numbering from the final version). China's comments included the following:

> **Article 2, paragraph 2, concerning tests for determining a commercial transaction**
>
> [...] A balance must be struck between the "nature" test and the "purpose" test to protect the property of States used for public purposes under exceptional circumstances. [...].
>
> **Article 18, concerning State immunity from measures of constraint**
>
> [...] The most serious concern is that article 18 fails to differentiate between pre-judgement measures of constraint and post-judgement measures of constraint. [...]. For post-judgement measures of constraint, the Government of China considers that, in principle, consent of the defendant State is also essential for the execution of such measures, especially in cases in which the defendant State is still contesting the jurisdictional immunity question. When a national court implements measures of constraint against the property of a defendant State without its consent, not only would such an action violate the famous legal axiom of *par in parem imperium non habet* but it could also strain relations between the two States. Therefore, there should be room for the Governments of the two States to resolve the question through diplomatic channels and the arbitrary enforcement of measures of constraint avoided.[259]

When signing the UNCSI, China was aware of the restrictive theory of immunity and that it extended to immunity from execution too. Notwithstanding this, before the FSIL entered into force and conversely because the UNCSI had not entered into force, the Chinese position on sovereign immunity remained absolutist and could be summarized as follows:

(1) Based on the sovereign equality of all states, sovereign immunity of states and their property is a principle of international law.

258. Wei, *supra* n. 254, at 780.
259. United Nations General Assembly, Fifty-sixth session, Convention on Jurisdictional Immunities of States and Their Property, Report of the Secretary General, Comments (reply from China, July 19, 2001) A/56/150.

(2) Unless a state voluntarily and expressly waives its immunity, all acts of a state per se or conducted on its behalf should be absolutely immune from foreign jurisdictions.
(3) A state-owned enterprise is an independent legal entity and should not enjoy immunities for its activities.
(4) Negotiations and international treaties should be utilized to deal with the differences among nations in relation to the issues of state immunity.
(5) China reserves its right to take counter-measures if any foreign state infringes upon sovereign immunities enjoyed by China and its property.[260]

Thus, despite the fact that China had signed the UNCSI, and despite the fact that such action was considered a sign that China was moving away from absolute immunity, it had not until the FSIL entered into force in 2024. Now it most definitely has. The *FG Hemisphere* case made it abundantly clear that China was firmly entrenched in the absolute immunity camp.[261] Similarly, the FSIL now makes it abundantly clear that China is firmly entrenched in the restrictive immunity camp. An award-creditor can under certain circumstances enforce an arbitral award in China by attaching and executing against an award-debtor state's assets.

Notably, China has also invoked sovereign immunity abroad in order to resist judgment or award enforcement.[262] For example, in *Walters v. Industrial and Commercial Bank of China*, the Chinese Ministry of Justice sent a letter to the judgment-creditor's counsel stating that "the execution of the request would infringe the sovereignty or security of the People's Republic of China."[263]

[3] Concluding Remarks

Conclusively, before the FSIL was implemented in 2024, China was a conservative—Red List—jurisdiction for award enforcement purposes. This did not mean that China was not a pro-arbitration jurisdiction for purely commercial matters, it was indeed. Despite the drastic changes with the implementation of the FSIL, and given that the law is relatively new and untested, it would be too early to conclude that China is a "liberal"—Yellow List—State. Taking its history into account, the rule of reciprocity, its invoking of sovereign immunity, and the fact that the law is untested, China falls in Level 1 and is an "Orange List" jurisdiction. However, it comes very close to being a "Yellow List" jurisdiction (*see* §1.2.2[2]).

§4.4.2 France

In France, arbitration is governed by Chapter IV of the French Code of Civil Procedure (Articles 1442-1527). French arbitration law is not based on the UNCITRAL Model Law.

260. Hobér, *supra* n. 247, at 507-508.
261. *Ibid.*, at 519.
262. *See, e.g.*, *Walters*, 651 F.3d at 280 ("Over the next ten years, the Walters unsuccessfully attempted to collect on the Missouri default judgment.").
263. *Ibid.*, at 285.

In France, there is a clear distinction between domestic and international arbitration law. France is widely considered arbitration-friendly.[264] France is a Member State to the New York and the ICSID Conventions and French courts have embraced a pro-arbitration attitude.[265] France has also signed ISDS clauses in most of its IIAs.[266] France has thus far not been in the position to voluntarily comply with an adverse arbitral award, but there is no reason to believe that it would not.

The question that this chapter deals with is whether the French approach to sovereign immunity from execution is "liberal" and/or "pragmatic." France has ratified the UNCSI. Moreover, given that the UNCSI has not entered into force, a separate law that closely follows the convention has been enacted—i.e., the "Loi Sapin 2," as it is called. Thus, the French law on sovereign immunity is nowadays statutory and embraces the "restrictive theory" on immunity both in the immunity from jurisdiction context and in the immunity from execution context. Despite this, the actual position on the law of sovereign immunity in France is largely to be found in and elucidated through case law. The French jurisdiction indeed embraces the restrictive theory of immunity, including in the execution context. However, French courts have not been as pragmatic when it comes to actually facilitating award-creditors in attaching and executing against State property through procedural rules.

France has: (1) signed the UNCSI; (2) enacted specific legislation on sovereign immunity; and (3) had a proactive court interpreting and applying the scope, degree, and nuance of the doctrine. The French law embraces the restrictive theory of immunity, but meanwhile makes a clear distinction between immunity from jurisdiction and execution. That being so, France has gone from being both liberal *and pragmatic* to adopting a more cautious, at times seemingly non-liberal, attitude.

[1] Legislation

France signed the UNCSI on January 17, 2007, and approved it on August 12, 2011. It has yet to enter into force (*see* Chapter 3). On November 9, 2016, the French Code of Civil Enforcement Procedures (CCEP) incorporated new rules on enforcement through the "Law on Transparency, Anti-Corruption and Modernization of Economic Life" (better known as the "Loi Sapin 2"). For the purposes of this chapter, it is enough to emphasize that Loi Sapin 2 incorporated Articles 18, 19, and 21 of the UNCSI on immunity from execution into French law.[267]

---

264. Marie-Laure Cartier, Alexandre Mayniel & Yann Schneller, *International Arbitration Laws and Regulations: France*, International Comparative Legal Guide § 1.3 (2021-2022), https://iclg.com/practice-areas/international-arbitration-laws-and-regulations/france.
265. *Ibid.*, at §§ 1.3, 11.1 and 14.1.
266. Julie Spinelli & Yann Dehaudt-Delville, *Investor-State Arbitration Laws and Regulations: France*, International Comparative Legal Guide § 1.1 (2022), https://iclg.com/practice-areas/investor-state-arbitration-laws-and-regulations/france.
267. *See* more in Ch. 5.

Article L.111-1-1 CCEP deals with post-enforcement matters before French courts. Article L.111-1-2 makes it clear that executing against State assets is only permissible where, *inter alia:* (a) the State has either waived its immunity from execution; or (b) the assets are used for a non-governmental commercial purpose. Thus, the code complies with public international law, in general, and UNCSI, specifically, in recognizing the restrictive principle of immunity from execution.[268] In this light, the CCEP also—like the UNCSI Article 21—establishes, in a non-exhaustive manner, the *ipso facto* "governmentally used assets" (*jure imperi* assets) that cannot be treated as attachable/executable commercial assets. Such assets include but are not limited to, diplomatic property, military property, assets of cultural heritage, assets forming part of an exhibition of scientific, cultural, or historical interest, and tax debts or social security debts.[269] Pursuant to Article L. 111-1-3, diplomatic missions enjoy extended protection. The relevant parts of Article L.111-1-2 and L.111-1-3 read as follows:

> **L.111-1-2**
>
> [...]
>
> Interim measures or measures of constraint over an asset belonging to a foreign State cannot be authorized by the judge unless one of the following conditions is met:
>
> [1.] the relevant state has expressly consented to the taking of such measure ...;
>
> [...]
>
> [3.] when a judgment or an arbitral award was rendered against the relevant State and that the asset in question is specifically in use or intended for use by the said State for other than governmental non-commercial purposes and provided that it has a connection with the entity against which the proceeding was directed.
>
> [...]
>
> For the application of [3.], are in particular considered as specifically in use or intended for use by the State for other than government non-commercial purposes, the following assets:
>
> (a) the assets, including any bank account, which are used or intended for use in the performance of the functions of the diplomatic mission of the State or its consular posts, special missions, missions to international organizations or delegations to organs of international organizations or to international conferences;
> (b) the assets of a military character or used or intended for use in the performance of military functions;
> (c) the assets forming part of the cultural heritage of the state or part of its archives and not placed or intended to be placed on sale;
> (d) the assets forming part of an exhibition of objects of scientific, cultural or historical interest and not placed or intended to be placed on sale;
> (e) labor or tax revenues of the state.

268. Robert Folloe & Guillaume Mezache, *Enforcement Against Foreign States: New Rules on Immunity Following the Loi Sapin 2*, Holman Fenwick Willan News (January 2017), https://www.hfw.com/Enforcement-against-foreign-states-Loi-Sapin-2-January-2017.
269. Code des procedures civiles d'exécution (CCEP), Art. L. 111-1-2 § 2 (Fr.).

L.111-1-3

> [...]
>
> Interim measures or enforcement measures may be taken against assets, including bank accounts, used or intended for the use in the exercise of the functions of diplomatic mission of foreign states, or of their consular posts, or of their special missions or missions to international organizations, only upon an express and specific waiver of the States.[270]

The law now requires a waiver to be both "express" and "specific" for Article L.111-1-3 purposes (i.e., with respect to diplomatic property), but arguably not so for Article L.111-1-2 purposes (i.e., with respect to commercial property). In other words, for diplomatic property to be attached and executed against, the waiver should be both: (i) written and free from ambiguity (the "express requirement"); and (ii) the assets to be attached and executed against should be clearly outlined (the "specificity requirement"). By contrast, for property with commercial purposes to be attached and executed against, the "express requirement" is arguably sufficient. A French author has taken note of the distinction as follows:

> [H]ad the Parliament wanted the waiver to be express and specific for both diplomatic immunity and immunity in general, it would have enacted one single section governing both types of immunities providing for the requirement of an express and specific waiver. This is not what it did; on the contrary, the Parliament chose to enact Section L.111-1-3 dealing with diplomatic immunity in general, which only requires the waiver to be express.[271]

Notwithstanding this, an award-creditor can execute against State assets held for a commercial purpose. However, such assets should belong to the entity against which the proceeding is directed.

As seen above, just as Article 21 of the UNCSI, the French legislation renders certain property immune *ipso jure*. Interestingly, however, central bank property is not mentioned in the French legislation and labor and tax revenues are added. That said, central bank assets are protected through special legislation. Section L.153.1 of the French Monetary and Financial Code renders assets of central banks, assets belonging to foreign monetary authorities, or assets managed for the State's own account or on behalf of foreign States, unattachable and inexecutable unless allocated for a commercial, private law activity.[272] Moreover, cultural assets that are placed in France on loan for public exhibits and certain specific assets of central banks are also not subject to seizure and execution.[273]

Through the new law, the legislative branch has introduced a new authorization procedure; that is, a creditor must first seek an order for either an interim relief or an

270. Translated in Fleur Malet-Deraedt, *The New French Legislation on State Immunities from Enforcement*, ASA Bull. 332 (2018) https://doi.org/10.54648/asab2018029.
271. *Ibid.*, at 344.
272. *See Ibid.*, at. 332.
273. *See* Law No. 94-679, Art. 61 (Fr., 1994) regarding cultural assets on loan and Code monétaire et financier (Monetary and Financial Code), Art. L. 153-1 (Fr.) regarding central bank assets.

enforcement measure against the State.[274] Such requirement is absent in the UNCSI. The procedural burden of judicial authorization prior to, or in advance of, the enforcement measures against State property, is indeed a procedural hurdle facing an aggrieved award-creditor.[275] Being cynical, it can prompt an award-debtor State to move assets, relocate assets (e.g., to SOEs), or "find a governmental use" for them.

Finally, Law No. 2016-1691 protects assets from speculative creditors (e.g., hedge funds): (a) where the debtor-State has benefited from OECD development assistance; (b) where the holder of the debt-security acquired the claim when the State was already in default or had proposed changed terms of the obligation; or (c) where the default status is less than 48 months at the time of seeking enforcement.[276] The law applies only to debt securities acquired after Loi Sapin 2 entered into force, and furthermore, the holder of the security must disclose the full financial terms of the acquisition in order to be certified by an auditor.[277]

[2] ***Case Law***

This book does not deal with immunity from recognition nor enforcement (i.e., what is known as "exequatur" in France).[278] The French terminology for recognition and enforcement may confuse the non-French speaker. Prior to Loi Sapin 2, France had no legislation to govern sovereign immunity. Therefore, the law on sovereign immunity was understood and created through case law.[279] Even after Loi Sapin 2, the court's role is one of developing the law by interpreting and applying it.

In 1984, the French Supreme Court (Cour de Cassation) ruled that State property can be executed against where it was "allocated for the economic or commercial activity governed by private law which gives rise to the proceedings."[280] Thus, the rule

274. Folloe & Mexache, *supra* n. 268; *see also* Xavier Nyssen & Emile Hu, *State immunity and arbitration in France*, Lexis PSL Arbitration (2017), https://www.lexisnexis.co.uk/legal/guidance/state-immunity-arbitration-in-france ("Under CCP Enforcement, art L 111-1-1, as introduced by the 'Sapin 2' law, a claimant seeking to seize a foreign state's assets located in France must seek an ex parte order (ordonnance sur requête) authorising the seizure from a juge d'exécution. Under the previous regime, provided that the creditor had title pursuant to inter alia a final award, the foreign state's assets could be seized directly through recourse to a bailiff, without recourse to a judge.").
275. Some have cautioned against this fear, *see, e.g.*, Malet-Deraedt, *supra* n. 270, at 335 ("prior judicial authorization should not be seen as too burdensome for creditors as ex parte applications are examined, pursuant to Section R.111-1 of the Code of Civil Enforcement Procedure, by judges in Paris with special expertise to deal with such matters and can be granted promptly, in a matter of days.").
276. *See* Folloe & Mezache, *supra* n. 268.
277. *Ibid.*
278. I have discussed the French approach to immunity from recognition and enforcement here: Ylli Dautaj & Maxime Chevalier, *A Liberal Push and The Sovereign Pull: Recognition, Enforcement, and Execution in The ICSID Convention*, 32 Am. Rev. Int'l Arb. 3 (2022). For a good shorter article, *see* Emmanuel Gaillard, *The Enforcement of ICSID Awards in France: The Decision of the Paris Court of Appeal in the SOABI Case*, 5 ICSID Rev. 1 (1990) https://doi.org/10.1093/icsidreview/5.1.69.
279. *See* Nyssen & Hu, *supra* n. 274.
280. *Eurodif et Sofidif v. République Islamoque d'Iran*, Cour de Cassation (March 14, 1984). For a translation, *see* Malet-Deraedt, *supra* n. 270, at 347.

lifting immunity for State assets used for a non-governmental commercial purpose was elaborated at an early stage.

The debates that have drawn considerable attention to the French jurisdiction have been largely focused on the so-called implied waiver doctrine, on the one hand, and on consent to execution through express waivers, on the other. Put simply, French courts have been instrumental in shaping the doctrine on what constitutes a waiver (implied or otherwise) of immunity from execution. In 2000, the French Cour de Cassation handed down the (in)famous *Creighton v. Qatar*[281] judgment, in which it held in unequivocal terms that:

> [T]he obligation entered into by the State by signing the arbitration agreement to carry out the award according to Article 24 of the [ICC Rules] implies a waiver of the State's immunity from execution.[282]

Thus, the highest court of the country had declared that an arbitration agreement (at least an ICC arbitration clause) constituted an implied waiver of immunity from both jurisdiction and, more importantly, from execution (i.e., a "double-waiver").

The *Creighton* award reversed a previous decision from the Paris Court of Appeals in *Republic of Iran v. Eirodif*,[283] in which it had been held that an arbitration agreement cannot be considered to constitute an implied waiver of immunity from execution.[284] The judgment in *Creighton* and its rationale have been the topic of intense debate ever since it was delivered. Leading French arbitration scholar, late Emmanuel Gaillard[285] noted that the *Creighton* doctrine stood "alone in comparative law and [was] in total contradiction with prevailing ICSID arbitration practice, as Article 55 of the [ICSID Convention] expressly preserves immunity from execution."[286]

Not unexpectedly then, the decision in *Creighton* was later reversed through case law. This reversed course was entrenched more recently by the legislative enactments of the Loi Sapin 2. In fact, not only was the decision overturned but the interpretation and application of explicit immunity waivers, even such referring explicitly to execution, were also questioned and debated with various outcomes.[287] For example, in 2000, the Paris Court of Appeals refused to entertain an express waiver of sovereign

281. Cour de Cassation, No. 98-19.068 (July 6, 2000), https://www.legifrance.gouv.fr/juri/id/JURITEXT000007043044/.
282. *See also* Gaillard, *supra* n. 255, at 179. This case was preceded by *Bec Frères v. Office des céréles de Tunisie*, Court of Appeals (June 20, 1996) (in which the court had endorsed a similar reasoning by stating that entering into an arbitration clause by the state constituted a waiver of immunity from execution since the agreement must be performed in good faith).
283. *People's Counsel v. Public Serv. Com'n*, 444 A.2d 975 (D.C. Cir. 1982).
284. Gaillard, *supra* n. 255, at 180. For a paper discussing the two contradictory positions in France prior to *Creighton v. Qatar*, *see* Nancy B. Turck, *French and US Courts Define Limits of Sovereign Immunity in Execution and Enforcement of Arbitral Awards*, 17 Arb. Int'l 3 (2001) https://doi.org/10.1023/a:1011295004421.
285. † May he rest in peace. Professor Gaillard was a big inspiration to this book's author, even though they never met. His scholarship lives in eternity.
286. Gaillard, *supra* n. 255, at 181.
287. This happened even the same year before the Paris Court of Appeals in *The Russian Federation v. NOGA* (August 10, 2000), where the court decided that an express waiver of immunity from execution was not to be construed as a waiver of immunity from attaching bank accounts that belonged to the debtor-state's diplomatic mission.

immunity by reasoning that a waiver of property being used for diplomatic purposes had to be both: (a) "express," and (b) "specific."[288]

In 2011, in *NML Capital v. République of Argentine,*[289] it was again held by the Cour to Cassation that an "express" waiver of immunity from execution was not enough to execute against bank accounts of a diplomatic mission due to the *jure imperii* element. According to the court, the waiver had to be both "express" and "specific." As a consequence, not only was *Creighton* reversed (at least in large parts) but the interpretation and application of waiver clauses were also radically narrowed. "Thus, absent an express and specific waiver, the only way to seize bank accounts of diplomatic missions is for a creditor to prove that such bank accounts are used for a commercial activity."[290]

However, one could say that the implied waiver doctrine laid down in *Creighton* referred to assets used for a commercial purpose and that the new more restrictive waiver doctrine focused more on assets used for diplomatic purposes. Hence, one could potentially argue that the case generated less contradiction than some seem to believe.

In 2013, the court doubled down on the narrow scope of an express waiver.[291] The Cour de Cassation held that:

> [P]ursuant to customary international law, as reflected in the [UNCSI], if states waive, in a written contract, their immunity from enforcement on property or categories of property used or intended to be used for governmental purposes, such a waiver must be express and specific, mentioning the property or category of property for which the waiver is granted.[292]

Thus, it was again made clear that even where award-creditors had included an express waiver of immunity from execution, they were effectively prevented from accessing bank accounts of diplomatic missions and assets used for public purposes where the clause was not specific enough.

In 2015, things took a slightly more liberal, yet unexpected, turn. In opposition to the 2011 and 2013 decisions, in *Société Commissions Import Export v. République du Congo,*[293] the Cour Cassation held that an express (but not specific) waiver of immunity was indeed to be construed as a waiver of immunity from execution, including from bank accounts of diplomatic missions. Thus, the contextually restrictive decisions handed down in 2011 and 2013 were overruled. Resultingly, the award-creditor was allowed to attach and execute against bank accounts held by the award-debtor State's embassy and its delegation to UNESCO in Paris, even though the clause was only

288. *See Russian Federation v. Noga*, Paris Court of Appeals (August 10, 2000).
289. Cour de Cassation, No. 09-72.057 (September 28, 2011), https://www.legifrance.gouv.fr/juri/id/JURITEXT000024617044.
290. Jaroslav Kudrna, *Fall of State Immunity from Execution in France: Let the States Beware,* 19 Int'l Arbitr. L. Rev. 6 (2016).
291. *NML Capital v. République of Argentine (3)* Cour de Cassation 1e civ. (March 28, 2013).
292. Malet-Deraedt, *supra* n. 270, at 340.
293. Cour de Cassation, No. 13-17.751 (May 13, 2015), https://www.legifrance.gouv.fr/juri/id/JURITEXT000030600444.

express and not specific. In its judgment, the Court reasoned that customary international law does not require a waiver of immunity to be specific, it only "requests that the waiver of immunity from enforcement be express."[294]

Whether the more restrictive decisions from 2011 and 2013 pertained strictly—or only—to diplomatic property has remained unclear. Some international lawyers were of the view that these decisions created a form of "autonomous regime" for diplomatic immunities, which was later crystallized through Article L.111-1-3 (discussed above), and others disagreed.[295] The broader regime on waivers—i.e., not only for diplomatic property—was later clarified through Article L.111-1-2, which states that a waiver (or consent rather) must be express.[296] Article L.111-1-2's waiver regime makes no mention of the specificity requirement. That said, Article L.111-1-2, however, definitely puts the *Creighton*, double-waiver doctrine to rest. Meanwhile, on a more liberal note, the same article put the cumbersome 2011 and 2013 holding to rest, too, by requiring a waiver to be "express" but not "specific." That said, award-creditors should exercise caution in their optimism; in practice, it may be less relevant that the specificity requirement is removed in Article L.111-1-2 since the double requirement is prevalent with respect to diplomatic property in Article L.111-1-3. Additionally, in practice, award-creditors are oftentimes able to trace central bank assets, which nowadays benefit from near absolute immunity pursuant to section L.153.1 of the French Monetary and Financial Code.

The French Cour de Cassation has already demonstrated this. In 2018, the court guided by Article L.111-1-3 disregarded the 2015 ruling that had removed the "specificity" element.[297] Thus, when the legislative branch codified parts of the law on sovereign immunity, it parted with the more regressive line of judicial authority, at least when dealing with diplomatic property.

Following this regressive evolution, in 2021 the Cour de Cassation held that central bank property (whomever held by) is unattachable assets, irrespective of any waivers, according to section L.153.1 of the French Monetary and Financial Code.[298] The Cour de Cassation had an opportunity to interpret the special legislation in light of Articles 19 and 21 of the UNCSI and customary international law. Instead of treating the

294. *See also* Nyssen & Hu, *supra* n. 274 and Malet-Deraedt, *supra* n. 270, at 337.

295. *See, e.g.,* Malet-Deraedt, *supra* n. 270, at 337 ("[T]he enactment of new Section L.111-1-3 clearly aims at overturning the 2015 ruling in *Commosimpex* and granting specific protection to diplomatic assets.") (cf. "To summarize the state of French case law after the 2011 and 2013 rulings in NML, the waiver of immunity from enforcement had to be not only express but also specific, whether it applied to diplomatic property or property used for governmental purposes.").

296. Malet-Deraedt, *supra* n. 270, at 343 ("[T]he wording of new Section 111-1-2, first paragraph, clearly marks the end of the *Creighton* solution [...] [and] this wording would also seem to mark the end of the 2013 ruling in *NML* [...].").

297. *See* Cour de Cassation, No. 16-25.190 (January 10, 2018), https://www.legifrance.gouv.fr/juri/id/JURITEXT000036670374/.

298. Cour de Cassation, No. 19-13.853 (May 12, 2021), https://www.legifrance.gouv.fr/juri/id/JURITEXT000043506796?init=true&page=1&query=19-13.853&searchField=ALL&tab_selection=all; *see also* Sally El Sawah, *Waiver of State Immunity over Central bank Accounts! Say No More!*, French Supreme Court Rules, EAPIL (August 5, 2021), https://eapil.org/2021/08/05/waiver-of-state-immunity-over-central-bank-accounts-say-no-more-french-supreme-court-rules/.

absolute immunity for central bank assets as a principle not yet settled under customary international law, and therefore entertaining an analysis of the purpose of the assets held in the specific bank accounts (i.e., functionally), the court went down a more categorical, absolutist route. In the 2021 case, not only were central bank assets treated with absolute immunity *ipso jure*, but not even an express waiver of immunity was considered to render such assets attachable and therefore able to be executed against. Commenting on the case, one French scholar opined that "it is important to attract foreign exchange reserves to the deposit of the [French Central Bank], yet, not at the high price of the Rule of Law."[299] This eloquently underscores the tension of the competing policies constituting the doctrine of sovereign immunity from execution as being conservative, liberal, or pragmatic.

Notwithstanding this, France has not walked away from holding award-debtor States accountable. Apart from the waiver case law, French courts also adopt the commercial purpose exception. Adopting such exception, the courts sometimes grant immunity and sometimes deny it—as is the practice in every liberal jurisdiction. Put simply, the rule is restrictive, not absolute. For example, in *Commisimpex v. Congo-Brazzaville*, the French Cour de Cassation dismissed the award-debtor State's plea of immunity from execution (and diplomatic immunity) when confirming the award in question against an aircraft (Falcon 7X) that was sold at public auction.[300] Congo-Brazaville had also invoked that the aircraft was used for the State's diplomatic mission, but the French court concluded that there was no proof of such use.[301] And at other times, the plea of immunity is granted. For example, in *N-Soft v. Chad*, the Paris Court of Appeal concluded that a property owned by Chad was protected by sovereign immunity for purposes of execution.[302] The court analyzed the use of the property and concluded that its future and intended use determines the status of the assets. Damien Charlotin has summarized the court's reasoning in a succinct manner as follows:

> For the court, however, French law recognised that sovereign immunities extended to the residential property of a foreign state designed to host its diplomatic personnel. The court further held that it was irrelevant that the property was not used as such at the time of the attachment, especially given evidence that Chad's new ambassador in fact desired to move there eventually. Moreover, given the residential nature of the property, the court also held that it made no difference that the property did not include any flag or other public indication of its function.
>
> Besides, the French foreign ministry had certified to the court its recognition of the building as a property designed to serve as the residency of Chad's ambassador—a recognition that had in fact predated the attachment by more than a decade. Lastly, Chad had produced evidence establishing that it had, in fact, never paid local taxes over the property at stake, the judges found.

299. *See* El Sawah, *supra* n. 298.
300. *See* West Africa Round-Up_ Tribunals in Place for Tax Dispute with Ghana, Enforcement Measures taken against Gabon and the Republic of Congo, and Developments in Cases Involving the Central African Republic and the Democratic Republic of Congo, IAReporter, April 3, 2024: https://www.iareporter.com/articles/west-africa-round-up-tribunals-in-place-for-tax-dispute-with-ghana-enforcement-measures-taken-against-gabon-and-the-republic-of-congo-and-developments-in-cases-involving-the-central-african-republi/.
301. *Ibid.*
302. *N-Soft Ltd v. Chad*, Paris Court of Appeal, September 12, 2024.

> As such, the appeal court confirmed the lower judgment that had lifted the attachment, and it made N-Soft bear the costs of the proceedings.[303]

Thus, the French court recognized the future and intended use as the prevailing one (i.e., not past or present use), showed significant deference to the State's certification of the intended use, and accepted the French executive branches' certificate of its perception of the intended purpose of the buildings.

Piercing the Corporate Veil

In practice, award-creditors often attempt to attach and seek to execute against an award-debtor State through its separate legal entities. Piercing the corporate veil manifests as a hurdle often unsurmountable to award creditors.

In 1985, the Cour de Cassation held that "assets of public entities, whether or not separate legal entities, distinct from the foreign State, when they belong to property that the foreign State allocated to a main activity governed by private law, can be seized by all the creditors, whoever they are, of such entities."[304]

Nowadays, for an award-creditor to be able to attach and execute against assets of, for example, an SOE, for the debt of an award-debtor State, the creditor needs to establish: (a) that there is a "lack of functional independence of the entity from the state"; and (b) that there is "an absence of a distinct estate."[305] The burden of proof is typically on the award-creditor and it is a high one indeed.

French courts have undertaken this exercise multiple times. For example, in *Winslow Bank & Trust Company Limited v. Société nationale des hydrocarbures*,[306] the Paris Court of Appeals held that:

> [E]ven though it is certainly established that SNH has its own separate assets comprised of real estate and securities, it results from [various factors] that SNH only appears legally and financially autonomous through the ownership of its own assets, with no real substance and without sufficient independence to take its own decisions, in its own interest, and cannot be considered to enjoy a legal or de facto autonomy from the State of Cameroon such that it could effectively be called a separate legal entity.[307]

---

303. Damian Charlotin, Chinese contractor obtains green light to enforce award and settlement agreement against Chad, but not against property found to be covered by state immunities, IAReporter, September 23, 2024: https://www.iareporter.com/articles/chinese-contractor-obtains-green-light-to-enforce-award-and-settlement-agreement-against-chad-but-not-against-property-found-to-be-covered-by-state-immunities/.
304. *Sonatrach v. Migeon*, Cour de Cassation (October 1, 1985). For a translation, *see* Malet-Deraedt, *supra* n. 270, at. 347-348.
305. Spinelli & Dehaudt-Delville, *supra* n. 266, at § 7.3.
306. *Winslow Bank & Trusk Co. Ltd. v. Société nationale des hydrocarbures*, Paris Court of Appeals (January 22, 2004). There are more recent instances where Parisian courts have refused enforcing arbitral awards against the assets of separate legal entities. *See, e.g.*, Ben Knowles, Khaled Moyeed, & Nefeli Lamprou, *The US$50 Billion Yukos Award Overturned: Enforcement Becomes a Game of Russian Roulette*, Kluwer Arbitration Blog (May 13, 2016), http://arbitrationblog.kluwerarbitration.com/2016/05/13/the-us50-billion-yukos-award-overturned-enforcement-becomes-a-game-of-russian-roulette/.
307. *See also* Gaillard, *supra* n. 255, at 191.

Thus, even though it is difficult to pierce the corporate veil, it is not impossible. That said, it should not be forgotten that in practice the piercing of the corporate veil in the context of execution remains a rare exception to the rule of presumed separability. It will in most cases not be enough to merely demonstrate that the award-debtor State owns most or virtually all of the shares in a company or that the State de facto controls the company. Piercing the corporate veil requires there to be a form of "alter ego" relationship or a fraudulent purpose behind the legal structure.

[3] Concluding Remarks

Gaillard and other leading French scholars have made the point that the recent legislative amendments in France have made the attachment and execution against State property nearly impossible.[308] The Loi Sapin 2 seemingly sought to adopt the universally agreed principles of sovereign immunity law as crystalized in the UNCSI. The objective of codifying customary international law into domestic legislation could be applaudable as such. However, the entirety of the UNCSI does not represent customary international law (*see* Chapter 3). Before Loi Sapin 2 and certain conservative court decisions as discussed above, France was "considered to be more liberal than [...] many other European countries which, meant, that under French law, it was relatively easy to enforce decisions against foreign States."[309] With Loi Sapin 2, France has made executing against award-debtor States more difficult than in many other trade-friendly and pro-arbitration jurisdictions in the world (cf., e.g., the United States and Sweden).[310] The onerous task of executing against State assets was already hard enough before Loi Sapin 2 with the burden of proof resting with the award-creditor, who has to trace, locate, and prove that assets are used for a commercial purpose. Such an obstacle is already difficult enough, especially considering that often the assets found are used for mixed purposes and there is generally a lack of general asset discovery.

For this author, it is nearly impossible to analyze the French evolution on the doctrine of sovereign immunity from execution without expressing an important cynical and contextual observation. How did France go from being liberal *and*

308. *See* Emmanuel Gaillard, *La Russie veut faire croire que ce sont les autres Etats qui violent le droit*, LES ECHOS (June 9, 2016), https://www.lesechos.fr/2016/06/e-gaillard-la-russie-veut-faire-croire-que-ce-sont-les-autres-etats-qui-violent-le-droit-208338; *see also* El Sawah, *supra* n. 298 ("In practice, it has become impossible to seize central bank accounts in France, regardless of their holder or the purpose of their use.") ("The legislative reform [i.e., the Loi Sapin 2] has *de facto* rendered any execution over foreign States' assets practically impossible. It is permissible in these circumstances to say that State immunity from execution in France has in fact become (quasi) absolute.").
309. Folloe & Mezache, *supra* n. 268.
310. *See, e.g.*, Phoebe D. Winch, "State Immunity and the Execution of Investment Arbitration Awards: A Review of the Plea of State Immunity and the Execution of Investment Arbitration Awards from the Viewpoint of the Forum State," in *Public Actors in International Investment Law, European Yearbook of International Economic Law* (Catharine Titi, ed.), 65, (2021) ("The enforcement landscape in France and Belgium has undergone legislative change, introducing procedural and substantive amendments which may have the effect of deterring, or at least rendering more difficult, enforcement proceedings going forward.").

pragmatic to now being moderately liberal and in some respects even conservative? This takes us back to politics and international policy. According to this author, it is difficult—if not impossible—to understand the evolution, theory, and practice of sovereign immunity without understanding its normative underpinning, i.e., what it is that justifies the doctrine. The ICJ has held that sovereign immunity rests on the principle of "equality" (*see* Chapter 2). This author has challenged such presumption and instead suggested that the doctrine seems to be more accurately justified against the backdrop of policy objectives and political concerns, i.e., a form of "comity." With this in mind, let us address the French evolution.

France has: (1) made it significantly more difficult for award-creditors to execute against award-debtor States; and (2) made it vastly more difficult for award-creditors to trade their claims to money in the open market by rendering it difficult for so-called speculators to acquire a debt instrument as security. This takes us to the political concerns and policy objectives in France that justified such pull from a more liberal and pragmatic place. The legislative changes came at a time when the political climate was anti-hedge funds buying claims against financially distressed States.[311] The practice of trading with State debt was said to be counterproductive to, *inter alia*, sovereign debt restructuring. Moreover, in the aftermath of the biggest investment arbitration award ever rendered (the USD 50 billion "Yukos case" against Russia),[312] the award-creditors sought to attach and execute against Russian property in France. This caused diplomatic tensions between France and Russia. It was in the aftermath of this, in 2015, that Russia enacted a new law on sovereign immunity which included a section on "reciprocity," i.e., threatening to "deprive foreign states of their immunity if they ignore Russia's immunity."[313] It has been suggested that the French legislative action with Loi Sapin 2 in 2016 was undertaken against this backdrop and that the provisions in the law were made with the aim to "grant more protection to foreign States' assets

311. Malet-Deraedt, *supra* n. 270, at 332 ("In recent years, certain creditors initiated in France aggressive strategies for the recovery of funds against foreign State property, which created increasing concern from the French Government as they were viewed as potential source of diplomatic conflicts."). For more on hedge funds and distressed states in the enforcement context, *see, e.g.*, John Muse-Fisher, *Starving the Vultures: NML Capital v. Republic of Argentina and Solutions to the Problem of Distressed-Debt Funds*, 102 Calif. L. Rev. 6 (2014); Stratos D. Kamenis, *Vulture Funds and the Sovereign Debt Market: Lessons from Argentina and Greece*, Crisis Observatory No. 13 (September 2014); Second Committee of the UNGA, *Sovereign Debt Restructuring: Lessons learned from legislative steps taken by certain countries and other appropriate action to reduce the vulnerability of sovereigns to holdout creditors*, UNCTAD (October 26, 2016), https://www.un.org/en/ga/second/71/se2610bn.pdf; Lucas Wozny, *National Anti-Vulture Funds Legislation: Belgium's Turn*, 2 Colum. B. L. Rev. (2017); Andrew Kelly, *Flight of the Condors: The Impact of Vulture Investors on Argentina's Sovereign Debt Default*, 30 Fla. J. Int'l L. 1 (2018); and Edette Lienau, *Sovereign Debt, Private Wealth, and Market Failure*, 60 Va. J. Int'l L. 2 (2020).
312. *Yukos Universal Ltd. (Isle of Man) v. The Russian Federation*, UNCITRAL, PCA Case No. 2005-04/AA227.
313. Federal Law No. 297-FZ, On the Jurisdictional Immunity of a Foreign State and the Property of a Foreign State in the Russian Federation. *See also* Victor Grandaubert, *France Legislates on State Immunity from Execution: How to Kill Two Birds with One Stone?*, EJIL TALK (January 23, 2017), https://www.ejiltalk.org/france-legislates-on-state-immunity-from-execution-how-to-kill-two-birds-with-one-stone/.

located in France."[314] Notwithstanding this, the French courts can still interpret and apply the sovereign immunity law with necessary pragmatism because the Loi Sapin 2 is not a comprehensive set of rules, "and therefore still leaves room for interpretation and further developments in French case law."[315]

We live in the real world, where the rules-based international order is still subject to policy objectives and political concerns. Some political and policy considerations are in fact too important for the maintenance of peace and security to cede to formalism or pure "legalism." Whatever position one takes, such considerations must be understood and at times even appreciated. As lawyers, we are bound to find comfort in the fact that we cannot see the entire picture, even though we fulfill an important purpose in civilization. In real life, some States push, and others are pushed. Our collective duty is to put this to a bare minimum. When this current tide of global skepticism is over, and multilateralism finds high standing again, France may eventually revitalize its former glory of being both liberal in theory and pragmatic in practice. Perhaps, the French jurisdiction will revisit the ethos expressed by its Advocate General in the *Islamic Republic of Iran v. Eirodif,*[316] where he eloquently expressed that:

> The necessarily voluntarist nature of the notion of the intended use of funds thus becomes a matter of pure discretion wherever, as here, the foreign government has not made its intentions known explicitly ... in practical terms the result will be tantamount to a return to the absolute nature of immunity from execution. The absolute nature of immunity in such circumstances would constitute a retreat to the time when governmental activity was confined to acts of public authority ... It would seriously endanger the security of international economic relations if States could, merely by remaining silent, protect themselves from any measure of execution aimed at securing compliance with their obligations.[317]

Thus, the French approach has swung like a pendulum from absolute immunity, to a liberal *and pragmatic* position, and then more recently back to a more cautiously liberal attitude with conservative features. One may submit that the French approach to sovereign immunity needs a little more liberté and egalité going forward, and a little less emphasis on sovereign-fraternité.

Conclusively, France could still be considered a Level 2, "liberal"—Yellow List—jurisdiction for award enforcement purposes (*see* §1.2.2[2]). France does not qualify for being considered "pragmatic" (Level 3, Green List). This is primarily a result of Loi Sapin 2, other special legislation protecting certain property as immune *ipso jure* and a series of relatively non-liberal and non-pragmatic case laws. In fact, France is closer to being on Level 1 (Orange List) than being on Level 3 (Green List).

314. Nyssen & Hu, *supra* n. 274. *See also* Grandaubert, *supra* n. 313 ("The recent decision to incorporate only Articles 18, 19 and 21 of UNCSI on immunity from execution was rather motivated by the fact that, first, the jurisprudence of the *Cour de cassation* had become unpredictable and, second, the French government was embroiled in diplomatic complications with foreign States.").
315. Malet-Deraedt, *supra* n. 270, at 350.
316. Cour de Cassation, No. 82-16.638 (March 14, 1984), https://www.legifrance.gouv.fr/juri/id/JURITEXT000007013942.
317. *Ibid.*

§4.4.3 India

India has a modern arbitration act (the 1996 Arbitration and Conciliation Act, as amended in 2015), which is modeled on the UNCITRAL Model Law. India is a Member State to the New York Convention but not to the ICSID Convention. Indian courts have recently started to embrace a so-called pro-arbitration attitude vis-à-vis ICA.[318] India has also signed ISDS clauses in most of its IIAs. However, the attitude toward IIAs, in general, and ISDS, in particular, has come to change. Traditionally, India settled and voluntarily complied with adverse arbitral awards but has more recently also refused to do so, including by invoking sovereign immunity.[319] India has also acted to terminate many IIAs. It may still be too early to assess India's overall attitude toward ITA, ISDS, and sovereign immunity in this context.

Now we move onto the analysis of whether India is "liberal" and/or "pragmatic" with respect to sovereign immunity from execution. India has no statute dealing with sovereign immunity. Historically, there was a requirement pursuant to section 86(3) of the Indian Code of Civil Procedure (CCP) to obtain a "prior-consent" from the executive branch before executing against State property. Such prior-consent is no longer a pre-requisite. India has embraced the restrictive doctrine of immunity, and it did so in 1982.[320] Already then, the High Court differentiated between sovereign acts and private acts and explained that the latter is identified by looking at the "nature" or "purpose" of the transaction.

Moreover, India has signed, albeit not ratified, the UNCSI. This clearly signals India's unequivocal adherence to a more liberal attitude with respect to sovereign immunity, including from execution. This position has been clarified in more recent case law.[321] Resultingly, the law of sovereign immunity in India is largely to be found

---

318. *See* Sumeet Kachwaha & Dharmendra Rautray, *International Arbitration Laws and Regulations: India*, ICLG § 11.3 (2021-2022) and *Vijay Karia v. Prysmian Cavi E Sistemi Srl*, Supreme Court, SCC Online 177 (2020). *See also Bharat Aluminium Company v. Kaiser Aluminium Technical Services Ltd.* (2012) 9 SCC 552; and *Union of India v. U.P. State Bridge Corporation Ltd* (2015) 2 SCC 52, which expressed India's emphatic policy favoring arbitration by comparing its arbitration act to that in England. The Court outlined the main or essential principles of arbitration law (e.g., the procedure being speedy, inexpensive, and fair; party autonomy; and minimum court intervention) and explained that arbitration law should be interpreted purposively with these principles in mind. This was a strong indication of India's pro-arbitration attitude and mimics very much the U.S. pro-arbitration policy, which too has been reflected in purposive pro-arbitration interpretation of the Federal Arbitration Act.

319. Emmanuel Gaillard & Ilija Mitrev Penusliski, *State Compliance with Investment Awards*, 36 ICSID Rev. 1, 38 (2021) https://doi.org/10.1093/icsidreview/siaa034; cf. Oiswarjya Basu & Shatrunjay Bose, *Cairn Moves to Seize Air India Assets to Recover Hefty Award Against India: Worthwhile Choice or a Futile Exercise?*, Kluwer Arbitration Blog (August 8, 2021), http://arbitrationblog.kluwerarbitration.com/2021/08/08/cairn-moves-to-seize-air-india-assets-to-recover-hefty-award-against-india-worthwhile-choice-or-a-futile-exercise/.

320. *See Uttam Singh Duggal & Co. Pvt. Ltd. v. United States of America, Agency of International Development*, *ILR* (1982) 2 Del. 273.

321. *See, e.g., Ethiopian Airlines v. Ganesh Narain Saboo*, (2011) 8 SCC 539 and *KLA Const Technologies PVT Ltd v. The Embassy of Islamic Republic of Afghanistan* and *Matrix Global PVT Ltd. v. Ministry of Education, Federal Democratic Republic of Ethiopia*, OMP (ENF) (COMM) 82/2019 & I.A. No. 7023/2019 (High Court of New Delhi, June 18, 2021) (hereinafter *KLA/Matrix v. Afghanistan/Ethiopia*).

in and elucidated through case law interpreting and applying customary international law. The Indian State has not taken actions contrary to the development of the restrictive theory of immunity in the execution context. Quite the contrary, Indian courts have elaborated for a rather strong exception for attaching and executing against State property, including by accepting the double-waiver doctrine (alternatively "implied waiver doctrine").

Whether India adheres to the restrictive doctrine of sovereign immunity as much in practice as in theory requires more data. India is new to the game.[322] With the limited data available, however, the substantive law seems to be supplemented by a pragmatic judicial attitude, culminating in case law that has effectively facilitated award-creditors in attaching and executing against State assets despite the plea of sovereign immunity. For example, the Delhi High Court has embraced an arbitration clause as an implied waiver of immunity from execution. Notwithstanding this, one needs to proceed with some caution to see whether the implied waiver doctrine actually stands the test of time and how it will be interpreted in scope, degree, and nuance (e.g., whether it will be understood as both an "express" and "specific" waiver, whether it applies for ITA awards, etc.). India is an interesting case because it could prove to be an orange list State as well as a green State. Time will tell.

[1] Legislation

India does not have an act specifically dealing with sovereign immunity. On January 12, 2007, India signed the UNCSI.[323] However, the convention has neither been ratified in India nor has it entered into force as a treaty. This notwithstanding, the convention holds significance in India as constituting in parts a codification of customary international law.[324] Both Indian senior advocates, as well as higher courts, refer to the UNCSI when dealing with the plea of sovereign immunity in India.[325] For example, in *KLA/Matrix v. Afghanistan/Ethiopia* (discussed more below), the petitioners argued that although the convention "*is yet to come into effect, India's assent thereto is significant and is an indicator of the espousal of a doctrine of restricted Sovereign Immunity.*"[326]

That being so, the starting point for an analysis of the doctrine of sovereign immunity in India is nevertheless section 86 of the CCP, which reads as follows:

> **86. Suits against foreign Rulers, Ambassadors and Envoys.—**
>
> (1) No foreign State may be sued in any Court otherwise competent to try the suit except with the consent of the Central Government certified in writing by a Secretary to that Government:

322. Ylli Dautaj, *Sovereign Immunity from Execution of Foreign Arbitral Awards in India: The "New" Kid on the (Super) Pro-arbitration Block*, 15 Arb. L. Rev. 19 (2024).
323. United Nations Convention on Jurisdictional Immunities of States and Their Property (UNCSI) adopted February 2, 2004.
324. *See, e.g., Jurisdictional Immunities of the State (Germany v. Italy: Greece Intervening)*, Judgment, ICJ Rep. (February 3, 2012), at 99 (hereinafter "*Jurisdictional Immunities*").
325. *KLA/Matrix v. Afghanistan/Ethiopia*, SCC Online Del. 3424, at para. 27 (petitioners invoking UNCSI).
326. *Ibid.* (reliance was placed on *Syrian Arab Republic v. A.K. Jajodia, ILR* (2004) 2 Delhi 704).

Provided that a person may, as a tenant of immovable property, sue without such consent as aforesaid [a foreign State] from whom he holds or claims to hold the property.

(2) Such consent may be given with respect to a specified suit or to several specified suits or with respect to all suits of any specified class or classes, and may specify, in the case of any suit or class of suits, the Court in which [the foreign State] may be sued, but it shall not be given, unless it appears to the Central Government that [the foreign State]—
(a) has instituted a suit in the Court against the person desiring to sue [it], or
(b) by [itself] or another, trades within the local limits of the jurisdiction of the Court, or
(c) is in possession of immovable property situate within those limits and is to be sued with reference to such property or for money charged thereon, or
(d) has expressly or impliedly waived the privilege accorded to [it] by this section.
(3) *Except with the consent of the Central Government, certified in writing by a Secretary to that Government, no decree shall be executed against the property of any foreign State.*[327] (authors emphasis) (articulation of inserted, substitutes and omitted words omitted)

In light of section 86(3), one outstanding issue has been whether an arbitral award is a decree in the sense that consent is required by the Central Government. This issue stems from the fact that section 36 of the 1996 Arbitration and Conciliation Act articulates that a final award "*shall be enforced in accordance with the provisions of the Code of Civil Procedure* [...] *in the same manner as if it were a decree of the Court.*" So, what does it mean for the award to be a decree? What does it mean for the award to be enforced in the same manner as a decree? Should the prior-consent requirement in section 86(3) of the CCP serve as a pre-condition to award execution?

One could argue that section 86 is a form of "virtually absolute immunity" and that it is not the court, but rather the executive branch that shall decide whether to revoke (i.e., condition) the privilege of immunity. Such reading would not be strange considering the time in which the section was adopted. Quite the opposite, such an understanding of section 86 would align with other developed States' approaches to the doctrine prior to the evolution of the theory of restrictive immunity. However, the Indian judiciary and the executive branch have made it clear that such an understanding is not accurate and does not reflect the law in India *de lege lata* (*see* below).

[2] *Case Law*

Two cases are of primary importance, namely, *Ethiopian Airlines v. Ganesh Narain Saboo*[328] ("*Ethiopia v. Saboo*") and *KLA Const Technologies PVT. Ltd v. The Embassy of Islamic Republic of Afghanistan*[329] ("*KLA/Matrix v. Afghanistan/Ethiopia*").

327. The Code of Civil Procedure, 1908, § 86, (India), https://www.indiacode.nic.in/show-data?actid=AC_CEN_3_20_00051_190805_1523340333624&sectionId=33423&sectionno=86&orderno=90.
328. *Ethiopian Airlines*, 8 SCC 539.
329. This was a consolidated matter, *see KLA Const Technologies PVT Ltd v. The Embassy of Islamic Republic of Afghanistan* and *Matrix Global PVT Ltd. v. Ministry of Education, Federal*

In *Ethiopia v. Saboo*, it was effectively reasoned that entering newer and more specialized statutes than the CCP may in some instances lead to implied repeal of certain parts of the code. On this line, it was held that being a member of a new and specialized convention may be interpreted as an implied waiver of immunity. In this case, the court also concluded that restrictive immunity prevails in India.

In that case, the Supreme Court dealt with a section 86(1) issue, i.e., immunity from jurisdiction. The question was whether Ethiopia could be brought before the Consumer Dispute Redressal Commission[330] (Redressal Commission), without a special consent pursuant to section 86(1). The Supreme Court not only classified the matter as a "suit" but also stated that section 86(1) did not apply because the CCP was an older and more general statute than the "more recent special statute, namely Consumer Protection Act, 1986 and the Carriage by Air Act, 1972."[331] The reasoning rested on the statutory interpretation principle that "specific statutes that come later in time trump prior general statutes."[332]

Importantly, it was also reasoned that Member States to the Warsaw Convention and signatories to the Carriage by Air Act have waived any immunity by entering into such instruments.[333] Thus, in *Ethiopia v. Saboo* case, the Supreme Court also ventured into a discussion on sovereign immunity under public international law, in general, and regarding the implied waiver doctrine, in particular. It relied on the decision in *The German Democratic Republic v. The Dynamic Industrial Undertakings Ltd.*[334] In that case, the Bombay High Court found that section 86 of the CCP does not "supplant" sovereign immunity pursuant to international law, rather it creates another exception to the plea of immunity.[335] Thus, the scope and extent of the doctrine on sovereign

Democratic Republic of Ethiopia, OMP (ENF) (COMM) 82/2019 & I.A. No. 7023/2019 (High Court of New Delhi, June 18, 2021).

330. A special body hearing claims pursuant to the Consumer Protection Act of 1986.
331. *Ethiopian Airlines* 8 SCC 539, at para. 72.
332. *Ibid.*, at para. 73.
333. *Ibid.*, at para. 76.
334. *German Democratic Republic v. The Dynamic Industrial Undertaking Ltd.*, AIR 1972 Bombay 27 (hereinafter *Germany v. Dynamic*).
335. *See, e.g., The United Arab Republic and Another*, AIR 1966 SC 230, para. 30 ("The effect of the provisions of section 86(1) appears to be that it makes a statutory provision covering a field which would otherwise be covered by the doctrine of immunity under International Law. It is not disputed that every sovereign State is competent to make its own laws in relation to the rights and liabilities of foreign States to be sued within its own domestic Courts. Just as an independent sovereign State may statutorily provide for its own rights and liabilities to sue and be sued, so can it provide for the rights and liabilities of foreign States to sue and be sued in its domestic Courts. That being so, it would be legitimate to hold that the effect of section 86(1) is to modify to a certain extent the doctrine of immunity recognised by International Law. This section provides that foreign States can be sued within the domestic Courts of India with the consent of the Central Government and when such consent is granted as required by section 86(1), it would not be open to a foreign State to rely on the doctrine of immunity under International Law, because the domestic Courts in India would be bound by the statutory provisions, such as those contained in the Code of Civil Procedure. In substance, section 86(1) is not merely procedural; it is in a sense a counter-part of section 84. Whereas section 84 confers a right on a foreign State to sue, section 86(1) in substance imposes a liability on foreign States to be sued, though this liability is circumscribed and safeguarded by the limitations prescribed by it ....").

immunity are to be found in public international law. This position was entrenched by referring to the English House of Lords in *Rahimtoola v. H.E.H. The Nizam of Hyderabad*[336] and the Court of Appeals in the *Trendtex Trading Corporation Ltd. v. Central Bank of Nigeria*,[337] after which the court concluded that restrictive immunity prevails and that a State cannot be immune with respect to commercial transactions.[338] Now, the question was whether such reasoning translated with equal force to the execution stage.

In *KLA/Matrix v. Afghanistan/Ethiopia*, the petitioners had argued, that the Ministry of External Affairs (MEA) had agreed, and the court later approved that there is no requirement under law for obtaining prior-consent of the executive branch under section 86(3) for execution of an arbitral award against an award-debtor State.[339] The court in *KLA/Matrix v. Afghanistan/Ethiopia* then went on to elaborate a double-waiver doctrine in light of the current standing of international arbitration as a preferred method of dispute resolution. The court reasoned that:

> [I]f Foreign States are permitted to stymie the enforcement of arbitral awards, which are the ultimate fruits of the above consensual process, on the specious ground that they are entitled to special treatment purely on account of being Foreign States, then the very edifice of International Commercial Arbitration would collapse. Foreign States cannot be permitted to act with impunity in this regard to the grave detriment of the counter-party in the arbitration proceedings.[340]

In *KLA/Matrix v. Afghanistan/Ethiopia*, the petitioners sought to enforce arbitral awards against the award-debtor States. Thus, the issue of sovereign immunity when enforcing and executing an arbitral award[341] against a State was implicated; that is, a section 86(3) issue. The court had to answer two questions:

(1) Whether the prior consent of the Central Government is necessary under section 86(3) of the CCP to enforce an arbitral award against a Foreign State?
(2) Whether a Foreign State can claim Sovereign Immunity against enforcement of arbitral award arising out of a commercial transaction?[342]

First, the court concluded, on well-settled principles of law, that "prior consent of the Central Government under Section 86(3) of the [CCP] is not required against the respondents" and that the award-debtor States should be "directed to deposit the respective award amounts with the Registrar General of this Court within four weeks"

336. *Rahimtoola v. Nizam of Hyderabad*, 1958 AC 379: (1957) 3 WLR 884: (1957) 3 All E.R. 441 (HL).
337. *Trendtex Trading v. Bank of Nigeria*, 1977 QB 529: (1977) 2 WLR 356: (1977) 1 All E.R. 881 (CA).
338. *Ethiopian Airlines*, 8 SCC 539, at para. 79. The court also looked carefully at American case law on the subject matter.
339. *KLA/Matrix v. Afghanistan/Ethiopia*, at para. 44.
340. *Ibid.*, at 50.
341. I am not using the term "foreign arbitral award" here since the arbitrations where conducted in India, even though it was still international commercial arbitrations. On this point, *see, e.g.*, *Bharat Aluminium Company v. Kaiser Aluminium Technical Services Ltd.*, (2012) 9 SCC 552.
342. *KLA/Matrix v. Afghanistan/Ethiopia*, at para. 2.

and if not, then the award-creditors shall be "at liberty to seek attachment of the assets of the [award-debtor States]."[343] The court went as far as to direct the award-debtor States to file affidavits of their assets in India (e.g., all assets owned and held in India, all bank accounts and bank statements held in India, all commercial transactions entered into by the respondents and their State-owned enterprises with Indian companies, etc.).[344]

On section 86(3), the Delhi High Court directed the Union of India to provide a statement as to whether consent of the Central Government was necessary pursuant to the code when enforcing arbitral awards. On this matter, the Central Government placed on record a statement from an under-secretary to the MEA, reading in relevant parts as follows:

> This has reference to your mail requesting consent to Matrix Global Pvt Ltd. Under Section 86 (3), Code of Civil Procedure, 1908 for execution of the arbitral award/decree against the Ethiopian Government. In this regard, I have been directed to convey the views of the Legal and Treaties Division of this Ministry that "the execution proceedings in respect of an arbitral award cannot be regarded as a suit for the purpose of Section 86 of the CPC. Thus, we understand that, for execution of an arbitral award, MEA's concurrence under Section 86 (3) CPC may not be required."[345]

It should be especially emphasized that the MEA was addressing specifically execution procedures.

Second, the court concluded that the doctrine of restrictive immunity prevails and that a State cannot claim sovereign immunity against enforcement of arbitral award arising out of a commercial transaction. Moreover, an arbitration agreement was said to constitute an implied waiver of immunity not only from enforcement but also from execution.

The court concluded that prior consent for the enforcement of an arbitral award against a foreign State is not necessary under section 86(3) and that section 36 of the Arbitration and Conciliation Act treats an arbitration award as a "decree" for limited award enforcement purposes.[346] It was held that treating it otherwise "would defeat the very underlying rationale of the Arbitration and Conciliation Act namely, speedy, binding and legally enforceable resolution of disputes between the parties."[347] Put simply, an award-debtor State cannot successfully plead the defense of sovereign immunity against the enforcement of an arbitral award arising out of a commercial transaction.[348] The court concluded that an arbitration clause in a commercial contract was considered an "implied waiver by the Foreign State so as to preclude it from raising

343. *Ibid.*, at para. 52.
344. *Ibid.*, at para. 55.
345. *Ibid.*, at para. 18. It is interesting to compare the statement from the MEA with that from China's MFA in the Hemisphere case, *see FG Hemisphere Associates LLC v. DRC* [2011] 14 H.K.C.F.A.R. 395.
346. *Ibid.*, at paras. 44, 46.
347. *Ibid.*, at para. 46.
348. *Ibid.*, at para. 45.

a defense against an enforcement action premised upon the principle of Sovereign Immunity."[349] The court reasoned that:

> In a contract arising out of a commercial transaction, such as the transactions which are subject matter of the present petitions, a Foreign State cannot seek Sovereign Immunity for the purpose of stalling execution of an arbitral award rendered against it. Once a Foreign State opts to wear the hat of a commercial entity, it would be bound by the rules of the commercial legal ecosystem and cannot be permitted to seek any immunity, which is otherwise available to it only when it is acting in its sovereign capacity. It is the purpose and nature of the transaction of the Foreign State which would determine whether the transaction, and the contract governing the same, represents a purely commercial activity or whether the same is a manifestation of an exercise of sovereign authority.[350]

Thus, the court had to first address whether consent was needed and then whether the foreign State nevertheless enjoyed immunity pursuant to international law on sovereign immunity. The court concluded that prior consent was not needed and that a foreign State does not enjoy immunity from execution when it has entered into a commercial agreement containing an arbitration clause for dispute resolution.

The Delhi High Court eloquently explained its justification for approving the double-waiver doctrine, i.e., that such logic is in "consonance with the growing principle of restrictive immunity, juxtaposed with the emergence of arbitration as the favored mechanism of international dispute resolution in the past few decades."[351] The one outstanding issue that was unfortunately not determined with sufficient clarity is whether entering into an arbitration agreement clearly and unmistakably constitutes a waiver of immunity from execution for all purposes. The case referred to "commercial transactions." For example, it is yet to be seen whether the implied waiver double-waiver doctrine includes the unilateral offers to arbitrate found in IIAs, namely, ISDS, and whether there are certain assets that cannot be touched *ipso jure*. Thus, we will have to wait and see whether Indian courts would offer the same pro-arbitration attitude also with respect to ITA. In such matters, States are sued for actions done in their public capacity as opposed to with respect to "commercial transactions"—compare *jure gestionis* with *jure imperii*.

Finally, one may wonder whether the court confused enforcement and execution. The use of the two otherwise different terms/concepts seems to be interchangeable and there is at least some reason to believe that there may have been a misunderstanding. Thus, we still need to figure out which assets can be attached and executed against, and which cannot be attached.

[3] Concluding Remarks

It is this author's submission that two fundamental questions, in two steps, must be asked and answered separately with respect to recognizing, enforcing, and/or executing an arbitral award in India:

349. *Ibid.*, at para. 47.
350. *Ibid.*, at para. 48.
351. *Ibid.*, at para. 50.

(1) *Question 1—Jurisdiction:*
   (a) Does section 86(1)-(2) of the CCP apply with respect to award recognition and enforcement matters; and if not
   (b) has the award-debtor State waived immunity or submitted to the jurisdiction of the court for purposes of recognition and enforcement?
(2) *Question 2—Execution:*
   (a) Does section 86(3) of the CCP apply with respect to award execution matters; and if not
   (b) has the award-debtor State waived immunity or submitted to the jurisdiction of the court for the purposes of execution?

The first part of both questions is based on domestic procedural law. The second part of both questions is based on the domestic courts' application of international law. In fact, it seems like the first part is yet another exception to sovereign immunity, and therefore can potentially override international law principles. That is the case if, for example, the Central Government of India consents to waive immunity, for which the second part of the questions above would be made redundant. Where consent is not needed, the courts must engage in an analysis of international law.

Indian courts have unequivocally and categorically removed the domestic procedural law hurdle from the equation by holding repeatedly that recognition, enforcement, and execution of an arbitral award is not to be equated with a "decree"/"suit" in the traditional sense of the meaning as understood in the CCP. The execution hurdle has not been discussed as extensively, but the Delhi High Court has ruled on the matter in an emphatically pro-arbitration manner more recently. Until the Supreme Court sounds-off, the situation in India could lay claim to be the most pro-arbitration worldwide—at least when it comes to enforcing international commercial arbitral awards against award-debtor States.

If one reads both the implied immunity waiver stemming from signing special statutes (*Ethiopian Airlines v. Ganesh Narain Saboo*),[352] together with the double-waiver doctrine pronounced in *KLA/Matrix v. Afghanistan/Ethiopia*, one could argue that both ICA and ITA awards (with the exception of ICSID awards perhaps) can be directly enforced *and* executed in India.

However, a major caveat remains India's difficult relationship with ISDS. As of 2024, 28 investment arbitrations had been initiated against India.[353] Initially, India complied with the adverse award rendered against it (*see*, e.g., *White Industries v. India*), but has more recently refused to comply voluntarily (*see*, e.g., *Cairn v. India*).[354]

352. *Ethiopian Airlines*, 8 SCC 539, at para. 76.

353. *See* Investment Policy Hub (India): https://investmentpolicy.unctad.org/investment-dispute-settlement/country/96/india/respondent and Gaillard & Penusliski, *supra* n. 319, at 38.

354. *Ibid. See also White Industries Australia Limited v. The Republic of India*, UNCITRAL, Final Award, (November 30, 2011) and *Cairn Energy PLC and Cairn UK Holdings Limited (CUHL) v. Government of India*, PCA Case No. 2016-7. Finally, *see, e.g., India Asks US court to reject Cairn Energy's $1.2 billion suit; cites "sovereign immunity,"* Business Today (August 17, 2021),

Conclusively, one could argue that India should be considered both a "liberal" and "pragmatic" jurisdiction. This is if one wishes to believe that the double-waiver doctrine will stand the test of time also in the ISDS/ITA context. However, for now, we need to proceed with relative caution and place India in Level 2, i.e., as a "Yellow List" jurisdiction (*see* §1.2.2[2]). This is because India has not really been tested on its stance that often, the position has not been clarified, and the Supreme Court has not delivered its opinion on the matter. This is especially so as pertains to ISDS/ITA. Whether India truly qualifies for being considered both "liberal" and "pragmatic" will be seen in due time. If the double-waiver doctrine stands the test of time, India could even lay claim to being the most pro-enforcement jurisdiction worldwide with respect to enforcing arbitral awards against reluctant State-debtors invoking sovereign immunity. Speculating cynically, it may be envisioned that India does not take such a strong pro-execution stance when it is asked to attach and execute against assets of a friendly or powerful State pursuant to an ISDS/ITA award (e.g., the U.S., the U.K., or Russia). If India changes course, it could fall down to Level 1 (orange list) because it is still relatively untested with the plea of immunity from execution in the international arbitration context.

§4.4.4 Russia

Russia has a modern arbitration act (Federal Law No. 5338-1 on ICA), which is largely based on the UNCITRAL Model Law (with some exceptions).[355] Russia is a Member State to the New York Convention. Russia has signed but not ratified the ICSID Convention. Russia has also signed ISDS clauses in most of its IIAs. Russia has, however, refused to voluntarily comply with adverse arbitral awards on multiple occasions.[356] Generally speaking, though, it can be said that Russia is a "pro-arbitration jurisdiction." Albeit Russia has indeed refused to comply with ISDS awards, it is a vivid user of ICA and has a robust system for both domestic and international arbitration. Russian investors, too, frequently participate in ITA, including SOEs, MNCs, wealthy private individuals, etc.

Is Russia "liberal" and/or "pragmatic" with respect to sovereign immunity from execution? During the USSR, the theory of absolute immunity reigned supreme.[357] When the USSR collapsed, the Russian Federation eventually came to adopt the restrictive theory of immunity.[358] Today, sovereign immunity is "based on a large

https://www.businesstoday.in/latest/corporate/story/india-asks-us-court-to-reject-cairn-energys-12-billion-suit-cites-sovereign-immunity-304409-2021-08-17.

355. Yulia Mullina, Valeriia Butyrina & Arina Akulina, *International Arbitration Laws and Regulations: Russia*, § 2.3 (2021-2022), https://iclg.com/practice-areas/international-arbitration-laws-and-regulations/russia.
356. Gaillard & Penusliski, *supra* n. 319, at 8, 32-34.
357. *See, e.g.*, Christopher Osakwe, *A Soviet Perspective on Foreign Sovereign Immunity: Law and Practice*, 23 Va. J. Int'l. L. 13, 14-15 (1982); and Kaj Hobér, *Enforcing Foreign Arbitral Awards Against Russian Entities*, 10 Arb. Int'l 17, 46 (1994) https://doi.org/10.1093/arbitration/10.1.17.
358. Andrey Panov, *Sovereign Immunity in Russia*, Lexology (July 31, 2019), https://www.lexology.com/library/detail.aspx?g=324495e8-844f-4e30-ad1f-6cb90417d206.

number of legislative provisions" that embrace the restrictive theory of immunity.[359] Moreover, Russia is a signatory to the UNCSI and even though the convention has not been ratified, Russia has enacted a statute dealing with sovereign immunity which is largely based on the UNCSI.[360]

Russia does embrace the theory of restrictive immunity. It can, however, be questioned whether Russia adheres to the restrictive doctrine as much in practice as in theory. The substantive law on sovereign immunity in Russia is not necessarily supplemented by a pragmatic judicial attitude and Russia's own actions when acting as an award-debtor State illustrates the opposite, more conservative attitude. As of 2021, there were 28 known investment arbitration cases brought against Russia under IIAs.[361] There are probably many more undisclosed ISDS and ICA matters. With the Russia-Ukraine war, the cases have increased significantly, and many are still "under the radar."[362]

The author of this book will not treat the Russia-Ukraine conflict as a scapegoat to express political opinions or seize the moment to articulate untested concepts of attaching/executing assets against a State. As unfortunate as the situation is, this author believes that the rule of law is one of three fundamental pillars of liberal capitalism/liberal democracies and does not wish to throw out the baby with the bathwater. For example, Ukraine's freezing and executing of assets against Russian SOEs will not be entertained in a book such as this, focusing strictly on law and legal application. Russia's categorization of "unfriendly States" will likewise not be mentioned more than necessary (e.g., as pertains to the matter of "reciprocity").

To this day, Russia has never complied with an adverse investment arbitral award rendered against it and has instead sought to annul/challenge awards and/or persistently resisted award-enforcement, including by invoking sovereign immunity from execution.[363] The last hurdle that an award-creditor may have to overcome in order to execute an arbitral award against Russia is sovereign immunity—and it is one that can indeed be expected.[364]

[1] Legislation

Federal Law No. 297-FZ on the Jurisdictional Immunity of a Foreign State and the Property of a Foreign State in the Russian Federation (Russian Law on Sovereign Immunity) accepts three exceptions to sovereign immunity from execution, namely, waivers, earmarking, and executing against property used for a non-governmental commercial purpose (resembling Articles 19 and 20 of the UNCSI). Moreover, as Article 21 of the UNCSI, the legislation contains a list of assets presumed to be immune *ipso*

359. *Ibid.*
360. Federal Law No. 297-FZ, *supra* n. 313.
361. *See* Investment Policy Hub (Russia): https://investmentpolicy.unctad.org/investment-dispute-settlement/country/175/russian-federation and Gaillard & Penusliski, *supra* n. 319, at 10.
362. Ten out of the 26 cases already initiated against Russia was due to the annexation of Crimea in 2014.
363. Gaillard & Penusliski, *supra* n. 319, at 33.
364. Hobér, *supra* n. 357, at 42.

jure. Thus, the law on sovereign immunity in Russia is nowadays based on the theory of restrictive immunity.[365]

The new law on sovereign immunity deals only with substantive law issues. In practice, the difficulty for an award-creditor, as in other jurisdictions endorsing restrictive theory, is that the "burden would be on the applicant to show [that] the property is used for commercial or other non-sovereign purposes."[366] However, in Russia, a court bailiff is empowered to search for assets owned by a debtor and owed to a creditor, and the doctrine of sovereign immunity is not an obstacle for such bailiff-search purposes.[367]

[2] Case Law

There is no decision directly dealing with sovereign immunity from execution. However, Russia's relative pro-arbitration attitude and the embracing of the restrictive theory of immunity can be distilled from a case dealing with the steps just prior to execution.

In 2017, the Court of Appeals held that an award-creditor cannot invoke sovereign immunity from recognition nor enforcement of an arbitral award because an arbitration clause effectively constitutes a waiver of jurisdictional immunity.[368] This reasoning was later repeated by the Commercial Court of the Stavropol Region, where the matter was re-heard because no assets were found in the Moscow region which could be executed against.[369] This was the first case on enforcement of an investment treaty award in Russia.[370] A Russian author described the rationale as follows:

> [T]he courts in Tatneft v Ukraine cases seem to have found that consent to arbitration results in waiver of immunity in relation to the proceedings for enforcement of the resulting award. At the same time, this waiver does not affect the ability of the claimant to cease [sic] assets of the state, which may be covered by sovereign immunity.[371]

A sharp distinction is drawn between immunity from jurisdiction (including incidental and ancillary enforcement jurisdiction) and execution. This is the position taken in most pro-arbitration jurisdictions: even though the award was recognized and enforced, some of the identified assets found in Moscow were protected as immune diplomatic property, and other assets were protected as immune cultural property (i.e.,

365. Noah Rubins, Maxim Kulkov, & Dmitry Vlasov, "Russia," in *Enforcement Of Investment Treaty Arbitration Awards, Globe Law And Business* (Julien Fouret, ed.), 566, (2021).
366. *See* Panov, *supra* n. 358.
367. *See Ibid.*
368. *See Tatneft v. Ukraine,* Court of Appeals, Russian Federation, Case No. 40-67511 (2017). *See also* Rubins, Kulkov & Vlasov, *supra* n. 365, at 566 ("The courts applied the general rules on enforcement of foreign arbitral awards [...], as well as the provisions on state immunity. Based on those provisions, the courts ruled that Ukraine's property was immune from enforcement, as the assets identified were diplomatic premises.") and Panov, *supra* n. 358.
369. *Tatneft v. Ukraine,* Supreme Court, Russian Federation, Case No. A63-15521 (2018). *See* Panov, *supra* n. 358.
370. *See also* Rubins, Kulkov & Vlasov, *supra* n. 365, at 566.
371. *See* Panov, *supra* n. 358.

immune *ipso jure*).[372] Interestingly, the Russian court did not really entertain a thorough analysis of the assets' mixed-use purposes.[373] Moreover, in Stavropol, the award was enforced, but also there the court held that "the question of the immunity of assets should be decided at the stage of execution, rather than at the stage of granting an application for recognition and enforcement of a foreign arbitral award."[374] There is no news that the author is aware of this matter.

When it comes to "veil-piercing," as a general rule the assets of SOEs cannot be attached and executed against the debt of the State.[375] The issue of piercing the corporate veil has been a long-standing issue for award-creditors against Russia; mainly because Russia frequently organizes its commercial activities through distinct legal entities.[376]

Practices in Foreign Courts and Political Pressure

Russia as an award-debtor State has vigorously refused enforcement and refuses to voluntarily comply with adverse arbitral awards. As a result, award-creditors are forced to spend years searching for commercial assets to attach and execute against.[377] The plea of sovereign immunity has complicated award enforcement against Russia, as is illustrated by the Sedelmayer and the Yukos sagas.[378] Award-creditors have been

372. Rubins, Kulkov & Vlasov, *supra* n. 365, at 566-567.
373. *Ibid.*
374. *Ibid.*
375. *See* Panov, *supra* n. 358.
376. *See, e.g.*, Osakwe, *supra* n. 357.
377. *See, e.g.*, the Sedelmayer saga and the Yukos saga. Mr. Sedelmayer won an arbitral award in *Mr Franz Sedelmayer v. The Russian Federation*, SCC, Award, 118 (July 7, 1998). The Yukos awards were decided in *Yukos Universal Ltd.*, *supra* n. 312. In both instances, the award-creditors have been forced to seek-out Russian assets across the globe and to engage in post-award proceedings, including facing the obstacle of sovereign immunity. *See, e.g.*, Gaillard & Penusliski, *supra* n. 319, at 33 ("[I]t took two decades, countless proceedings and important resources for Mr Sedelmayer to receive partial satisfaction.") and Evan Drake, *Sovereign Immunity for Russia's Rocket Engines? Enforcing the "Yukos" Award*, 45 Brook. J. Int'l L. 367, 367-368 (2019) ("In 2014, the former shareholder of Yukos Oil Company celebrated a major victory in their ongoing legal battle against the Russian Federation. After nearly a decade of litigation, the Permanent Court of Arbitration (PCA) awarded Yukos shareholders US $50 billion in compensation for Russia's expropriation of Yukos assets in violation of the Energy Charter Treaty (ECT).").
378. *See* Noah Rubins & Azizjon Nazarov, *Investment Treaties Ad the Russian Federation: Baiting the Bear?*, 9 Bus. L. Int'l 100, 107 (2008) ("It soon became clear that the Russian Government was not about to honour the Sedelmayer award voluntarily. Mr Sedelmayer sought out Russian state-owned assets in a number of Western European countries, but faced initial difficulties overcoming local laws on sovereign immunity of assets."). Drake, *supra* n. 377, at 368 ("In order to collect their award, the shareholders must convince national courts to attach Russian assets located within their jurisdiction. Most of these assets are shielded from attachment by 'sovereign immunity' ..."). Another such "saga" is the "NOGA case." The decision was handed down in *Compagnie Noga v. The Russian Federation*, SCC, Award (February 1, 1997) and has been followed by enforcement procedures in many jurisdictions, including France, Switzerland, and the U.S. *See also* Winch, *supra* n. 310 ("For example, the *Tribunal de grande instance de Paris* upheld Russia's immunity from execution in respect of land near the Eiffel Tower on which Russia was constructing a cathedral. The award-creditors were similarly met with mixed success in Belgium.").

forced to initiate enforcement proceedings all over the world, including in the U.S., the U.K., France, Belgium, Germany, and Sweden.

Apart from legislation and judicial activity, the Russian executive branch has been involved in expressing Russia's attitude vis-à-vis sovereign immunity. In practice, political pressure seems to have been successfully used to block the enforcement of arbitral awards.[379] For example, in the aftermath of the biggest investment arbitration award ever rendered (USD 50 billion), the award-creditors (Yukos) sought to attach and execute against Russian property in France.[380] This caused diplomatic tensions and "Russia vigorously opposed enforcement of the Yukos awards [and engaged in] diplomatic pressure and lobbying."[381] On this note, in 2015, Russia enacted the law on sovereign immunity which included a section on "reciprocity."[382] Russia immediately made good on this reciprocity threat and has, for example, issued diplomatic notes that any enforcement over Russian property would result in reciprocal seizure in Russia.[383] Thus, The Russian MFA is now "required to give recommendations on the extent of [sovereign] immunity granted to the Russian Federation in the foreign State in question before a Russian court makes a determination on jurisdictional immunity."[384]

Considering the chain of events in Russia and France juxtaposed, it has been suggested that the French legislative action in 2016 was made against the backdrop of Russia's political pressure and organized lobbying and that the provisions in the law were made with the aim to grant more protection to foreign States' assets located in France, including Russian assets.[385]

As one author described it, Russia has shown its willingness "to pursue an aggressive strategy of litigation to protect its assets abroad."[386] The plea of sovereign immunity from execution has proved to be an instrumental tool in this aggressive litigation strategy, manifested in various post-award proceedings. Russia has directed much energy and costs at shutting down award-creditors and persuading States where attachment and execution are sought in refusing to apply the doctrine of sovereign immunity in a liberal and pragmatic fashion. One cannot deny that, thus far, Russia has been successful in pushing its policy objectives and political concerns by threatening reciprocal treatment. All in all, Russia is using legal venues—both post-award proceedings and the plea of sovereign immunity are legal mechanisms that can be used by award-debtor States.

[3] Concluding Remarks

Russian law experts have noted that even a total victory against Russia in an investment arbitration is unlikely to lead to voluntary payment for the award-

379. Drake, *supra* n. 377, at 376.
380. *Yukos Universal Ltd.*, No. 2005-04/AA227.
381. Gaillard & Penusliski, *supra* n. 319, at 33.
382. Federal Law No. 297-FZ, *supra* n. 313.
383. Gaillard & Penusliski, *supra* n. 319, at 33.
384. Shan & Wang, *supra* n. 249, at. 64-65.
385. Nyssen & Hu, *supra* n. 274.
386. Drake, *supra* n. 377, at. 376.

creditor.[387] Moreover, it has been noted that even if domestic court practices and the legislation itself may be slightly more liberal than previously, "there is little sign that the Russian Government has changed its recalcitrance with respect to arbitration awards rendered against it."[388] Some authors have likened an award-creditor's asset-hunt against Russia to a game of "Russian Roulette."[389] Two scholars noted Russia's ambivalent approach to sovereign immunity as follows:

> Interestingly, in 2016 China and Russia signed a Declaration on the Promotion of International Law in which both countries "assert[ed] that international obligations regarding immunity of States, their property and officials must be honored by States at all times. Violations of these obligations are not in conformity with the principle of sovereign equality of States and may contribute to the escalation of tensions." Thus, it is clear that in spite of its new Federal Law on Jurisdictional Immunity (discussed above), Russia also reaffirmed the importance of State immunity.[390]

Thus, despite the theoretical endorsement of restrictive immunity through legislative enactment, the action of Russia through political pressure, bilateral agreements, and repeated pleas of sovereign immunity demonstrates a different and more conservative attitude.

Conclusively, Russia could be considered liberal in theory for award enforcement purposes but conservative in practice. For the combined reasons, Russia falls in Level 1—an "Orange List"—jurisdiction (*see* §1.2.2[2]).

§4.4.5 Sweden

Sweden has a modern arbitration act (the 1999 Swedish Arbitration Act), which is not modeled on the UNCITRAL Model Law but is nevertheless based on it and is indeed considered arbitration-friendly.[391] Sweden is a Member State to the New York and the ICSID Conventions and Swedish courts have embraced a pro-arbitration attitude.[392] Sweden has also signed ISDS clauses as seen in most of its IIAs.[393] Sweden has thus far

387. Rubins & Nazarov, *supra* n. 378, at 112.
388. *Ibid.*
389. Knowles, Moyeed & Lamprou, *supra* n. 306.
390. Shan & Wang, *supra* n. 249, at 66.
391. Lina Bergqvist & Maria Zell, *International Arbitration Laws and Regulations: Sweden*, ICLG § 2.3 (2021-2022), https://iclg.com/practice-areas/international-arbitration-laws-and-regulations/sweden.
392. Ulf Franke et al., *International Arbitration in Sweden* 296 (2013) ("Sweden has a modern arbitration law and a very well-functioning legal system. A long tradition of arbitration practice gives it the foundation to offer not just reliable, but also a responsive, arbitration service. This is also reflected when it comes to recognition and enforcement of foreign arbitral awards"). The court rejects enforcement in very few cases. *See Compilation of enforcement decisions of the Court of Appeal (2000-2012)* in *Ibid.*, at 300-302.
393. Ylli Dautaj & Rolf Åbjörnsson, *Investor-State Arbitration Laws and Regulations: Sweden*, ICLG § 1.1 (2022), https://iclg.com/practice-areas/investor-state-arbitration-laws-and-regulations/sweden.

not been in the position to voluntarily comply with an adverse arbitral award, but there is no reason to believe that it would not.[394]

The question of this chapter is whether Sweden is "liberal" and/or "pragmatic" with respect to sovereign immunity from execution. There is no legislation on sovereign immunity in Sweden.[395] The UNCSI has been ratified but has yet to enter into force. Thus, the Swedish law on sovereign immunity remains non-statutory, but it is clear from case law that the "restrictive theory" on immunity has been embraced—from jurisdiction as well as from execution.[396] The Swedish Supreme Court has emphatically endorsed parts of the UNCSI as a codification of customary international law.[397] Swedish courts have elaborated a rather strong exception for attaching and executing against property used for commercial purposes.[398]

Sweden adheres to the restrictive doctrine of sovereign immunity as much in practice as in theory. The substantive law is supplemented by a pragmatic judicial attitude, culminating in case law that has effectively facilitated award-creditors with attaching and executing against State assets despite the plea of sovereign immunity. By illustration, Swedish courts have not placed the burden of proof onerously high for award-creditors and have in specific instances even reversed the burden of proof on the State. Moreover, Swedish case law has demonstrated a highly award-creditor-friendly stance on so-called mixed-use assets as well as elaborated a less rigid approach vis-à-vis property considered immune *ipso jure*.

[1] *Case Law*

In practice, there two major exceptions to the general rule of immunity from execution that become relevant in the arbitration context are: (a) "waivers"; and (b) "property used for a commercial purpose" (i.e., the commercial purposes exception). There has been no case law on the "waiver" regime in Sweden. The focus has been on the commercial purposes exception and on property that may be considered immune *ipso facto*, on mixed-use assets, and on the burden of proof. There is no relevant case law on veil piercing in this context.

394. Furthermore, there is no known case where the Swedish state has engaged through diplomacy to assist Swedish award-creditors. *See Ibid.*, at §4.2 (2022), https://iclg.com/practice-areas/investor-state-arbitration-laws-and-regulations/sweden.
395. Ove Bring, Said Mahmoudi & Pål Wrange, *Sverige Och Folkrätten* 97 (2011).
396. *See, e.g., Västerås kommun v. Republic of Iceland*, (Swedish Supreme Court, NJA 1999), at 821; *Bostadsrättsföreningen Villagatan 13 v. Kingdom of Belgium*, Case No. Ö 2753-07, (Swedish Supreme Court, NJA 2009), at 95; *Sedelmayer v. The Russian Federation*, Case No. Ö 170-10, (Swedish Supreme Court, NJA 2011), at p. 475; and *Ascom, Terra et al v. The Republic of Kazakhstan*, Case No. Ö 3828-20, (Swedish Supreme Court, NJA December 10, 2021), s. 850.
397. *See Sedelmayer*, Case No. Ö 170-10, at 475 and *Ascom*, Case No. Ö 3828-20, s. 850.
398. *See generally* Kaj Hobér, *International Commercial Arbitration in Sweden* (2021); Ylli Dautaj, *Sovereign Immunity from Execution of Foreign Arbitral Awards: Sweden's Liberal and Pragmatic Contribution*, SAY, Ch. 13 (2020); and Ylli Dautaj, *Verkställighet av utländska skiljedomar mot statsgäldenärer I ljuset av immunitetsspörsmålet. Ascom v. Kazakstan*, JT 975 (2021/22).

In the arbitration context, two cases are of primary importance, i.e., the *Sedelmayer v. The Russian Federation*[399] (the "*Sedelmayer* case") and the *Ascom, Terra et al v. The Republic of Kazakhstan*[400] (the "*Ascom* case"). These are the only cases where the Swedish Supreme Court has dealt with the matter of immunity from execution of a foreign arbitral award. Both times the court ruled in a liberal and pragmatic manner.

The issues pertaining to sovereign immunity from execution of foreign arbitral awards were heard before the Swedish Supreme Court in the *Sedelmayer* case between Mr. Sedelmayer and the Russian Federation.[401] The award-creditor, Mr. Sedelmayer, had won an ITA against Russia. Russia did not comply voluntarily and as a result, the award-creditor had to engage in an "asset-hunt" in various jurisdictions. Following a long search for commercial assets, he was successful with attaching and executing against real estate in Cologne, Germany. The award-creditor continued and sought to attach and execute against real estate in Sweden. Thus, the issue at hand was whether the property owned by Russia in Sweden, including the rent that was generated, was used for commercial purposes or for sovereign purposes. Approximately sixty individuals were registered as residents in the property and two companies.[402]

The Swedish Supreme Court started by treating the UNCSI as a stepping-stone. It reasoned that "[t]he convention is largely—but not entirely—a codification of customary law."[403] The Court pointed to the fact that Sweden had ratified the convention and that parts of it could be viewed as a codification of customary international law.[404] Moreover, the Court "broke from the traditional commercial/noncommercial dichotomy and held that State-owned property used for noncommercial uses may not be immune from attachment."[405] The court reasoned that the commercial purposes exception in Article 19(c) of the UNCSI has been considered a codification of customary international, albeit that its contours must be given meaning.[406] The court reasoned in a liberal manner and one that in considerable ways lowers the burden of proof on the award-creditor and perhaps in some instances reverses it to the award-debtor State. The court stated that the phrase used for other purposes than government non-commercial purposes "cannot be considered to mean that immunity from enforcement measures can be successfully claimed solely based on the fact that a property is owned by a State and used for government non-commercial purposes."[407] The court continued and stated that there are some property of "a more specific nature" that can be cloaked in immunity, i.e., "such particular nature as stated in Article 21 of the UNCSI."[408] The fact that the court accepted the distinction in Article 19(c) as customary international

399. *Sedelmayer,* Case No. Ö 170-10.
400. *Ascom,* Case No. Ö 3828-20.
401. For a good analysis, *see* Pål Wrange, *Sedelmayer v. Russian Federation,* 106 Am. J. Int'l L. 347 (2012) https://doi.org/10.5305/amerjintelaw.106.2.0347.
402. *Sedelmayer,* Case No. Ö 170-10, at para. 2.
403. *Ibid.,* at para. 12.
404. *Ibid.*
405. *Ibid.,* at paras. 21-23.
406. *Ibid.,* at para. 14.
407. *Ibid.*
408. *Ibid.*

law was itself a major step in the direction of approving the restrictive theory of immunity in the execution phase.

The property in dispute was a building which had 48 apartments, out of which Russian diplomatic staff used 15 apartments. In other words, some were used for "governmental non-commercial purposes," but that was not entirely so because most apartments were used for commercial purposes (i.e., sublet for lease). First, the court noted that "[a]n individual property may be used for several, various purposes" and then noted that the real estate had mixed uses as it was partly resided by diplomatic staff (i.e., for "diplomatic purposes").[409] The court also explained that the possible diplomatic immunity is not to be conflated with sovereign immunity—i.e., that "the limits of state immunity and diplomatic immunity do not coincide."[410] When the property is tied to the representation of carrying out diplomatic functions, it enjoys immunity, but not necessarily otherwise. The Court then moved on to highlight the difficulty in mixed-use situations.[411] The property at hand was not a property where diplomatic functions were carried out and it was used partly for commercial purposes and partly for sovereign purposes. However, and despite such governmental use, the court ultimately concluded that the property was mainly used for "non-official," non-governmental purposes. The court presented the question as:

> [W]hat applies if the real property is used to some extent for official purposes or purposes nearly linked to the official purposes [...], but is mainly used for other purposes represented by the foreign state, for purposes that are a prerequisite to or consequence of a state run operation that is commercial or otherwise non-official in nature, or both.[412]

In undertaking this exercise, the court noted the onerous burden on an award-creditor because States cannot be forced to hand over information and therefore that regular rules on evidence in enforcement matters cannot fully be upheld.[413] The court focused on "the actual use of the property"; that is, the time when the application was received by the enforcement authority and not a time in place thereafter.[414] This is important because otherwise, the award-debtor State could turn non-immune property immune ex post facto. In this case, the most compelling fact was that apartments in this large complex were sublet for rental purposes. At the relevant time for assessment—i.e., when the enforcement authority received the application—the property was not used for governmental purposes exclusively, or rather *substantially*.[415] Consequently, the court held that Russia could not successfully invoke sovereign immunity from execution. The court finally concluded that:

> In light of the above, it is clear that the property ... was not to a substantial part used for the official purposes of the Russian Federation. The nature of the use has

409. *Ibid.*, at para. 15.
410. *Ibid.*
411. *Ibid.*, at para. 16.
412. *Ibid.*
413. *Ibid.*
414. *Ibid.*, at para. 20.
415. *Ibid.*, at paras. 21, 23.

> not otherwise been of such specific nature as to grant the property immunity from enforcement in the present enforcement matter.[416]

Thus, the court had adopted the commercial purposes exception and reasoned liberally on the burden of proof and the possibility of attaching and executing against assets of mixed-use. It is important to note that the court underscored that the UNCSI is largely—but not entirely—a codification of customary law. Moreover, the court noted that it forms a compromise between the opinions of different States.[417] That being so, the court reasoned that the commercial purposes exception in Article 19(c) of the UNCSI has been considered a codification of customary international law but that "there is an apparent disagreement ... on what should be considered a holding for government non-commercial purposes."[418] The emphasis on disagreements among various jurisdictions that was highlighted in *Sedelmayer* would prove instrumental when the court was asked to attach and execute against such possible *jure imperii* assets that are listed in Article 21 of the UNCSI. We now turn to this matter in the *Ascom* case.[419]

In the *Ascom* case, like the *Sedelmayer* case, the investors had won an ITA against the State in question (the Republic of Kazakhstan). Kazakhstan did not comply voluntarily with the award. As a result, the investors had to engage in an "asset-hunt" to execute the award against the award-debtor State. In this case, the Supreme Court concluded that assets held by the NBK did not enjoy immunity from execution.[420]

The court, as in *Sedelmayer*, started by analyzing the significance of the UNCSI and whether and to what extend its articles represent a codification of customary international law.[421] Like in the *Sedelmayer* decision, the court analyzed the purpose of the assets by focusing on Article 19(c) of the UNCSI and weighed situations where assets could be attached and executed against with situations where such execution should not be allowed, e.g., due to *ipso jure* limitations in Article 21 of the UNCSI. The Court reasoned as follows:

> 21. Article 21 (1) (c) is intended to provide central banks and other monetary authorities with special protection from enforcement measures. However, the extent of this protection appears unclear in international customary law. This applies in particular in light of the fact that, during the negotiations that preceded the Convention, there were different views on the issue and that no clear state practice has subsequently been developed.
>
> [...]
>
> 24. There is no clear support for the position that absolute immunity under international customary law also applies in respect of property which a central bank has at its disposal without any connection to the bank's monetary policy tasks. Furthermore, such far-reaching entitlement to immunity does not appear to be justifiable. The special level of protection to be enjoyed by central banks should

---

416. *Ibid.*, at para. 23.
417. *Ibid.*, at para. 12.
418. *Ibid.*, at para. 14.
419. *Ascom*, Case No. Ö 3828-20.
420. *Ibid.* Cf. *AIG Capital Partners Inc*, EWHC 2239.
421. *Ascom*, Case No. Ö 3828-20, at para. 14.

therefore be limited to such property as has a clear connection with the central bank's activities in the area of monetary policy. The extent to which other property owned by or at the disposal of the bank is protected from enforcement measures should instead be determined in accordance with the principles expressed in Article 19 of the Convention.

This discussion must be put into the broader public international law debate on assets of central banks or other monetary authorities. In international law three schools of thought have emerged:

(1) some States' legislation provides near absolute immunity from execution of central bank property (i.e., the *categorical approach* adopted in the UNCSI);
(2) some States protect central bank property only when it is used for central bank functions or for governmental purposes (i.e., the *functional approach*); and
(3) some States provide no special protection at all.[422]

The bottom line question for the court was whether Article 21(c) should be applied, and if so whether it was to be applied categorically or functionally. The Svea Court of Appeals went with the categorical approach. The Svea Court of Appeal had concluded that the attached property is absolutely immune because it constitutes central bank property and because such property is categorically immune *ipso jure* pursuant to Article 21(c) of the UNCSI.[423] Thus, the Svea Court held that Kazakhstan and the National Bank enjoyed immunity pursuant to Article 21(c), and therefore, that there was no need to analyze Article 19(c) of the UNCSI any further.

The Supreme Court, however, reasoned diametrically opposite and concluded that the scope of Article 21(c) of the UNCSI has not been firmly established in customary international law. Put differently, there is no general unification (state practice and *opinio juris*) on whether immunity for central bank assets should be treated as immune either categorically or functionally. The court reasoned that the *ipso jure* immunity approach was justified against the backdrop of the core central bank functions and that it was not applicable to all spheres where the central bank (or other monetary authority) may be active. The court elaborated a form of "connection test," whereby the bank must show a "clear" connection with the bank's core functions in order for immunity to be granted. In order to demonstrate such connection, the assessment is made by looking at Article 19(c) of the UNCSI, i.e., by looking at the purpose of the State's holding of the financial assets in question.

The court then proceeded to determine the purpose of the holding in the financial assets. The court held that financial assets that are bought and sold on the capital market oftentimes lack "an actual use," and therefore that an assessment of the

422. Ingrid Wuerth, "Immunity from execution of Central Bank Assets," in *Cambridge Handbook on Immunities and International Law* (Tom Ruys, et al., eds.), 266 (2019).
423. *See The Republic of Kazakhstan and the National Bank of Kazakhstan v. Stati, Ascom et al*, Case No. ÖÄ 7709-19 (June 17, 2020), at 14-15.

purpose cannot easily be done. Therefore, the assessment must proceed differently.[424] The court proceeded to analyze the motives behind the State's placement of capital on the capital market. The court explained that such motive and purpose can be reflected in, and elucidated from, the investment strategy undertaken and the possible risk and reward in such practice.[425] The court reasoned as follows:

> 28. An investor in listed shares and similar securities is indirectly exposed to the same business risks as the companies in which the investments are made. A state's primary motive for exposing itself to such risks can typically be assumed to be the same as that of other equity investors, namely better value development and higher returns than an investment that only aims to secure the real value of the assets. If the state's motive for the investment is not more developed than that, it cannot generally be regarded as an outflow of the state's sovereign actions. In order for immunity to continue to apply to such property, it must therefore be required that, over and above motives which are basically of a commercial nature, there are qualified purposes of a sovereign nature that are expressed concretely and clearly in the state's regulation of how the property is to be used. The mere fact that the state will be able to use the value of the property for government activities in the future or that the savings are intended for future generations cannot be considered to be enough.
>
> 29. A state's saving in financial assets on the international capital market may, like other government saving, per se serve a general macroeconomic function. However, this does not mean, without more, that such saving is to be regarded as a sovereign activity. For this to be the case, a more concrete link between, on the one hand, the form of saving and, on the other hand, the state's monetary policy or other acts of a sovereign nature must be required.

In the case at hand, the Supreme Court had to determine whether Article 21(c) was to be interpreted categorically (as the Court of Appeals had considered), or whether it was to be interpreted functionally (i.e., by looking at the function of the central bank vis-à-vis the assets). The non-commercial governmental purpose can only be demonstrated if there is a "qualified purpose of governmental character," which according to the court is "clearly" and "concretely" (i.e., clearly and unmistakably) reflected in the State's regulation of how the assets are used. Thus, in order to enjoy immunity, the financial assets shall have a concrete connection between the: (a) placement plan, and (b) the State's monetary policy or other non-commercial and governmental undertaking (i.e., *jure imperii* performance). The court reasoned as follows:

> 40. The special treatment of central bank property in terms of immunity is linked to the activity of central banks in the area of monetary policy. A question then is whether the attached property has a clear connection with the bank's central monetary policy function. (Cf. paragraphs 20-24.)

The court explained that the *ipso jure* immunity of central bank assets is connected to core central bank functions. Therefore, a functional analysis is instead entertained unless assets are held for such a core function/purpose. To determine

424. *Ascom*, Case No. Ö 3828-20, at para. 25.
425. *Ibid.*, at para. 27.

which is which, the court is guided by Article 19(c) of the UNCSI. In this case, the court considered the assets to be used in a commercial nature, and therefore the court had to determine the immunity issue in accordance with its already elaborated test, i.e., whether there was such a concrete and clear connection to a non-commercial governmental purpose (*jure imperii*) that the assets nevertheless, despite its otherwise commercial nature, were covered by immunity from execution.[426] The court reasoned as follows:

> 45. What Kazakhstan and the National Bank have stated regarding future state purposes is framed in very general terms and the presented regulation of the National Fund does not specifically express what those purposes are. Nor has it otherwise come to light that, prior to attachment, it had been decided that the attached property should be used for any specified state purpose. A clear connection between the attached property and a qualified purpose of a sovereign nature is therefore lacking. In this context it should be noted that long-term savings for future—as-of-yet specified—needs cannot be regarded as being of a sovereign nature. (Cf. paragraph 28.)
>
> 46. The National Fund, which includes the savings portfolio, is per se also intended to "ensure macroeconomic stability." The underlying idea seems to be that the long-term savings in the savings portfolio should create the conditions for taking budgetary stabilizing and similar measures even in the future perspective. However, the link between the attached property and this stabilization purpose must, however, be described as weak. A fulfillment of this purpose requires not only the sale of the shares, but also—as the Kazakh regulation has been described in the case—that the value of what has been sold is subsequently transferred from the savings portfolio to the stabilization portfolio in order, in the next step, to be transferred to the state budget. This link cannot be considered concrete enough to justify immunity in respect of property of the present kind (cf. paragraph 29).

Thus, the Supreme Court has lowered the burden of proof for award-creditors in order to demonstrate that the assets are used commercially. Moreover, the burden of proof is reversed on the award-debtor State to show that the assets are *clearly and concretely* connected to the use of a non-commercial governmental purpose (*jure imperii*).

The court concluded, in line with the precedent already set in *Sedelmayer* that the substantial purpose of the asset, at the date of execution, was on a more general plane to contribute to the economy of Kazakhstan long-term and that such use and purpose is not enough to qualify as being in use for a non-commercial governmental purpose (*jure imperii*) in accordance with the law of sovereign immunity.[427]

[2] Concluding Remarks

The *Sedelmayer* decision leaves us with two main takeaways: (1) the Swedish courts treat parts of the UNCSI as a manifestation of customary international law, and thus a stepping-stone for further analysis of the law of sovereign immunity; and (2) the

426. *Ibid.*, at para. 36.
427. *Ibid.*, at para. 47.

Swedish courts interpret the UNCSI liberally and pragmatically as was demonstrated by the "substantial part" test with respect to property used for mixed-purposes. The *Ascom* decision entrenches the liberal and pragmatic reasoning in the *Sedelmayer* case by widening the pool of assets that can be executed against and lowering the burden of proof for the award-creditor.

Conclusively, Sweden could be considered both a liberal and pragmatic jurisdiction—in theory and in practice—for award enforcement purposes. Sweden falls in Level 3 and is a "Green List" jurisdiction (*see* §1.2.2[2]).

CHAPTER 5
Legal and Non-legal Solutions to Immunity from Execution

This book has investigated whether the doctrinal understanding of sovereign immunity from execution (in *theory*) and its interpretation and application in the international arbitration context (in *practice*) sit well with a twenty-first-century global marketplace.

To answer the question, this book has investigated doctrinally (a) whether and how domestic legislators and courts have contributed to shaping the law on sovereign immunity from execution, in general, and in the arbitration context, in particular. Following such exploration of the substantive law, this book investigated in a more practically driven study (b) whether and how domestic legislators and courts have facilitated award execution through its procedural rules and court practices.

This chapter will succinctly re-articulate the substantive law and procedural rules solutions identified in Chapter 4 and additionally explore (c) potential non-legal solutions that can assist an award-creditor against a reluctant award-debtor State. Such non-legal solutions can be more immediate (e.g., market-based solutions) and long-term (e.g., norms-based solutions).

This chapter will outline various substantive law-based solutions (§5.1), procedural rules-based solutions (§5.2), market-based solutions (§5.3), and norms-based solutions (§5.4).

§5.1 SUBSTANTIVE LAW-BASED SOLUTIONS

§5.1.1 Immunity from Jurisdiction and Immunity from Execution

One distant solution would be to treat immunity from jurisdiction and execution in the same manner, i.e., not having different tests and exceptions. In such a world, if a State cannot invoke immunity from jurisdiction, neither can it invoke immunity from execution. This proposition treats the distinction between immunity from jurisdiction and immunity from execution as fictional and as an idea not really anchored in legal theory. This idea would not be suggesting that States should not be able to invoke immunity for "any" property, but rather it suggests that there should be no immunity from execution if there is no immunity from jurisdiction, in a first step, and then moving onto the fact that certain property may be protected *ipso jure*.

Treating the two stages in conjunction—i.e., that execution should result automatically (with some exceptions) from the removal of jurisdictional immunity—is practiced by the Swiss court for litigation purposes. Thus, in Switzerland, if the court has adjudicatory jurisdiction, the same court cannot be said to lack execution jurisdiction.[1] As a matter of law, such practice makes a lot of sense. Such idea, however, is rather perplexing where the product to be executed was not the product of that State's courts but rather by a Tribunal (often sitting in a foreign jurisdiction).

Put simply: a legal reform could be to treat the sovereign immunity regime as one and therefore refrain from making the artificial distinction between immunity from jurisdiction and immunity from execution. This is not likely to happen anytime soon—and where it is, it will likely mimic the Swiss approach whereby if the courts have jurisdiction and render a judgment, the same courts/authorities have powers vis-à-vis execution. That does not preempt the question of foreign judgments and (international) arbitral awards.

§5.1.2 Nature or Purpose

It has been noted with quite rigor that "[t]here is a general rule that, even if judgment against a State based on an act *jure gestionis* has been entered, measures of execution against that State's property may not be taken without the foreign State's consent if the asset in question serve governmental purposes."[2] Thus, due to the difference in treatment of immunity from jurisdiction and immunity from execution, the prevalent test to decide whether the asset is commercial is different too. When dealing with immunity from jurisdiction, the prevalent test is the Nature Test. When dealing with immunity from execution, the prevalent test is the Purpose Test. The former is easier to overcome for award-creditors, while the latter places quite an onerous and high burden on the award-creditor. Thus, the treatment of immunity from jurisdiction and execution separately leads to different tests, which leads to differences in the burden of proof.

Thus, a possible legal reform would be to embrace the Nature Test also in the context of immunity from execution, i.e., to focus on the nature of the underlying use of a State's assets as opposed to the current or intended use of the assets. Additionally, one could explore allowing the attaching and executing against assets that are used "in connection with" or "related to" a commercial activity, and therefore not only those directly "used for" such activity.

1. Hazel Fox & Philippa Webb, *The Law of State Immunity* 1 (2015).
2. Roy Goode, et al., *Transnational Commercial Law, Text, Cases, And Materials* 522 (2015).

§5.1.3 Certain Property Immune *Ipso Jure*

As explained in Chapters 2-4, proving that property is in use or intended to be used for commercial purposes is indeed challenging to begin with. This becomes aggravated when the few assets that are typically located are protected categorically (or at least nearly so). Such assets protected *ipso jure* often include diplomatic assets and the assets of central banks. In real life, States generally deposit assets "in accounts held in the name of their diplomatic missions or of their central banks."[3]

Here, the law can step in in two major ways: (1) the law can shorten the list of assets/property protected *ipso jure*; and (2) the law can clarify that only parts of such assets are protected categorically and thereby embrace a functional test looking at the actual use of the assets. This point can be illustrated by looking at central bank assets. Today, States are divided among those that: (i) provide for "near-absolute immunity" from execution; (ii) adopt a "middle-approach"; and (iii) offer "no special protection." i.e., conditioning immunity on a commercial *purposes* exception only. Many of the jurisdictions analyzed in Chapter 4 would go with the first approach (e.g., France and the U.K.). However, the Swedish courts have taken the opposite approach and treated assets held by a central bank as commercial assets if used for a commercial purpose.

Rejecting a categorical approach to immunity from central bank assets is one possible reform that would make a big difference for award-creditors. Similarly, focusing on a diplomatic mission's actual use of the property/assets instead of adopting a categorical immunity stance would achieve the same aims.

§5.1.4 Legislation/Model Law

Another legal reform that could prove fruitful would be the codification of sovereign immunity law. There was such an attempt with the UNCSI. As of today, the UNCSI is probably the informal model law since it is referred to domestically and internationally and is even said to—at least in parts—codify customary international law.

However, it could prove fruitful to give UNCITRAL a renewed mission to elaborate a Model Law on sovereign immunity. Such law could then, like the UNCITRAL Model Law for arbitration, be implemented in whole or in parts in various domestic settings.

Given the wide divergences in the theory and practice of sovereign immunity law that exist worldwide, it is probably more feasible to suggest a model law only for the enforcement and execution of foreign arbitral awards. This is because the jurisdictional immunity is less of an issue, there is more uniformity, and immunity from execution presents as a more serious obstacle to award/judgment-creditors. Fox proposed this already in 1996, where she suggested that:

> Rather than leave the matter [of sovereign immunity] to be codified through the auspices of the ILC and the UN conference planned for 1987-88, I suggest that

3. Philippa Webb, "International Immunities in English Law," in *The Oxford Handbook of Comparative Foreign Relations Law* (Curtis A. Bradley, ed.), 8 (2019).

> UNCITRAL should mount a separate initiative and draft a Model Law, not a treaty, containing rules relating to attachment of state property in enforcement of arbitral awards. The advantage of such an initiative is that it would separate the much less controversial topic of enforcement of arbitral awards to which a state is a party from the general question of proceedings in national courts concerning state activities.[4]

In fact, some States already have a codified law. Such laws also serve as a form of model law for other jurisdictions. In most of the codified versions (e.g., as seen in Chapter 4: France, Russia, the U.K., and the U.S.), the arbitration exception is codified, meaning that arbitration agreements are being treated as waivers of ancillary enforcement jurisdiction.

However, the nearly universal move toward the restrictive immunity from execution renders a Model Law a bit outdated unless it does something more, e.g., converts an arbitration agreement or award into a full waiver of immunity from execution, embraces the Nature Test for immunity from execution, narrows the list of property protected *ipso jure* or treats such property/assets functionally, includes procedural features that enable award execution (rules on mixed-use assets, burden of proof, standard of proof, discovery, injunctions, etc.).

§5.1.5 Implied (Double) Waiver Doctrine

Another legal solution could be to accept the implied (double) waiver doctrine. Even though an arbitration agreement is considered to be a waiver of immunity from jurisdiction, it is a generally held view that an arbitration clause does not represent an implied waiver of immunity from execution.[5] There has been a longstanding and well-established proposition that a waiver of immunity from jurisdiction does not automatically entail a waiver of immunity from execution.[6] This debate regained attention in the arbitration context. Lew, Mistelis, and Kröll noted that:

> The fact that a state cannot claim immunity from jurisdiction does not necessarily mean that the state is not immune from the actual execution of the award. In most laws the exceptions to immunity from execution are narrower than the exceptions to immunity from jurisdiction.[7]

4. Hazel Fox, *State Immunity and Enforcement of Arbitral Awards: Do We Need an UNCITRAL Model Law Mark II for Execution Against State Property?*, 23 Arb. Int'l 89, 93 (1996) https://doi.org/10.1093/arbitration/12.1.89.
5. The most notable exception to this presumption was presented in France, *see Creighton v. Qatar* Case No. 98-19.068 (Court of Cassation, July 6, 2000) where the Court held that the arbitration agreement constituted a waiver for purposes of execution because the ICC rules provided for a duty to carry out the award and waive any appeal of it, too. In other words, the court accepted the theory on "double waiver of immunity."
6. *See, e.g.*, James Crawford, *Execution of Judgments and Foreign Sovereign Immunity*, 75 Am. J. Int'L L. 820, 860 (1981) https://doi.org/10.2307/2201355.
7. Julian D.M. Lew et al., *Comparative International Commercial Arbitration* 750 (2003).

It is generally accepted that an implied waiver of jurisdictional immunity extends to a court's "jurisdiction to grant measures in support of arbitration proceedings."[8] Such measures in support could be recognition and enforcement (i.e., the making of a judgment). This is the implied waiver doctrine. However, it does mostly not reach beyond waiving jurisdictional immunity (i.e., single waiver) and into waiving immunity from execution (i.e., double waiver).

One might reasonably ask whether there really is, or should be, a difference in treatment between waiving immunity from jurisdiction and execution. Does a justification for waiving the former indeed rest on the same premises as the possible justification for the latter? Was it not the parties that freely entered this commitment to engage in trade, commerce, investment, and to arbitrate any dispute stemming therefrom? But, States may respond that a commitment merely to permit arbitrating a dispute cannot result in a permit to attach an Embassy building or central bank assets. If the sovereign has acted "commercially," should it nevertheless be able to turn around subsequent to unsuccessful adjudication in order to shield itself from asset realization? If so, from any and all assets? Would a domestic court be uncomfortable for political reasons to attach and execute against assets used for public purposes? Does it matter? Should courts be (or feel) bound by policy objectives and political concerns? Should courts disregard such balancing and focus on enforcing the rule of law? Should a court use its coercive powers to force disclosure of where the award-debtor holds commercial assets? Should courts reverse the burden of proof? Should courts entertain a nature or purpose test to identify the use of the assets?

The very bottom line is whether the State, by entering into an arbitration clause voluntarily, has consented to honor the arbitral procedure, including its award. Put differently, is the voluntarily undertaken commitment to arbitrate a good faith expression to honor the means and the ends of the arbitral procedure? If so, should such commitment be entrenched and enforced by general principles of law, such as *good faith* and *pacta sunt servanda*? Regardless of one's logical presupposition and therefore analytical preference of a theory on the implied double waiver debate, the double waiver theory through an ordinary arbitration clause has found little support in legislation and case law.[9] The very bottom line is that the *de lege lata* in international comparative law is that an arbitration clause does not constitute a waiver of immunity from execution. However, there may be a good *de lege ferenda* case to be made for a future broadening of the waiver doctrine to encompass a double waiver doctrine. In fact, it seems that India has recently endorsed such approach and France did so historically but redirected its course later on (*see* Chapter 4).

As things stand, investors are recommended to include express waivers of immunity from execution in investor-State contracts if they have such leverage.[10] Even then, whether such contractual waivers would cover awards rendered on the basis of

8. *Ibid.*, at 746 ("Only in very exceptional circumstances can it be assumed that the waiver is limited to the proceedings before the arbitration tribunal. In all other cases the waiver could also cover the court proceedings necessary for a proper and efficient conduct of an arbitration.").
9. *Ibid.*, at 751.
10. ICSID provides for a Model Clause in this respect, it reads as follows: "The Host State hereby waives any right of sovereign immunity as to it and its property in respect of the enforcement

IIAs is not clear. Moreover, there are three major caveats for the reader to consider before entertaining this academically easy-to-make and obvious recommendation of including express waivers when contracting with States. First, the bargaining power is often tilted in favor of the State, especially for small- and medium enterprises. Second, given the nature of investments that qualify for treaty protection (often public utilities and exploitation of natural resources), there is careful consideration in not creating unnecessary tension with the State at the negotiation, drafting, and implementation stages.[11] The success of the investment will often depend on the host-States' attitude and to some extent satisfaction with the investor. Third, jurisdictions differ on whether express waivers nevertheless include execution against assets used for public purposes.[12] Moreover, an implied waiver doctrine may not be needed where the "commercial purposes" exception is already embraced (*see* Chapter 3) unless the implied waiver is considered both express and specific (*see* more in Chapters 4 and 5).

The idea of treating a waiver of immunity from execution in the same manner as immunity from jurisdiction is not novel. Today, the two regimes are treated separately. However, the double waiver doctrine's theoretical appeal and practicality are obvious from the standpoint of an award-creditor. The champions of the double waiver doctrine have welcomed it as honoring the principle of good faith, pacta sunt servanda, and strengthening the resort to arbitration. However, the doctrine has also been criticized as being contrary to the requirements of waivers being express/explicit or specific/certain.

Practically speaking, given the large endorsement of the restrictive immunity theory the practical utility of the double waiver doctrine is lessened, especially if the implied waiver is not treated as both "express" and "specific."

§5.1.6 Broadly Construed Waivers

Even waivers negotiated and included by investors in contracts with States have at times been frustrated by court practice. As seen in Chapter 4, courts have stated that express and even specific waivers cannot be used to waive immunity of certain property that is considered "specifically protected" (e.g., such assets as found in Article 21 of the UNCSI).[13]

In some jurisdictions, like the U.S., express waivers have been treated as yet another exception to the general rule of immunity, inviting the next step to identify assets in the U.S. that are used for commercial purposes. Thus, the waiver manifests as

---

and execution of any award rendered by an Arbitral Tribunal constituted pursuant to this agreement." *See* ICSID/5/Rev 2, cl. 15 (April 2006).

11. An investment that qualifying for protection under investment treaties is often one that extends over years and requires a lot of initial monetary input. *See, e.g.*, the generally applicable criteria outlined in *Salini v. Morocco* (i.e., the "Salini Criteria"); that is, the investment must have a financial contribution, performance of project must be for a certain duration, there must be an existence of risk, and there must be a significant contribution to the economic development of the Host State.
12. For an extensive discussion comparing several approaches over many jurisdictions, *see* Ch. 4.
13. *See also* ILC Commentary (8), UNCSI, Art. 19, at 59.

a first step much like the commercial purpose exception. Put differently, in this double key-hole test, the award-creditor first must show that the assets are used for a commercial purpose or that the award-debtor State has waived immunity and then show that the assets are used for a commercial purpose. Thus, the waiver has limited importance where the enforcement forum has embraced the restrictive theory on immunity from execution.

As suggested above, a practical solution is to include an express and specific waiver of immunity from execution when dealing with States. Including a waiver of immunity from execution in investor-State contracts when dealing with a State is one of the most reliable ways of avoiding an effective plea of immunity.[14] For example, ICSID recommends the following clause:

> The Host State hereby waives any right of sovereign immunity as to it and its property in respect of the enforcement and execution of any award rendered by an Arbitral Tribunal constituted pursuant to this agreement.[15]

The generally held view with respect to waivers is that: (1) an arbitration clause constitutes a waiver of immunity from jurisdiction (mostly enforcement jurisdiction, too); (2) an arbitration clause does not constitute a waiver of immunity from execution; (3) the scope of a general waiver of sovereign immunity does not include immunity from execution; (4) the scope of a clause waiving immunity from execution can be interpreted restrictively or liberally.

For an award-creditor, it would be preferable if courts treated waivers (implied or express) as a waiver of immunity from execution, for all State property. It would then be for the award-debtor State to prove that: (1) the specific asset/property is protected *ipso jure;* and (2) that it is used exclusively for governmental purposes.

§5.1.7 Mixed-Use Assets

Another pragmatic legal reform would be to clarify the law on "mixed use" assets and clarify the rules for attaching and executing against such assets. The rule could be that mixed-use assets/property can be executed against unless the substantial (or predominant) purpose of the assets is governmental at the time for enforcement of the arbitral award.

A pragmatic approach would be to either sever-out the assets used for a commercial purpose (is possible; e.g., if the assets are in a bank account) or execute against the entire asset/property where the assets are predominantly used for a commercial purpose (e.g., where the asset is real estate, an airplane, etc.).

---

14. Inna Uchkunova & Oleg Temnikov, *Enforcement of Awards under the ICSID Convention: What Solutions to the Problem of State Immunity?*, 29 ICSID Rev. 187, 202 (2014) https://doi.org/10.1093/icsidreview/sit038.
15. *ICSID Model Clause 15*, ICSID—Model Clauses, http://icsidfiles.worldbank.org/icsid/icsid/staticfiles/model-clauses-en/15.htm.

§5.1.8 Piercing the Sovereign Veil

Another legal solution to the award-creditor issue could be if jurisdictions clarify the law, or at least put forth succinct legal tests, for when, where, why, and how to pierce the sovereign veil and attach and execute against SOE's assets for the debt of an award-debtor State.

There are two situations that can be of importance in the immunity context: (1) where the award-debtor is the SOE and that entity claims immunity; and (2) where the award-debtor is the State and the award-creditor seeks to attach and execute against SOE assets. This book looks only at the latter situation, namely, piercing the corporate veil in order to execute against assets held by a State's separate legal entity. As demonstrated throughout this book but primarily in Chapter 4, such is a difficult task and for good legal reasons. The general rule is that "a legal entity's separate status may be disregarded only under exceptional circumstances."[16] Therefore, it has been difficult to convince States to disregard the presumption of separateness.[17]

Because States often undertake commercial affairs through separate entities and therefore have most of their non-governmental assets controlled and owned by those entities, the alternative route of tracing/locating commercial assets held by SOEs has gained increased traction and popularity.[18] These assets are especially attractive because they are more readily identifiable and more easily seized given their commercial nature.[19] Additionally, attaching and executing against SOE assets makes the number of assets available for satisfaction of the arbitral award significantly higher.[20]

Organizing State commercial affairs through State enterprises (owned, controlled, funds, and otherwise) has caused fear that States could shield responsibilities and frustrate a claim, in general, and award-enforcement, in particular. As stated by Gaillard, "there does exist an incompatibility between the principles of [a] effectiveness of arbitral awards, [b] state immunity from execution, and [c] autonomy of state entities."[21] Furthermore, he made the point that when any two of the competing principles are respected, the third is sacrificed.[22]

Thus, seen in this light, an award-creditor faces two significant legal barriers: (1) the public international law barrier of immunity from execution; and (2) the corporate law barrier of "separateness." Conversely, the State's effective commercial organization can lead to legally efficient planning around liability or effective legal sanctioning. Gaillard wrote that:

16. Kaj Hobér, *Enforcing Foreign Arbitral Awards Against Russian Entities*, 10 Arb. Int'l 17, 42 (1994) https://doi.org/10.1093/arbitration/10.1.17.
17. *Ibid.*
18. Mevelyn Ong, *The Interplay of Sovereignty and Consent in the Execution of Arbitral Award Debts Against Non-party State-Owned Enterprises*, 4 McGill J. Disp. Resol. 22, 25 (2018).
19. *Ibid.*
20. *See* Brian King et al., "Enforcing Awards Involving Foreign Sovereigns," in *International Commercial Arbitration in New York* (James H. Carter & John Fellas, eds.), 433, (2010).
21. Emmanuel Gaillard, "Effectiveness of Arbitral Awards, State Immunity from Execution and Autonomy of State Entities: Three Incompatible Principles," in *State Entities in International Arbitration* (Emmanuel Gaillard & Jennifer Younan, eds.), 181 (2008).
22. *Ibid.*

> Quite often, states organize their *jure gestionis* activities by creating as many distinct legal entities as they have activities. The intent in so doing is not necessarily malicious. Such organization usually corresponds to the requirements of effective management, enabling the profitability of each commercial activity to be valued individually. Yet the end result is that the state is effectively shielded from its creditors: when creditors try to enforce a decision against a state through assets allocated to *jure imperii* activities, the state will raise its immunity from execution; when creditors try to seize assets allocated to *jure gestionis* activities, they will be told that they are not pursuing the right debtor.[23]

Thus, many have suggested that there are at times good reasons to pierce the corporate veil under certain (albeit limited) circumstances. If not, there may be unfair incentives to create separate entities to avoid execution or other liabilities.[24] Courts and parties are guided by the reasoning in the *Barcelona Traction* case:

> Forms of incorporation and their legal personality have sometimes not been employed for the sole purposes they were intended to serve; sometimes the corporate entity has been unable to protect the rights of those who have entrusted their financial resources to it; thus inevitably there have arisen dangers of abuse, as in the case of many other institutions of law. Here, then, as elsewhere, the law, confronted with economic realities, has had to provide protective measures and remedies in the interests of those within the corporate entity as well as those outside who have dealings with it ... It is in this context that the process of "lifting the corporate veil" or "disregarding the legal entity" has been found justified and equitable in certain circumstances or for certain purposes. The wealth of practice in municipal law indicates that the veil is lifted, for instance, to prevent misuse of the privileges of the corporate personality, as in certain cases of fraud or malfeasance, to protect third persons ... or to prevent the evasion of legal requirements or responsibilities.[25]

This statement is as important and influential today as it was in 1970. The most important question is: when is it warranted for courts to pierce the corporate/sovereign veil? This is a delicate balance, and it remains important that the exceptions are not allowed to swallow the rule of separateness.

§5.1.9 Nexus Requirement and Minimum Contacts

Award-debtor States have at times raised the defense that there needs to be a territorial connection with the underlying dispute or at least that the property needs to be linked to the subject matter that gave rise to the underlying dispute. The argument is simply that there must be a "substantial link" to the enforcement/execution jurisdiction in order to meet an exception to sovereign immunity from enforcement and/or execution. Most jurisdictions would refuse to entertain such arguments, holding that the signing of multilateral enforcement conventions (such as the New York Convention and the

23. *Ibid.*, at 183.
24. *See* Uchkunova & Temnikov, *supra* n. 14, at 209.
25. *Case Concerning Barcelona Traction Light Power Co.* (*Belgium v. Spain*) ICJ Rep. (1970), at 3.

ICSID Convention) is sufficient to establish such connection for enforcement purposes and that the enforced award itself is sufficient for execution.

In Switzerland, there needs to be a "substantial link" to the jurisdiction in order to meet an exception to sovereign immunity from execution. To illustrate this, in *Oxus Gold v. Uzbekistan*, the Swiss Federal Supreme Court "reasoned that foreign states benefitted from immunity from execution under public international law, which had been integrated into Swiss law. The court added that, according to its standing practice, this immunity from execution could only be disregarded if the foreign State acted iure gestionis in the underlying dispute, and if the underlying dispute presented a sufficient link with Switzerland."[26] What a "substantial link" is will be determined from one jurisdiction to another—e.g., some require the arbitration to be seated in the jurisdictions, other do not.

In the U.S., there has been a debate on minimum contacts in the enforcement phase, that could possibly venture into the execution stage too. The U.S. Supreme Court has granted *a certiorari* to hear a matter in which the 9th Circuit concluded that a minimum contacts analysis is necessary in order for U.S. courts to exercise personal jurisdiction over States in actions seeking recognition/enforcement of foreign arbitral awards pursuant to the New York Convention.[27] It is more likely than not that the Supreme Court will reverse the decision.

§5.1.10 Post-Award Interest

States can impose (high) interest on awards that are recognized and enforced, but not executed. Separate laws/rules can be implemented for such awards/judgments. Thus, the cost of not paying voluntarily by shielding assets through immunity may be too cumbersome and an unadvisable path.

§5.2 PROCEDURAL RULES-BASED SOLUTIONS

§5.2.1 Burden of Proof

A possible procedural solution to the obstacle of immunity from execution could be to either lower the burden of proof for award-creditors or at some reasonable point reverse the burden of proof and place it on the award-debtor State. Bjorklund argues

---

26. Jarrod Hepburn & Lisa Bohmer, *Swiss Federal Supreme Court Declines Enforcement of Investment Treaty Award, Finding No "Substantial Link" to Switzerland in Underlying Dispute*, IAReporter, October 14, 2018: https://www.iareporter.com/articles/swiss-federal-supreme-court-declines-enforcement-of-oxus-award-finding-no-substantial-link-to-switzerland-in-underlying-treaty-dispute/.
27. *Devas Multimedia Private Ltd. v. Antrix Corp.*, 2023 U.S. App. (9th Cir., August 1, 2023). For an excellent take on how the Supreme Court should change the outcome, *see* Brief of Amicus Curiae Professor George a Bermann in Support of Petitioners (December 11, 2024), at: https://www.supremecourt.gov/DocketPDF/23/23–1201/334870/20241211145023226_23-1201%20CC%20Devas%20Mauritius%20Limited%20v%20Antrix%20Corp%20Ltd%20Bermann%20Amicus%20Brief%20in%20Support%20of%20Petitioners.pdf.

that such shifting of the burden of proof "could represent an enormous benefit to creditors who will find it difficult to establish the commercial nature of assets absent the cooperation of the state."[28]

The general rule is one of immunity. The rule is qualified by exceptions—e.g., waiver, earmarking, and the commercial purposes exceptions. The most important exception is the commercial purposes exceptions. Generally speaking, it is the Claimant that bears the burden of proof that the property/assets is/are used for a commercial purpose, or as it turns out in practice that the property/assets is/are not used for a governmental non-commercial purpose.[29] This is logical due to the structure of the law, i.e., because sovereign immunity is the rule, and attaching and executing against State property and its assets is the exception. The party seeking to rely on the exception has the onus of proving it.[30] Proving that real property is used entirely, or if allowed, predominantly for commercial purposes is difficult. Proving that tangible assets are first controlled by the State and then used for a commercial purpose is also very difficult, especially since ownership so easily can change hands (e.g., to an SOE) and purpose perhaps easier so (e.g., from investments on the capital market to buying dollar reserves). Moreover, proving the use (or future use) of intangible property is even more cumbersome.

Furthermore, the burden and standard of proof is extremely difficult to overcome when the assets are used for mixed purposes. For example, funds in the name of a diplomatic mission could be used in the performance of diplomatic functions and for other commercial purposes. Judge Crawford underscored this problem already in 1981, where he highlighted the evidentiary problems and difficulties vis-à-vis indivisible, mixed-use property without allowing extensive discovery.[31] Adding to this problem is the fact that heads of diplomatic missions enjoy immunity from cross-examination.

In some jurisdictions, the burden is exacerbated by being engraved statutorily. In the U.K., for example, section 13(5) of the SIA treats a certificate from the ambassador of the State as a presumption of whether the property is used for commercial or non-commercial governmental purposes.

§5.2.2 Discovery

As has rightly been noted, "[a] basic requirement for executing against property is finding it."[32] Therefore, the procedural solution of making it possible for award-creditors to seek post-judgment discovery in terms of the disclosure of the whereabouts of commercial assets would prove of intrinsic value in aiding award-creditors with

28. Andrea K. Bjorklund, *Sovereign Immunity as a Barrier to the Enforcement of Investor-State Arbitral Awards: The Re-politicization of International Investment Disputes*, 21 Am. Rev. Int'l Arb. 211, 231 (2011).
29. Fox & Webb, *supra* n. 1, at 517.
30. Uchkunova & Temnikov, *supra* n. 14, at 199.
31. Crawford, *supra* n. 6, at 863.
32. Mark M. Cymrot, "Enforcing Sovereign Arbitral Awards: State Defences and Creditor Strategies in an Imperfect World," in *The Cambridge Handbook of Immunities and International Law* (Tom Ruys et al., eds.), 372 (2019).

execution. As of today, there are very few jurisdictions that effectively offer discovery rules to assist award-creditors.

Notably, the U.S. has endorsed such approach in the *NML* case (*see* Chapter 4). Scholars noted that the case "demonstrates that judgment creditors have adopted novel tools to enforce judgments against sovereigns—and that courts have endorsed the practice."[33] Others are unhappy with such procedural assistance and instead argue that it runs counter to established principles of international law and that it may even jeopardize U.S. interests abroad.[34] However, such procedural reform may be necessary—even crucial—in assisting award-creditors "finding assets which are covered by exceptions to immunity from execution," and therefore such procedural ease may be "essential for the successful enforcement of an [investment arbitration] award."[35] It is inevitably the case that extraterritorial discovery against the debtor States' assets without the need to specify them will alleviate the daunting challenge of finding such assets.[36]

There are other such procedural rules available in attaching and executing against assets of a non-sovereign award/judgment-debtor that may be deployed in the context where the award-debtor is a State. For example, as we saw in Chapter 4, the High Court of India directed the award-debtor States to file affidavits of their assets in India. If properly sanctioned, such procedural rule may prove to be an instrumental tool to award-creditors. Another tool is the so-called examination orders. This is a tool that can be used to examine State officials on the whereabouts of commercial assets. However, this raises an issue of diplomatic immunity.

§5.2.3 Interim Relief and Injunction Orders

The general prohibition of interim relief, in general, and through injunctions, in particular, can prove cumbersome for award-creditors.[37] For example, to deny a party the right to a *Mareva Injunction* (i.e., a freezing order) "will frequently render proceedings nugatory and deprive a successful plaintiff of the fruits of his victory."[38] This is because award-debtor States may, *inter alia*, move assets out of the country, move them to a separate legal entity, or re-direct their use from commercial to governmental.

As we saw in Chapter 4, however, a U.S. Circuit Court did affirm an injunctive relief requesting Argentina to refrain from making payments with respect to its

33. Adriana T. Ingenito & Christina G. Hioureas, *Carving Out New Exceptions to Sovereign Immunity: Why the NML Capital Cases May Harm U.S. Interests Abroad*, 30 Md. J. Int'l 118 (2015).
34. *Ibid.*, at 119.
35. Tomoko Ishikawa, *Extraterritorial Discovery in Aid of Execution and State Immunity: Case Comment on Republic of Argentina v. NML Capital, Ltd., 573 U.S. (2014)*, 5 Acct. Econ. L. 173, 187 (2015) https://doi.org/10.1515/ael-2014-0016.
36. *Ibid.*
37. Frederick Alexander Mann, *The State Immunity Act 1978*, 50 BYIL 43, 59 (1979) https://doi.org/10.1093/bybil/50.1.43.
38. *Ibid.*, at 60.

restructured bonds and not also make payments on the defaulted bonds.[39] Such specific performance was ordered because no adequate monetary remedy was considered available.[40] The injunction proved instrumental for the judgment-creditor because monetary damages were ineffective, and because Argentina simply refused to pay despite judgments. Hence, the court effectively assisted the judgment-creditor without undercutting the substantive law on sovereign immunity through procedural rules available to it.

§5.2.4 Contempt of Court and Court-Ordered Sanctions

Generally speaking, courts have broad discretionary powers to make sure that judgment/award-creditors comply with judgments/awards. One such effective procedural tool to effectuate compliance is holding the faulting party in "contempt of court" followed by monetary sanctions. Such contempt orders coupled with sanctions could potentially be ordered against defaulting States.

Notwithstanding this, invoking sovereign immunity is not such a situation that *ipso facto* invites contempt of court. Invoking immunity is a legal right, just as much as seeking to enforce an arbitral award. However, refusing to comply with procedural orders ancillary to enforcement or incidental to execution may lead to a contempt of court. For example, where an award-debtor State refuses to comply with court-ordered injunctions or general asset disclosure could.

§5.2.5 Security for Cost

Often, award-creditors are forced into enforcement proceedings in many parts of the world. Even when successful in recognition/enforcement, or even in attaching/executing against a part of the outstanding debt, the legal costs are accruing, and the award-debtor State may refuse to comply voluntarily with such costs. Therefore, a security-for-cost order may be an effective tool used by courts to level the playing field and preserve the integrity of the court. However, such orders can raise problems of sovereign immunity and at times even diplomatic immunity.

Security for costs could also be delivered by ICSID ad hoc committees. ICSID ad hoc committees could request security for the award in the form of, for example, a bank guarantee in order to accept a stay of enforcement pending the annulment phase.

§5.2.6 The Right to a Fair Trial and Execution

In relevant parts, Article 6(1) ECHR reads as follows: "In the determination of his civil rights and obligations or of any criminal charge against him, everyone is entitled to a fair and public hearing within a reasonable time by an independent and impartial

39. *NML Capital, Ltd. v. Republic of Argentina (Equal Treatment Case I)*, 699 F.3d 250 (2d Cir. 2012).
40. *Ibid.*, at 261.

tribunal established by law …" Moreover, the European Court of Human Rights has reasoned that:

> 66. Execution of court decisions: Article 6 § 1 applies to all stages of legal proceedings for the "determination of … civil rights and obligations," not excluding stages subsequent to judgment on the merits. Execution of a judgment given by any court must therefore be regarded as an integral part of the "trial" for the purposes of Article 6 (Hornsby v. Greece, 1997, § 40; Romańczyk v. France, 2010, § 53, concerning the execution of a judgment authorising the recovery of maintenance debts) …
>
> 67. Article 6 § 1 is also applicable to the execution of foreign judgments that are final (exequatur—see Avotiņš v. Latvia [GC], 2016, § 96 and case-law references cited) … .[41]

An important problem in this light is the treatment of certain property as immune *ipso jure*, without looking at the distinction between the use for governmental or commercial purposes (i.e., the functional test), and thus potentially interfering with the award-creditor's right of access to effective execution and peaceful enjoyment of their judgment.

In *AIG Capital Partners Inc v. Kazakhstan*, the High Court of Justice in England heard a case that concerned the claim for sovereign immunity for the State and its central bank (the NBK).[42] More specifically, the case dealt with the *ipso jure* immunity of central bank assets. The court heard arguments on whether section 14(4) SIA has an adverse impact on the meaning of Article 6(1) ECHR so that the former should be reconstructed in a purposive manner.[43] The court determined whether the "restriction on execution" by treating certain property as effectively absolutely immune is legitimate and proportionate. The court looked at the UNCSI which does the same thing in Article 21. The court concluded that section 14(4) SIA does impinge the rights of access to the enforcement jurisdiction and thus that Article 6(1) ECHR is relevant.[44] However, the court concluded that the restriction "on the right of a party to enforce a judgment on the property of a central bank or other monetary authority that is imposed by section 14(4) is both legitimate and proportionate."[45] Aikens J explained that this is so because: (1) the UNCSI, which is the most important guide on the state of international opinion, restricts enforcement on certain properties; (2) there is no international consensus on limited immunity; (3) section 14(4) is sensible and easy to apply, and therefore promotes comity and good relations; and (4) the arbitral award is neither a nullity nor ineffective since other assets can be executed against.[46] Conclusively then, Aikens J held that "although section 14(4) does affect the Claimants' rights of access to

41. European Court of Human Rights, *Guide on Article 6 of the European Convention on Human Rights* (December 31, 2021), paras. 66-67, https://rm.coe.int/1680700aaf.
42. *AIG Capital Partners Inc. v. Kazakhstan* [2005] EWHC 2239 (Comm).
43. *See Ibid.*, at paras. 62-88.
44. *Ibid.*, at para. 78.
45. *Ibid.*, at para. 79.
46. *Ibid.*, at paras. 80-83.

the courts, the interpretation that I have given it is consistent with their Article 6(1) rights; it is legitimate and proportionate in the circumstances."[47]

This outcome may potentially be revisited by English or other courts in the future. It may then very well be the case that treating property as categorically immune is at odds with Article 6(1) ECHR, and therefore in conflict with general principles of law (e.g., access to justice, good faith, or pacta sunt servanda). It is also likely that courts will continue to confirm that certain property can be immune *ipso jure* but not others on the basis of what is reasonable/proportionate. Seeing it this way, the current "fair trial argument" or "access to justice argument" only brings one as far as revealing the standard of immunity already found in most jurisdictions which is based on the restrictive theory. However, it seems unlikely. Similar to the English courts, in *Geotehnika v. Sudan*, the Paris Court of Appeals reasoned that the rights in Article 6(1) ECHR of access to justice/court were not jeopardized by a State's successful plea of sovereign immunity.[48]

§5.3 MARKET-BASED SOLUTIONS

§5.3.1 Hedge Funds ("Holdout Creditors") and Assignment

Given the nature of the substantive law on sovereign immunity from execution and the overall lack of procedural rules to assist award-creditors, the award-creditor may at times turn to the market to sell or assign her award to a hedge fund, also known as "holdout creditors" or "vulture funds." Due to legal shortcomings, award-creditors "are growing increasingly creative in their efforts to collect."[49]

Award-creditors increasingly turn to the market that in turn increasingly has shown an interest in investing in acquiring and recovering distressed and outstanding debts from award-debtor States.[50] The market actors purchase arbitral awards at a discounted value, with accruing post-award interest, and act to enforce them in full.[51]

To illustrate, in 2001 Argentina defaulted on its external debt. Following the "Argentinean crisis," a U.S. hedge fund called "NML" purchased defaulting international bonds and started claiming full repayments with interest. NML pursued litigation in various jurisdictions, including a stream of cases in the U.S. NML that were largely

47. *Ibid.*, at para. 84.
48. *See* case analysis by Lisa Bohmer, *French Court Refuses to Hear Claims Against Sudan and Its State Entities, but Claims Against ICC Stemming from Forced Discontinuance of Arbitration will Move Forward*, July 1, 2024: https://www.iareporter.com/articles/french-court-refuses-to-hear-claims-against-sudan-and-its-state-entities-but-claims-against-icc-stemming-from-forced-discontinuance-of-arbitration-will-move-forward/.
49. King et al., *supra* n. 20, at 431.
50. For example, in 2004 a major award-creditor against the Democratic Republic of Congo transferred the benefit of the interest payable under two awards to FG Hemisphere, an American Vulture Fund. *See* Shu Shang & Wei Shen, *When the State Sovereign Immunity Rule Meets Sovereign Wealth Funds in the Post Financial Crisis Era: Is There Still a Black Hole in International Law?*, 31 Leiden J. Int'l L. 915, 922 (2018) https://doi.org/10.1017/s0922156518000420.
51. *See, e.g.*, *Kensington International Ltd v. Republic of Congo* [2005] EWHC 2684.

successful in the initial litigation phases.[52] Overall, Argentina was the subject of a USD 81 billion lawsuit, some 40 ICSID arbitrations, and likely many more commercial arbitrations due to their various defaults against the backdrop of the financial crisis (primarily defaulting on sovereign bonds).[53] This is nowadays common and routine practice for hedge funds dealing in arbitral awards against award-debtor States. To give another example, FG Hemisphere Associates LLC purchased two substantial ICC awards against the Democratic Republic of Congo and sought to enforce the awards in various jurisdictions across the world.[54]

These kinds of hedge funds often "purchase highly discounted sovereign bonds and sue for full recovery as holdouts."[55] For that reason, some have labeled them "vulture funds" praying on distressed States. For example, in *NML Capital Limited v. Republic of Argentina*, Lord Phillips opined the following in the U.K. Supreme Court: "[Vulture funds] feed(s) on the debts of sovereign States that are in acute financial difficulty by purchasing sovereign debt at a discount to face value and then seeking to enforce it."[56]

There are two ways of looking at these market creatures. One approach is that the funds rescue award-creditors and as a result are at best rewarded for their "hold-out" capabilities and patience. The other approach is that they make possible additional pressure on already distressed nations, forcing the States to a total surrender in an inequitable manner. The first approach cherishes the hedge fund as enabling access to justice, while the other approach argues that they are unethical actors working injustice. Cymrot described this debate as one between those "who view opportunistic creditors as vultures preying on poverty and those who view the resistant States as irresponsible and a detriment to financial markets."[57]

In this light, Belgium, France, and the U.K. have all enacted legislation to "prevent hedge funds from profiting by acquiring claims against States in financial difficulty."[58] Thus, many leading and indeed trade-friendly nations have opted in favor of the viewpoint that hedge funds are vulture funds that must be stopped.

Some could argue that it is unfair to overplay the "greed" or "vulture" card. Hold-out strategies can be adopted—and indeed frequently are—by States too. The strategy just looks a bit different for States. For example, an award-debtor State understands that oftentimes award-creditor will settle for much less by not paying

52. *See* Ishikawa, *supra* n. 35, at 178 ("NML, the leading holdout creditor in the sovereign debt despite against Argentina, filed 11 actions against the country in the SDNY for the recovery of the debt and prevailed in each of these actions.").
53. *See* Cymrot, *supra* n. 32, at 363.
54. *See La Générale des Carrières et des Mines v. F.G. Hemisphere Associates LLC*, [2012] UKPC 27.
55. *See* Ishikawa, *supra* n. 35, at 175.
56. *NML Capital v. Argentina* [2011] UKSC 31.
57. *Ibid.*
58. Robert Folloe & Guillaume Mezache, *Enforcement Against Foreign States: New Rules on Immunity Following the Loi Sapin 2*, Holman Fenwick Willan News (January 2017), https://www.hfw.com/Enforcement-against-foreign-states-Loi-Sapin-2-January-2017. *See* Law No. 201 6-1691 (Fr.); Debt Relief (Developing Countries) Act 2010 (U.K.); and Law dated April 6, 2008 aiming to prevent seizing or transfer of public funds intended for international cooperation, in particular through the vulture funds technique M.B. May 16, 2008/Law dated July 12,2015 against the activities of vulture funds, M.B., September 11, 2015 (Belgium).

voluntarily and instead engage in post-award negotiations and proceedings. The truth of the matter is that, compared to States, most investors do not plan and execute their budget and liquidity needs in decades or centuries, but rather in year(s).[59] Thus, the award-creditor may "feed" those who "feed on the debts of sovereign states that are in acute financial difficulty"[60] because they themselves are put in that very same position and want to focus on growing their businesses rather than restructuring, liquidation, or bankruptcy. There is a moral claim on all three sides—the award-creditor, the award-debtor State, and the hedge fund. All actors can claim the moral high ground.[61]

Practically speaking, hedge funds may be more effective in overcoming the sovereign immunity hurdles due to monetary means, other resources, and increasing expertise and experience. Additionally, the greatest strength of hedge funds may be leverage in the fact that they can "hold-out" for longer and therefore accrue interest rates at good profit margins. States are well aware. Thus, in the strict legal sense immunity from execution is not less of an obstacle for hedge funds, but in a more practical sense, they can deal with it differently because it is part of their business model. Investors are not in the business of enforcing arbitral awards. All that has been said with respect to hedge funds can be equally applied to other expert actors that trade in arbitral awards or take an interest in them and that have the necessary expertise in or knowledge about award enforcement, e.g., certain third-party funders.

§5.3.2 Insurance, Letter of Credit, and Third-Party Funding

First, to hedge against risks an investor may turn to the market to get insurance prior to investing abroad. Investor insurance comes in two categories; that is, political risk insurance and BIT award insurance.[62] There are multiple insurance providers, e.g., the World Bank offers insurance through MIGA and the U.S. offers insurance through OPIC. It is important to note that some insurance companies only offer recovery of the book value of the investment, i.e., not "loss of business," expectation damages (e.g., based on discounted cash flow methods), and other types of damages.[63]

Second, another market mechanism that can be utilized by investors with stronger negotiating power is bonds or letter of credits as a form of waiver or earmarking against the State in case of a favorable arbitral award.[64] Practically speaking, such earmarking may be either difficult to obtain or perhaps a bit embarrassing to ask for in a negotiation for an investor-State contract.

Finally, third-party funders can fund, purchase or invest in post-award procedures. There are different ways of doing this, but most likely it would be for some part of the total amount that is awarded to the award-creditor including post-award interests. Obtaining such funding may allow the award-creditor to afford the asset-hunt

59. Fox & Webb, *supra* n. 1, at 485.
60. *NML Capital v. Argentina*, UKSC 31.
61. *See* Cymrot, *supra* n. 32, at 351.
62. *See* Bjorklund, *supra* n. 28, at 234.
63. *See Ibid.*
64. *See* King et al., *supra* n. 20, at 414.

while also providing the necessary experience and expertise that third-party funders may have in-house or in their pool of network.

§5.3.3 International Finance and Development Houses

A market remedy that can be imposed on an award-debtor State by the international community or other States could be the taking of penalizing measures against the State, such as the refusal to provide international financing or to buy bonds. Award-debtor States should consider the implications of international finance when deciding between voluntary compliance and non-compliance.[65]

Put differently, international lending houses could use the "big-finance-stick" to enforce a rules-based international order through market pressure. For example, the World Bank Group and IMF have the power to make it difficult—if not impossible—for award-debtor States to take part in international financing schemes where in repeated default with no good excuse. For example, the World Bank can limit lending to a State that has expropriated property or failed to honor and fulfill its contractual obligations.[66] On the same lines, IMF and other development banks and financial institutions can take non-compliance into account in their assessment of the award-debtor State's overall creditworthiness.[67]

Thus, a failure to pay an investment award (in particular, ICSID) may have an indirect political consequence with consequential market action adversely affecting the award-debtor State's access to funding (e.g., World Bank funding) or its overall creditworthiness.[68]

As outlined in Chapter 2 States mostly comply with adverse arbitral awards. Such compliance may be the result of market factors more than possible legal remedies. For example, a possible "explanation for this high compliance rate is the fear of the debtor states that they may not be able to obtain further loans from the World Bank."[69] Notwithstanding this, due to the potential adverse effects of external stakeholders (primarily the citizens of a State), the World Bank has been hesitant to let defaults affect development aid.[70]

---

65. Phoebe D. Winch, "State Immunity and the Execution of Investment Arbitration Awards: A Review of the Plea of State Immunity and the Execution of Investment Arbitration Awards from the Viewpoint of the Forum State," in *Public Actors in International Investment Law, European Yearbook of International Economic Law* (Catharine Titi, ed.), 73-74, (2021).
66. Cymrot, *supra* n. 32, at 374.
67. Bjorklund, *supra* n. 28, at 238.
68. *See* King et al., *supra* n. 20, at 415.
69. Ishikawa, *supra* n. 35, at 185.
70. Cymrot, *supra* n. 32, at 374. *See also Orascom Telecom Holding v. Chad and Sotel Tchad,* [2008] EWHC 1841 (Comm) 2 Lloyds Rep 396, [2009] 1 All ER (Comm) 396 ("The monies are not the London assets of a national fund of Chad and are not being operated or traded in London pursuant to a global custody or any other agreement between Chad and Citibank. The monies are in London because they were required to be channeled through the mechanisms expressly set up by the RMP, in order to preserve them so that Chad's direct oil revenues pursuant to the oil contracts were not simply passed direct to Chand, and so that there could be security and protection for the World Bank and the European Investment Bank to allow for their loans to Chad to be safely and transparently repaid.").

§5.3.4 State Insolvency, Restructuring, and the Paris Club

When a company cannot meet its liabilities, it is insolvent. The result is either restructuring, liquidation, or bankruptcy. There is no law dealing with insolvent States.[71] At best, the State can engage in some form of restructuring of its debt, but there is no liquidation or bankruptcy. As a result, the award-creditor can either "hold-out," assign/sell the award or hope for a restructuring process and accept the outcome of it. The leading group working to coordinate solutions for insolvent States is the so-called Paris Club which is:

> an informal group of official creditors whose role is to find coordinated and sustainable solutions to the payment difficulties experienced by debtor countries. As debtor countries undertake reforms to stabilize and restore their macroeconomic and financial situation, Paris Club creditors provide an appropriate debt treatment. Paris Club creditors provide debt treatments to debtor countries in the form of rescheduling, which is debt relief by postponement or, in the case of concessional rescheduling, reduction in debt service obligations during a defined period (flow treatment) or as of a set date (stock treatment).[72]

Paradoxically, a major obstacle to State restructuring is international arbitration, litigation, and even award/judgment enforcement and execution. In the *NML* case discussed in Chapter 4 (U.S. jurisdiction), the United States submitted an *amicus curiae* regarding the injunctive relief and stated among other things that the decision "could enable a single creditor to thwart the implementation of an internationally supported restructuring plan, and thereby undermine the decades of effort the United States has expended to encourage a system of cooperative resolution of sovereign debt crises."[73] One author articulated the concern as follows:

> The assessment of the impact of this decision on future [sovereign debt restructuring] starts with the recognition that the success of holdout creditors implies a lower chance of success for [sovereign debt restructuring]. Creditors will not be willing to accept the restructuring offer knowing that holdout creditors have a good chance to obtain full and practically enforceable compensation, whereas their new credits under the exchange offer they took will not eventually be paid (the latter is the consequence of *NML v. Argentina* (Second Circuit, August, 2013)). Therefore, successful holdout litigation will "encourage parties to hold out and make restructurings harder to achieve." Given the increase in the frequency of sovereign debt litigation, this approach adopted by the US courts in the NML-Argentina disputes casts concerns over the future of [sovereign debt restructuring].[74]

---

71. In 2002, the IMF elaborated the idea of introducing a sovereign debt restructuring mechanism. For a good paper on the IMF's role in sovereign debt restructuring, *see* European Central Bank, *The IMF's Role in Sovereign Debt Restructurings*, Occasional Paper Series No. 262 (September 2021), https://www.ecb.europa.eu/pub/pdf/scpops/ecb.op262~f0e9e1e77e.en.pdf.
72. *See* Club de Paris, https://clubdeparis.org/.
73. Brief for the United States of America as Amicus Curiae in Support of Reversal 5. *See* more in Ch. 4 (U.S. jurisdiction).
74. Ishikawa, *supra* n. 35, at 182.

The NML procedures, in general, and the ones in the U.S.,[75] in particular, have "given rise to sufficient alarm to cause the UN General Assembly to adopt a resolution requiring the UN to create a 'multilateral legal framework for sovereign debt restructuring'."[76] On September 9, 2014, the U.N.G.A. adopted resolution 68/304 to work "towards the establishment of a multilateral legal framework for sovereign debt restructuring processes."[77] Notwithstanding this attempt, some ten years later, the project must be considered a failed aspiration. The U.N. failed to implement the framework.[78]

It has been argued that the procedural ease at which award or judgment creditors can attach and execute against State property in certain jurisdictions can "have potentially serious consequences for future [sovereign debt restructuring]."[79] Such legitimate fear and concern must be weighed against liberalizing award execution and the right balance must be struck. When discussing the law of sovereign immunity, on the one hand, and the effectiveness of an arbitral award, on the other hand, one should not too easily dismiss the State's perspective as well, which includes the interest of other stakeholders (primarily its citizens). It is the citizens of an award-debtor State that ultimately pay the bill. Like the investors, these very citizens may themselves be victims of unstable, inexperienced, repressive, corrupt, or even rogue governments. International cooperation is required to strike the right balance between the rights of the award-creditor and the financial difficulty that an award-debtor State may find herself in.[80]

This is not a book on sovereign debt restructuring, but for illustrative purposes, it is worth mentioning that *SerVaas Incorporated v. Rafidain Bank and Others* from the U.K. Supreme Court (as analyzed in Chapter 4) dealt with a matter where the Iraqi government through work with the Paris Club had started restructuring with its creditors.[81] When the award-creditor—that was not part of the restructuring plan—sought to attach and execute against Iraqi property, the process of restructuring was slightly frustrated. As the court noted, the ultimate question was whether Iraq "bought the debts in order to make a profit and as part of a commercial venture, or whether ... they were bought in the exercise of sovereign authority as part of a huge restructuring of debts incurred in the Saddam Hussein era."[82] To this author, this underscores another important tension and reality that perhaps justifies some sentiments for a more conservative doctrine of immunity from execution, i.e., that many underdeveloped and

75. *See Republic of Argentina v. NML Capital, Ltd.*, 134 S.Ct 2250 (2014).
76. Fox & Webb, *supra* n. 1, at 503.
77. United Nations General Assembly, Resolution 68/304 (September 9, 2014) U.N. Doc. A/RES/68/304, https://www.un.org/development/desa/financing/sites/www.un.org.development.desa.financing/files/2020-03/N1453005.pdf.
78. There are other solutions to this particular problem, but that does not fall within the scope of this dissertation, e.g., the inclusion of "Collective Action Clauses" in the contractual terms of bonds. However, also this may face issues with vulture funds pursuing investment treaty arbitration for the way a state conducts its restructuring. *See* Ishikawa, *supra* n. 35, at 183-184.
79. *Ibid.*, at 177.
80. *See* Katherine Reece Thomas, *State Immunity. Insight* 30 (2016).
81. *SerVaas Inc. v. Rafidan Bank* [2012] UKSC, para. 4.
82. *Ibid.*, at para. 12.

developing States have suffered at the hands of unstable, inexperienced, repressive, corrupt, or even rogue governments and leaders. The Paris Club and sovereign debt restructuring regimes are meant to relieve States and ultimately its citizens of financial distress by giving them a relatively fresh start. Enforcing huge monetary awards can frustrate such fair and well-intended procedures. Thus, ironically for the message of this book, sovereign immunity can prove an important shield for States to get some wiggle-room to set their affairs straight. More ironically perhaps, policy objectives and political concerns in this regard may well underscore that the law and rules-based order is one dimension among others. State-centric approaches may be equally valid and perhaps even a dogma with a bad name.

It has been noted that a State that has defaulted on its debt has no incentive to pay voluntarily because such would create coordination problems in restructuring plans and perhaps even incentivize "hold-out" creditors.[83] Given this dynamic, "it would make no sense to pay the successful litigants voluntarily" as that would "encourage holdouts and potentially derail the restructuring."[84] This is another practical obstacle to consider carefully.

§5.3.5 Forum-Shopping

The award-creditor should decide where to enforce its award based on market chances of success. Saunders and Salomon suggested that "[b]efore deciding against which assets to enforce an award, it is worth researching the enforcement history of the relevant country, as some countries ... do not have a good enforcement record."[85] Moreover, it has been noted that a "practical consequence resulting from this divergence in approach [is] a sort of 'forum shopping' by award-holders in determining the optimal forum in which to seek the enforcement and, ultimately, the execution of an award."[86]

Forum-shopping may be absolutely necessary for award-enforcement aspirations. To illustrate, in *Stati/Ascom v. Kazakhstan* (*see* "saga 2" in Chapter 1 and on the Swedish jurisdiction in Chapter 4) the Swedish Supreme Court's decision to grant execution against State assets did not mean the end of the road for the award-creditor. The award-creditor had commenced several enforcement procedures to make up for the entire USD 500 million award (e.g., in Sweden, the U.K., the U.S., Italy, the Netherlands, Belgium, and Luxembourg). And while successful with part of the amount in Sweden, the award-creditor found themselves unsuccessful in other jurisdictions. In 2022, the Hague Court of Appeal lifted the attachment of the SWF's shares

83. Mark C. Weidemaier, *Sovereign Immunity and Sovereign Debt,* 14 U. Ill. L. Rev. 67, 89 (2014) https://doi.org/10.2139/ssrn.2180228.
84. *Ibid.*
85. Matthew Saunders & Claudia Salomon, *Enforcement of Arbitral Awards Against States and State Entities* 476 (2007).
86. Winch, *supra* n. 65, at. 62.

in Samruk Kazyna JSC valued at USD 5.2 billion.[87] The attachment had been ordered by the Court of Appeal and later quashed by the Supreme Court and sent back for reconsideration. In the reconsideration, it was reasoned that the award-creditor had not shown that the ownership was not intended for *jure imperii* purposes—e.g., by increasing the national welfare of the State.[88] After many years of "asset hunting," the parties settled. Surely the fact that some courts embrace a liberal (and at times pragmatic) approach to sovereign immunity from execution, coupled with the award-creditors persistence and effective "forum-shopping" were factors that contributed to reaching the settlement.[89]

§5.4 NORMS-BASED SOLUTIONS

§5.4.1 Competing for Business and Reputational Damage[90]

In order to attract business and generate economic development, a State undertakes efforts to create a hospitable environment for commerce, trade, and investment. Such efforts include the elaboration of business-friendly topics touched upon in this book—i.e., IIL, ISDS, and the evolution toward the restrictive doctrine of immunity from execution. The very bottom line is an attempt to promote and attract FDI in order to foster economic development. An incidental good to such mission is peace through interdependence and interconnectivity. Resultingly, award-debtor States should be motivated to comply with arbitral awards because the alternative could send signals that the State is "anti-business" or an "inhospitable environment." Such reputation could have serious repercussions on the international investment community and adversely impact the competition for business.[91]

To illustrate how norms underpinned by the desire to attract business push States to create a favorable business environment, we may analyze the aftermath of the U.S. enactment of the FSIA in 1976. As a response, the U.K. shortly thereafter passed the SIA 1978. White explained the passing of the SIA as "in part due to the concern of the city [of London] (and the Government) that valuable business would be lost to New York [and U.S.] as a consequence of the passing by the [U.S.] Congress of the [FSIA]."[92] In the debate of the bill in the U.K., then Solicitor-General Archer expressed the following:

> The position now obtaining in the courts of the [U.S.] accords with the interests of all those who, in commerce or finance, engage in transactions with foreign States.

---

87. Vladislav Djanic, *CIS Round-Up*, IAReporter, October 6, 2022: https://www.iareporter.com/articles/cis-round-up-russian-court-deems-arbitration-clauses-unenforceable-against-sanctioned-entities-new-cases-concluded-disputes-and-an-ecthr-ruling/.
88. *Ibid.*
89. Paolo Sorbello, *The Stati v Kazakhstan Saga Ends*, The Diplomat (July 18, 2024), at: https://thediplomat.com/2024/07/the-stati-v-kazakhstan-saga-ends/.
90. This section could equally be placed under § 5.3 as a market-based solution. It operates in between norms-based and market-based solutions.
91. *See* King et al., *supra* n. 20, at 416.
92. Robin C.A. White, *The State Immunity Act 1978*, 42 Modern L. Rev. 72, 72 (1979) https://doi.org/10.1111/j.1468-2230.1979.tb01511.x.

> Unless we change our law, much of the work connected with these transactions—an important invisible export—could be lost to this country.[93]

In a speech about the SIA from 2018, Lord Lloyd-Jones expressed similar views, where he stated that:

> There was an urgent need to bring domestic law in the [U.K.] into line with the new international reality. There was a need to establish certainty in what is predominantly an area of commercial law. There was a real danger that if the [U.K.] continued to apply an absolute theory of immunity or if the position remained unclear while the precise limits of a new restricted immunity were worked out in the cases, the adjudication and arbitration of commercial disputes would move away from London.[94]

While States can push each other in a more pro-business direction, sometimes the opposite is true as well. States can indeed push each other in a more regressive direction. For example, if influential and powerful States practice isolationist and protective measures of their own (e.g., favoring higher tariffs, conservative rules on immunity from execution, interventionist policies with respect to international arbitration, etc.), the idea of a more State-centric policy orientation may gain ground in global competition.

Meanwhile and paradoxically, the reality is that sometimes a more conservative and protective approach elevates the positioning for global business. For example, there is a valid economic reason as to why both the FSIA and SIA specifically protect diplomatic and central bank property *ipso jure*. Mann stated that the special protections afforded to central banks and other monetary authorities were "no doubt due to the wish to attract foreign funds to the City of London [and New York] by assuring their owners that they have nothing to fear from their creditors."[95] Powerful States carefully balance their actions when competing for business (economic dominance) and political influence.

Another intrinsically linked aspect is the reputational factor. A State must preserve its reputation in order to compete for global business. Thus, one major reason why award-debtor States generally comply voluntarily with adverse arbitral awards is undoubtedly the reputational harm of defaulting.[96] Professor Weidemaier notes that even if an award-creditor's efforts to find and seize sovereign assets have failed, "the attempt itself might disrupt the [award-debtor State's] trade relations and thereby penalize[s] default."[97] Thus, the reputational cost of non-compliance may cost more

93. *Ibid.*, at 73 (1979) (referencing H.C. Deb., Vol. 949, col. 412 (May 4, 1978)).
94. David Loyd Jones, *Forty Years On: State Immunity and the State Immunity Act 1978*, 4 (October 18, 2018).
95. Mann, *supra* n. 37, at 62. *See also* Reece Thomas, *supra* n. 80, at para. 19 ("As befits London's status as one of the world's most important financial centres of a large number of states maintain bank accounts in London in the name of their central bank.").
96. *See, e.g.*, Winch, *supra* n. 65, at 63 ("In the context of investor-state dispute settlement, the incentive of protecting reputation encourages host states subject to investment treaty claims to comply with such awards.").
97. Weidemaier, *supra* n. 83, at 104.

than it tastes. Consequently, sovereigns do in most cases pay their debt because doing otherwise could turn the investment community and global community against the State.[98] One may think that reluctant States do not care, but over time such attitude may come to change. This is especially true where market factors are at play (*see* §5.3). As renowned practitioners have noted, "[i]n the short term, states may consider themselves to be immune from such pressure, but history has taught claimants to take a longer view."[99]

§5.4.2 Trends and Anchoring States

Another factor to consider is that States watchfully observe each other's conduct. I call this an "anchoring State phenomena," i.e., that some (often economically, politically, or militarily powerful) States influence other States with similar ideological, historical or cultural inclinations. Such influence can be both conservative and liberal/pragmatic as the case may be. For example, the U.S. adopting the FSIA led to the U.K. adopting the SIA, which in turn has "served as the model for many jurisdictions, including Singapore, Pakistan, and South Africa."[100]

When powerful award-debtor States refuse to comply with adverse arbitral awards, including by invoking immunity from execution, such practice may spread quickly. Why would Sri Lanka comply with an adverse award when India is not? Why would Belarus comply with an adverse award when Russia and Ukraine are not? Why would the Dominican Republic comply with an adverse award when Spain does not? Gaillard and Penusliski have gathered data on the outcome of investment arbitrations involving 32 States that have been sued more than 10 times as of December 31, 2019, and concluded that "the instances of non-compliance have increased and, by all accounts, are likely to continue to do so, especially where disputes are burgeoning, intra-EU or political."[101] This is a trend to monitor closely, in particular through the lens of the "anchor State phenomena."

§5.4.3 Diplomatic Protection and Diplomatic Pressure

If a State refuses to pay its debt, the home State of the award-creditor may turn to diplomatic means, i.e., diplomatic protection. Avoiding diplomatic protection and thereby the politicization of investment disputes was one of the main reasons for

98. *See* King et al., *supra* n. 20, at 415.
99. *Ibid.*
100. Webb, *supra* n. 3, at 2.
101. Emmanuel Gaillard & Ilija Mitrev Penusliski, *State Compliance with Investment Awards*, 36 ICSID Rev. 1, 52 (2021) https://doi.org/10.1093/icsidreview/siaa034,at 8 and 54. Moreover, the diplomatic pressure can yield legislative changes that makes it more difficult for an award-creditor to execute against state assets. *See, e.g.*, the recent legislative amendments in France and Belgium—Loi no 2016-1691 du 9 décembre 2016 relative à la transparence, à la lutte contre la corruption et à la modernisation de la vie économique and Article 1412 quinquies of the Belgian Code Judiciaire, respectively. *See also* Winch, *supra* n. 65, at 64-65.

ISDS/ITA and any such reversion to diplomatic protection may re-politicize investor-State disputes.[102] That being said, there is undoubtedly an important and real role for home State governments to play in assisting their investors in foreign countries. Believing otherwise would simply be naïve; it is not even a matter of being cynical, but rather of being a realist.

For example, in *De Letelier v. Republic of Chile*, the 2nd Circuit refused to pierce the corporate veil of a State-owned airline in order to satisfy the credit of the holder of a decision against Chile.[103] In a footnote to the conclusion, the court explained that even if tenuous, "other remedies may still be possible," such as that Chile can decide to pay as "an act of international good-will to honor the judgment" or the U.S. "may be persuaded to bring this claim before some international tribunal."[104]

At the end of the day, whether such belief is written or stated, or not, does not matter. Such underlying policies lurk behind the curtains. States are involved, period. If award-debtor States refuse to pay and the law is unable to assist, there may simply be no other viable alternative left. This is too obvious to mention, but there are also situations prior to arbitration where the home State's assistance may be necessary to avoid arbitration, to begin with. Fox and Webb rightly note, "short of resort to war, there is ... little alternative even today but to make settlement of judgment debts with the cooperation of the debtor State and by diplomatic means."[105]

Unfortunately, while diplomatic protection could commence in a well-intended manner, it can over time escalate into quite significant pressure. For example, in the aftermath of the Argentinian crisis, the Obama administration criticized Argentina publicly.[106] Furthermore, the U.S. suspended Argentina from the General System of Preferences for reduced tariffs and began voting against new loans for Argentina from various development banks.[107] The U.S. Senate went as far as suggesting that Argentina should be excluded from G20.[108] Finally, Argentina gave in and settled their investment arbitration cases, including those against so-called vulture funds (*see* §5.3 above).[109] As a result, the U.S. withdrew its trade sanctions and did not put obstacles in the way of much-needed loans from the World Bank.[110] The U.S. diplomatic pressure was not the sole factor in pushing Argentina to "faithfully observe the rule of law," but it surely was an important one. Sometimes, the multilateral pressure may be even more assertive whereby States impose sanctions on a defaulting State (e.g., as is currently the case against Russia and Iran).[111] However, too aggressive diplomatic pressure may be unproductive. For example, increasing tariffs or implementing sanctions may lead to an escalation and trade wars.

102. *See generally* Bjorklund, *supra* n. 28.
103. *Letelier v. Republic of Chile*, 748 F.2d 790, 799 (2d Cir. 1984).
104. *Ibid.*, at 799 (fn 4).
105. Fox & Webb, *supra* n. 1, at 486.
106. Cymrot, *supra* n. 32, at 375.
107. *Ibid.*
108. *Ibid.*
109. *Ibid.*
110. *Ibid.*
111. *See* Bjorklund, *supra* n. 28, at 238.

§5.4.4 Policy Objectives and Political Concerns

Despite what has been said in law, an enforcement forum's reluctance to attach and execute against assets of another sovereign State appears not primarily rooted in law. Fox and Webb underscored this by writing that "[e]ven where attachment of State assets located in the forum State is legally possible, the political consequences to the friendly relations of the forum State with the foreign State may discourage the forum State's support for such enforcement."[112]

Put differently, whether a State is conservative, liberal, or liberal and pragmatic depends largely on its theoretical understanding of sovereign immunity (as discussed in Chapter 3). This author has argued that the theoretical preference—albeit justified by concepts such as equality, dignity, independence, and comity—is actually better explained through policy objectives and political concerns. Such approach accounts not only for the rule of immunity and major exceptions such as waiver and commerciality but also includes the various directions in scope, degree, and nuance that the law may undertake. Whether a State endorses the theory of absolute immunity or of restrictive immunity is binary and largely a matter of ideological preferences. For example, the Soviet approach was based on the "dogmatic notion that there [were] two antagonistic systems in the modern world, and that the choice between the restrictive and the absolute theories of sovereign immunity translates into a choice between the free-market and the centrally-controlled economic systems."[113] Whether a State is quasi-liberal, liberal, or liberal and pragmatic is not binary—rather it takes many shapes.

The fact that policy objectives and political concerns play a not insignificant part in shaping the law of sovereign immunity even in liberal democratic and liberal capitalist societies is undoubtedly the case. Just look at France with Loi Sapin 2 (Chapter 4), the Obama administration's response to Argentina's behavior following its financial crisis (§5.4.3), the various responses to "vulture funds" (§5.3), and so on. This attitude is reflected in scholarship, which often plays a prolific role in changing law. By way of illustration, arguing against the U.S. Supreme Court decisions in the *NML* cases, the authors wrote that:

> Perhaps most importantly, the Supreme Court's decision on discovery, the Second Circuit's upholding of injunctions, and the use of contempt sanctions and contempt orders "could lead to reciprocal adverse treatment of the United States in foreign courts," where the United States may now also be subjected to same treatment [citing U.S. amicus curia brief]. As the United States noted in its amicus brief, the "judicial seizure" of a foreign state's property "may be regarded as an affront to its dignity and may ... affect our relations with it." As a result, foreign states and the U.S. itself (because of reciprocity) may be burdened by litigation over the scope and manner of discovery, running afoul of one of the principles of the FSIA.[114]

112. Fox & Webb, *supra* n. 1, at 486.
113. Christopher Osakwe, *A Soviet Perspective on Foreign Sovereign Immunity: Law and Practice*, 23 Va. J. Int'l. L. 13, 14 (1982).
114. Ingenito & Hioureas, *supra* n. 33, at 130.

This is not an uncommon position to hold. Many practitioners share such a point of view.[115] The Supreme Court did in fact respond to this alarm-belling too. The Court reasoned as follows:

> Nonetheless, Argentina and the United States urge us to consider the worrisome international relations consequences of siding with the lower court. Discovery orders as sweeping as this one, the Government warns, will cause "a substantial invasion of [foreign states'] sovereignty," Brief for United States as Amicus Curiae ..., and will "[u]ndermin[e] international comity," ... Worse, such orders might provoke "reciprocal adverse treatment of the United States in foreign courts," ... and will "threaten harm to the United States' foreign relations more generally," ... These apprehensions are better directed to that branch of government with authority to amend the Act—which, as it happens, is the same branch that forced our retirement from the immunity-by-factor-balancing business nearly 40 years ago.[116]

Thus, preferences in a specific legal outcome may be rooted less in strict legal reasoning and more in policy objectives and potential political consequences. This can be illustrated by yet another more practical and behind-the-curtain example. Lawyers operating in the U.S. oil industry may be unhappy with allowing execution of awards against nonmonetary obligations of oil and gas.[117] In exchange for extraction of natural resources, the host State can often either opt for cash royalties or a share of the production in-kind.[118] Underscoring a problematic situation, two authors highlighted the following scenario:

> Had the Fifth Circuit [in *Af-Cap Inc. v. Republic of Congo*, 462 F.3d 417 (5th Cir. 2006)] found that Texas law allows garnishment of CMS Nomeco's nonmonetary obligations, CMS Nomeco would have found itself in a thorny situation. On the one hand, a U.S. court ordered CMS Nomeco to turn over the Congo's royalty oil and the SNPC's oil entitlement to the Congo's judgment creditors. On the other hand, a Congolese court found that the U.S. orders were not enforceable in the Congo and demanded that CMS Nomeco deliver to the Congo its in-kind royalty oil and to the SNPC its oil entitlement as mandated by law and the concession contracts.[119]

The point being made here is that it is not only "altruistic" well-doers who have an interest in retaining sovereign immunity. Multinational corporations, even fossil fuel enterprises, may have an interest in foreign assets being protected, unless, of course, it is they, themselves, that are the award-creditors. In this example, the companies' royalties being subject to attachment makes them less competitive in the fight for concession contracts in the developing world—i.e., business they want and need. The world of business and governance presents all sorts of unexpected paradoxes.

115. *See, e.g.*, Brief Encounters, *A Cautionary Tale on the Interplay of Sovereign Immunity and International Arbitration*, Podcast (September 21, 2022).
116. *Republic of Argentina*, 134 S.Ct at 2258.
117. *See, e.g.*, Andrew B. Derman & Andrew Melsheimer, *Recent Developments in Foreign Sovereign Immunity and Texas Garnishment Law: A New Threat Facing U.S. Oil and Gas* Companies, 29 Hous. J. Int'l L. 277 (2007). *See Af-Cap Inc. v. Republic of Congo*, 462 F.3d 417 (5th Cir. 2006).
118. *Ibid.*, at 278.
119. *Ibid.*, at 284-285.

§5.4.5 Scholarly Work, Social Change, and an Inclusive Debate

Scholars have an important role to play in pushing social change. Not only is scholarly work a source of public international law—even prolific in the field of sovereign immunity law—but it also affects policy and eventually change. Through scholarship, we can "nudge" the choice-architectures in a particular direction.[120]

For many years, the courts and legislators of politically influential and economically strong Western States have been the driving force in creating the public international law doctrine on sovereign immunity. In fact, in shaping public international law more broadly speaking too. The dominant scholarship underpinning much of the evolution is Western-based. Thus, the normative framework of public international law may lack diversity and inclusiveness. As a result, it may serve the interests of some, and not others. This could be said for many areas of public international law, including IIL, ISDS, and sovereign immunity law. Western hegemony in dictating the policy orientation and therefore in shaping these legal frameworks may have myriads of explanations—some logical (economic, military, and political power) and yet perhaps anchored at least in part on a dark post-colonial, post-imperialist legacy.

When analyzing the doctrine of sovereign immunity, many Western scholars, legislators, and judges appear to be favoring a liberal and pragmatic doctrine vis-à-vis sovereign immunity. The disagreements are mostly in scope, degree, and nuance—often presented as whether to endorse yet further liberalization and pragmatic procedural rules.

We must ask: Can the law be legitimate if not uniform, or at least approved by large parts of the diverse world? Can the evolution of the law gain real and meaningful approval if major players such as China, Russia, Brazil, India, and many others are left out of the debate when shaping its contours? What role should TWAIL scholars and voices from the Global South have? Can a reform even take place without an inclusive and diverse debate?

The truth of the matter is simple; that is, one ideology has prevailed so emphatically, until recently at least, that the rest of the world has been idle, mainly watching from a distance while the debate unfolds in international bodies created by (and largely for) the capital-exporting, Western world, while those mostly in need have had little incentive—let alone power—to voice their concerns or shape the debate. For good and obvious reasons, there has been a great measure of cynicism directed toward exclusively Western practices in shaping public international law. Accordingly, we must now seriously address the question of whether the creation of what we now perceive to be international law, most notably customary international law, is actually a result of State practice, *opinio juris*, and legislative work, or whether it is the manifestation of centuries of hegemonical-like practice?

And one is bound to ask: If these forceful Western-dominant practices continue unhindered and unhinged, will we forever be stuck in a scenario where—as the cynics have often asserted—the UN and similar Western-led projects remain an imposed

120. Richard H. Thaler & Cass R. Sunstein, *Nudge: The Final Edition* (2021).

"catch-22" boot on the neck by which the developing world can only break free from poverty by intensifying its dependence on the West? There is a similar question, of somewhat milder import (a proverbial dog that caught the car scenario) as to what happens once these projects reach the intended goals of relative interdependence.

Meanwhile, it remains important that the West should not deviate from its firmly entrenched and well-elaborated values that so effectively improved stability, reduced wars, and lifted millions out of poverty post-WWII. These virtues are manifested in various international bodies, such as the UN, EU, World Bank, IMF, WTO, and so on. The economic models that underpin liberal capitalism and the values central to liberal democracy are good and workable ideas, even if there is merit in choosing other methods of governance too.

CHAPTER 6

Conclusions: Sovereign Immunity from Execution and International Arbitration

§6.1 CONCLUDING REMARKS

Having identified the underlying problem of sovereign immunity law when intersecting with international arbitration law in Chapter 2 and then outlined the theory and sources of sovereign immunity law in Chapter 3, this book explored and analyzed the doctrinal understanding of sovereign immunity from execution, as well as various domestic courts' interpretation and application of the doctrine in Chapter 4. Having undertaken such doctrinal and comparative exercise, the author was able to illustrate shared and unique problems as well as offer various possible legal and non-legal solutions in Chapter 5.

Here, in Chapter 6, the author concludes with some regret perhaps, but no surprise, that the plea of immunity from execution remains a serious obstacle to award-creditors in international arbitration where the award-debtor is a reluctant State. Even though most States nowadays have a liberal theory on the substantive law of sovereign immunity, many of the same States are nevertheless often less pragmatic in their interpretation and application of the doctrine of immunity from execution. Most jurisdictions have little procedural ease to make award-execution possible, with some notable exceptions.

Having undertaken a rather robust comparative exercise, the overall conclusion to the research question put forth in Chapter 1 is that the law of sovereign immunity from execution in the context of international arbitration, as currently understood, interpreted, and applied, does not sit well with the expectations of a twenty-first-century global marketplace. That being said, there are competing, non-market-oriented, interests that pull the capitalist-oriented liberal push due to policy objectives and political concerns. In legal theory, these considerations have been called "equality," "dignity," "independence," "comity," and equivalent. Depending on the overall political climate, the competing sides have different leverages, and the operators in the system have different bravery or actual perceptions when applying the doctrine or such procedural rules ancillary and incidental to it. As with much else in this world, the doctrine of sovereign immunity from execution manifests and is interpreted and applied against the backdrop of cultural identity and ideological preferences or inclinations.

All in all, the plea of sovereign immunity from execution remains a strong and powerful shield for award-debtor States unwilling to comply voluntarily with adverse arbitral awards. The doctrinal understanding of sovereign immunity from execution is mostly based on the restrictive theory of immunity but is nevertheless applied on the basis of a Purpose Test and is often coupled with exceptions to the exceptions—e.g., treating certain State assets as immune *ipso jure*. Moreover, it is only a few States that interpret and apply the substantive law in such a pragmatic manner as to facilitate award execution through procedural rules—e.g., through lowering or reversing the burden of proof, dissecting and attaching parts of mixed-use assets, allowing for discovery, piercing the corporate veil, and so on. This book has shown many problems, legal and practical barriers, that an award-creditor faces when the award-debtor State invokes sovereign immunity from execution. Meanwhile, this book has also shown many ways in which award-creditors can achieve success—both in terms of legal and non-legal solutions. Below is a list of the author's general observations and conclusions.

Enforcement of international arbitral awards is its main advantage over litigation and other types of alternative dispute resolution. There is no multinational convention dealing with enforcement of foreign judgments. The New York and ICSID Conventions make international arbitration the preferable venue for settling transborder disputes stemming from trade, commerce and investment.

For the ends of international arbitration to be as effective as the means, award-creditors must be able to rely on domestic courts' coercive means through attachment and execution. A lack of effective execution undermines ISDS/ITA and frustrates the otherwise effective machinery of international arbitration. As Brower II put it, "although the point should be obvious, no system for the adjudication of private claims against States can secure the confidence of potential users by adopting post-judgment proceedings that consistently threaten to rob them of the fruits of their victories."[1] Professor Schreuer described the potential plea of sovereign immunity as the "Achilles' heel" of the ICSID Convention.[2] The New York Convention is no different. It is silent on the topic. Overall, the ISDS "has its weak point when it comes to the actual execution against States of pecuniary obligations under awards."[3] Thus, in certain situations,

1. Charles H. Brower II, *Mitsubishi, Investor-State Arbitration, and the Law of State Immunity*, 20 Am. U. Int'l Rev. 907, 923 (2005).
2. Christoph H. Schreuer et al., *The ICSID Convention: A Commentary* 1154 (2nd ed. 2009).
3. *Ibid. See also* Matthew Saunders & Claudia Salomon, *Enforcement of Arbitral Awards Against States and State Entities* 476 (2007) ("The greatest restriction on obtaining satisfaction of an arbitral award against a state therefore remains domestic rules on sovereign immunity, a restriction which applies in equal measure to court judgments."); Hazel Fox, *State Immunity and Enforcement of Arbitral Awards: Do We Need an UNCITRAL Model Law Mark II for Execution Against State Property?*, 23 Arb. Int'l 89, 90 (1996) https://doi.org/10.1093/arbitration/12.1.89 ("But there still remain grave deficiencies in the effectiveness of international commercial

award-creditors have a right but no remedy.[4] As we have seen in this book, it is not easy to execute an arbitral award where the award-debtor State invokes sovereign immunity. Therefore, the ends of international arbitration are far less effective than the means. International lawyers should work so that the last link is not allowed to be its weakest. We cannot tolerate situations where "sovereign defaults are legion and where governments rarely repay debts in full."[5]

International arbitration, as well as IIL, facilitates and enables a rules-based international legal order. An adjudicatory process that is rules-based should not threaten to deny the award-creditor the fruit of their victories, and therefore of the promise in ISDS/ITA. The object and purpose of international arbitration with States should not be reduced to a paper commitment.[6] If international arbitration cannot deliver for investors, then what is the alternative? The alternative is re-politicization through diplomatic means, which is paradoxically an institution that ISDS/ITA was meant to replace.[7] Things could be even worse; for example, a re-emergence of power politics and gunboat diplomacy.[8] Put simply, the alternative to a rules-based international order is a power-based world order. And in the jungle, the strong win. Thus, both the regime of ITA/ISDS and the retreat of the absolute immunity doctrine were indications of a trend away from a State-centric international law order and instead a move toward a rules-based international order.[9] The supporters of a rules-based international order "must do not more, but also no less, than to rediscover a handful of sensible principles that we once knew, but seem to have forgotten along the way."[10] Such principles are embedded in the post-WWII landscape and gave birth to international economic law and with it inevitably ab increased reliance on international arbitration.

The law and legal trajectory of sovereign immunity is fluid and changes are inevitable. The doctrine of sovereign immunity has not been static. It will likely remain fluid. The lack of global consensus is exacerbated by the fact that the normative

arbitration. Effective implementation of foreign arbitral awards by national courts remains patchy and fraught with obstacles ... One obstacle to effective implementation of awards is the ability of a state or state entity as a party to an arbitration to renege on its undertaking to implement the award by pleading state immunity."); and Brian King et al., "Enforcing Awards Involving Foreign Sovereigns," in *International Commercial Arbitration in New York* (James H. Carter & John Fellas, eds.), 413 (2010). ("Sovereigns generally enjoy a number of immunities not applicable to private individuals, so that sovereigns that decide not to pay have powerful weapons at their disposal to shield their assets from enforcement ...").

4. *See* Mark M. Cymrot, "Enforcing Sovereign Arbitral Awards: State Defences and Creditor Strategies in an Imperfect World," in *The Cambridge Handbook of Immunities and International Law* (Tom Ruys et al., eds.), 350, (2019).
5. Michael Waibel, *Sovereign Defaults Before International Courts and Tribunals* 13-16 (2011).
6. *See* Brower, *supra* n. 1, at 927.
7. Andrea K. Bjorklund, *Sovereign Immunity as a Barrier to the Enforcement of Investor-State Arbitral Awards: The Re-politicization of International Investment Disputes*, 21 Am. Rev. Int'l Arb. 211, 241 (2011).
8. *Ibid.*
9. Stephan W. Schill, *Cross-Regime Harmonization Through Proportionality Analysis: The Case of International Investment Law, the Law of State Immunity and Human Rights*, 27 ICSID Rev. 87, 91 (2012) https://doi.org/10.1093/icsidreview/sis002; Brower, *supra* n. 1, at 913.
10. *Ibid.*, at 927.

justification for the doctrine rests on different underpinnings—e.g., equality, dignity, independence, comity, or a combination of the mentioned. To reflect changed priorities historically, the theory underpinning the doctrine of sovereign immunity has moved from being "absolute" (i.e., absolute immunity), to being "restrictive" (i.e., restrictive immunity). Notwithstanding this, simply treating the theory of absolute immunity as "a thing of the past" is not completely accurate.[11] First, the general rule is still absolute immunity, albeit exceptions have been elaborated. Second, many States still adhere to absolute immunity. Third, most jurisdictions approve de jure absolute immunity for certain State property. Finally, because the law on sovereign immunity is not static and history is indeed cyclical—absolutist sentiments may swing back in taste like a pendulum. Capitalist countries are keener to align with a liberal, market-oriented theory on sovereign immunity than, for example, socialist or communist States. Perhaps liberal democracies, even more so. Today, State capitalism and other political theories have once more manifested as serious contenders to liberal capitalism/democracy. Such trends will likely affect the interpretation and application of sovereign immunity, in general, and with respect to execution, in particular.

While there is a relative divergence of States' approaches to sovereign immunity, there is also a relative uniformity. Domestic practice has developed differently, and divergent practices exist. The differences are theoretical, substantive and procedural. Despite this divergence, there is some level of consensus in theory and therefore on broader substantive law points. These developments have been reflected in customary international law and highlighted by the ICJ and domestic case law. Moreover, The UNCSI harmonizes the law in many important ways. Most notably, by codifying the restrictive theory of immunity in the jurisdiction and execution contexts. No matter what exceptions are eventually endorsed and how they are to be interpreted and applied, the debate on sovereign immunity encapsulates and underscores much of the complexity of establishing harmony in transnational adjudication. It is inevitably the case that the complex subject matter of sovereign immunity will keep on throwing up nuanced problems of, among other things, legal theory, methodology, interpretation and application, statutory interpretation, policy objectives, political concerns, and equivalent.[12] To this end, Professor René David's take on the role of comparative law in leading to convergence, unification, and harmonization in a modern world seems to have partly come to fruition in this specialized area of public international law. The "transnationalization" of sovereign immunity law should not be rejected, it is better to be embraced. David famously stated that:

> There are those who, rooted in nineteenth-century thinking, decry such an ambition [of international unification of law] as pure fantasy. But it may be more fanciful to think that the present anarchy in international relations can be tolerated any longer in the modern world.[13]

11. Xiodong Yang, *State Immunity in International Law* 3 (2012).
12. *See* Thomas E. Carbonneau, *The Law and Practice of Arbitration* 108 (2020).
13. René David & E.C. Brierley, *Major Legal Systems in the World Today* 11 (1985).

It is this author's opinion that the statement is as true today as it was then.

Domestic case law is the leading source of sovereign immunity law, but the UNCSI plays an instrumental role and often serves as a stepping-stone for further analysis. "Immunity exists as a rule of international law, but its application depends substantially on the law and procedural rules of the forum."[14] Even though the UNCSI has not yet entered into force, the ICJ and domestic courts have treated the convention as partly codifying customary international law, and therefore to be used as a stepping-stone for further analysis of the substantive law of sovereign immunity. Article 19(c) UNCSI accepts the restrictive theory of immunity for execution purposes (i.e., the commercial purposes exception), while Article 21 is designed to offer heightened protection—virtually absolute immunity—to certain specific property *ipso jure*. Article 19(c) represents a codification of customary international law. Thus, it has rightly been noted that the convention is an "epoch-making document" that "marks the final establishment of restrictive immunity as the prevailing doctrine in international law."[15] Whether Article 21 represents a codification of customary international law is debated. This author's position is that it does not represent a codification of customary international law, but can indeed be treated as a stepping-stone for further analysis.

The ICJ has an important role to play in developing the law on sovereign immunity. There is no doubt that the ICJ has had an enormous impact on the development of the law of sovereign immunity. While domestic courts and legislators establish state practice and *opinio juris*, it is the ICJ's role to consolidate the law and crystalize principles.

There is a distinction between immunity from jurisdiction and execution. In the *Jurisdictional Immunities* Case, the ICJ made it clear that there is a distinction between enforcing a judgment (or an award for that matter) and executing against State property. On the topic of execution, the court held that "the rules of customary international law governing immunity from enforcement are distinct from and go further than those governing jurisdictional immunity, and must be separately applied."[16] The reason for treating immunity from jurisdiction differently than immunity from coercive measures (including execution) is that "[e]nforcement against State property constitutes a greater interference with a State's freedom to manage its own affairs and to pursue its public purposes than does the pronouncement of a judgment or order by a national court of another State."[17] The allocation of public funds is considered a vital and integral part of sovereignty.

The commercial exception operates differently in the jurisdiction and execution contexts. Sovereign immunity is qualified based on the Nature Test vis-à-vis immunity from jurisdiction, while the Purpose Test is prevalent with respect to immunity from execution. Even though most commercial hubs have embraced the restrictive theory of immunity also with respect to execution, in practice it has a limited effect because the

14. James Crawford, *Brownlie's Principles of Public International Law* 1934 (8th ed. 2012, e-book). *See also* Hazel Fox & Philippa Webb, *The Law of State Immunity* 423, 505 (2015).
15. Yang, *supra* n. 11, at 441.
16. *Jurisdictional Immunities of the State (Germany v. Italy: Greece Intervening)*, Judgment, ICJ Rep. (February 3, 2012), at para. 131 (hereinafter "*Jurisdictional Immunities*").
17. Fox & Webb *supra* n. 14, at 486.

exceptions to jurisdictional immunity is based on the Nature Test (i.e., nature of the use of assets) while the exceptions to execution immunity is based on the Purpose Test (i.e., purpose for which the State assets are used). Put differently, it is more difficult to attach and execute against State property than it is to get the State into court or to initiate award recognition and enforcement procedures against it.

Some State assets are treated as immune ipso jure even where the restrictive theory of immunity is adopted. For example, Article 21 UNCSI outlines five, non-exhaustive categories of properties/assets considered immune *ipso jure*. In fact, most States that have codified the law on sovereign immunity include a list of *ipso jure* protected assets/property. As does States that have not codified the law—through case law. The fact that certain assets are treated as immune *ipso jure* is undoubtedly part of customary international law. What and how the virtually absolute immunity for certain assets applies is, however, much disputed.

Award-creditors could benefit from various domestic procedural features/rules. States have different procedural rules that may enable award-creditors in the execution context. It is true that sovereign immunity exists as a rule of public international law, but it is equally true that its application depends substantially on the law *and* procedural rules of the enforcing domestic court.[18]

The burden of proof is typically onerous and high for award-creditors. There is an undeniably difficult and high burden of proof on the award-creditor when seeking to attach and execute against State assets. The burden of proof is neither discharged nor reversed easily.

The fact that award-debtor States hold assets as mixed-use complicates execution. Oftentimes, State assets are found in "mixed accounts" or for "mixed use." Jurisdictions differ in how they treat mixed accounts or properties. The differences can be whether they allow attaching and executing against the assets altogether, whether parts can be severed, whether the asset can be attached and executed against if it is majorly used for commercial purposes, etc.

An arbitration clause generally constitutes a waiver of immunity from jurisdiction but not from execution. An arbitration clause is nowadays treated as a waiver of immunity from jurisdiction. Such court jurisdiction generally includes recognition and enforcement of an international arbitral award. However, the State still retains the right to invoke immunity from execution. Few courts have concluded that an arbitration clause is considered to be an implied waiver of immunity from execution. This was the position in France in 2000 before it was later reversed. This seems to be the position in India today, but it is unclear (e.g., whether it applies also to ISDS/ITA awards). Even where applied, the waiver doctrine, like the commercial purposes exception, comes with limitations of certain property/assets protected *ipso jure*.

Even an express waiver may prove of limited use for an award-creditor seeking to attach and execute against State assets. For example, in the U.S., the 9th and 5th Circuits have held that an explicit waiver of immunity from "suit, execution, attachment, or other legal process" was an exception pursuant to section 1610(a)(a) to the

18. *See, e.g.*, Crawford, *supra* n. 14, at 489.

general rule of immunity found in section 1609 and that a "waiver merely triggers the exception to the immunity from execution that would otherwise be in effect."[19] Thus, the waiver means that the court must still continue the inquiry to determine: (1) whether the property is in the U.S.; and (2) whether the property is used for a commercial activity in the U.S. In other jurisdictions, there is often a requirement that the waiver (at least for purposes of attaching and executing against assets protected *ipso jure*) should be both *express* and *specific*. Thus, in many instances, it seems that what is effectively requested is a form of earmarking.

An award-creditor cannot expect to easily pierce the corporate veil of an SOE in order to attach and execute against the debt of award-debtor State. There is a strong presumption of separability, but it may be overcome under certain exceptional circumstances. As a general matter of law, SOEs and the State itself are treated separately for purposes of responsibility. There is a very strong presumption that a State-owned entity is a distinct legal person and should not be liable for the debt of the State.[20] However, on some rare occasions, the law does not allow this distinction to stand because such could, for example, work injustices. Therefore, the piercing of the corporate veil has been granted under (highly) exceptional circumstances.

Few States would allow discovery against an award-debtor State, especially general asset or extraterritorial discovery. However, in *Republic of Argentina v. NML Capital, Ltd*,[21] the U.S. Supreme Court reasoned that "the FSIA does not restrict the discovery of a foreign State's extraterritorial assets in aid of post-judgment attachment." It was clarified that "[t]here is no ... provision forbidding or limiting discovery in aid of a foreign-sovereign judgment debtor's assets ..."[22] Accordingly, post-judgment discovery should be no different when the award-debtor is a sovereign State compared to a private award-debtor. This is a rare exception to the situation in (most, if not all) other States worldwide.

Courts could order injunctions against an award-debtor State in order to ultimately assist the award-creditor. In the *NML Capital, Ltd. v. Republic of Argentina* (*Equal Treatment Case I*), the 2nd Circuit Court affirmed an injunctive relief requesting Argentina to refrain from making payments with respect to its restructured bonds and not also make payments on the defaulted bonds.[23] Specific performance was ordered because no adequate monetary remedy was available.[24]

Many legal determinations considered "conservative" in this book are actually anchored in valid policy objectives and political concerns. The doctrine of sovereign immunity functions as a tool enabling mutual intercourse and global governance by not putting States on bad terms or in financial difficulties. Sovereign immunity assists in stabilizing global affairs and allows States to exercise the rule of law as opposed to acting rogue. Put differently, States can invoke a legal shield (immunity) instead of simply ignoring their legal obligations. Thus, even if this book spends many pages

19. *Af-Cap Inc. v. Republic of Congo*, 475 F.3d 1080, 1087 (9th Cir. 2007).
20. *See* Ch. 4.
21. *Republic of Argentina v. NML Capital, Ltd.*, 134 S.Ct 2250 (2014).
22. *Ibid.*, at 2256.
23. *NML Capital, Ltd. v. Republic of Argentina (Equal Treatment Case I)*, 699 F.3d 250 (2d Cir. 2012).
24. *Ibid.*, at 261.

explaining why the doctrine of sovereign immunity puts obstacles in the road for award-creditors, it is important to underscore (and understand) the policy objectives and political concerns that justify the heightened protection for State assets. There is much important nuance, scope, and degree to the fuller understanding of sovereign immunity from execution, in general, and as it intersects with international arbitration law, in particular.

The legislative and executive branches matter, but it is the judicial branch that interprets and applies the international law on sovereign immunity. Similarly, it must be understood that the law of sovereign immunity is public international law, even where the law has been codified domestically. By way of example, in the legislative work leading up to the FSIA it was stated that the legislative branch had "decided to put [their] faith in the U.S. courts to work out progressively, on a case-by-case basis ... the distinction between commercial and governmental" activities.[25] In so doing, it was said that the judge must bear in mind that the rules on sovereign immunity as found in the FSIA expressly reflect and codify principles of international law.[26] Moreover, it should be understood that the FSIA not only was based on principles of international law but also that it "continues to reflect basic principles of international law."[27] Finally, it must be noted that in some jurisdictions the role of the executive branch is still prevalent in determining whether or not to grant sovereign immunity.[28]

The debate on the direction of the law on sovereign immunity may not be as inclusive and diverse as one would wish. The traditional opposition to a restrictive theory with respect to immunity from measures of constraint stems from either non-capitalist political theories or third-world reservations. Analyzing the ILC work, Dr. Bankas wrote that: "Coupled with the Third World's opposition to the idea of subjecting State property to execution or attachment by domestic courts or local courts. The increase in the number of nationals from the developing countries on the International Law Commission has given these nations immense strength to ventilate their grievances in respect of those laws which militate against their interests, and to shape the development of international law."[29] The "articulation of the Third World interest did crystallize into a forceful unity of aggregation that could not be defeated" initially, and therefore the disagreements prolonged the work of the General Assembly (GA) Working Group significantly.[30] The divergences represented in the third world, as well as in socialist and communist States, complicated the progression of the UNCSI.

25. Monroe Leigh, *Jurisdiction of U.S. Courts in Suits Against Foreign States: Hearings on H.R. 11315 Before Subcomm. On Admin Law and Governmental Relations of the House Comm. on the Judiciary*, 94th Cong. 24, at 53 (1976).
26. *Bolivarian Republic of Venezuela, et al., Petitioners v. Helmerich & Payne International Drilling Co., et al.*, 137 S. Ct. 1317 (2017) ("The Act for the most part embodies basic principles of international law long followed both in the United states and elsewhere."). *See* David P. Stewart, "International Immunities in U.S. Law," in *The Oxford Handbook of Comparative Foreign Relations Law* (Curtis A. Bradley, ed.), 626, (2019).
27. *Bolivarian Republic of Venezuela, et al., Petitioners*, 581 U.S. 1317.
28. E.g., in Spain the courts still request an opinion from the MFA regarding whether a party can rely on a sovereign immunity plea (Ministerio de Asuntos Exteriores, Informe No. 23.520 DBO, Madrid December 14, 2022).
29. Ernest K. Bankas, *The State Immunity Controversy in International Law* 176 (2005).
30. *See Ibid.*, at 189.

Resultingly, albeit the substantive law on sovereign immunity has moved toward the restrictive theory of immunity, the UNCSI does indeed demonstrate a culmination between two opposite sides. The UNCSI is the product of competing ideologies, where divergent States had to give in to each other's views, and therefore have a meeting of minds through concessions. Whatever preference one endorses, it is important that all voices are heard.

1. Moshe Hirsch, *The Arbitration Mechanism of the International Center for the Settlement of Investment Disputes*, 1993 (ISBN 07-923-1993-1).
2. Aida B. Avanessian, *Iran-United States Claims Tribunal in Action*, 1993 (ISBN 18-533-3902-4).
3. Isaak I. Dore, *The UNCITRAL Framework for Arbitration in Contemporary Perspective*, 1993 (ISBN 18-533-3573-8).
4. Vesna Lazić, *Insolvency Proceedings and Commercial Arbitration*, 1998 (ISBN 90-411-1115-8).
5. Joachim Frick, *Arbitration in Complex International Contracts*, 2001 (ISBN 90-411-1662-1).
6. Katherine Lynch, *The Forces of Economic Globalization: Challenges to the Regime of International Commercial Arbitration*, 2003 (ISBN 90-411-1994-9).
7. Christoph Liebscher, *The Healthy Award: Challenge in International Commercial Arbitration*, 2003 (ISBN 90-411-2011-4).
8. Hamid G. Gharavi, *The International Effectiveness of the Annulment of an Arbitral Award*, 2003 (ISBN 90-411-1717-2).
9. Abdulhay Sayed, *Corruption in International Trade and Commercial Arbitration*, 2004 (ISBN 90-411-2236-2).
10. Gabrielle Kaufmann-Kohler & Thomas Schultz, *Online Dispute Resolution: Challenges for Contemporary Justice*, 2004 (ISBN 90-411-2318-0).
11. Christopher R. Drahozal & Richard W. Naimark (eds), *Towards a Science of International Arbitration: Collected Empirical Research*, 2005 (ISBN 90-411-2322-9).
12. Ali Yeşilirmak, *Provisional Measures in International Commercial Arbitration*, 2005 (ISBN 90-411-2353-9).
13. Christian Bühring-Uhle, *Arbitration and Mediation in International Business*, second revised edition, 2006 (ISBN 978-9-041-12256-8).
14. Bernard Hanotiau, *Complex Arbitrations: Multi-party, Multi-contract and Multi-issue – A Comparative Study*, Second Edition, 2020 (ISBN 978-94-035-1261-7).
15. Loukas A. Mistelis & Julian D.M. Lew (eds), *Pervasive Problems in International Arbitration*, 2006 (ISBN 978-9-041-12450-0).
16. Julian D.M. Lew & Loukas A. Mistelis (eds), *Arbitration Insights – Twenty Years of the Annual Lecture of the School of International Arbitration, Sponsored by Freshfields Bruckhaus Deringer*, 2006 (ISBN 978-9-041-12606-1).
17. Mark Kantor, *Valuation for Arbitration: Compensation Standards, Valuation Methods and Expert Evidence*, 2008 (ISBN 978-9-041-12735-8).
18. Christoph Brunner, *Force Majeure and Hardship under General Contract Principles: Exemption for Non-Performance in International Arbitration*, 2009 (ISBN 978-90-411-2792-1).

19. Loukas A. Mistelis & Stavros L. Brekoulakis (eds), *Arbitrability: International & Comparative Perspectives,* 2009 (ISBN 978-90-411-2730-3).
20. Sam Luttrell, *Bias Challenges in International Commercial Arbitration: The Need for a 'Real Danger' Test,* 2009 (ISBN 978-90-411-3191-1).
21. Monique Sasson, *Substantive Law in Investment Treaty Arbitration: The Unsettled Relationship Between International Law and Municipal Law,* Second Edition, 2017 (ISBN 978-90-411-6103-1).
22. Ileana M. Smeureanu, *Confidentiality in International Commercial Arbitration,* 2011 (ISBN 978-90-411-3226-0).
23. Won Kidane, *China-Africa Dispute Settlement: The Law, Economics and Culture of Arbitration,* 2011 (ISBN 978-90-411-3674-9).
24. Karel Daele, *Challenge and Disqualification of Arbitrators in International Arbitration,* 2012 (ISBN 978-90-411-3799-9).
25. Crina Baltag, *The Energy Charter Treaty: The Notion of Investor,* 2012 (ISBN 978-90-411-3428-8).
26. Alexandra Diehl, *The Core Standard of International Investment Protection: Fair and Equitable Treatment,* 2012 (ISBN 978-90-411-3869-9).
27. Manuel Indlekofer, *International Arbitration and the Permanent Court of Arbitration,* 2013 (ISBN 978-90-411-4766-0).
28. Günther J. Horvath & Stephan Wilske (eds), *Guerrilla Tactics in International Arbitration,* 2013 (ISBN 978-90-411-4002-9).
29. Albert Badia, *Piercing the Veil of State Enterprises in International Arbitration,* 2014 (ISBN 978-90-411-5162-9).
30. Nadja Erk, *Parallel Proceedings in International Arbitration: A Comparative European Perspective,* 2014 (ISBN 978-90-411-5264-0).
31. Simon Vorburger, *International Arbitration and Cross-Border Insolvency: Comparative Perspectives,* 2014 (ISBN 978-90-411-5419-4).
32. Ahmad Ali Ghouri, *Interaction and Conflict of Treaties in Investment Arbitration,* 2015 (ISBN 978-90-411-5417-0).
33. Reto Marghitola, *Document Production in International Arbitration,* 2015 (ISBN 978-90-411-5159-9).
34. Alfonso Gómez-Acebo, *Party-Appointed Arbitrators in International Commercial Arbitration,* 2016 (ISBN 978-90-411-6671-5).
35. Jonas von Goeler, *Third-Party Funding in International Arbitration and Its Impact on Procedure,* 2016 (ISBN 978-90-411-5015-8).
36. Dean Lewis, *The Interpretation and Uniformity of the UNCITRAL Model Law on International Commercial Arbitration: Focusing on Australia, Hong Kong and Singapore,* 2016 (ISBN 978-90-411-6700-2).
37. Stavros Brekoulakis, Julian D.M. Lew & Loukas Mistelis (eds), *The Evolution and Future of International Arbitration,* 2016 (ISBN 978-90-411-7004-0).
38. Rémy Gerbay, *The Functions of Arbitral Institutions,* 2016 (ISBN 978-90-411-6217-5).

39. Maximilian Clasmeier, *Arbitral Awards as Investments: Treaty Interpretation and the Dynamics of International Investment Law*, 2017 (ISBN 978-90-411-8357-6).
40. Tony Cole (ed.), *The Roles of Psychology in International Arbitration*, 2017 (ISBN 978-90-411-5921-2).
41. Pietro Ferrario, *The Adaptation of Long-Term Gas Sale Agreements by Arbitrators*, 2017 (ISBN 978-90-411-8232-6).
42. Jacob B. van de Velden, *Finality in Litigation: The Law and Practice of Preclusion – Res Judicata (Merger and Estoppel), Abuse of Process and Recognition of Foreign Judgments*, 2017 (ISBN 978-90-411-8342-2).
43. Dolores Bentolila, *Arbitrators as Lawmakers*, 2017 (ISBN 978-90-411-8354-5).
44. Giacomo Marchisio, *The Notion of Award in International Commercial Arbitration: A Comparative Analysis of French Law, English Law, and the UNCITRAL Model Law*, 2017 (ISBN 978-90-411-8391-0).
45. Csaba Kovács, *Attribution in International Investment Law*, 2018 (ISBN 978-90-411-9675-0).
46. Mary Mitsi, *The Decision-Making Process of Investor-State Arbitration Tribunals*, 2019 (ISBN 978-90-411-9600-2).
47. Ahmet Cemil Yıldırım, *Interpretation of Contracts in Comparative and Uniform Law*, 2019 (ISBN 978-94-035-1130-6).
48. Beata Gessel-Kalinowska vel Kalisz, *The Legal, Real and Converged Interest in Declaratory Relief*, 2019 (ISBN 978-94-035-1244-0).
49. Maximilian Pika, *Third-Party Effects of Arbitral Awards: Res Judicata Against Privies, Non-mutual Preclusion and Factual Effects*, 2019 (ISBN 978-94-035-1273-0).
50. Yulia Levashova, *The Right of States to Regulate in International Investment Law: The Search for Balance Between Public Interest and Fair and Equitable Treatment*, 2019 (ISBN 978-94-035-0931-0).
51. Flavia Marisi, *Environmental Interests in Investment Arbitration: Challenges and Directions*, 2020 (ISBN 978-94-035-1723-0).
52. Martina Magnarelli, *Privity of Contract in International Investment Arbitration: Original Sin or Useful Tool?*, 2020 (ISBN 978-94-035-2020-9).
53. Xu Qian, *Water Services Disputes in International Arbitration: Reconsidering the Nexus of Investment Protection, Environment, and Human Rights*, 2020 (ISBN 978-94-035-2203-6).
54. Nobumichi Teramura, Ex Aequo et Bono *as a Response to the 'Over-Judicialisation' of International Commercial Arbitration*, 2020 (ISBN 978-94-035-2073-5).
55. Bruno Guandalini, *Economic Analysis of the Arbitrator's Function*, 2020 (ISBN 978-94-035-2265-4).
56. Zena Prodromou, *The Public Order Exception in International Trade, Investment, Human Rights and Commercial Disputes*, 2020 (ISBN 978-94-035-2031-5).

57. Jürg Künzle, *Multiple Contracts and Coordination in International Construction Projects: A Swiss Law Analysis*, 2020 (ISBN 978-94-035-2024-7).
58. Cornel Marian, *The State's Power to Tax in the Investment Arbitration of Energy Disputes: Outer Limits and the Energy Charter Treaty*, 2020 (ISBN 978-94-035-1752-0).
59. Luke Nottage, Shahla Ali, Bruno Jetin & Nobumichi Teramura (eds.), *New Frontiers in Asia-Pacific International Arbitration and Dispute Resolution*, 2021 (ISBN 978-94-035-2855-7).
60. Eva Litina, *Theory, Law and Practice of Maritime Arbitration: The Case of International Contracts for the Carriage of Goods by Sea*, 2021 (ISBN 978-94-035-3035-2).
61. Franco Ferrari & Friedrich Rosenfeld (eds), *Autonomous Versus Domestic Concepts under the New York Convention*, 2021 (ISBN 978-94-035-3173-1).
62. Doğan Gültutan, *Moral Damages under International Investment Law: The Path Towards Convergence*, 2022 (ISBN 978-94-035-4025-2).
63. Simon Foote QC, *The Bona Fide Investor: Corporate Nationality and Treaty Shopping in Investment Treaty Law*, 2022 (ISBN 978-94-035-4185-3).
64. George A. Bermann, *Twilight Issues in International Arbitration: Latent Choice of Law Challenges*, 2023 (ISBN 978-94-035-1746-9).
65. Emmanuel Obiora Igbokwe, *Dealing with Bribery and Corruption in International Commercial Arbitration: To Probe or Not to Probe*, 2023 (ISBN 978-94-035-2066-7).
66. Peter Sester, *Contract Law in International Commercial Arbitration*, 2023 (ISBN 978-94-035-1036-1).
67. Julian Bickmann, *Fact-Finding in International Arbitration: The Emergence of a Transnational* Lex Evidentiae, 2023 (ISBN 978-94-035-1886-2).
68. Giovanna E. Gismondi, *International Environmental Law and International Human Rights Law in Investment Treaty Arbitration: The Contribution of Host States' Argumentation in Re-Shaping International Investment Law*, 2023 (ISBN 978-94-035-3047-5).
69. Fabricio Fortese, *Early Determination of Jurisdiction*, 2024 (ISBN 978-94-035-0268-7).
70. Sabrina Pearson-Wenger, *Good Faith in International Commercial Arbitration: Its Application by Arbitral Tribunals to the Parties' Contract and the Arbitration Agreement*, 2024 (ISBN 978-94-035-0738-5).
71. Charalampos Tagaroulias, *International Investment Law and the Law of the European Union: How Regionalism and Interregionalism Have Shaped the Relationship in the Post-Lisbon Era*, 2024 (ISBN 978-94-035-0708-8).
72. Dan Xie, *Transnational Due Process and Article V(1)(b) of the New York Convention: Grounding Interpretation and Application of the Due Process Defence in the Public International Law Framework for Treaty Interpretation*, 2024 (ISBN 978-94-035-2437-5).
73. Thomas Lehmann, *Investment Arbitration and International Climate Change Law: Revaluing Legitimate Expectations*, 2025 (ISBN 978-94-035-2799-4).

74. Ylli Dautaj, *Sovereign Immunity from Execution and International Arbitration: Theory and Practice*, 2025 (ISBN 978-94-035-0858-0).